CASTLE AND CATHEDRAL
IN MODERN PRAGUE

CASTLE AND CATHEDRAL IN MODERN PRAGUE

Longing for the Sacred in a Skeptical Age

BRUCE R. BERGLUND

Central European University Press
Budapest-New York

Published in 2018 by

Central European University Press
Nádor utca 11, H-1051 Budapest, Hungary
Tel: +36-1-327-3138 or 327-3000
Fax: +36-1-327-3183
E-mail: *ceupress@press.ceu.edu*
Website: *www.ceupress.com*

On the cover:
Granite bowl in the Paradise Garden, Prague Castle, designed by Jože Plečnik.
(Photo courtesy of the Jože Plečnik Collection,
Museums and Galleries of Ljubljana, Slovenia)

Book design by Sebastian Stachowski

ISBN 978-963-7326-43-1 paperback

Library of Congress Cataloging-in-Publication Data

Names: Berglund, Bruce R., author.
Title: Castle and cathedral in modern Prague : longing for the sacred in a
skeptical age / Bruce R. Berglund.
Description: New York : Central European University Press, 2016. | Includes
bibliographical references and index.
Identifiers: LCCN 2016031542 (print) | LCCN 2016041625 (ebook) | ISBN
9789633861578 (hardcover : alk. paper) | ISBN 9789633861585 (pdf : alk.
paper) | ISBN 9789633861585 (pdf)
Subjects: LCSH: Prague (Czech Republic)—Religion. | Prague (Czech
Republic)—Religious life and customs. | Sacred space—Czech
Republic—Prague—History—20th century. | Church buildings—Czech
Republic—Prague—History—20th century. | Pražský hrad (Prague, Czech
Republic) | Czechoslovakia—History—20th century.
Classification: LCC BL980.C94 B47 2016 (print) | LCC BL980.C94 (ebook) | DDC
200.94371/209042—dc23
LC record available at https://lccn.loc.gov/2016031542

Printed in Hungary

Table of Contents

Illustrations

Abbreviations

AGM	Alice Garrigue Masaryková
CGM	Charlotte Garrigue Masaryková
TGM	Tomáš Garrigue Masaryk
AHMP	Archiv hlavního města Prahy (Archive of the City of Prague)
AKPR	Archiv Kanceláře prezidenta republiky (Archive of the Office of the President of the Republic)
APH KPR, SV	Archiv Pražského hradu, Kancelář prezidenta republiky, Stavební věci (Archive of Prague Castle, Office of the President of the Republic, Facilities Administration)
LA PNP	Literarní Archiv, Pamatník národního pisemnictví (Literary Archive, Museum of [Czech] National Literature)
Lilly Library	Lilly Research Library, Indiana University, Bloomington
MÚA AV ČR	Masarykův ústav a archiv Akademie věd ČR (Masaryk Institute and Archive, Academy of Sciences, Czech Republic)
PC MGL	Jože Plečnik Collection, Museums and Galleries of Ljubljana, Slovenia

Acknowledgements

This book had its origins over a decade ago in the office of Antonín Klimek, senior researcher at the Historical Institute of the Czech Army in Prague. At the time, Klimek was the leading scholar of interwar Czechoslovakia. His two-volume political history of the First Republic, *Boj o Hrad* [The Battle for the Castle], had gained wide attention and stirred much debate at its release in 1996 and 1998. After its publication, Klimek became a regular commentator on Czech history and politics, appearing on television and contributing opinion essays to the respected daily newspaper *Lidové noviny*. Our first meeting was when I was a graduate student. All the lessons about proper formalities I had gained in my Czech language classes went out the window. He insisted that I call him "Tonda" (Tony), and that I use the familiar form of address. As I began my dissertation research, Klimek went out of his way to provide guidance and assistance, accompanying me across the city to archives, contacting journal editors about publishing my first essays, and translating those essays from English into Czech. I remember when he praised my writing style. Coming from a historian who wrote with color and humor, I valued the compliment. Most importantly, he complimented my instincts as a historian. He said that I understood Czech history well. For a young graduate student there could be no better words of encouragement.

After finishing my dissertation, I visited Klimek whenever I returned to Prague. During one of these visits, I asked if he ever planned to write a biography of Tomáš Masaryk, the revered first president of Czechoslovakia. Long before the revolution of 1989, Klimek had gained access to Masaryk's archive through the help of a friend. Years of surreptitious research in those materials became the foundation for his book *Boj o Hrad* as well as a biography of Masaryk's successor, Edvard Beneš (co-authored with Zbyněk Zeman), and another two-volume work, a comprehensive history of the First Republic. Nobody knew the life of Masaryk better than Klimek. But he had no desire to write a biography of the President-Liberator. "I would have to leave the country!" he exclaimed. Having withstood the critical response to his history of the First Republic, Klimek judged that there was no way he could write a truly scholarly biography of Masaryk, based on the materials he had seen in the formerly closed archive. Were there scandals or skeletons hidden in the documents? That wasn't the cause of Klimek's concern. Instead, he said of Masaryk: "He wanted to start a new religion!" Klimek had spent years in Masaryk's personal papers. He had written volumes about Masaryk the politician. But it was clear, as his voice rose, that this was something he could not comprehend about Masaryk the man. How could someone presume to start a new religion? As I conducted my research, this question stayed with me. Tonda passed away in 2005, so I was unable to pester him with questions, ask his advice, and borrow his wisdom. But this work is certainly inspired by him. Antonín Klimek had seen Masaryk's religious ideas as some kind of key to his life and work. This book is an attempt to follow upon that clue, and it is dedicated to the memory of the scholar who encouraged me at the start of my career.

Most of the sources for this book were found in archives and libraries in Prague and in Ljubljana, Slovenia, the home of architect Jože Plečnik. A year-long stay in these cities was funded by the US Department of Education's Fulbright-Hays Faculty Research program. Shorter, follow-up visits were made possible by grants from the Calvin College Alumni Association and the Calvin Center for Christian Scholarship.

In Ljubljana, I received an education in Slovene cultural history over cups of coffee with Peter Krečič, former director of the city's Architectural Museum. Plečnik's contemporaries in Ljubljana—figures such as Izidor Cankar, France Kralj, and Ivan Vurnik—had roles in early drafts of this book. Even though their sections ended up on the cutting-room floor, this project is colored by my understanding of their work, gained from Peter, art historian Igor Kranjc, and the late Ervin Dolenc. Archivist Ana Porok at Plečnik's house and museum was always a welcoming host and exceedingly helpful with my requests for plans and materials. I will always remember my visits to the house in Trnovo with fondness.

In Prague, I visited several collections, including the National Library, the National Archive, the Architectural Archive of the Czech Technical Museum, the archive of the National Gallery, and the archive of the Art History Institute. The bulk of my time was spent at the Archive of the T. G. Masaryk Institute, part of the Czech Academy of Sciences, both at its former location near Masarykovo nádraží and its current building in Prague 8. Thanks to the archive's current director, Helena Kokešová, and former director Jan Bílek for making available documents and photographs, and to the various staff members in the research rooms, who were always gracious and helpful. Special thanks go to Dagmar Hájková, senior researcher in the Institute's Department for Research and Source Editions. She shared her insights into the relationship between Joze Plečnik and Alice Masaryková, whom she knows better than any historian. I spent many afternoons at the Literary Archive at Strahov Monastery (sometimes after giving directions to wayward tourists in search of the monastery library). My thanks to Iva Prokešová and her staff there, who were always patient with my awful spoken Czech. Michal Šula and the staff at the Prague Castle Archive were gracious and helpful during my visits to Hradčany as well as with follow-up requests for photographs. And I am grateful to Zdeněk Lukeš for leading me on a personal tour of the castle and its grounds and pointing out aspects of Plečnik's work that only someone of his expertise could identify.

During stays in Prague and Ljubljana, my family and I enjoyed the support of many friends. Jason and Olga Kuiper have welcomed us during both of our long-term stays in Prague. I am grateful for their friendship, dating back to my first visit to Prague as a student in 1995. The Špaček family graciously welcomed a noisy American family who moved into the upper floor of their villa. They became dear friends. Their children shared their backyard play area (and their collection of

Harry Potter DVDs), Mirka was the kind and generous anchor of the house, and Frantisek was a patient and understanding landlord. He also passed along a welcome supply of new music, and to the end of my life I will thank him for introducing me to Čechomor's *Proměny*. Through the Špačeks, we became friends with Bořek and Miša Tydlitát and their children. They welcomed us to their family home in the countryside and have offered their hospitality and assistance whenever I return to Prague. Miša provided me with books from Masaryk's library during her tenure at the Institute, and she and Bořek have answered several emailed requests for materials inaccessible in the States. Their daughter Lída translated some passages of Czech that were particularly tricky.

Thanks also to Hanka Ripková and her staff at the Fulbright Commission of the Czech Republic. They have hosted me twice—as a student Fulbrighter in 1997-98 and then as faculty researcher on a Fulbright-Hays grant—both times arranging unique opportunities for me during those stays. For over two decades, they have done great work for students and scholars from the United States and the Czech Republic. They deserve much gratitude and respect for their service to international education in both countries.

The earliest threads of this project date back to my time at the University of Kansas. Funding from the KU Center for Russian and East European Studies allowed for an early research trip and travel for conferences. The center's former director, Maria Carlson, was a mentor as I started my academic career and a model of the kind of wide-ranging yet grounded cultural historian I hoped to become. Marc Greenberg of KU's Slavic Languages Department gave his time to tutor me in Czech and Slovene, and he and his wife, Marta Pirnat-Greenberg, have been encouraging supporters of mine. My research has allowed me to spend some wonderful moments in Europe, enjoying good food and good company in settings of extraordinary beauty. The day I spent in Slovenia with Marc, Marta, and their children years ago is certainly one of those moments.

As the book took shape, I was able to draw upon the expertise and wisdom of a number of colleagues. In 2005-06, I helped organize two academic meetings, along with Brian Porter-Szűcs and Andreas Kossert, that brought together scholars from the U.S. and Europe who were conducting research on religion in twentieth-century Eastern Europe. This present book would be pretty thin if not for the insights I gained from these colleagues during our meetings in Grand Rapids and Warsaw. Particular thanks to: Jim Bjork, John Connelly, David Doellinger, James Felak, Paul Hanebrink, Katharina Kunter, Patrick Patterson, and Anca Şincan. These meetings led to a volume of essays, published in 2010 by Central European University Press. I so appreciated working with the press that I returned with this project. Thank you to my editor, Nóra Vörös, director Krisztina Kós, and copyeditor Adela Hîncu for their good work in bringing this book to print.

I worked on this project in the collegial, supportive, and often jovial environment of the Calvin College History Department. My fellow historians commented on drafts and provided helpful advice. Eric, Will, Kristin, Dan, Doug, Jim, David, Bill, Bert, Kate, Frans, Karin, Bob, and Dan: you have been terrific colleagues. I offer sincere thanks as well to the former coordinator of interlibrary loans at Calvin's Hekman Library, Kathleen Struck, who answered my ceaseless stream of ILL requests—even securing copies of periodicals from the National Library in Prague. Two of my all-time best Calvin students helped in the project at its beginning and end. Melissa Smith served as a summer research assistant in the project's early stages, and Jenna Hunt proofread the complete draft and edited the endnotes. Their contributions were invaluable.

Fellow historians of interwar Czechoslovakia offered their critiques of early chapters. This book would be much the poorer if not for the valuable comments of Thomas Ort, Andrea Orzoff, and Cynthia Paces. Their research on interwar Prague was essential to my work, and I lift my cap to them in gratitude and respect. I also owe a great debt to Martin Putna. His knowledge of Czech literature, culture, and religion is unsurpassed. After I presented my early research findings in a public lecture in Prague, he immediately exclaimed: "This is exactly the kind of work we need!" His encouragement affirmed that my project was on the right track.

Apart from the comments of readers or the help of librarians or the careful work of editors, this project has depended upon friends and family in Minnesota, Michigan, and Kansas, who over the years provided much help to my family and me. At the top of the list are my parents, Bill and Pat, my sister Collette and her family, and my wife's large family, the Blonigan clan. These and others gave their support in many ways—traveling to Prague to visit, giving rides to the airport, sending care packages while we were overseas, showing hospitality to my family while I was away, and much more. They showed great patience for the curious life of a historian. But certainly not as much patience as my children, who spent a year in a strange country so their dad could work on some book. Will, Marta, Nils, and Vera: I will always appreciate your adaptability, your openness to new adventures, and your ability to have fun in any environment. And above all else, thanks to Megan, for so much. You're a good sport.

Introduction

This is book about Something. Something sacred. Something eternal. Something higher.

Surveys regularly show the Czech Republic as being one of the least religious countries in the world, with anywhere from a third to two-thirds of the population declaring themselves as atheists. However, scholars of religion point out that most Czechs actually do hold some belief. This faith is not directed to God as defined in any traditional, creedal sense, nor is it affiliated with any church or religious institution. Instead, it is a belief in something that is sacred or supernatural or simply "up there." Catholic priest and sociologist Tomáš Halík, the 2014 Templeton Prize laureate, coined a term to describe this belief. From the Czech word for "something" (*něco*), Halík labeled this type of religious feeling as *něcismus*, meaning the "belief in something" or, literally, "something-ism." According to Halík, Czechs who follow Somethingism are reluctant to even associate the object of their belief with the word "God," let alone with a particular religion.[1] But this privatized spirituality does have traceable patterns. Along with having the highest rates of atheism in Europe, the Czech Republic also has large percentages of people who declare themselves as "very superstitious" and who believe in amulets and fortune tellers. Even among Czechs who claim affiliation with a church, belief in the occult is common while adherence to traditional Christian teaching is inconsistent. According to one survey, twenty percent of Czech atheists believe in

---

[1] Halík, "O ateismu, pochybnostech a víře."

faith healers, while twenty-seven percent of regular Catholic church-goers believe in reincarnation.[2]

Somethingism has a history. Halík's longtime friend Václav Havel expressed belief in Something in his essays on morality and politics, as did nineteenth-century nationalists like Karel Havlíček, who confronted the alliance of church and state in the Habsburg Empire. There are common aspects of Somethingism repeated over the decades in the writings of Czech intellectuals: belief in a providential movement to history, appreciation of the moral teachings of Jesus, and the insistence on a spiritual element to human existence. Halík observes that it was important for these intellectuals to describe their belief in a "vertical or transcendental aspect of human life, a providential dimension to the history of 'the horizon of horizons,' 'the perspective of eternity,' and the like." Since the nineteenth century, leading Czech writers and thinkers had been very sensitive to the moral principles of Christianity. But, Halík added, "none were willing to use the traditional terminology of the church to express these values."[3]

The aim of this book is to investigate a pivotal period in the history of Somethingism: the two decades of interwar Czechoslovakia, known as the First Republic. This period has been idealized as a golden age.[4] Prague at the time was a hub of early modernist culture. It was the city of Jaroslav Hašek, creator of the Good Soldier Švejk, and Karel Čapek, who introduced the Czech word "robot" to the rest of the world with his phenomenally successful play *R.U.R.* Prague's cubists, surrealists, and avant-garde functionalists adopted styles originating in Western Europe and turned them in distinctive directions. Composers, theatre directors, photographers, and designers created works of striking originality, earning the attention of artists from Europe West and East. Beyond the realm of art and culture, interwar Czechoslovakia boasted a prosperous industrial economy, technological innova-

---

2   Nešpor and Nešporová, "Religion: An Unsolved Problem for the Modern Czech Nation"; and Nešpor, "Religious Processes in Contemporary Czech Society." See also Hamplová, "Čemu Češi věří: dimenze soudobé české religiozity."

3   Halík, "O ateismu, pochybnostech a víře."

4   An example of this view of Prague is the last chapter of Peter Demetz's book *Prague in Black and Gold*. The idea of "golden age" Czechoslovakia colors most popular guides to Prague, aimed particularly at tourists.

tion, high rates of literacy, an effective public health system, and a functioning, if flawed, parliamentary democracy. The Czechs of interwar Prague saw their state, their city, and themselves as modern, as European. But what exactly that meant—being modern Europeans—was the subject of much discussion.

In First Republic Prague the conventional notion of the modern age carried images of cities and factories, rising skyscrapers and sleek automobiles. As Czech writers of the time observed and periodicals illustrated, the stuff of modern life consisted of movie theatres and football stadiums, assembly lines and economic forecasts, exercise clubs and ads for the latest fashions. At the same time, modern life brought a new way of seeing and comprehending the world: it meant putting off narrow, traditional outlooks and accepting the pluralistic reality of society; seeking truth through evidence and analysis, while at same time acknowledging that there can be multiple perspectives; and understanding the workings of the world in material and mechanical terms. At its root, this modern outlook was secular. Religious institutions constrained the autonomy of the modern individual; religious doctrine defied the advance of modern learning; religious teaching was unsuited for the reality of modern life.

Or so people claimed. In Prague of the early twentieth century, the place of religion in modern life was subject of ardent debate. Czech cultural and political figures wrote about the role of church institutions in a democratic state, the relevance of religious education in an age of science and technology, the contemporary legacy of the nation's religious heritage, and the value of faith for individual morality and civil society. There were some—both believers and skeptics—who argued that modernity and religion were fundamentally incompatible, and that one side had to win out. Others, however, saw some form of religious belief as a valid, even necessary, part of modern life. Yet these advocates of religion also insisted that religion had to change, in some way, in order to speak to the times. Individual believers and institutions had to adapt their practices and expressions, whether in the realm of religious ethics, religious art, the design of churches, or even the fundamental conception of God. Some Catholics and Protestants asserted that these changes could be made within the frameworks of their churches. Indeed, they often justified contemporary adaptations as being a return to core beliefs. Meanwhile, there were others who saw the traditional churches and doctrines as irrevocably obsolete, even as they defended personal belief. They professed instead a belief in Something. In their view, this was an affirmative statement at a time when traditional religion was in decline. People still longed for transcendence amidst the confusion of modern life, they claimed. According to these prophets of Something-ism, an indefinable object of belief offered a source of meaning and moral direction. To clarify: these intellectuals did not use the term Somethingism (*něcismus*). Some continued to use the word God (*Bůh*), but others spoke of belief in "something higher" (*něco vyššího*) or "something eternal" (*něco věčného*). This faith in Something, they argued, was a freer form of belief, stripped of all that was constraining or premodern in religion, while at the same time giving an individual solace, hope, and inspiration.

Somethingism was challenged by defenders of the One Thing: the True God, the True Church, the Truth as Absolute. There were Catholic and Protestant writers in interwar Prague who recognized Somethingism as a strong current in Czech culture and a threat to creedal, trinitarian Christianity. Their objection was not simply that Somethingism went against tradition. Indeed, some of these Catholics and Protestants were critical of their own churches' inability to respond to the needs of the times. However, they criticized this supposedly progressive form of belief as insufficient for the adversities of modern life. These religious intellectuals were tenacious and compelling in arguing for the continued relevance of traditional faith. They were also heard in the public arena. Just as today, there were religious journals and publishing houses marketed specifically to the faithful. But in Prague of the 1920s and 1930s, leading Catholic and Protestant intellectuals also contributed regularly to prominent, secular periodicals, and they engaged in debates with leading nonreligious intellectuals. As an analogy, imagine in the contemporary United States an outspoken, theologically conservative Catholic writer winning the Pulitzer Prize for fiction, and then engaging the lead columnist of the *New York Times* in regular feuds over religion and politics. Or imagine an evangelical philosopher chairing international academic conferences, serving as editor of a leading university press, and sparring with the editor of *The Atlantic*, all while organizing summer Bible camps and student ministry meetings. These scenarios are a rough approximation of what took place in interwar Prague, as skeptics, professing Christians, and believers in Something sought to define the role of religion in the modern, democratic state.

Culture wars are fought on broad fronts. Appropriately, this book is a work of cultural history that draws from a broad selection of sources: novels and reviews, academic lectures and political speeches, architectural plans and paintings, and the letters of mystics and moralists, traditionalists and doubters. The subject of the book is theology in the fullest sense of the term—that is, thinking about God. As Benjamin Lazier writes in *God Interrupted*, his award-winning book on Jewish and Christian theologians in interwar Europe, thinking about God needs to be included in the cultural and intellectual history of the twentieth century. Lazier bases his study on the assertion that we must "appreciate theology as a vehicle for commentary on the political, aesthetic, and philosophical present common to us all, and not merely as the parochial pursuit of like-minded, if fractious believers."[5] During the 1920s and 1930s, the ways in which Europeans spoke of the divine overlapped with the ways in which they spoke of themselves, their nations, and their civilization. There was, Lazier insists, "a theological dimension to interwar life," one that can be seen in the arts and letters of the period.

My study explores this theological dimension in an important city of interwar Europe. This is not a comprehensive history of religion in Prague or First Republic Czechoslovakia. Kateřina Čapková and Hillel Kieval have published acclaimed studies of Jewish identity and Judaism in Prague and the Czech Lands.[6] James Felak and Jaroslav Šebek have written extensively about Catholic Slovaks and Germans in interwar Czechoslovakia.[7] On the subject of Christianity and Czech cul-

---

5   Lazier, *God Interrupted*, 3.

6   Čapková, *Czechs, Germans, Jews?*; Kieval, *The Making of Czech Jewry*.

7   Felak's many works on Catholicism and Slovak politics include: *"At the Price of the Republic": Hlinka's Slovak People's Party*; and *After Hitler, Before Stalin: Catholics, Communists, and Democrats in Slovakia*. Šebek is author of *Od konfliktu ke smíření: Česko-německé vztahy ve 20. století očima katolické církve* and *Mezi křížem a národem: Politické prostředí sudetoněmeckého katolicismu v meziválečném Československu*.

ture, Martin Putna's two volumes on Catholic literature and thought
are magisterial, while Pavel Marek and Martin Schulze Wessel have
detailed the roles of the Catholic and Protestant Churches in Czechoslovakia's political and social history.[8] This book instead will focus at
the level of individual religious experience. My subjects were all part
of the Czech political or cultural elite of the interwar republic (the one
non-Czech subject gained access to these circles at the highest level). I
look at professing Catholics and Protestants as well as Czechs who
were baptized into the Catholic Church as children but were not adherents as adults. The aim is to explore what these particular people
believed, how they expressed those beliefs, and how they applied religious conviction—or lack of conviction—to questions of morality,
politics, art, and social welfare. In short, how did these prominent figures in the culture and politics of interwar Prague think about God?

Toward this end, the book takes a more biographical approach, focusing on three principal subjects. The first is Tomáš Garrigue Masaryk (1850–1937): philosophy professor, cultural critic, and member
of the Austrian parliament, who became Czechoslovakia's first president when the country gained independence in 1918. Scholars agree
that Tomáš Masaryk is central to the development of contemporary
Czech religion, but they do not examine his role in a historical context.
This book takes up that task, looking at Masaryk's personal religious
philosophy, his desire to establish that set of beliefs as the civil religion
of Czechoslovakia, and his disappointment at seeing the failure of
those efforts. I argue that Masaryk's political program for the Czechoslovak Republic was rooted in his idea of a "new religion," which he
had formulated at the turn of the century. Adapted from German romantic philosophy, liberal Protestant theology, and American Unitar-

---

8   Putna, *Česká katolická literatura v kontextech, 1918–1945.* His book is the second volume of a study of
    Czech Catholic literature in the modern period, following *Česká katolická literatura v evropském kon-
    textech, 1848–1918.* Marek's work has focused on Catholic political movements in the Czech lands.
    See *Český katolicismus, 1890–1914* and *Politické programy českého politického katolicismu 1894–1938.*
    Schulze Wessel has edited several books of essays on religion, politics, and society in Czechoslova-
    kia and Eastern Europe. Most valuable is the volume he edited with Martin Zückert, *Handbuch der
    Religions- und Kirchengeschichte der böhmischen Länder und Tschechiens im 20. Jahrhundert,* partic-
    ularly Schulze Wessel's introductory essay: "Religion und Politik in den böhmischen Ländern und
    Tschechien im 20. Jahrhundert."

ianism, Masaryk's new religion held that God existed and set an eternal measure for the actions of people and nations. Because the new religion would be freed from churches and doctrines, Masaryk insisted that it would better allow people to act in love and service. On becoming president, he expected that this new religion would be accepted by all Czechs; it would provide the unifying conviction that would inspire them to civic engagement, much as he understood the function of religion in America.

The second subject is Slovene architect Jože Plečnik (1872–1957), whom Masaryk commissioned in 1921 to direct the renovation of Prague Castle. Plečnik had left his native Ljubljana in the early 1890s to learn a trade in Austria. A decade later, after studying under Otto Wagner, he was hailed in Vienna as one of the most promising young architects of the modern style. Plečnik was a regular contributor to exhibitions at the Secession House in Vienna, earned the admiration of artists and architects in Vienna and Prague, and became an important influence on the Czech cubists. At the same time, he remained a devoted Catholic, continuing to attend mass regularly. Catholic imagery fired his imagination: his drawings include sketches of chapels, wayside shrines, altars, and communion chalices. Yet he also believed that all architecture was sacral, whether a church or the home of a noble patron. This understanding of architecture—and his own responsibility as an artist in service of God—shaped his two major projects in Prague: the Church of the Sacred Heart, one of the great works of twentieth-century church architecture, and the gardens and courtyards of Prague Castle, which millions of tourists visit each year. Although the city's secular atmosphere rankled him, Plečnik saw his tasks in Prague as guided by Providence. He came to have an important role in shaping Prague's landscape, with his work on the monumental, modern cathedral that stands in one of its most prominent districts and the ancient castle that serves as presidential seat.

The last of the three main subjects is Alice Garrigue Masaryková (1879–1966), eldest child of Tomáš Masaryk and his American wife, Charlotte. After Czechoslovakia gained independence, Alice Masaryková became the founding director of the new state's Red Cross organization. She had been a student at the first gymnasium for girls in the Austrian Empire and then one of the first female students at the university in Prague. Motivated to serve society, she spent a year in Chicago, working with poor immigrant workers at the city's settlement houses. Masaryková returned home determined to introduce what she had learned in America—the disciplinary methods of social work and the civic altruism of social gospel Protestantism—for the improvement of Czech society. This aim, along with her father's ideas on religion and politics, later motivated her work with the Red Cross. As director, Masaryková sought to bridge religious conviction with social scientific analysis and democratic civic engagement. Like Tomáš Masaryk and Jože Plečnik, she believed in the synthesis of the traditional and the modern, the immediate and the eternal, and she saw this synthesis as the hope of Europe in the aftermath of the World War.

At the center of the book is the one lasting manifestation of these three figures' shared ideals: Prague Castle. Studies of Plečnik's work at the castle in the 1920s and 1930s have typically cast the project as an effort to transform a neglected relic of the Habsburg Monarchy into the seat of authority for an independent republic, a "democratic castle." Often cited is Masaryk's charge that Prague Castle must become "a symbol of our national democratic ideals."[9] However, in addressing how Plečnik the architect translated the vision of his patron, we must clarify what Masaryk understood those ideals to be. We must also recognize that the ideals Masaryk claimed as "ours," as belonging to the Czechs, were distinctly *his*.[10] Upon becoming the first president of independent Czechoslovakia in 1918, Masaryk announced a far-reaching vision of political and moral renewal, the components of which he had already forwarded in previous decades as philosopher, politician, and cultural critic. Fundamental to this political and moral program was his religious philosophy. As he later explained in an interview with Karel Čapek, Masaryk viewed his work as parliamentarian and president in a religious light: "I saw in politics an instrument. The aim for me was religious and moral. Still today I do not say that the state will

---

9   Masaryk, address to the National Assembly, 28 October 1923, in *Cesta demokracie I*, 483.
10 Eva Schmidt-Hartmann discusses Masaryk's belief that his ideas were scientifically correct because he best fulfilled his own criteria of honesty, independence, and rationality. See *Thomas G. Masaryk's Realism*, 141–43.

be the fulfillment of a cultural mission. Instead, we must work toward the building of the City of God."[11] In serving as the liaison between the president and the castle architect, Alice Masaryková translated her father's vision into a conception of the castle as a "sacred acropolis." She insisted to Plečnik that the castle must embody the principles of her father, creating a link between the world and the eternal. This charge corresponded to Plečnik's own understanding of architecture as a sacral art, a means of connecting humanity and God. The renovations of Prague Castle thus were intended to create a sacred space, not only for the city and the republic but also for all of Europe.

Jože Plečnik's work at Prague Castle in the 1920s–30s has received much attention from historians of architecture. For this book, I have relied on the research of Plečnik scholars such as Peter Krečič, Zdeněk Lukeš, Irena Žantovská-Murray, and Damjan Prelovšek.[12] But I am a historian, rather than an architectural historian. The relationship of Plečnik, Alice Masaryková, and Tomáš Masaryk and the renovation of Prague Castle are at the core of the book—that is why a photograph of the castle is on the cover. This work, however, does not delve into the details of Plečnik's design, the provenance of his ideas, or the theoretical foundations of his architecture; other scholars have accomplished that. Instead, I look at this major architectural project as an expression of the three principal characters' beliefs about God, art, politics, and the future of Europe. All three were idealists and visionaries. Their ideals are evident in particular elements of the castle's courtyards and gardens—they are visible today to visitors at the castle. As it still does today, the citadel served as the seat of the head of state: a site of polit-

---

11 Čapek, unpublished manuscript, appendix to *Hovory s T. G. Masarykem* (1990), 517.

12 Krečič is author of a comprehensive study of Plečnik's life and work, in Slovene, titled *Jože Plečnik*. A shorter translation of that book was published as *Plečnik: The Complete Works*. Prelovšek's major volume on the architect was also translated into English as *Jože Plečnik, 1872–1957: Architectura perennis*. Zdeněk Lukeš organized a major exhibition in Prague in 1997 devoted to Plečnik's work at the castle. The catalog, edited by Lukeš, Prelovšek, and Tomáš Valena, is an exhaustive study of Plečnik's architecture: *Josip Plečnik: An Architect of Prague Castle*. Irena Žantovská-Murray, former Sir Banister Fletcher Director of the British Architectural Library, wrote her dissertation in the history of architecture on Plečnik: "'Our Slav Acropolis': Language and Architecture in the Prague Castle under Masaryk." Also important is a volume of essays translated into English, published in connection with the 1986 exhbition of Plečnik's work in Paris, which sparked interest in the architect outside of Slovenia: Burkhardt, Eveno, and Podrecca, eds., *Jože Plečnik, Architect: 1872–1957*.

ical symbolism and real political authority in a major European city. This book looks at Prague Castle within this broader context. If the castle was meant to be, as Masaryková wrote to Plečnik, an expression in stone of her father's ideals, then how were those ideals—and their architectural expression—received and understood?

Tomáš Masaryk had a grand vision for Czechoslovakia. The founding of the republic was part of what he called the "world revolution," in which politics and religion would be transformed. He expected that the leaders of the new state and its citizens would conduct their daily affairs *sub specie aeternitatis*—under the perspective of eternity. But in 1938, a year after Masaryk's passing, this grand vision of a moral republic came to ruin, as Britain and France allowed Nazi Germany to annex territory on the Czech borderlands. The failure of the First Czechoslovak Republic is most often cast as a drama of power politics and internal divisions. These political analyses of Czechoslovakia's failure typically do not address the more fundamental element of the president's program: his religious and moral philosophy. Here as well we must recognize failure. The religious revolution that Masaryk proclaimed did not take place, at least not in the Czech Lands. Even Masaryk recognized by the early 1930s that the Czechs had not fulfilled the calling of their religious heritage, the calling he had set before them. Why not?

In order to understand the failure of this civil religion *sub specie aeternitatis*, this book discusses other figures prominent in Czech culture during the interwar period. In looking at liberal intellectuals such as Karel Čapek and journalist Ferdinand Peroutka, we see their appreciation for the emphasis on civility and civic responsibility in Masaryk's philosophy. However, they could not accept its religious foundation. Protestant philosopher Emanuel Rádl recognized this as a problem. Regarded at the time as one of the nation's leading critics and thinkers, Rádl saw Czechoslovakia's political problems, particularly tensions between Czechs and Germans, as a result of this disconnect between Masaryk's principles and the day-to-day actions of his supposed disciples. In contrast to the president's backers, such as Rádl and Čapek, Catholic writer Jaroslav Durych was an opponent of the republic from the start. Durych's literary brilliance won him critical acclaim and readers, including Čapek, who saw him as one of the most original and talented Czech writers. Durych, in contrast, viewed Čapek as an example of the republic's well-mannered atheism. The Catholic author opened a literary feud with Čapek that lasted until the latter's death in 1938, just weeks after the Munich Agreement brought an end to the state that Čapek had loved and Durych despised.

In looking at Prague of the 1920s–30s, this book can be placed on the shelf with other works of Czech and East Central European studies. First, it offers a revised portrait of Tomáš Masaryk, one of the towering figures of the region's history.[13] There are streets and squares named in Masaryk's honor in Ljubljana, Zagreb, Geneva, Tel Aviv, and Mexico City. He is commemorated with statues in Washington, DC, Chicago, and San Francisco, as well as in towns and cities across Slovakia and the Czech Republic. There is no end to the scholarly literature about him. However, as Andrea Orzoff points out, much of that literature views Masaryk as a "statue, not a person."[14] This book is an attempt to look at Masaryk as a man instead of a monument. Rather than doing this by looking at his political decision-making, as other scholars have, it looks at his lifelong struggle to form, articulate, and gain adherents to his philosophy of religion and morality. This struggle is especially apparent when we view Masaryk within his family. Masaryk's wife Charlotte had a decisive role in shaping his view of the world and his own sense of mission. His daughter Alice was determined to understand and act upon Masaryk's religious and moral ideals, especially in her work as Red Cross director. Yet while Alice venerated her father, even she recognized that his ideals were not set in stone. "I think that you want to come to some worldview," she wrote to him in 1906, when he was fifty-six years old, "but perhaps it is not yet

---

13 Recent biographical works on Masaryk generally view him in heroic terms, yet they are still valuable portraits. See Skilling, *T. G. Masaryk: Against the Current*; and Soubignon, *Tomáš Garrigue Masaryk*. The seven-volume biography by Stanislav Polák is based on exhaustive research in the Masaryk archival collections: *T. G. Masaryk: Za ideálem a pravdou*. Interpretations of Masaryk's thought generally take a more critical approach. Especially useful are the three-volume collection of essays *T. G. Masaryk (1850–1937)*: vol. 1, *Thinker and Politician*; vol. 2, *Thinker and Critic*; and vol. 3, *Statesman and Cultural Force*; Szporluk, *The Political Thought of Thomas G. Masaryk*; Van den Beld, *Humanity: The Political and Social Philosophy of Thomas G. Masaryk*; Schmidt-Hartmann, *T. G. Masaryk's Realism*; and Funda, *Thomas Garrigue Masaryk*.

14 Orzoff, "O mimoparlamentní politice meziválečné ČSR zatím víme dost málo."

clear in itself."[15] Years later, during Masaryk's presidency, Alice Masaryková saw it necessary to remind others of her father's ideals—and
to remind Masaryk himself.

Second, like other studies of Czech and East Central European
history, an important theme of this book is how its subjects understood the identity and contemporary development of the nation. At
the same time, the book looks beyond nationalism. The figures I researched were in no way indifferent to the nation—they were political
and cultural elites in the capital city of a newly established nation-
state. I found, though, that the nation was only one area of concern
for them; it was not the sole lens through which they viewed the
world. Thus, the book places the nation in a horizontal, overlapping
relationship with their other loyalties, commitments, and concerns,
rather than in a vertical, hierarchical relationship, with the nation at
the apex. In taking that approach, I heed the caution of Tara Zahra,
who advised historians to not "replace the national with something
else."[16] For the subjects of this book, the nation was alongside something else—or more accurately, *somethings* else. A case in point is novelist Jaroslav Durych, who was at once a vehement Czech nationalist
and a vehement Catholic. As moderns, Durych and the other figures
in this book understood themselves as fulfilling multiple roles, heed-
ing multiple influences, and having multiple loyalties. Indeed, one
cause of their searching was the question of how to bring these dif-
fuse aspects of modern life—patriotism, citizenship, family, morality,
knowledge, faith, skepticism—into some kind of harmony. These individuals looked up, they looked within themselves, and they looked
around—to the health of communities, the conduct of politics, and
the currents of art and thought. Their searching, I maintain, is an appropriate subject of historical inquiry, one that offers a more complex
and more complete understanding of the nation, the region, and the
era in which they lived.

In looking at these subjects' ideas about religion, this book also
speaks to another field of scholarship. For the last two decades, histo-

---

15 AGM to TGM, 6 December 1906, MÚA AV ČR, TGM Collection, Korespondence III, box 54, fold-
    er 2.
16 Zahra, "Imagined Noncommunities," 111.

rians of religion in twentieth-century Europe have completely revised the standard narrative of secularization. This narrative states that developments dating back to the eighteenth and nineteenth centuries—industrialization, urbanization, the embrace of rationalism and empiricism—brought the steady, inexorable decline of religious practice in Europe. In short, secularization was a necessary product of modernization. In contrast, historians like Hugh McLeod, Callum Brown, and others have argued that, in the cases of Britain, France, and the Low Countries, Christian affiliations and practices continued to have an important place in social and cultural life well into the mid-twentieth century.[17] This book draws upon their body of work on religion in Western Europe. In applying these scholars' questions and insights, I likewise found that religion in interwar Prague was not as moribund or marginal as is typically thought. Certainly, the Christian churches in Prague and Bohemia saw fewer and fewer people enter their doors in the twentieth century. And we can argue that this decline was linked to broader social and economic changes. But when looking at religious decline in the Czech Lands and across Europe, an appropriate approach is that of sociologist José Casanova, who views secularization as related more to identity and culture than the processes of modernization. Casanova writes:

> We need to entertain seriously the proposition that secularization became a self-fulfilling prophecy in Europe, once large sectors of the population ... accepted the basic premises of the theory of secularization: that secularization is a teleological process of modern social change; that the more modern a society, the more secular it becomes... If such a proposition is correct, then the secularization of Western European societies can be explained better in terms of the triumph of the knowledge regime of secularism, than in terms of structural processes of socio-economic development.[18]

---

17 See, for example, Brown, *The Death of Christian Britain*; the collected essays in McLeod, ed., *European Religion in the Age of the Great Cities*; McLeod, *Secularisation in Western Europe*; and McLeod, *The Religious Crisis of the 1960s*.

18 Casanova, "Religion, European Secular Identities, and European Integration," 84.

In looking at interwar Prague, we find that this "knowledge regime of secularism" was not yet fully established. As the book shows, there were Czech intellectuals who believed that modernization would bring the inevitable decline of religious faith and practice. Others, however, insisted that there was a place in modern life for belief. Indeed, some suggested that modern life made the need for belief even more pressing. But how should that belief be expressed in a modern, democratic society? Did that belief require connection to a religious organization? And, most basic of all, what was the object of that belief: the God defined in traditional creeds and doctrines, the God of modernist theology and religious reform movements, or simply Something eternal yet inexplicable?

A word about organization: The book is divided into two parts. The first part consists of three biographical chapters introducing the principal characters: Masaryk, Plečnik, and Masaryková. The chapters focus on the first years of the new century, providing necessary background by looking at their lives in the years before and during the First World War. These are not simply recitations of their life events. Instead, the chapters look at how these figures came to define their religious convictions and devise an outlook on the world based on those convictions. It is inaccurate to say that any of the three experienced a conversion or a "coming to faith" during this time. Instead, each demarcated a redefined religious identity. Certainly, internal reflection contributed to their pledges of conviction, but correspondence with friends and family shows that their thinking on religion was also sparked by observation of external trends: for Plečnik, changes in art; for Masaryková, urban poverty and social dislocation; and for her father, the cultural, even civilizational upheaval of an age that had lost its sense of God. Unnerved by the trends of the times, all three found personal assurance—and a path for their work in the world—in the convictions they defined at the start of the new century.

The second part, comprised of four chapters, looks at the three principals in the context of interwar Prague. The title of this part, "Czechoslovakia under the Perspective of Eternity," refers to Masaryk's insistence that individual citizens and the state's leaders had to conduct their affairs *sub specie aeternitatis*. The first chapter in the section explores Masaryk's ideal for the Czechoslovak state, and the work of Masaryková and Plečnik to give expression to this ideal. Subsequent chapters examine the main subjects' views and activities relative to the religious history of 1920s–30s Czechoslovakia and to the broader question of thinking about God. In addition, this section investigates the views of other cultural and political figures of the time, looking at their understanding of Masaryk's moral-religious republic and the place of religious belief in twentieth-century life. In sum, these chapters look at how some of Prague's writers, academics, and artists—as well as the architect of Prague Castle, the founder of the Red Cross, and the republic's philosopher-president—answered the big questions: Does God exist? Does religion still have meaning and purpose? Can we know what is true and good in the modern age? In taking account of these questions and the longings behind them, we better understand the cultural and social life of the period as well as the limits of nationalist and state-building projects, from the early decades of the twentieth century down to the present age of European unification and globalization.

Part One

Three Portraits
of the Modern Believer

Chapter One

The Philosopher in Search of Truth

In his long career as academic, critic, and politician, Tomáš Garrigue Masaryk cast his attention on an encyclopedic range of subjects. He read in several languages, founded three journals, published books on historical and contemporary questions, and spoke regularly in public fora. One theme was constant in this body of work—religion. Masaryk was fascinated with the contemporary study of religion: the work of modern scholars in the history of religions, literary and historical criticism of scripture, sociology of religion, even theology. At the same time, his thinking was shaped on these and all issues by a sustained religious sentiment that had its roots in the baroque churches of his childhood. Throughout his life, he held to the conviction—as he insisted on calling it—that God existed, that people could relate personally to God, and that this relationship then compelled people to act in kindness and sympathy toward others. Jan Patočka, the foremost Czech philosopher of the twentieth century, observed that this conviction was "the central axis" of Masaryk's thought. "It sets the mood of his entire life. From the earliest, religious feeling plays the role of the moving spirit of his entire life."[1]

Masaryk was fixed on what he called the "religious question." Influenced by philosopher Auguste Comte and his professor at the University of Vienna, Franz Brentano, Masaryk saw the nineteenth centu-

---

[1] Patočka, "Spiritual Crises of European Humanity in Husserl and Masaryk," 109. René Wellek likewise stresses the religious foundations of Masaryk's thought, stating that "Masaryk's philosophy is incomprehensible unless we know that it is ultimately based on the religious assumption." See Wellek, "Masaryk's Philosophy," 18–9.

ry as a time of crisis. In an age of industry, urbanization, science, and technology, he asked, how could the individual man or woman live a fully authentic life, a life of concrete moral knowledge and active responsibility? How could modern society come to a harmony of views, a consensus on right and wrong? The answer Masaryk offered in his thesis on suicide as a social phenomenon, submitted in 1879, remained his creed for the rest of his academic and political career. The modern European individual, the modern European society, and the modern European state had no moral foundation without a convinced awareness of God and the eternal. Masaryk did not seek to save souls (although he did briefly consider entering ministry); instead, his concern was for the present and future, in this world, not the hereafter. At times, though, he took up this message with evangelistic fervor. Masaryk often slipped from measured academic language into acerbic barbs and sloppy arguments. As a self-made man who had risen from low station through hard work and discipline, he was quite sure of himself. Masaryk offered his way of doing things as the right way of doing things, and with his academic training in philosophy, he claimed to base his judgments on unassailable logic.[2] His critics disagreed, labeling him a preacher or a cheap journalist. Even a few of his admirers, past and present, acknowledged the limits of his philosophizing. In the judgment of English philosopher Roger Scruton, Masaryk was in over his head with his sweeping theories on morality and religion. "It is a mistake to attribute to him a philosophical profundity," Scruton remarked.[3] Nevertheless, Masaryk was convinced he was waging a lonely fight for truth.

After Masaryk became president, the standard portrait of him at the turn of the century was that of a resolute, courageous iconoclast, standing against forces of reaction. To be sure, Masaryk did take on

---

2   Masaryk's 1898 lectures on work are the best example of his tendency to point to his personal habits as universally valid. They are published in English as "How to Work," in *The Ideals of Humanity and How to Work.*

3   Scruton, "Masaryk, Kant, and the Czech Experience," 44. Jan Patočka was likewise critical of Masaryk's attempts at a grand, moral-religious-political philosophy: "His synthesis is a theistically corrected [version of] Comte's objectivist positivism together with intrinsic moralism, i.e., the concept of the world from the viewpoint of morally free people. Such elements are metaphysically incompatible, fundamentally contradictory." Patočka, "An Attempt at Czech National Philosophy and Its Failure," 13–4.

conservative Catholics, both at home and in the Austrian parliament, and he became a target of abuse from the Catholic press. But the religious environment of turn-of-the-century Prague and Bohemia was much more unsettled than this simple picture suggests. Within the Church, a group of priests and lay artists calling themselves *Katolická moderna* proposed new literary and visual expressions of the faith; their attempts at reforming religious art inspired other members of the Czech clergy to deliberate ecclesiastical reforms. Spiritual themes were visible in exhibitions of modern art, as Czech painters and sculptors adopted the aesthetics of decadence and symbolism. Acclaimed poets Julius Zeyer and Otokar Březina published works full of mystical and religious imagery. Occultism, theosophy, and other forms of esotericism attracted the curious, as in other European cities. Meanwhile, the political and business leaders of Prague espoused a brand of liberal nationalism that held religious reformer Jan Hus as a hero and marked Jews and Germans as enemies. As Tomáš Vlček describes it, the culture of Prague in 1900 was characterized by both spiritual searching and critical rationalism, by longings for transcendence and debates about the nation's purpose.[4] In this context, Tomáš Masaryk set down a challenge to Czechs (and reaction against his challenge nearly drove him from Prague). At the same time, his religious ideas were a product of the times. Decades of thinking about religion, science, morality, and modern life crystallized in turn-of-the-century Prague. As the new century opened, Masaryk called for a different kind of religion that would free people from clergy and point them in the direction of a more humanitarian society. This "new religion," as he called it, emerged from his observations of contemporary religiosity and studies of modernist theology, as well as his own religious experiences and far-reaching, utopian visions. In public lectures and pamphlets, he gave these visions a gloss of scholarship and expressed them with forceful, sometimes effective arguments. Initially, he gained only a few converts. But after 1918, when he became president of Czechoslovakia, Masaryk offered these same ideals as the civil religion of the newly independent state.

---

4   Vlček, *Praha 1900*, 182–83.

Imagining a New Religion

Masaryk had not been a stranger to controversy since arriving in Prague in 1882 to take a professorship. But in 1900, the year he turned fifty years old, Masaryk found himself at the center of a storm. The previous year, a young Jewish vagrant named Leopold Hilsner had been put on trial for the death of a nineteen-year-old woman from a south Moravian village. Czech Catholic and liberal newspapers charged that Hilsner had killed the girl to use her blood in Jewish rituals, an accusation the lawyer for the victim's family—a leading politician in the liberal nationalist Young Czech Party—even made in the trial. Antisemitism was a strong current in the Czech nationalism of the 1890s, and Hilsner's conviction was the catalyst for violence against Jews in more than a hundred towns in Bohemia and Moravia.[5] Professor Masaryk looked into the case after the trial, with some encouragement from a former student. After reviewing the forensic evidence, he filed an appeal on Hilsner's behalf, arguing that the facts of the case disproved the charge of ritual murder. Masaryk also went public; in pamphlets and newspaper articles, he condemned the speculation of ritual murder as a primitive superstition and criticized the prosecution's faulty handling of the case. Legal and medical experts from outside the Bohemian Lands joined Masaryk in denouncing the verdict, and Hilsner's conviction was annulled and a new trial ordered in 1900. The state prosecutor was no longer able to claim ritual murder as a motive in this second trial (although the lawyer for the victim's family continued to make that claim). Once again, however, Hilsner was convicted of murder and sentenced to death.[6]

After Hilsner's second trial, Masaryk experienced a fierce reaction against his intervention in the case. Austrian authorities fined him for

---

5   Czech antisemitism at the turn of the century was fueled by Czech-German tensions, with Jews believed to be allies of the Germans, and economic nationalism, which warned against putting Czech money into Jewish hands. On the antisemitism of the times and the Hilsner affair, see Kieval, *The Making of Czech Jewry*, 67–83; Kieval, "Death and the Nation"; Frankl, "The Background of the Hilsner Case"; and Miller, "The Rise and Fall of Archbishop Kohn."

6   Hilsner's sentence was later commuted to life in prison, and he was pardoned in 1916. On Masaryk's role in the Hilsner affair, see Beller, "The Hilsner Affair," 52–76; and Skilling, *T. G. Masaryk*, chapter six. Stanislav Polák discusses the Hilsner affair and its aftermath through the first three chapters of his biography, *T. G. Masaryk: Za ideálem a pravdou*, vol. 4, *1900–1914*.

FIGURE 1.1. Portrait of Tomáš Masaryk by Max Švabinský, 1902.
Masaryk Institute and Archive, Academy of Sciences, Czech Republic.

his statements against the courts, and nationalist and Catholic newspapers charged that he was a stooge of Jewish money—or a Jew himself. Students shouted against him in classrooms and even below the windows of his apartment. On one occasion, a group of young men accosted Masaryk on a Prague street and started beating him over the head. Masaryk was able to slip into a nearby hotel, but the gang followed and smashed a window.[7] News of the furor over the Hilsner affair spread throughout the Habsburg Empire and the rest of Europe. Masaryk was more than a controversial figure; he was notorious. The scandal was too much for administrators at the Czech Charles-Ferdinand University in Prague. Tired of their professor's reputation and wary of any more classroom confrontations, the university put Masaryk on leave for the upcoming term, the winter semester of 1901.

---

7   Polák, *T. G. Masaryk: Za ideálem a pravdou*, 4:53.

After Masaryk became president of Czechoslovakia in 1918, the Hilsner affair became a key episode in his hagiography; it was another example of his resoluteness, his unshakeable morality, and his willingness to stand against popular opinion no matter the cost. In Masaryk's own version of the affair, as later relayed by Karel Čapek, he had dared the student protestors to make their case against him, but they had withered at the challenge.[8] In the midst of the scandal, Masaryk received letters from supporters in the Bohemian Lands, Austria, and elsewhere in Europe, who applauded his principled stand. As one Viennese attorney wrote, "You will be judged only *sub specie aeterni*."[9] In recounting the episode to Čapek years later, Masaryk cast the opposition to his stance as little more than a rude annoyance. "I felt very bad about the whole affair not so much for myself as for the low level of it all."[10] But in the years 1900–1, the Hilsner affair brought Masaryk to the breaking point. His health suffered, his mood darkened, and he contemplated leaving Prague. "America is still most alluring to me," he wrote to a friend, "to sit peacefully somewhere, to write what I'm able to, and rest a bit."[11]

Masaryk did go to America. He spent the summer of 1902 giving lectures at the University of Chicago, with the support of the American business owner Charles Crane. At the end of that short sabbatical, he returned to Prague and again entered public life, giving lectures, writing about contemporary events for the periodical *Naše doba* (Our Times), which he had founded, and eventually standing for a seat in the Austrian parliament in 1907. But in the years following his Chicago sojourn, his activities took a new turn. In the crucible of the Hilsner affair, Masaryk had devoted himself to the study of theology and church history. He began the readings over the summer holiday of 1901 and devoted himself to intensive study for the next year, continuing through his stay in Chicago. In addition to reading the works of

---

8   Čapek, *Talks with T. G. Masaryk*, 167–68.
9   Polák, *T. G. Masaryk: Za ideálem a pravdou*, 4:14; and Skilling, *T. G. Masaryk: Against the Current*, 86. Polák discusses the letters of support that Masaryk received.
10 Čapek, *Talks with T. G. Masaryk*, 168.
11 Masaryk, letter to poet J. S. Machar, 25 October 1901, quoted in Polák, *T. G. Masaryk: Za ideálem a pravdou*, 4:450 n24. See also Skilling, *T. G. Masaryk: Against the Current*, 85–6.

contemporary theologians and scholars of religion, Masaryk also corresponded with representatives of Protestant Churches in Germany and Austria, as well as British Unitarians.[12] Rather than simply providing personal consolation, his readings led him to form a comprehensive view of the historical development of religion and its warrant and function in the contemporary world. Masaryk came to a determined diagnosis: modern individuals still needed religion, but religion had to be transformed in order to earn their adherence. This determination became a consistent theme of his writing and speaking after his return from Chicago. On the one hand, he criticized the persistent influence of the Catholic Church in the Austrian Empire, particularly in education. At the same time, he expressed a vision of religious life liberated from churches and doctrines, a form of religion that was suited for modern life. Although Masaryk drew upon theological ideas present in German liberal Protestantism and American Unitarianism since the early nineteenth century, he cast his religious thinking as a decisive turn, what he called the "new religion."[13]

Masaryk premiered this new religion in public lectures in Prague in summer 1904, later published in a book titled *V boji o náboženství* (In the Battle over Religion). The lectures commemorated the execution in 1415 of Jan Hus, and Masaryk opened by discussing the religious significance of the Bohemian church reformer. Since his arrival in Prague, Masaryk had dedicated himself to restoring the religious meaning of Hus's life and career, in contrast to the commonly held view of the reformer as simply a Czech national hero. But he did not use the example of Hus to lead Czechs back to church. Modern people could no longer blindly follow churches, clerics, and doctrines, he insisted. Yes, the teachings of Hus and the Czech reformers were still to be valued, as was the Bible, but religion had to be based on a new foundation. Science, rather than theology, was the basis of knowledge in the modern world. "We also base our religion on this thesis: there are not two truths; there is only one truth," he declared. "Truth is scientific truth, critically examined and substantiated; therefore, the religion

---

12 Polák, *T. G. Masaryk: Za ideálem a pravdou*, 4:465n70.
13 See Axt-Piscalar, "Liberal Theology in Germany," especially 469–80, on the motifs in liberal Protestant thought, many of which correspond directly to Masaryk's ideas.

of the modern person must also rely upon scientific truth. His religion will rely upon conviction, in no way upon faith."[14]

Masaryk maintained that the new religion was still grounded in the teachings of Jesus. But he consciously avoided the term "Christ," with its connotation of divinity; instead, he pointed to the human, historical Jesus as teacher and example. Masaryk added, however, that the ethical teachings of Jesus had to be framed by contemporary philosophical and social-scientific analysis.[15] In other writings on the new religion, Masaryk stated that the New Testament was a work of literature rather than revealed scripture; nobody believed any longer that it had been written by the apostles.[16] Likewise, he declared that traditional Christian theology was an amalgam of Asian religion and Greek and Roman mythology. In contrast, the new religion would rest only on teachings that withstood the test of reason. Masaryk thus defined the creedal beliefs of Protestant and Catholic Christianity as myth. The divinity of Christ, the triune God, the divine inspiration of scripture, the miraculous events recorded in the Gospels: all were excised from the new religion.

According to Masaryk, the new religion would offer a clear and comprehensible understanding of God without the accumulation of ritual and dogma. He spoke of God (*Bůh*), but he did not encourage worship of the deity. Instead, God was a fixed point for comprehending the natural and moral order. Masaryk wrote of the hope for "eternal life," but the aim of the new religion was not to enter the presence of the divine after death. Rather, it was to bring the moral progress of the individual in this life. "The longing for eternity is the main spring of our moral development," he stated, "the hope of immortality strengthens our spirituality."[17] Masaryk adopted the Latin phrase *sub specie aeternitatis*, from the perspective of eternity, as his ethical motto. In the new religion, people would live their daily lives with awareness of the eternal, rather than under fear of a church's strictures or the pressures of modern life. This would be the source for true moral-

14   Masaryk, *V boji o náboženství*, 12–3.
15   Ibid.
16   Masaryk, *Přehled nejnovější filosofie náboženství*, 18.
17   Masaryk, *V boji o náboženství*, 38.

ity.[18] According to Masaryk, people would measure their actions not out of fear of damnation or hope of reward, but by the understanding that they are part of something greater. As one of his interpreters explains: "Eternity does not begin after death, eternity is now, we are living in it. It is possible to live one's life truly and fully only as an immortal soul among kindred souls."[19] In Masaryk's view, this awareness that existence transcends the immediate circumstances of life would lift people from selfishness to service.

Masaryk formulated a narrative of European religious history as a progressive, evolutionary development. The Reformation—which began not in sixteenth-century Germany with Martin Luther but in fourteenth-century Bohemia with Jan Hus—had broken the authority of the Catholic Church. Adherents to Protestantism had gained autonomy in religious belief, thus making their faith more genuine, and the creation of multiple denominations had limited the authority of institutions. To Masaryk, a necessary part of the progressive development was that religion would become "de-ecclesiasticized" (odcírkevováni).[20] This "natural process of evolution" would bring an advance in humanity's understanding of and relation to the divine. Masaryk's vision of the next step in humanity's religious development mixed ideas from German liberal Protestantism, American Unitarianism, and the Bohemian reform movements from the fourteenth through sixteenth centuries, in particular the Unity of the Brethren and their leader Jan Amos Komenský. Nevertheless, Masaryk was convinced that he was on to something wholly original, something epochal and universal. He declared the significance of it all at the close of his 1904 Prague lecture: "Just as the Old Testament was surpassed by the New, so are we surpassing the New Testament. Except this step from a revealed God to an un-revealed God, from revealed religion to un-revealed, is much more difficult."[21]

In the following decade, Masaryk took up the difficult work of declaring and defining his new religion. He appeared frequently before

---

18 Ibid., 22.
19 Hajek, *T. G. Masaryk Revisited*, 41.
20 Masaryk, *The Spirit of Russia*, 1:263.
21 Masaryk, *V boji o náboženství*, 42.

community gatherings and student groups, speaking about the importance of secular education in the empire, the need to emphasize science over religion, and the unholy alliance of clerics and the Habsburg
Austrian state. In addressing these topics, he would slip in references
to "our" modern religion. His words could be provocative. Churches
were "surrogates of religion," insufficient for the spiritual needs of the
modern age.[22] Ritual and sacraments were vestiges of primitive religion—in essence, pagan rites. Catholicism was "the most highly developed form of classical and Asiatic polytheism."[23] But Masaryk tried to
present himself as a reasonable, even moderate figure. At the turn of
the century, he was not alone in debating the place of religion in the
Bohemian Lands, the Austrian Empire, and modern Europe. Commentators of the time used the term "culture war" to describe these debates. Liberals, freethinkers, socialists, and conservative and progressive Catholics waged this war in journals, pamphlets, and public
lectures throughout the country. In October 1906, for example, Masaryk took the stage in the Bohemian city of Hradec Králové for a debate on religion with five other intellectuals: two editors of the secu-
larist journal *Volné myšlenky* (Free Ideas), two theologians from the
local Catholic seminary, and the Jesuit pastor of the St. Salvátor
Church, adjacent to the university in Prague. In addressing the reasons that intellectuals were leaving the Church, Masaryk raised one
controversial issue after another: the declaration of papal infallibility
in 1870, the Church's opposition to modern science and philosophy,
celibacy of the clergy, the continued existence of the Index of Prohibited Books, an authoritarian ecclesiastical structure that prevented reform. But Masaryk insisted, as he typically did when criticizing the
Church, that he was not an opponent of religion. "I have one opponent
in the question of religion and that is indifference," he declared, "indifference in the church, indifference outside of the church." The philosopher insisted that he was Catholic "to the bone"; he knew the Church's
history and teachings inside and out. If his adversaries saw him as a
foe of religion, then they did not comprehend him or his message. As

---

22 Ibid., 27.
23 Masaryk, *The Spirit of Russia*, 2:501.

he stated in the debate: "My Catholic adversaries are unable to understand that I work for religion."[24]

Masaryk typically took this stance whenever someone accused him of criticizing religion: It is a mistake to say I'm opposed to religion, because I am religious myself and see religion as important. This was his defense, for example, in the spring of 1906, when he was brought in on formal charges of slandering the Catholic Church. The charges stemmed from a student meeting at a Prague restaurant, where Masaryk had spoken on the controversy over a Moravian teacher's published criticism of religion and the heated Catholic response to those comments.[25] As Masaryk spoke about the episode, a police agent in the audience suddenly announced the event over and officers cleared the room. Catholic newspapers again scorned their old enemy. The clerical daily *Čech* (The Czech) suggested that the inspiration behind Masaryk's statements against the Church was his alliance with the Jews. Another paper saw a more insidious source: "We see in this attack only one part of the systematic attack against Christ and his teachings by the camp of the Antichrist."[26] More threatening to Masaryk were the legal challenges that followed. He reckoned beforehand that if he lost the case, he would be forced to leave Prague. Nonetheless, he did not back down from his accuser. From the start of the proceedings Masaryk went on the counterattack, accusing the police agent (a German whose knowledge of Czech was lacking) of taking his words out of context. Masaryk insisted that he had not criticized religion but had argued against religious education and against the Church's association with the state. The judge asked him to explain a quotation attributed to him in the periodical *Čas* (Time): "I do not

---

24 Masaryk, *Inteligence a náboženství*, 141–42.

25 The scandal began in December 1905, when a priest in the city of Prostějov, Karel Dostál-Lutinov, who was one of the founders of the *Katolická moderna* movement, responded to an article in the catalog of a modern art exhibition in Prague. The article, which discussed artist František Kupka's cycle of paintings called "Religion," was signed by Kara Ben Jehuda, but Dostál-Lutinov knew that this was the pen name of local high school teacher Karel Juda. Dostál-Lutinov wrote a letter to the Prostějov newspaper, pointing out Juda's critical comments on religion and questioning how a teacher could do that. Dostál-Lutinov's letter opened a storm of debate in Moravia and Bohemia about religion in schools, the freedom of thought and expression allowed to teachers, and restrictions on education. See Marek, *Český katolicismus, 1890–1914*, 511–26.

26 Quoted in Polák, *T. G. Masaryk: Za ideálem a pravdou*, 4:178.

stand against religion, but against a decadent religion that needs politicians for its defense." Yes, he had used the phrase "decadent religion," Masaryk admitted. What he had meant, though, was that a faith weakened by clericalism required the power of the state to uphold it. He turned to the police agent and asked a question: Why does God need the police? *That* was the insult, Masaryk stated, to suggest that God needed the state.[27]

Masaryk then added his standard defense: "I did not speak against Catholicism. I did not speak against religion. I spoke against the contradiction of theology and science. And I only asserted something. In no way did I criticize."[28] His attorney followed this approach, introducing as evidence the front-page article in a recent issue of *Die Christliche Welt*, a Lutheran newspaper published in Marburg, Germany. The article denounced as absurd the suggestion that Masaryk was waging a campaign against religion. Masaryk was a man of deep religious conviction and piety, wrote the article's author, a German Lutheran pastor named Walter Schmidt. In fact, as someone who prayed and read scripture daily, the professor was an example for all Czechs concerned with religion. The claim that Pastor Schmidt's appraisal was something like an objective confirmation of Masaryk's religiosity was disingenuous: Schmidt was a frequent visitor at the Masaryk house in Prague, and he had provided the text of the article to Masaryk before the trial.[29] It is unclear whether the argument had any effect with the judge. Most likely, the charges fell apart when the prosecution's two witnesses, students who had been at the restaurant meeting, could not confirm the police agent's accusation that Masaryk had slandered the Church. At the end of the day-long proceeding, Masaryk was acquitted. He emerged from the court building to the cheers from his students.

Masaryk saw himself as a religious man standing for a rational, tolerant understanding of God and humanity, someone who wanted to save religion from the churches. Any strong words he may have spoken

---

27 Stenographic record of the judicial proceedings against Masaryk, 23 May 1906, pp. 10–11, MÚA AV ČR, TGM Collection, Osobní, box 534, folder 16.

28 Ibid., 13.

29 Polák, *T. G. Masaryk: Za ideálem a pravdou*, 4:183.

were necessary. Years later he recalled his struggles over religion: "It's true that a long time ago, before the war, I came into bitter conflicts with Catholic theologians, writers, and journalists. But the documents prove that I did not provoke those disputes."[30] Despite insisting on his moderate stance, Masaryk would not allow himself any room for collaboration with any Catholics—even those who likewise deplored the authoritarian structure and antimodern viewpoints of the Church. Masaryk was initially supportive of the *Katolická moderna* movement in the Bohemian Lands, an effort of progressive priests to have the Church speak more relevantly to the contemporary age. But he later turned against the movement with bitter hostility and privately mocked the priest who led it. Masaryk saw Catholic and modern as fundamentally incompatible.[31]

Similarly, during a 1907 parliamentary debate on the Church's involvement in Austrian education, Masaryk showed little regard for one Catholic deputy's suggestion of a settlement in the culture war.[32] This deputy, Janez Evangelist Krek of Slovenia, was perhaps a model of Masaryk's idea of an active religion. He wrote novels and theological essays, and edited the influential cultural journal *Dom in Svet* (Home and the world). As a priest, Krek was a tireless advocate of Christian socialism, promoting the creation of savings and loan cooperatives for Slovene peasants and workers. Masaryk's statements in the education debate brought shouts and slurs from other deputies, but Krek was a solitary voice of reason and charity. He agreed with Masaryk that the Church's role in education could not be maintained by political intervention. He did defend Catholic teaching, particularly in a time of such social and economic change. Yet Krek also insisted, "If people stand up openly with a contrary viewpoint—good, we must welcome

---

30 Masaryk, "Filosofický náčrt" [Philosophical sketch], letter to Karel Čapek, dated October 1927, corrected 19 November 1930, p. 44, contained in the file of draft manuscripts of Čapek's *Hovory s TGM III*, "Nezjištení verse," MÚA AV ČR, TGM Collection L, no. 95, box 654.

31 Šmid, "Vztah Tomáše Garrigua Masaryka k české Katolické moderně na přelomu 19. A 20. století"; and Marek, *Český katolicismus, 1890–1914*, 400–408.

32 The debate was part of the political scandal known as the Wahrmund affair, first stirred by Vienna's mayor and leader of the Christian Social Party, Karl Lueger. John Boyer discusses the broader scandal and Masaryk's part in it in the context of Viennese politics in *Culture and Political Crisis in Vienna*, 186–99.

this." The priest declared that Catholics must not fight against free-thinkers and social democrats, but work with them for the higher development of people. "We have a bridge, by which we can reach the freethinkers." Krek clarified that this did not mean accepting a freedom of thought that allowed for intellectual laziness or smugness. Instead, Catholics should reach out to those secular thinkers, whether philosophers or socialists, who have sympathy for others and an understanding of reality, of the difficulties of life. To these freethinkers, aware of the emotional struggles of people, a bridge was possible, "a bridge founded on the sense for truth and justice."[33]

Masaryk appreciated Krek's words, and repeated that he was not against religion. He rebutted, however, that the role of religion in society could only be established on natural and scientific foundations, not on supernatural mysteries or the notion of revelation. If Krek was willing to teach that to people, then yes, Masaryk could work with him. "Yes, certainly there is this bridge," Masaryk acknowledged, "equity and truth!" But that bridge was to be built not on the freethinkers' and socialists' recognition of the Church's standpoint, but on the Catholic priest recognizing the standpoint of the freethinkers and socialists. "You had very good things to say about social democracy and the secular worldview," declared Masaryk to Krek. "Here apparently is the possibility of a bridge."[34] The exchange in the Austrian parliament was indicative of Masaryk's stance toward clergy and theologians throughout his life. A bridge of understanding was possible and, indeed, desirable. But Masaryk would set its pillars.

The Spiritual Pastor

What leads someone to propose a new religion? The immediate circumstances of Masaryk's crusade at the turn of the century were his experiences during the Hilsner affair and his time of concentrated study in recent theology and religious studies. But his desire for a different kind of religious belief and practice was a constant throughout

---

33 Krek's comments in parliamentary debate of 4 December 1907, quoted (in Czech translation) in Kovtun, *Slovo má poslanec Masaryk*, 206.

34 Masaryk speech, parliamentary debate of 4 December 1907, in *Parlamentní projevy, 1907–1914*, 71.

his life. Masaryk's deliberate rejection of Catholicism was the familiar story of a young European deciding that the church of his childhood could not stand against scientific learning and the realities of modern society. Yet despite this turn from the Church, Masaryk refused to turn away from God. Masaryk repeatedly insisted—as he did in the debate in Hradec Králové, his trial in Prague, and the debate in Vienna—that he was a religious person. "All the money in the world could not unhinge in me the belief in a personal God," he declared in an interview with two priests, while the embers of the Hilsner affair still smoldered. "The intentionality of the universe bears so powerfully on the soul that one must recognize God. I am much closer, for example, to you Catholic priests than I am to some university professor who is a pantheist or materialist."[35]

Once he had formulated his idea of the new religion, Masaryk was careful to distinguish himself not as a man of faith (*víra*) or a believer (*věřící*) but as a man of conviction. Masaryk clarified that belief amounted to passive acceptance of catechisms and dogma. Once he had lost that simple faith, it could be replaced only with conviction, which was rooted in firm knowledge (the Czech word for conviction, *přesvědčení*, includes the common Slavic root for knowledge or science: *věd*). As was his custom, Masaryk extrapolated from personal experience. He described his move from uncritical belief to conviction as characteristic of modern individuals, and he translated his own spiritual and intellectual biography into the roadmap to the new religion.

Raised in villages of southeastern Moravia, near the present boundaries of the Czech Republic, Slovakia, and Austria, Masaryk was steeped in the traditions of village Catholicism. His mother was a model of folk religiosity, taking her son to mass, processions, and pilgrimages. Memories of those experiences remained deeply embedded. In his 1902 interview with the two priests, published in a Catholic newspaper, Masaryk stated: "The impressions from my youth, the memories, their center is my mother, a devout Catholic. As of yet, they

---

35 "Návštěvou u prof. Masaryka" [A visit with Prof. Masaryk], interview with priests Emil Dlouhý-Pokorný and Ladislav Kunte, *Katolické listy*, 28 January 1902, in *Ideály Humanitní a Texty z let 1901–1903*, 171.

have not faded from my mind. More often than not I feel myself a Catholic."[36] The male examples of religious practice for Masaryk were the young priest in his home village and one of his gymnasium teachers in Brno (Brünn), both of whom offered books from the library to the inquisitive boy. The teacher in Brno, Father Matěj Procházka, was a particular influence, presenting to Masaryk the example of a learned priest who was committed to social change.[37] At the same time, however, Masaryk encountered priests in Brno whose example of worldly living drove him first from the confessional booth and then from the doors of the Church.[38] The First Vatican Council's declaration of papal infallibility, occurring when Masaryk was a twenty-year-old university student, confirmed his view of Catholicism as an institution at odds with the times. He judged the Catholic Church as ruined in both intellectual and moral terms. Decades later, Masaryk still revered his mother's example of devotion, and he recalled fondly the splendor of his village's baroque church.[39] Yet he also described the faith he had shared with his mother as "primitive," undisturbed by the realities of the larger world. He came to see Catholicism, with its mysticism and sensuality, its reverence of tradition and authority, as a remnant of Europe's premodern past. "This childhood has passed away forever," Masaryk insisted, referring to himself and to Europe, "simply because childhood must yield to maturity."[40]

As a younger man, Masaryk often was not so poetic in his opinions. The aspiring academic could be a fierce critic of Catholicism. Still,

---

36 Ibid.
37 Masaryk, "Filozofie," in *Světová revoluce*, 421. This final chapter of Masaryk's memoirs, written in 1925, was not published until the 1938 edition. Roman Szporluk discusses the particular importance of the priest in Brno, Father Procházka, on the subsequent development of Masaryk's religious ideas. See Szporluk, *The Political Thought of Thomas G. Masaryk*, 12–5.
38 See the diary notes of Charlotte Garrigue on letters she received from Masaryk during their engagement. The notes of 17 December 1877 refer to Masaryk's dim view of the priests in Brno as a factor in his break with the Catholic Church. Diary of 1877–78, MÚA AV ČR, CGM Collection, box 2, folder 7D. In the 1938 edition of his memoirs, Masaryk explained that the Brno priests were interested only in food, drink, and money. "Filozofie," in *Světová revoluce*, 422. In the 1902 interview with Catholic priests Emil Dlouhý-Pokorný and Ladislav Kunte, Masaryk went into greater detail explaining his disenchantment with the church, including his concerns about Catholic dogma and the declaration of papal infallibility: "Navštěvou u prof. Masaryka," 171–73.
39 "Our church was heaven on earth to me," Masaryk recalled in his memoirs. *Světová revoluce*, 422.
40 Masaryk, *The Spirit of Russia*, 1:5.

even though Masaryk scorned the Church as unsuited for the modern age, he did not renounce belief in God. "I did not want to declare myself as being without a religious affiliation," he recalled in his 1902 interview for the Catholic newspaper, "since this means for me a negation."[41] As a student of philosophy in Vienna under the young professor and priest Franz Brentano, Masaryk could not conceive of an ethics or ontology without a deity as its center. These speculations inclined him to Plato, and he adopted from Platonic thought a conception of God as the rational, integrative capstone of the cosmos.[42] At the same time, he held to a Catholic belief in a personal God, and his interest in religion remained lively and committed, rather than only abstract and philosophical. Masaryk read theology during his postgraduate studies in Leipzig in the 1870s, sharing with Brentano the belief that the modern individual suffered from a spiritual crisis, rooted in the loss of faith and sense of meaning.[43] In his subsequent habilitation thesis, a study of suicide in modern European society, he saw this absence of religious conviction as the cause of a cultural sickness that manifested itself in an increase in suicides. Masaryk even engaged in what we might call evangelistic activity, at least with one notable acquaintance. In Leipzig he met a mathematics student from Moravia, Emund Husserl, and guided the younger man's initial forays into philosophy. When Husserl moved to Vienna to continue his studies under Brentano, Masaryk served as something of a mentor while working to complete his thesis. Already in Leipzig, Masaryk had shared his vision of an ideal state, in which citizens would be united by culture, morality, and love of homeland; in Vienna, he gave a Bible to the Jewish-born Husserl and encouraged him to read the New Testament. Husserl was later baptized into the Lutheran Church, and the Bible he received

---

41 Masaryk, "Navštěvou u prof. Masaryka," 171.

42 On the formation of Masaryk's philosophy as a student, see Polák, *T. G. Masaryk: Za ideálem a pravdou*, 1:293–98. On Masaryk's thinking relative to Herder, Kant, and Descartes, see Barnard, "Humanism and Titanism: Masaryk and Herder"; and Scruton, "Masaryk, Kant, and the Czech Experience." On Masaryk's relationship with Brentano and the professor's other students, see Novák, "Masaryk and the Brentano School"; and the collection of essays Zumr and Binder, eds., *T. G. Masaryk und die Brentano-Schule.*

43 Novák, "Masaryk and the Brentano School," 36–7.

FIGURE 1.2. Tomáš Masaryk, 1882, after his move to Prague.
Masaryk Institute and Archive, Academy of Sciences, Czech Republic.

from Masaryk remained in his library to the end of his life.[44] After
Masaryk became president, Husserl wrote admiring letters to his old
friend, expressing hope that Czechoslovakia would fulfill Masaryk's
ideals and lead to an ethical renewal of Europe. As Michael Gubser
notes, Husserl and other phenomenologists regarded Masaryk as one
of their own, even though Masaryk's own philosophical writings did
not necessarily influence their work. Masaryk and Husserl shared the
prognosis of Europe in moral and intellectual crisis, fueled by relativ-

---

44   Schuhmann, "Husserl and Masaryk," 155–56. Patočka discusses the different views on religion held by
     Masaryk and Husserl in "Spiritual Crises of European Humanity in Husserl and Masaryk," 100–4.

ism and skepticism, and they insisted on devotion to truth and ethics as the source of renewal. Already in Vienna, the two young philosophers—one, whose interest in mathematics led to logic and epistemology, and the other, who would be drawn to sociology and then to politics—saw themselves as engaged in a common struggle.[45]

Masaryk's own reading of scripture and theology led him to convert to the Reformed Church in 1880. In long conversations with the pastor of the southern Moravian congregation where he was received, Masaryk declared his intention of becoming a minister. The pastor, however, suggested that Masaryk would have greater influence on Czechs not as a minister but as a believing professor.[46] Masaryk took up this vocation. In 1882 he and his family moved to Prague, where he accepted a professorship at the newly established Czech-language university. From the start, Masaryk's academic activities showed a missionary intent. Prague was unknown to Masaryk, and when he arrived he was struck by the indifference to religion in the city. "Everywhere I saw a frightful deadness," he recalled decades later.[47] He judged the Czechs of the Bohemian capital as being in a state of "half-Catholicism," holding a nominal connection to the Church with no significant intellectual or ethical meaning. Masaryk was also critical of liberal nationalists' appropriation of the Hussite movement of the fourteenth and fifteenth centuries, which they stripped of all religious meaning. In this atmosphere of religious detachment, Masaryk offered his first university lectures in Prague on the thought of Blaise Pascal. The seventeenth-century philosopher and mathematician, a man of both science and Christian conviction, was influential for Masaryk. But Masaryk saw religion not simply as a source of personal assurance in changing times; religious awareness could also repair current social problems. He followed the lectures on Pascal by speaking on what he called a "practical philosophy," proposing religious conviction and the Christian principle of love as a solution to the ills of contemporary society.[48] Masaryk quickly

---

45   Gubser, *The Far Reaches*, 140–44.
46   On his visits with Císař in the town of Klobouky and Masaryk's conversion, see Polák, *T. G. Masaryk: Za ideálem a pravdou*, 1:314–17.
47   Gašparíková-Horáková, *U Masarykovcov*, 110.
48   On Masaryk's first lectures in Prague, see Polák, *T. G. Masaryk: Za ideálem a pravdou*, 2:77–85, 103–5.

gained a reputation as the philosophy professor who spoke seriously of religion and Jesus, gaining the nickname of "spiritual pastor." Given his frequent run-ins with colleagues in his first years on the faculty, it is likely that the name was not entirely complimentary.[49]

Masaryk's first major academic work, his habilitation thesis on suicide in modern society, set the template for much of his later writing on religion. Trained as a philosopher but drawn to the emerging field of sociology, Masaryk weaved together evidence from literary texts and statistics on suicide from various countries. He also diverged to distant subjects and launched into sweeping pronouncements, which he presented as the self-evident conclusions from his empirical research. At the root of Masaryk's interpretation of contemporary suicide was his belief that connection to the divine was essential to human nature. "Man needs religion to live as much as he needs air to breathe."[50] In countries such as France, Germany, and Austria, belief in God and the social links that religion provided had eroded, leaving only skepticism, indifference, and pessimism in their wake. Meanwhile, in England and the United States, freedom of religion had encouraged genuine, personally held belief, thus keeping suicide rates relatively low. Masaryk's solution to the problem of suicide was a restoration of religion. He did not mean a revival swelled by individual conversions. Instead, Masaryk looked to the presumably harmonious society of the Middle Ages, when a shared religious worldview ordered social relations and individual behavior. Of course, he did not propose the restoration of medieval Catholicism. Instead, Masaryk closed his first book with speculation about a new religion that would shape society and culture just as fully as Catholicism did in the Middle Ages, while at the same time maintaining the individual faith emphasized in Protestantism. This new religion, he wrote,

> could inaugurate a new and better Middle Ages, after which a new period of free thought would begin again, until at last, through alternating periods of belief and disbelief, "one flock and one shep-

---

49 Polák, *T. G. Masaryk: Za ideálem a pravdou*, 2:214–15. On Masaryk's difficulties at the university, see Skilling, *T. G. Masaryk: Against the Current*, 1–3.

50 Masaryk, *Suicide and the Meaning of Civilization*, 223.

herd" would appear. Or it may happen quite differently... It is possible that a new upswing of religious feeling would take place without ecclesiastical unification. Perhaps the Congregational or some similar method could even bring to a definitive conclusion and stabilize that religious individualism to which Protestantism has so far attained.[51]

Tomáš Masaryk was not unlike other intellectual dreamers of the mid-nineteenth century. Observing a society and culture in turmoil, the young academic sought the return of a supposedly lost world, one of social accord and unity in moral purpose. The foundation to this idyll would not be political revolution or the scientific understanding of history. Masaryk disagreed with these tenets of Marxist thought, as well as its wholly materialist basis. Politics and economics were fields that concerned the body; Masaryk was fixed upon the soul—this was the core of the concrete human being.[52] Whereas Marxism dissolved the individual human into a deterministic system, Masaryk insisted upon the active, autonomous, and spiritual human subject as central to his social and political thought.[53] In his view then, the cure to modernity's ills was religious. His work as the "spiritual pastor" in Prague, the professor who talked about Jesus, was not simply a matter of ministering to students or spurring a rethinking of belief in a climate of liberal nationalism. Already as a young professor, Masaryk's thinking on religion had a much broader aim. In the mid-1890s, when he wrote a series of articles on religion, later published in book form as *Moderní člověk a náboženství* (Modern man and religion), Masaryk again described European civilization as suffering from a spiritual sickness. Surveying the intellectual and cultural currents converging at the end of the nineteenth century, Masaryk saw only confusion in modern Europeans' thinking about basic concerns. What does it mean to be hu-

---

51 Ibid., 256. On Masaryk's ideas on religion in his writings on suicide, see Page, "The Social Philosophy of T. G. Masaryk."

52 Masaryk makes this analogy of body and soul in *Modern Man and Religion*, 51.

53 Theologian Jan Milič Lochman discusses Masaryk's opposition to Marx's materialism—as well as other points of disagreement and agreement—in his essay "Masaryk's Quarrel with Marxism," 120–33, especially 128–31. Masaryk's 1899 counter to Marxism is translated as *Masaryk on Marx*.

man? What is the purpose of life? What is the root of morality, the object of hope, the source of contentment? According to Masaryk, the absence of answers to these questions had brought his contemporaries to despair. The loss of a coherent religious outlook, he wrote, "means intellectual and moral disquietude and anarchy." Europe at the turn of the century was at a passage in its history, a period of struggle "between the incomplete new outlook and the old one." Humanity in its modern state was not yet complete, but attaining that completeness required resolution to the question of religion. "The old religion of the people is dying out and modern man is trying to find a substitute for it." Masaryk's solution to the uncertainty of modern life in the 1890s was the same as it had been twenty years earlier. "It may be a new, or at least a renovated, religion."[54] What he had to do—and what he set to do in the first years of the new century—was to determine the contours of this new religion.[55]

Care for the Soul of the Nation

The new religion that Tomáš Masaryk proposed was like the old in that it included a special role for particular peoples, and especially the Czech nation. Yet, rather than mixing an exclusive nationalism into his religion, Masaryk sought to integrate the distinctive identity of the Czechs—and every other nation—into an all-embracing theory of historical and moral development. This view of a special role for nations came only after he had lived several years in Prague and involved himself in Czech cultural and political life. Prior to that time, Masaryk's thinking on religion, ethics, and other questions had been broad in scope. He criticized Catholicism in the Austrian Empire, he pointed to social and cultural trends in Europe, and he cited religious freedom in the United States; but his statements about the necessity of religion always referred to humanity in general. Like other intellectual dreamers

---

54 Masaryk, *Modern Man and Religion*, 37–38.

55 One of Masaryk's foremost interpreters, Antonie van den Beld, writes that his *Modern Man and Religion* "leaves us mostly groping in the dark." Van den Beld, *Humanity*, 33. While Masaryk made plenty of critiques and raised plenty of questions, there was little in terms of a positive explication of what modern religion should be.

of nineteenth-century Europe, he understood his solutions to the problems around him as being universally applicable. Initially, his broad prognoses and prescriptions did not allow room for small collectives of people competing with each other. In the words of one of Masaryk's foremost interpreters, Roman Szporluk: "We might say that against the *ethnos* Masaryk asserted the rights of the *logos*."[56] By the 1890s, however, Masaryk applied his thinking on religion and civilization to the specific social and political situation of the Czechs. As a moral and religious thinker, he believed that the Czechs needed moral and religious direction. In Masaryk's view, that was the solution to the "national question."[57]

Thinking in terms of nationality did not come easily for Masaryk. Szporluk points out that Masaryk's family background was fundamental in shaping his sense of national identity, or lack thereof. His mother was from a German family and spoke the language to her children, while his father spoke the local West Slavic dialect. After Masaryk's birth in 1850, the family moved from one imperial estate to another in a region called Slovačko, a rural area crisscrossed by the boundaries of Austria, Moravia, and Upper Hungary, the name at the time for Slovakia. Like other border regions, this was a backwater of mixed marriages, mixed languages, and uncertain ethnic identities: a source of frustration for geographers, census takers, and politicians who sought to draw distinct lines among national groups. As Szporluk observes, Masaryk was a citizen of nowhere, so he was able to adapt himself wherever he lived.[58] His eventual move to Prague was by no means foreordained by some long-held Czech nationalist sentiment. If anything, Masaryk was a Slovak, and later in life he identified himself as such both privately and publicly.[59] When he first came to the Bohemian capital at age thirty-two, Masaryk had little knowledge of the city. He even had trouble writing in Czech.[60]

56 Szporluk, *The Political Thought of Thomas G. Masaryk*, 62.
57 Pynsent, introduction to *T. G. Masaryk (1850–1937)*, vol. 2, *Thinker and Critic*, 3–4; and Vlček, *Praha 1900*, 61.
58 Szporluk, *The Political Thought of Thomas G. Masaryk*, 20–1.
59 Gašparíková, diary entry of 3 October 1931, in *U Masarykovcov*, 126.
60 Polák, *T. G. Masaryk: Za ideálem a pravdou*, 2:17.

Masaryk was an outsider in Prague. He had lived for years in Vienna, the cosmopolitan imperial capital; he had studied in Leipzig in the powerful new German Empire; and he had even been to New York City. He was someone who had seen the world, whereas a charitable description of Prague and its intellectual environment at the time was provincial. In Masaryk's view, the Czechs of Prague had replaced a narrow-minded and intolerant Catholicism with a narrow-minded and intolerant nationalism. He saw his task as casting the light of science and reason into this muddle, prompting Czech society—not simply the students in his lectures—to an increase in rational thinking and morality.[61] With his lectures and particularly his founding of the academic journal *Athenaeum*, Masaryk brought a needed critique to Czech intellectual life and opened windows to scholarship outside of Bohemia and Austria. But in the process, the young professor stepped on many toes.

In addition to his bumps and scrapes with Czech intellectuals, young Masaryk had difficulty fitting the idea of the nation, and nations in general, into his fundamental view of the world. When Masaryk eventually began writing about the Czech nation in the 1890s, it came only after a shift in his ethical and religious thought. He came to acknowledge that individuals were part of nations, rather than wholly autonomous agents. Membership in a nation placed historical and cultural parameters on an individual's moral outlook. And the nations themselves, Masaryk determined, were more than the sum of their individual members. They were organic entities with their own distinctive characters. Each nation's character—manifest in history, literature, and the arts—was potentially a force for greater good, for universal regeneration. Masaryk thus brought the *ethnos* and *logos* together: nations were instruments of Providence, and the character of each nation was more than historical or cultural—it was spiritual. The nation had a soul.

Masaryk plumbed the Czech soul in his writings of the 1890s, most notably his book *The Czech Question*. He identified an underlying meaning or sense (*smysl*) of Czech history and culture, from the medi-

---

61   Ibid., 32–33.

eval period to the national revival of the mid-1800s. This meaning was found in asking the basic question of the nation's existence: How can a small nation, at the very center of Europe, remain substantive and autonomous? How can it survive? With violence? By following the example of the Poles, with their repeated uprisings? "Not with violence, but peacefully," was Masaryk's answer, speaking in the language of the spiritual shepherd, "not with the sword but with the plow, not with blood but with work, not with death but with life leading to life—that is the answer of Czech genius, that is the meaning of our history and the legacy of our great ancestors."[62]

For Masaryk, the meaning of the Czech nation was found specifically in its religious heritage. The shining moment of the nation's history was the "Bohemian Reformation" of the fifteenth through seventeenth centuries: Jan Hus's challenge to the Catholic Church, which led to his execution; the armed struggle of Hus's followers after his death, led by the general Jan Žižka; the criticism of that armed conflict by lay theologian Petr Chelčický and the founding of the Unity of the Brethren Church on Chelčický's ideas; and finally the intellectual and spiritual leadership of the Brethren by the great bishop and philosopher Jan Amos Komenský. For Masaryk, these chapters of religious history were moments when the Czechs stood independently, offering resistance to the Catholic Church and the growing power of the Germans in Central Europe. It was also an instance when Czech thinkers offered truly compelling, innovative ideas which earned the attention of other Europeans. Martin Luther declared himself and all reformers as Hussites, Masaryk pointed out. So if Luther's Reformation was commonly seen as integral to the development of modern Europe, and Luther saw himself as following Hus, then this meant that the Hussite movement, a movement of Czechs, was the *real* beginning of the modern age. According to Masaryk, these religious movements in Bohemia and Moravia manifested the virtues of modernity: the cultivation of reason, altruistic service for one's neighbors, and a democratic, nonhierarchical form of social organization. Moreover, these virtues were

---

62 Masaryk, "Česká otázka," in *Česká otázka, Naše nynější krize, Jan Hus*, 106. A slightly different English translation is in the collection of Masaryk's essays on Czech history and culture, *The Meaning of Czech History*, 111.

not simply those of a small Christian sect. They were the essence of Czechness. As Masaryk stated in 1910, on the anniversary of Hus's martyrdom: "We see in the Czech Reformation a deeper manifestation of the Czech soul and our national character."[63]

The Czech soul was revealed not only in the nation's history; it was also exemplified in the heroes of that history. Like other Czech nationalists, Masaryk adopted the practice of referring to figures in the national pantheon in his speeches and writings. For example, he declared in his first speech to the Austrian parliament after his election in 1907: "We in Bohemia, our nation, we are the nation of Hus, Žižka, Chelčický, and Komenský. You in Vienna have not a whit of understanding of these figures."[64] In Czech political culture of the time (and indeed, throughout contemporary Czech history), mere mention of these historical characters evoked the virtues of the nation. But what, specifically, were these virtues? Masaryk found that there was little understanding of what the leaders of the Bohemian Reformation represented. They were simply slogans. "We are the nation of Hus, and we like to call ourselves such," he observed in his 1896 book on the reformer. "However, are we the nation of Hus in truth and in fact? We are not. Not yet."[65]

Masaryk took it upon himself to explain the significance of these figures. In his interpretation of the national heroes, Hus stood high as the unwavering proclaimer of truth. Masaryk closed his 1910 speech honoring the reformer with a recitation of Hus's well-known prayer: "'Seek truth, listen to the truth, learn the truth, love the truth, speak the truth, keep the truth, defend the truth with your very life!'"[66] Throughout his life, Masaryk cited Hus's devotion to truth as a model, and he had the reformer's model "Pravda vítězí" (Truth prevails) em-

---

63 Masaryk, *The Meaning of Czech History*, 10. Schmidt-Hartmann offers a critical analysis of Masaryk's thinking on the Reformation and its connections to Czech national character in *Thomas G. Masaryk's Realism*, 121–25.

64 Masaryk, speech in parliamentary session of 20 July 1907, in *Parlamentní projevy, 1907–1914*, 29.

65 Masaryk, "Jan Hus: Naše obrození a naše reformace" [Jan Hus: Our revival and our reformation] (1896), in *Česká otázka, Naše nynější krize, Jan Hus*, 314.

66 Masaryk, "Jan Hus and the Czech Reformation," from his speech delivered in 1910 at Kozí Hrádek, in *The Meaning of Czech History*, 14. Masaryk lectured on each of the leading figures of the Bohemian reformation at the University of Chicago. See *The Lectures of Professor T. G. Masaryk at the University of Chicago, Summer 1902.*

blazoned on his presidential flag. In contrast, Masaryk's reference to Jan Žižka in the parliament speech was rare for him. The innovative military leader of the Hussite rebellion represented strength, bravery, and fortitude, but as someone inclined to pacifism, Masaryk was drawn more to Žižka's contemporary, Petr Chelčický, who had opposed the Hussites' use of force, even in self-defense. Masaryk interpreted Chelčický as a man of unbendable morality, someone who held to his convictions in the face of popular opinion, yet who was also a radical—even an anarchist.[67] Most important to Masaryk was Jan Amos Komenský. Certainly, Hus was the primary figure of the Czechs' religious heritage, someone who revealed traits of the national soul in his life and example, but Komenský represented the whole of the Bohemian Reformation. Bishop, theologian, pedagogue, and philosopher, Komenský had proposed—in Masaryk's view—a higher form of religion, one that embraced reason over mysticism and humble service over hierarchical institutions. In his voluminous writings and his leadership, Komenský offered spiritual wisdom and practical direction to the nation, synthesizing the ideals of both Hus and Chelčický and anticipating the efforts of the nineteenth-century awakeners.[68] "Hus attracts by his example," Masaryk stated, "but in the end I must admit that the Reformation progressed beyond Hus, and I choose Komenský." Masaryk was drawn to the harmony of Komenský's life and thought, and he sought for a similar harmony for himself and the nation. "We must find the kind of harmony advocated by Komenský, a harmony that would unify all the beautiful elements of our reformation."[69]

Indeed, a large part of Masaryk's attraction to Komenský was the bishop's advocacy of education. Outside of the Czech Lands, Komenský—or, as he is more widely known, Comenius—is recognized as one of the founders of modern education (in his lifetime, this reputation led to an offer to serve as president of a newly founded college in Britain's American colonies; in the mid-1600s, though, the draw of Harvard was not yet strong enough to lure Komenský across the Atlantic). Masaryk likewise saw education as vital to the continued development

---

67   *The Lectures of Professor T. G. Masaryk*, 70–5.
68   Polák, *T. G. Masaryk: Za ideálem a pravdou*, 3:28–9.
69   Masaryk, "Jan Hus and the Czech Reformation," 11.

of the Czech nation. Many of his activities as a public intellectual, beyond his writing and teaching, aimed at building institutions to advance education in the Bohemian Lands.[70] Like Komenský, Masaryk took on the role of the educating leader responsible for enlightening the nation. This task meant more than imparting knowledge to the Czechs. His writings and lectures on the national question were aimed at discerning the underlying purpose of Czech political and cultural life. According to Masaryk, it was not enough to have a Czech name and speak the language. Before a person could act as a Czech, he had to know what it meant to be Czech.[71] This was particularly true for the nation's politicians as well as its writers, artists, journalists, and teachers. Their efforts in leading the nation had to be grounded in knowledge of the nation's fundamental purpose. Of course, as enlightener of the nation in the tradition of Komenský, Masaryk best understood this purpose.

With his emphasis on knowledge before action, Masaryk showed his debt to Platonic philosophy. Throughout his life, Masaryk expressed his love for Plato. "The philosopher who influenced me the most was Plato," he told Karel Čapek in their conversations, adding the declaration: "Yes, to this day I am a Platonist."[72] The principles of Platonic thought were evident in Masaryk's writings on the national question. He saw the pursuit of knowledge as the foundation of ethics: if we know what is good, we will do what is good. Even though a constant theme in Masaryk's political and ethical thought was work, meaning active service for the good of others, he stressed that one first needed to know the aim and process of that work in order for it to be effective.[73] Masaryk also followed the Platonic principle that

---

70 Masaryk founded the academic journal *Athenaeum* in 1883 and the cultural periodical *Naše Doba* (Our Times) in 1893, with the aim of introducing Czech readers to current intellectual trends in Europe. In his first speeches and proposals after his return to the Austrian Parliament in 1907, Masaryk challenged the hold that the imperial government, dominated by German Austrians and the Catholic Church, had on education in the Bohemian Lands. He called for the founding of additional universities that offered instruction in Czech (Emperor Francis Joseph had closed the entire university in Olomouc in 1860, due to the strength of Czech nationalism there) and the publication of textbooks in the language.

71 See Szporluk, *The Political Thought of Thomas Masaryk*, 63–4, 82–3, and 98–9.

72 Čapek, *Talks with T. G. Masaryk*, 105.

73 When Masaryk delivered a series of lectures in 1898 on the subject of how to work, most of his remarks

knowledge was not simply the means to an ethical life; real knowledge was virtue.[74] This idea was particularly important to his understanding of nation-building. According to Masaryk, people who were engaged in politics had to be aware of the fundamental, common principles of the nation.[75] The primary aim in Czech politics, he argued, "is not to decide whether we should proceed more or less towards the left, but whether or not we are right."[76] Only after they first comprehended what was correct, what was good, what was truthful, could politicians then move on to specific programs and strategies. In this sense, as his interpreters have noted, Masaryk followed the example of Socrates.[77] His writings and lectures on Czech nationality were an exhortation to this principle, a call for politics—in a Platonic and Socratic sense—as care for the soul. We can summarize his understanding of the Czech question with a rephrasing of the famous question Socrates addressed to a fellow Athenian: "Good sir, you are a member of the Czech nation, the nation of Hus and Komenský; are you not ashamed of your eagerness to possess as much wealth and honor as possible while you do not give thought to wisdom or truth, or the best possible state of your soul?"[78]

For Masaryk, though, care for the soul was not simply an individual matter. He held that the nation, like a person, also had spiritual and material parts.[79] Masaryk spoke of the soul of the nation as its lasting, fundamental character. "As when I am looking at a man, in looking at

---

were devoted not to the practical tasks that Czechs should undertake but to education: the need for universities, the benefit of seminars and lectures, the value of a private library, even the proper method for taking notes. "All enthusiastic work has similar characteristics, whatever its scope," he told the audience at the university in Prague. "Sound preliminary education is needed, not a summary collection of information. The whole man must be educated, formed by his education; later, in practice, this will reveal itself." Masaryk, "How to Work," in *The Ideals of Humanity and How to Work*, 185.

74   Van den Beld, *Humanity*, 20.

75   Masaryk, "How to Work," 170.

76   Ibid., 188.

77   On Masaryk as a Socratic figure, see Page, "The Social Philosophy of T. G. Masaryk," 49.

78   On Masaryk's Platonism, see Kohák, "Masaryk and Plato in the 20th Century"; and Funda, *Thomas Garrigue Masaryk*, 98–100. On the idea of "care for the soul" in Masaryk's political thought, see Scruton, "Masaryk, Patočka, and the Care of the Soul."

79   Masaryk, "Czechs and Slavs: The Time of Kollár and Jungmann," from chapter two of *Česká otázka*, translated in *The Meaning of Czech History*, 63. On this dualistic aspect of Masaryk's Platonist thought, see Funda, *Thomas Garrigue Masaryk*, 98–99.

a nation I am mainly concerned with soul and spirit," he stated in his book on the Czech question.[80] A nation could not change its soul, nor deviate from it.[81] But the dispositions of a nation's soul could be occluded at points in its history. Over-attention to material concerns, the harmful influence of foreign elements, and the contaminating influence of the times could all adversely affect the nation's soul. The antidote was to recognize those forces. Once again, knowledge would bring virtue. Masaryk explained: "There is no other alternative but to embark on the most painstaking and conscientious self-analysis and examination of foreign influences and thus replace unconscious, instinctive behavior with deliberate, purposeful action."[82] For Masaryk, a nation—just like a person—had to lead an examined life.

Masaryk's Platonic thinking also led him to conceive of the nation in its ideal form. The nation as ideal was a timeless entity that gave purpose to history and meaning to daily life, cultural expressions, and political trials.[83] Masaryk acknowledged that the Czech nation, like all nations, had its faults and throughout history various representatives of the nation made missteps. But he insisted that part of seeking truth was to counter false patriotism with an awareness of the nation's ideal form and to constantly strive toward that ideal.[84] Masaryk labeled and defined the ideal of the Czech nation: he called it *humanita*, a word that has been translated variously as "humanity," "humanism," and "humanitarianism." I will use Masaryk's term *humanita*, as it retains both the breadth and ambiguity of his idea. *Humanita* encompassed the virtues that we would associate with humanitarianism: sympathy for the marginalized, altruism over force, respect for rights and equality, uplift through education, selfless work in the interests of social progress. Unlike the English term, however, Masaryk's *humani-*

---

80 Masaryk, *Česká otázka*, 53.

81 Szporluk, *The Political Thought of Thomas Masaryk*, 86.

82 Masaryk, "Czechs and Slavs: The Time of Kollár and Jungmann," 64–65.

83 Kohák writes, "The Czech ideal for Masaryk is not merely an epiphenomenal product of historical accident, but a normative ideal, which nudges our present and gives it direction and meaning. Here we see Masaryk's basic Platonism, the emphasis on the ideal not merely as a mystic ideal in the sense of German idealism, but the real basis which gives unity and meaning to our life." "Masaryk and Plato in the 20th Century," 290.

84 René Wellek, introduction to Masaryk, *The Meaning of Czech History*, xvi.

ta was, at root, a religious idea: it was the Czech nation's providential purpose.[85] Indeed, it was the purpose of all nations. Masaryk insisted that God did not favor the Czechs, or any nation, over others. Instead, all nations developed toward the same ideal, *humanita*, but they each did so in distinct, God-ordained ways.

Here, with his idea of *humanita*, Masaryk integrated the *logos* and the *ethnos*, bringing together his dreams of a universal, religious regeneration with his specific concerns for Czech political and cultural life. Looking broadly at European history, Masaryk saw the manifestation of *humanita* in the flowering of Renaissance humanism, the development of science, the emergence of individual rights, and the expansion of democracy and social legislation. But particular nations also manifested *humanita* at various times in their histories, with unique, national qualities. According to Masaryk, the Czechs expressed *humanita* religiously and morally, manifesting the ideal most fully during the Bohemian Reformation.[86] Meanwhile, the English demonstrated the ideal of *humanita* in the realm of individual ethics, the French in philosophy and political principles, and the Germans in social ethics.[87] There were distortions and deviations at different points in history, he admitted. Darwinism tended toward elitism, positivism toward a determinism that eliminated individual agency, and Nietzsche's philosophy toward the chaos of subjectivism. In contrast, Masaryk envisioned fulfillment of *humanita* as bringing the universal enlightenment and renewal of which he had dreamed since his days as a student. Guided by reason and love, individuals would act in the spirit of *humanita* to lift their neighbors and live in morality. Nations would develop in distinct ways, but also harmoniously, embraced and guided by a world organization as they strove toward *humanita*.[88] Just

---

85 Masaryk, *Česká otázka*, 106–8.

86 Masaryk, "The Ideals of Humanity," in *The Ideals of Humanity and How to Work*, 15–16.

87 While the ideal of *humanita* was unchanging, Masaryk's analysis of it was not. His views of the characters of different nations changed from 1898, when he described them in this lectures on *humanita*, and the early 1920s, when he wrote about them in his memoir. Compare "The Ideals of Humanity," 15–16, and *Světová revoluce*, 391.

88 Masaryk, "The Ideals of Humanity," 18. On *humanita* as the root of Masaryk's ideas on individual ethics and the history and purpose of nations, see Funda, *Thomas Garrigue Masaryk*, 109–12, 159–70, and 187–89; and van den Beld, *Humanity*, chapters three and four.

as the Neoplatonists of antiquity posited the ultimate Good as the source and goal of all things, Masaryk proposed his single ideal as the fundamental essence and common end of all nations—and indeed, of all historical development.

"Our Czech idea is truly a world idea," Masaryk wrote at the turn of the century, "an existential question, the most existential of all: it is the idea that the relation of man to man, of nation to nation, must be determined in the most profound sense, *sub specie aeternitatis*." Like an individual measuring his actions by the perspective of the eternal, so must the nation "ever yearn for the infinite."[89] In a series of lectures explaining the ideal of *humanita*, given at the university in Prague in 1898, Masaryk concluded in the tone of a preacher. He cited Milton, Turgenev, and Seneca, but at the core of his remarks was the teaching of the gospels: "True love rests on hope, the hope of eternal life."[90] Some five years later, when Masaryk began preaching his new religion, *humanita* was at its center. This was the "higher morality" that modern religion had to encourage: a combination of Christian love and rational inquiry. As Masaryk explained: "If *humanita* is the end of all our thought, then it must also be the end of all our striving. We will attain *humanita* only through the means of *humanita*: with an enlightened head and a warm heart."[91] In his theory of Czech history and *humanita*, Masaryk thus sought a grand synthesis, a harmony like that of Komenský: the Christian virtue of love and the Platonic ideal of knowledge, the fulfillment of an individual community and the regeneration of all humanity, attention to immediate, practical needs and awareness of the eternal.

"She Formed Me"

At the turn of the century, in the midst of the Hilsner affair, Masaryk had debated whether or not to leave his country for good. His biogra-

---

89 Masaryk, "The Mind of František Palacký," from an 1898 article published in *Naše Doba*, in *The Meaning of Czech History*, 139.

90 Masaryk, "The Ideals of Humanity," 95.

91 Masaryk, *Česká otázka*, 105. A different English translation in "The Completion of the Czech National Renascence," in *The Meaning of Czech History*, 110.

phers agree that the decision to stay in Prague and remain committed to Czech public life was largely due to the influence of his wife. One might have expected Charlotte Garrigue Masaryková to support her husband's thoughts of leaving for America, given that she had been born and raised in Brooklyn. She had married and moved to Europe intent on forming a partnership with a man who envisioned great transformations—in marriage, in religion, in social organization. As Masaryk acknowledged, his wife played an integral part in shaping his views of the world. "I taught her much," he later said of their relationship, "but she formed me."[92]

Charlotte Masaryková was certain of her husband's mission to the Czech nation. She exhorted Masaryk in his work, convinced that he played a singular role in the nation. One letter to her husband, written in 1897, offered encouragement at a time of doubt—and revealed her sense of purpose. "In the depth of your heart you don't care for worldly triumph," she reminded Masaryk. "The only triumph worth having is the triumph of Christ & of Hus: rather die than be untruthful. Then your name may be, to future generations, their healthy daily bread." She pointed to their shared aim. "We two shall live for the praise of God and not of man," she wrote and underlined twice. She urged him to speak truth boldly. "Darling, if you say all that you know here without fear & trembling, you will be acknowledged even in your lifetime by many honest Bohemian souls."[93]

Masaryková was far more than a supportive wife. Masaryk himself described her as his partner. When he met Charlotte Garrigue in Leipzig, where he was studying and she was visiting friends (she had studied piano there years earlier), Masaryk had been impressed with her intelligence and independence. Their relationship began with readings of John Stuart Mill at the boarding house where they both were staying. After her return to America, they exchanged intellectual self-portraits in dozens of letters, sharing their views on subjects like music, morality, God, the Good, Plato, Mill, marriage, democracy, and the telephone. Masaryk wrote of how he wanted his wife to also be

---

92　Ludwig, *Duch a čin: Rozmluvy s Masarykem,* 170.
93　CGM to TGM, 12 April 1897, MÚA AV ČR, TGM Collection, Korespondence III, box 54, Sign. 1. Underlining in original.

FIGURE 1.3. Charlotte Garrigue, 1877. Masaryk Institute and Archive,
Academy of Sciences, Czech Republic.

his friend.[94] But there remained hints of the prejudices of the times. "Women are more religious than men because they think less deeply," he wrote during their courtship, a rare slight of the abilities of women.[95] Garrigue, meanwhile, wrote in her diary of her inadequacy compared to Masaryk and her fear that he would be disappointed. These doubts were compounded by episodes of depression and debilitating headaches: ailments she would suffer throughout her life. "Terribly blue," she wrote in November 1877. "Cannot imagine that Thomas should love me. Am afraid I shall be a burden to him—that he will be disappointed." Garrigue's anxiety went beyond that of any young per-

---

94 The letters have not survived. However, Charlotte Garrigue wrote a summary of each letter she received in her diary. Diary of 1877–78, MÚA AV ČR, CGM Collection, box 2, folder 7D. A thorough account of Charlotte and Tomáš's courtship is in their daughter's memoir of the family: Masaryková, *Dětsví a mladstvi*, 1–4.

95 Charlotte Garrigue, diary entry of 17 December 1877, recording Masaryk's 59th letter. Diary of 1877–78, MÚA AV ČR, CGM Collection, box 2, folder 7D.

son in love. She recorded her changes in mood and mental acuity, from "mind active" to "mind sluggish."[96] Her feelings of inadequacy remained after their wedding in Brooklyn and their move to Vienna. "Compared myself with Thomas as we now stand," she wrote only two months after their wedding, "felt depressed by my inferiority, the sense of it paralyzed my thought."[97] Masaryk, however, showed his respect by adopting his wife's family name as part of his own, an unusual step that would later bring derision from his political opponents. "He did this because he was fully aware that from the day of their marriage, his own life work and hers were complementary and inseparable," explained their daughter, Alice Garrigue Masaryková.[98]

Charlotte Garrigue Masaryková surely shaped her husband's views—which were extraordinary for a man of his times—on women's political rights, education for girls and women, and the value of housework.[99] Her influence was also notably apparent in the development of his religious views. According to reminiscences of her family, Charlotte Masaryková was a woman of unshakeable and manifest religious belief, who read and thought intently on religious questions.[100] Like Masaryk, she had been surprised—and offended—by the dormant religiosity they observed after their move from Vienna to Prague in 1872. She shared with Masaryk the determination that the Czechs liberate themselves from the remnants of Catholicism, renounce their pettiness and small-mindedness, and achieve the holiness promised by God.[101] In his later interviews with Karel Čapek, Masaryk stated that his wife had given him "the best Protestantism has to offer: the unity of religion and life, that is, religious practicality, religion for every

---

96 Charlotte Garrigue, diary entry of 7 November 1877, Diary of 1877–78.

97 Charlotte Garrigue, diary entry of 17 May 1878, Diary of 1877–78.

98 Mitchell, *Alice Garrigue Masaryk, 1879–1966*, 20. Alice Masaryková recalled that Masaryk's decision to adopt "Garrigue" as a middle name had precedent in Charlotte Garrigue's family.

99 On Masaryk's views of women's rights and gender relations, see chapter one of Feinberg, *Elusive Equality*.

100 Charlotte's diary from 1877–78 records her visits to lectures and services, and a later, undated fragment of a diary lists various books, published in the 1890s, offering scientific critiques or explanations of religiosity.

101 The summary of Charlotte Masaryková's views is taken from Alice Masaryková, who read through her mother's diaries and letters in the months after her death. See AGM to TGM, 6 June 1923, MÚA AV ČR, TGM Collection, Korespondence III, box 54, folder 2.

day."[102] One thing in particular that Masaryk appreciated was his wife's path to mature belief. Growing up in a wealthy and well-established home, Charlotte and her siblings were not instructed in a church under the influence of her parents. Tomáš Masaryk later recalled: "Each family member was of a different faith, having been brought up in religious freedom and encouraged to make a personal commitment."[103] As parents themselves, Charlotte and Tomáš Masaryk continued this practice, applying the model of American religious liberty to the family. Their children attended religious education classes, as was a requirement in schools of the time, and they also held membership in the Austrian Reformed Church after their father's conversion. But as Alice Masaryková later recalled, while her parents sent the children to church, they did not go along.[104]

Charlotte Masaryková did join the Reformed Church after her husband. And we know that she did attend services when her children were older, because the minister wrote a letter of complaint to Masaryk when she had stopped going.[105] In general, though, Masaryková shared her husband's skepticism of churches. "The real church is everywhere," she later wrote to Alice, during the war. "It is a spiritual church."[106] In the tolerant atmosphere of her Brooklyn home, she had come to be an adherent of Unitarianism. She believed in a personal God who was an active presence in the lives of her and her husband. In the months before her wedding, she repeatedly closed her diary entries with prayers for God to "bless Thomas," and she wrote that the purpose of her marriage was "to find God."[107] But she followed the teaching of nineteenth-

---

102 Čapek, *Talks with T. G. Masaryk*, 117.

103 Ibid., 116.

104 Skilling, *T. G. Masaryk: Against the Current*, 26. In a later letter to her father, after she had completed her studies and a stint of social work in Chicago, Alice Masaryková seemed to disagree with Masaryk's views on religion in the family: "I know that you had to undergo severe change in your makeup in this thing," she wrote. "Religion is necessary in the relationship of a parent to his children." AGM to TGM, 3 May 1906, MÚA AV ČR, TGM Collection, Korespondence III, box 54 (740), sign. 2. Underlining in original.

105 The letter, written in 1899, also mentioned that Charlotte had attended along with one of Masaryk's daughters (most likely Alice), who was also delinquent. Polák, *T. G. Masaryk: Za ideálem a pravdou*, 4:4.

106 CGM to AGM, 21 April 1916. Translation in Lilly Library, Alice Masaryk Collection, box 1, 1968 English ms.

107 Charlotte Garrigue, diary entry of 17 May 1878, Diary of 1877–78.

century Unitarianism in the belief that God was not found in the shared rituals or worship of a church service. Rather, Masaryková wrote of God speaking to her through the beauty of nature, and she insisted that God was present everywhere and in everything. Along with her husband, she rejected the dogmas of traditional Christianity and imagined a new kind of religion.[108] In the spring of 1902, just after Masaryk had left for his sojourn in Chicago, she expressed her views of the new religion in a sketch for a proposed women's association (presumably the beginnings of the Czech Women's Club that was formed in 1903). Masaryková wrote of issues such as women's suffrage and access to education, but she also envisioned a religious foundation to the group's work. "The old religion, the old science, does not teach equality of the sexes," she wrote. "The old religion teaches that woman was created for man. The new religion must teach that man and woman are children of God, and they have to seek his laws." Just as her husband connected political developments to the advent of the new religion, Masaryková held that a transformed religious understanding of men and women would bring political and social equality. Therefore, one of the tasks of the women's club was to convince "religious bodies to recognize the development in religion and correct the old mistakes."[109]

Masaryková took interest in her husband's explorations in religion and theology in the wake of the Hilsner affair, and she shared her own thinking on the new religion. Writing to him during his time in Chicago, she offered a short catechism, which showed the influence of her Unitarian background as well as her determination to move in a different direction:

You have been to many churches in England & America, did you find the one fault common to them all?

---

108 Masaryk did not believe in the doctrine of the Trinity, which placed him at odds with a fundamental tenet of Reformed Protestantism. When he entered the church in 1880, the minister asked him to recite the Apostle's Creed, which includes declarations of belief in the Trinity. Masaryk did say the creed, but he admitted later to another minister that he did so "with self-denial." He was also never inclined as an adult to collective worship and did not attend services. See Skilling, *T. G. Masaryk: Against the Current*, 95.

109 Charlotte Masaryková, notebook entry dated 3 April 1902, AÚTGM, CGM Collection, box 2, folder 5. Underlining in original.

1. They all have authority directly revealed by God in the Bible. This is true of all denominations from the most clerical Catholics to the most liberal Protestants.

2. The Unitarians no longer stand on the divine authority of the Bible, but they talk from the Bible the person of Christ the perfect man. Here they are mistaken, for Christ was not a perfect man & it remains for the:

3. New Religion to reverently criticize Christ.

Then we shall see, & only then, that we have done with the Bible as a divine authority. The Bible will thereby be placed in the ranks of all other books. It will thereby not be lost to us. It has been our education & will continue to be so. <u>It is the best book I know.</u>[110]

The principles of the Masaryks' new religion were nothing new in the nineteenth century. We find their sources in American Unitarianism, in historical-critical scholarship on the Bible published in both Europe and the United States, and in German historical theology and liberal Protestantism. But the ethical foundations of the new religion, its grounds for validity, came from the house of Masaryk. Both Tomáš and Charlotte Masaryk were people of will, determination, and discipline. Tomáš Masaryk had been raised in the backwaters of an empire. He was the son of a laborer on an imperial estate and had gone to earn a doctorate in the capital; he became a professor, a scholar, and a member of parliament. His wife meanwhile had been a child of privilege, with a patrician outlook and an American sense of individual freedom.[111] Her obstacle was the mental illness she suffered throughout her life. Charlotte Masaryková sought to overcome her depression with the same determination that had lifted her husband out of rural backwardness. After one bout in her first year of marriage, in which she had suffered from anxiety, fevers, and excessive thirst, she plotted

---

110 CGM to TGM, 11 July 1902, AÚTGM, TGM Collection, Korespondence III, box 54, folder 1. Underlining in original. It should be pointed out that Masaryková wrote notes to herself in her adopted language of Czech and wrote to her husband in English. As the mistakes show, her written English developed tics during her decades of living in Prague.

111 Alice Masaryková recalled of her parents: "Father appreciated that his wife came from a free country. Truly free, she was a great help and comfort to him." Quoted in Mitchell, *Alice Garrigue Masaryk*, 20.

the antidote in her diary: "Fearlessly I search for the truth, with a manly spirit, studying my body and my mind, glad to find the existing faults & determined to eradicate them, & then of good material to build up a character." Tomáš and Charlotte Masaryk saw themselves as people of character, built through resolve, hard work, and the seeking of God. "It is in character that I have been lacking," Charlotte determined.[112] If she could overcome that failing and her illness, if her husband could rise from humble station, then others could lift themselves in the same way. There was no need for worship, for gathering with a congregation in a building. The goal of becoming a moral, autonomous individual, with an awareness of the eternal, was a matter of outlook and intent, achieved by the application of intellect and action.

The new religion was also the product of the Masaryks' own sense of mission. "Shall we dream together?" Tomáš Masaryk asked Charlotte Garrigue before their marriage.[113] Her record of his letters, sent in the months after she had returned to America, reveals how grandiose those dreams were. Masaryk envisioned their marriage as a union of hearts and intellects, of two people who shared the earnest belief that they could change the world. Charlotte summarized one of Tomáš's letters: "Begin with ourselves to improve [the] condition of society." He knew from the start that such a path would require them to oppose the trends of the age. "We will stand firmly & not allow ourselves to be misled by the floods of the times," he wrote.[114] In the letters, Masaryk expressed his idea of a universal moral philosophy grounded in empirical knowledge: a "perfect concordance in Science & Morality," as Charlotte described it.[115] He wrote of his plans for a book on this philosophy. And he thought even bigger. According to Charlotte's notes on his letters, Masaryk pondered a unity of churches and governments as a means of moral renewal, "the saving of mankind."[116] Already as a twenty-seven-year-old graduate student, his head swelling with thoughts of love and

112 Charlotte Garrigue, diary entry of 17 May 1878, Diary of 1877–78. Underlining in original.
113 Charlotte Garrigue, diary entry of 17 December 1877, on Masaryk's 60th letter, Diary of 1877–78.
114 Charlotte Garrigue, diary entry of 10 December 1877, on Masaryk's letter of 27 November, Diary of 1877–78.
115 Charlotte Garrigue, undated diary entry (February–March 1878?) on letter 91, Diary of 1877–78.
116 Charlotte Garrigue, diary entry of 10 December 1877, on Masaryk's letter of 27 November, Diary of 1877–78.

philosophy, Tomáš Masaryk imagined a fusing of politics and religion—a new religion—aimed toward the universal "regeneracy of society." Yes, they were dreams. But Charlotte Garrigue believed in them, and she believed in the intentions and abilities of Masaryk. "Thomas is very serious," she observed after his sixty-first letter in just over two months apart. Garrigue was herself a dreamer. In the spring of 1878, she returned with Masaryk to Vienna to begin their partnership. In a diary entry from a few weeks after their arrival in Europe, she wrote that she could "see a method of building a new life from the foundation—our love the foundation, to find God our aim."[117]

Conclusion

When war began in 1914, Tomáš Garrigue Masaryk knew what it meant. Just the year before, he had published a monumental study of Russian intellectual and cultural history. The product of more than a decade's work, including three research trips to Russia, the two-volume book was recognized as one of the most complete studies of Russian culture in any Western language.[118] Originally published in German as *Russland und Europa* (the English translation followed in 1919), the book was not simply about the Romanov Empire. Typical of Masaryk's other academic writings, the research served as a platform for his pronouncements. More than a learned survey of the main currents of Russian thought, the book was a diatribe against the Orthodox religion

---

117 Charlotte Garrigue, diary entry of 17 May 1878, Vienna, Diary of 1877–78.

118 The original kernel of the project was the fiction of Fyodor Dostoevsky. At the turn of the century, Dostoevsky's novels were first translated into Czech and other European languages and gained the attention of readers. Masaryk, however, had been reading Dostoevsky in the original Russian since the mid-1880s. He had appreciated the novelist for the realistic studies of characters living through the modern crisis of faith. Masaryk recognized that the questions Dostoevsky probed in his literature were the same that he was examining in his scholarly writing. Masaryk originally intended to write a study only of Dostoevsky, but he recognized the need to write something of a prelude to his discussion of the novelist. This background study became volumes one and two of *Russia and Europe*, published in 1913 (the English translation, published in 1919, is titled *The Spirit of Russia*). Volume three, focusing on Dostoevsky, was not finished until after the war. Masaryk, by that time president, turned the manuscripts over to his literary secretary, Vasil K. Škrach, who edited his writings into a complete book. Ironically, the first volumes stand far better than the intended volume on Dostoevsky, which is more of a polemic against the novelist's religious philosophy (which Masaryk despised) than a literary study. See Trensky, "Masaryk and Dostoevsky."

FIGURE 1.4. Tomas Masaryk in his study in Prague, 1913.
Masaryk Institute and Archive, Academy of Sciences, Czech Republic.

and the imperial state. It was also a summation of Masaryk's ideas on Europe's past, present, and future, weaving together his views on history, literature, religion, politics, economics, and philosophy. In his view of European religious history as a process of necessary and natural development, Masaryk maintained that the primitive churches, such as Orthodoxy and Catholicism, could only pass away. He expected that this religious evolution of Europe would also have its political counterpart. Protestantism had allowed for the development of democracy. Democracy, in turn, would bring an end to absolutist theocracy—the form of government underpinned by myth and opposed to science, democracy, and individual freedom. The rule of hierarchs and nobles could not withstand the democratic ethic, which called all citizens to cooperation and loosed humanity's creative energy. Yet even after the authority of churches and priests was swept away, religion would remain essential. "Democracy is not inimical to religion per se," Masaryk averred in his book, "if by religion we understand the new religion and not ecclesiastical religion, not ecclesiastical Christianity."[119]

119 Masaryk, *The Spirit of Russia*, 2:514–15.

This conflict between democracy and reaction was the lens through which Masaryk viewed Europe's Great War. Granted, the war required some adjustments to the theory: democratic France was not very Protestant, and it was fighting on the side of theocratic Russia. Meanwhile, Masaryk had praised Protestant Germany in his book but then included the empire among the reactionary theocracies during the war. Nevertheless, when he launched the movement for an independent Czech state with a speech in Geneva in July 1915, on the 500th anniversary of Hus's martyrdom, the ideas at the core of his book—ideas he had been expressing for decades—were all present. The ideals of the Czech nation were those of its religious reformers, while Habsburg Austria was an agent of the Counter-Reformation and conservatism. Czech ideals were founded upon the principle of *humanita*. Even though *humanita* rejected force, the Czech reformers had recognized that *humanita* had to be defended, when necessary, "with iron." The ideal of *humanita*, Masaryk declared, "seeks life, a life that is fully affirming, in no way death. Life overcomes death. That is the hope, that is the obligation— the legacy of the Czech reformation."[120]

In the three years after his speech in Geneva, Masaryk worked to gain Allied support for an independent state for the Czechs and Slovaks. His triumph at the war's end was the result of tireless and strategic political work. Indeed, throughout his life, Tomáš Masaryk showed the ability for shrewd maneuvers.[121] At the same time, Masaryk the pragmatic politician was also a philosopher devoted to the sweeping ideals he had devised. During his years in London, he had continued to nourish his fascination with the religious question. He clipped articles from newspapers and journals: reviews of books, commentaries by clergy, even curious bits from the religious side of the war (a photo of soldiers queuing for communion, a piece about a wayside cross on the Somme battlefield that had remained undamaged). And he was drawn to pieces that supported his own vision of a future religion without

---

120 Masaryk's Geneva speech of 6 July 1915 is reprinted in Polák, *Za ideálem a pravdou*, 5:79–80.

121 Karel Čapek's biography of the president rested on the famous story of how Masaryk, when caught in an exchange of gunfire on the streets of revolutionary Moscow, refused to falsely announce himself as a guest in order to gain safe entrance to a locked hotel. Masaryk's explanation, "I didn't want to lie," became a cornerstone of the myth built around him. See Orzoff, *Battle for the Castle*, 182–3.

sectarian divisions. With a blue or red pencil, he highlighted statements that corresponded to his own. One of these was an excerpt from
the Gifford Lectures at the University of Aberdeen, delivered by the
former British Prime Minister, Arthur James Balfour—like Masaryk,
a philosopher who had entered politics:

> My desire has been to show that all we think best in human culture,
> whether associated with beauty, goodness, or knowledge, required
> God for its support, that <u>Humanism without Theism loses more
> than half its</u> value... If we would maintain the value of our highest
> beliefs and emotions, we must find for them a congruous origin.
> Beauty must be more than an accident. <u>The source of morality must
> be moral. The source of knowledge must be rational.</u> If this be
> granted, you rule out Mechanism, you rule out Naturalism; and a
> lofty form of Theism becomes, as I think, inevitable.[122]

---

122 Clipping from W. R. Sorley, "Theism and Humanism," a review of Arthur James Balfour's Gifford
Lectures, 1913–1914, *The Sunday Times*, 3 October 1915. Masaryk's underlining. MÚA AV ČR, TGM
Collection, Válka, box 309, folder 1.

Chapter Two

The Architect Creating for the Ages

"The modern school can boast of only a handful of such original artists."[1] This was the assessment of the architect Jože Plečnik made in 1906 by the Czech architectural journal *Styl*. The statement is noteworthy because Plečnik was a devout, even mystical Catholic. As a student in Vienna, working in the studio of the famous architect Otto Wagner, he had stood out from his classmates because of his ascetic habits and a firm devotion to his beliefs. The author of the *Styl* piece was quite familiar with Plečnik's faith and its tendencies toward moralism and discontentment: "his relationship to contemporary life is full of misunderstanding and sorrow."[2] Still, this writer and Plečnik's other supporters observed that the architect was a distinctive talent in turn-of-the-century Vienna, and that what made him a great artist was his religiosity: his profound belief in the eternal, his self-criticism, his reflective character. "Plečnik is a believer whose creative production is determined by his faith," stated the profile in *Styl*.

Plečnik's standing in the Vienna art scene is a reminder that "modern" and "religious" did not have firmly drawn lines, as we often expect today. Certainly, there were freethinkers and socialists who insisted that Catholicism in any form was incompatible with the modern. Likewise, there were many Catholics in turn-of-the-century Vienna who denounced current trends in culture and society. But the frontier between these worldviews—or knowledge regimes, to use José Casano-

---

1   A., "Jože Plečník," *Styl* 1 (1906): 130, translation in Šlapeta, "Jože Plečnik and Prague," 85.
2   Ibid.

va's term—could be inexact. For example, the Christian Social party of Vienna mayor Karl Lueger proclaimed traditionalist values while at the same time touting its progressive and technological advances in urban planning.[3] Plečnik navigated this borderland during his time in Vienna and then afterward in Prague. He mixed with artists of the Secession, but seethed at the art shown at the famous exhibition hall. He took commissions from the Church, but came under attack from conservative Catholics who saw his designs as motley concoctions. He openly expressed his traditional Catholic faith, yet people who did not share that faith were drawn to him. His contemporaries remarked on the firmness of Plečnik's convictions. At the same time, he took surprising steps that seemed to confound those convictions, or even contradict them.[4]

Plečnik's path was not easy. In the first years of the century, before the war, he was unsettled and searching for his place. While still in the capital, he took note of Tomáš Masaryk's 1907 speech in parliament, the one in which the newly elected deputy cited Hus, Žižka, and Komenský and declared: "You in Vienna have not a whit of understanding of these figures." Plečnik identified with Masaryk's larger point that the Czechs were strangers to the Austrian Germans. "The same applies to me," he wrote; "it arouses a great feeling of foreignness— and it fills me with horror."[5] Even after nearly two decades there, Plečnik found himself an outsider in Vienna, as Catholic traditionalists criticized his designs and animosity rose against the Slavs. Yet when he moved to Prague to live among a Slavic people he had long admired, Plečnik felt isolated. In a time of hardening boundaries, in an East Central Europe being divided according to nation and ideology, he avoided any restricting label. One might read his decisions in this period as motivated simply by ambition and practical need. But Plečnik was mindful of a greater purpose. As the Czech writer of the profile in *Styl* wrote, Plečnik the architect took elements from various sources

---

3 Boyer, *Culture and Political Crisis in Vienna*, 10–11.

4 Martin Putna discusses Plečnik in the different religious-cultural contexts of late nineteenth-century Slovenia, *fin-de-siècle* Vienna, and First Republic Czechoslovakia in his essay "Plečnikovo místo mezi náboženskými kulturami."

5 Plečnik to Jan Kotěra, 1907, letter 64 in *Kotěra/Plečnik: korespondence.*

and then integrated them into a distinct whole, according to his creative aim. "The decisive factor for him is not the form as such, but its logic and intention. Thus we find historical elements juxtaposed without the slightest interest in history, brought in simply because they lend themselves to his goal." The same remark can apply to Plečnik the modern believer. In his personality, Plečnik was a mix of contradictions—he was aware of this and racked himself in self-criticism. Yet he held to a goal. He saw himself as an instrument of God, and he sought to create art that was sacred and eternal.

Finding a Path in Fin-de-Siècle Vienna

In November 1905, the Secession House held its first exhibition after the departure of its most famous artist and one of its founders. Just a few months earlier, Gustav Klimt had judged that the Secession was becoming too conventional and left with a circle of like-minded artists to form a new association. While the Secession pressed on without Klimt, continuing to offer regular exhibitions (as it still does today), the exhibition hall lost its place at the leading edge of modern art, in the judgment of art historians. Unlike the important shows of its first years, exhibitions at the Secession after 1905 gain little mention in accounts of early twentieth-century art. This first exhibition after Klimt's departure that November seems to confirm this judgment. The show featured work devoted to religious, and particularly Christian, subjects. There were paintings of Biblical scenes and lives of the saints, designs for stained-glass windows and models of churches, altarpieces, monstrances, and chalices. The exhibition included artists from the various lands of the Habsburg Empire as well as across Europe. There were artists long associated with the Secession, such as the Pole Józef Mehoffer, whose religious paintings incorporated decorative motifs standard to the Viennese *Jugendstil*. But the featured artists, whose work occupied the central galleries, were from a German monastery: the Benedictine monastery at Beuron, in Baden-Württemberg. In the exhibition hall that bore the motto "To every age its art and to art its freedom," in galleries that had shown paintings and sculptures scandalous for their sensuality and jarring visuals, the Secession presented

FIGURE 2.1. Józef Mehoffer, *Angels* (drawings for stained-glass windows). Catalog of the 24th Secession Exhibition, 1905. Jože Plečnik Collection, Museums and Galleries of Ljubljana, Slovenia.

the paintings of Catholic monks—whose supporters included the pope. Surely, Klimt had been correct in bolting.

From our contemporary perspective, an exhibition of modern art devoted to religious art, featuring Catholic monks, seems absurd. Yet even in the context of turn-of-the-century Vienna, where socialists and freethinkers challenged the cultural authority of the Church and the political power of the Christian Social party, the mixing of the

FIGURE 2.2. Desiderius Lenz, *Baptism of the Ethiopian*, Catalog of the 24th Secession Exhibition, 1905. Jože Plečnik Collection, Museums and Galleries of Ljubljana, Slovenia.

modern and the religious in art was not the contradiction that we now assume.[6] Prior to the 1905 exhibition, the monks of Beuron, led by Desiderius Lenz, had gained respect in broader artistic circles in Vienna. Following publication in 1898 of Lenz's book on the art produced at the monastery, the founding artists of the Secession had embraced the monks' ideas. Lenz had criticized naturalism and the reliance on perspective in painting, advocating instead the geometric interpretation of form, the use of gold as a foundation, and the integration of archaic

---

6   John Boyer discusses conflicts between the Christian Social party and various anticlerical politicians on matters of education in the empire in *Culture and Political Crisis in Vienna,* chapter one.

sources, such as Egyptian and Byzantine art. All of these elements subsequently appeared in the early art of the Secession, particularly in the famous works of Klimt's "Golden Style."[7] Thus, the Secession exhibition featuring the Beuron monks was not some kind of retreat in the wake of Klimt's departure. Rather, the show featured artists who were held in high regard by the leading figures of the modern school. Critics wrote positively of the exhibition and of the treatment of religious themes in contemporary art. Klimt and his circle likewise agreed with the choice of theme. Following the Secession show, their first exhibition in Vienna was also dedicated to religious art.

The organizer of the November Secession exhibition was the thirty-three-year-old architect Jože Plečnik. In the seven years since completing his architectural studies under the Viennese master Otto Wagner, Plečnik had worked to establish himself as an independent designer in the capital. He had a reputation as one of Wagner's most talented and innovative protégés, and he had been involved with the Secession since 1901 as a designer of exhibition galleries and member of planning committees.[8] The 1905 exhibition was his first as director, and the theme of religious art was one that he had proposed. With the exhibition devoted to religious art, Plečnik was able to pursue an idea particularly important to him: the creation of art that was both sacral and modern. He was interested not simply in recognized modern artists doing an occasional commission for the church, or in religious artists copying contemporary styles. Instead, he sought an art that was sacred in subject matter and in inspiration, an art that would draw upon traditional forms but was also original in vision. He was dismissive of current styles and theories, but at the same time he rejected historicist mimicry. Plečnik sought a sacred art that defied periodization, that could not be placed in either past or present. He wanted an art that would not be modern or traditional, but timeless.[9]

---

7   Warlick, "Mythic Rebirth in Gustav Klimt's Stoclet Frieze," 121–23.

8   Plečnik kept the catalogues of the Secession exhibitions in which he participated. They are collected in the archive at his house, PC MGL.

9   Prelovšek discusses Plečnik's reform-minded approach to religious art in *Jože Plečnik: Architectura perennis*, 72–8; and *Plečnikova sakralna umetnost*, 29–38. Helena Čižinská points out the lasting influence of the Beuron monks on Plečnik's sacral architecture, including his later designs for Prague's Church of the Sacred Heart, in "Zbožnost a liturgie v díle Josipa Plečnika," 28–9.

FIGURE 2.3. Plečnik, drawing of a shrine from his years in Vienna.
Jože Plečnik Collection, Museums and Galleries of Ljubljana, Slovenia.

Plečnik's ambiguous stance toward modern art was evident in his links with the Secession. Although he contributed to various exhibitions and regularly attended shows at the Secession House, the architect had a somewhat instrumental view of the association. "I am like a spider," he wrote in 1901 to his brother Andrej, a priest and teacher in Slovenia, "I spin my web around the Secession—curious, whether I will succeed more—when it rips—I will spin anew."[10] Over the years, he praised the work of artists he encountered at the exhibitions. For

---

10   Jože Plečnik to Andrej Plečnik, February 1901, quoted in Prelovšek, *Josef Plečnik: Wiener Arbeiten*, 56–7.

FIGURE 2.4. Plečnik in Vienna, 1910.
Jože Plečnik Collection, Museums and Galleries of Ljubljana, Slovenia.

example, Plečnik raved to his friend Jan Kotěra, a Czech classmate in Otto Wagner's studio, about paintings in the 1901 show by Spanish, French, and Italian artists. At the same time, he abhorred many pieces exhibited at the Secession Hall. The same 1901 exhibition also featured the work of German sculptor Max Klinger, which appeared to Plečnik like the "lesions of a skin disease."[11] Plečnik particularly scorned the famous centerpiece of the 1902 show: Klinger's sculpture of Beethoven, surrounded by Klimt's series of murals.[12] Plečnik had a dim view of the contemporary architectural designs on display in the wave of new building constructions in Vienna. "They are all a Tower

---

11   Plečnik to Kotěra, January 1901, letter 20 in *Kotěra/Plečnik: korespondence.*
12   Prelovšek, *Josef Plečnik: Wiener Arbeiten,* 58. Carl Schorske remarks upon the sacral intent of the Klinger exhibition, with the Secession artists seeking "to provide in art a surrogate religion offering refuge from modern life." Schorske, *Fin-de-Siècle Vienna,* 254.

of Babel," he complained to Kotěra. "It is worse than sad."[13] He rejected the slogan "art for art's sake," the founding statement of the Seces-
sionists and modern artists across Europe. "To hell with the reverie
and *l'art pour l'art*," he wrote to Kotěra in 1908. The idea satisfied only
base instincts and produced "heartless rabble, unwashed tombs."[14] In
contrast to the "tortured sewage" he saw in contemporary art, Plečnik
longed for simplicity. The aim of art had to be the same as any other labor: yes, to create something out of one's own ingenuity, but something of use, something of benefit. The simpler the better, he insisted
to Kotěra. The motivation of the artist should be a "childlike, pure joy
of natural creation."[15]

Throughout his life, Plečnik was a man of firmly stated and often
biting opinions. In addition to disparaging the art of the times, his letters on occasion also turned against the broader cultural and social environment of turn-of-the-century Vienna. Plečnik felt himself engulfed by the immoral spirit of the age, by a crushing, godless din in
the capital. "I live here in a center of horrors, of a pestilent herd," he
wrote to Kotěra.[16] In scattered letters to his friend in Prague and his
brother Andrej in Slovenia, he complained of the influence of "femi-
ninity," the politics of the Social Democrats, and Jewish capitalists.
The harsh tone of his letters sometimes echoed the anti-semitic, anti-
liberal rhetoric of Karl Lueger's Christian Social movement.[17] Above
all, however, Plečnik turned his harsh criticism inward. He would follow a judgment on some modern trend with a reflection on his own
failings. For instance, after condemning the modern architecture of
Vienna as a Tower of Babel, he conceded that perhaps he misunderstood the designs owing to his own lack of education.[18] He acknowledged his own doubt and loneliness. In letters to Kotěra, Plečnik de-

---

13   Plečnik to Kotěra, September 1902, letter 35 in *Kotěra/Plečnik: korespondence.*
14   Plečnik to Kotěra, 1905, letter 58 in *Kotěra/Plečnik: korespondence.*
15   Ibid.
16   Ibid.
17   Putna, "Plečnikovo místo mezi náboženskými kulturami," 48. Although critical of trends of the
times, Plečnik was representative of the younger generation of Christian Social activists that emerged
after 1907 in his willingness to engage with modern developments. On the intellectual and political
shift in the Christian Social movement, see Boyer, *Culture and Political Crisis in Vienna,* chapter six.
18   Plečnik to Kotěra, September 1902, letter 35 in *Kotěra/Plečnik: korespondence.*

scribed himself as an unlucky wretch buffeted by misfortune and pain, with an "unbalanced soul," unable to find peace.[19] He warned his friend to not be misled into thinking that Plečnik was spiritually content. "You deceive yourself that I live in peace," Plečnik wrote in 1907. "In no way, my friend. I live in anxiety and struggle, above all with myself."[20]

Plečnik's personal turmoil and his disapproval of modern Vienna were compounded by his professional struggles. After leaving Otto Wagner's studio in 1900, his first commissions were the mundane jobs common to any young architect: the renovation of a flat, the layout of a villa garden, plans for a few family houses and apartment buildings in the suburbs. His first major commission came from the wealthy founder of an insecticide company, Johann Zacherl. From 1903 to 1905, Plečnik designed the new building in the center of Vienna that housed the Zacherl family's apartments and offices, beginning a relationship with the industrialist that would be both friendly and profitable for the young architect. Zacherl was a convert to Catholicism and, like Plečnik, a member of the Leo Society, an organization named in honor of Pope Leo XIII that promoted science and art "on a Christian foundation."[21] Plečnik spoke highly of his patron. "I would wish that you could get to know Zacherl," he wrote to his brother. "He is really a Catholic man, a father, and shows himself to all as a man who is at home in this world."[22] With Zacherl's support, Plečnik had the opportunity for the first time in his career to exercise his ideas about architecture. He was pleased with the result. "When my building is finished, you absolutely must see it," he wrote to Andrej. "There will be nothing like it, whatever people say about it."[23]

19 Plečnik to Kotěra, spring 1903, letter 43; and Plečnik to Kotěra, 1904, letter 49 in *Kotěra/Plečnik: korespondence*.

20 Plečnik to Kotěra, 1907, letter 64 in *Kotěra/Plečnik: korespondence*.

21 Putna discusses the Leo Society and its influence on Plečnik in "Plečnikovo místo mezi náboženskými kulturami," 47–8. As Boyer explains, the Leo Society was founded by theologian Franz Martin Schindler, who drew upon contemporary social science in his moral theology and acknowledged the pluralism of modern society. See *Culture and Political Crisis in Vienna*, 304–6.

22 Plečnik to Andrej, undated letter (March 1903), quoted in Prelovšek, *Josef Plečnik: Wiener Arbeiten*, 81.

23 Quoted in Krečič, *Plečnik: The Complete Works* 38. On Plečnik's relationship with Zacherl and his design of the Zacherl house, see also Prelovšek, *Jože Plečnik: Architectura perennis*, 45–62.

As the remark indicated, Plečnik was aware that the response to his design would not be entirely favorable. Indeed, reviews were mixed, in large part because the Zacherl House broke from the norms set by Otto Wagner and followed by his more dutiful students. Plečnik took pride that his building was *not* Viennese. The Zacherl House was a statement of artistic independence; however, its unconventional design did not bring more commissions. Plečnik longed for work, but he was hired only for small-scale renovations in the years following completion of the Zacherl House.[24] The one notable commission he gained was dissatisfying. In 1906 artist Josef Engelhart, one of the leaders of the Secession after Klimt's departure, invited Plečnik to collaborate on a monument honoring Vienna mayor Karl Lueger: a fountain to be placed at Karl-Borromäus-Platz. Engelhart sculpted the figures, while Plečnik designed the fountain and basin. Plečnik appreciated the opportunity to work in a new medium, but the collaboration left him unsettled. Engelhart had married into money, and Plečnik was offended by his lavish studio.[25] And as the project progressed, Engelhart intervened in Plečnik's side of the project too often for the architect's liking. In the end, Plečnik came to see the fountain, and the collaboration as a whole, as a failure. In a letter to his brother, he dismissed the fountain as "chaotic, without harmony, without purpose. I don't know whether it is a waltz, a polka, or a mazurka."[26] Plečnik joked that he would have to emigrate after its unveiling. Critics, however, praised it.

The episode with the Vienna fountain confirmed Plečnik's disenchantment with secular art, and contributed to the maturing of his own architectural vision. In his subsequent designs, he took further steps away from the style of his contemporaries. Plečnik experimented with classical forms for a series of minor projects completed in 1908–9 in Vienna: another private villa, a Catholic orphanage, and renovations of Zacherl's villa. The designs followed upon a desire Plečnik had expressed years earlier to Kotěra: "I have been wishing for a long time

---

24 Plečnik discussed his professional disappointment in a 1907 letter to Kotěra, number 67 in *Kotěra/Plečnik: korespondence*.
25 Plečnik to Kotěra, 1908, letter 68 in *Kotěra/Plečnik: korespondence*.
26 Plečnik, undated letter to Andrej Plečnik (1909?), quoted in Prelovšek, *Wiener Arbeiten*, 114.

that someone would start building in the 'classical style.' That would be our only salvation."[27] Plečnik's admiration for architecture of the past extended to other periods, especially the Romanesque and Baroque. He did not seek to simply mimic these styles, in the manner of a historicist. Instead, he integrated historical elements into his own designs. For a Franciscan monastery in Croatia, for instance, he submitted a design in 1909 that incorporated existing structures into new construction. Plečnik's later work in Prague and Ljubljana would feature both of these ideas: the use of classical elements, and the integration of older structures into his own designs.

At the same time, Plečnik's interests turned from secular to sacral architecture. In the autumn of 1905, at the time he was preparing the exhibition of religious art, he had expressed dissatisfaction with the design work he had been doing. "I am an appallingly fragmented and sick soul," he wrote to Kotěra. The reason for this condition, he explained, was that all of his work was "fundamentally the same as the rest." He wrote of the need for a solid core to his architecture—and all of art.[28] Three years later, in 1908, he came to an understanding of this core, an "absolute" that would be at the foundation of his architecture. "All things must be made with 'reverence,'" he declared to his brother Andrej, "anything not so made has no value."[29] Reverence, morality, harmony: these were the watchwords of the artistic philosophy that Plečnik adopted for himself. An artist must help others, he insisted, while at the same time cultivating a childlike faith in divine Providence. "We are artists," Plečnik stated to Jan Kotěra. "We are God's elect, a blessing to the nations. But we must understand that we are not artists because we would create artistic works, even exquisite artistic works, but because we alone, in our struggle and agony and in the search for what is beautiful and good, come as close as possible to God, bringing the embodiment of justice, and engendering people who are good, just, and as perfect as possible."[30]

---

27 Plečnik to Kotěra, September 1902, letter 35 in *Kotěra/Plečnik: korespondence*. On Plečnik's use of classical forms in these designs, see Prelovšek, *Jože Plečnik: Architectura perennis*, 69.

28 Plečnik to Kotěra, 1905, letter 58 in *Kotěra/Plečnik: korespondence*.

29 Quoted in Prelovšek, *Jože Plečnik: Architectura perennis*, 72.

30 Plečnik to Kotěra, 1908, letter 68 in *Kotěra/Plečnik: korespondence*.

Plečnik expressed his philosophy in positive terms (the passage above was written as encouragement to Kotěra, who was experiencing health problems and his own professional dissatisfaction at the time). But Plečnik also defined his view against an idea of what an artist should not be. The negative example was his former teacher, Otto Wagner. In 1907, construction had concluded on Wagner's project for St. Leopold's Church in Vienna (known as the Kirche am Steinhof). Both architectural critics and Catholic writers regarded the church as a model of modern sacral design, with its double-shell dome, sloping floor in the sanctuary, and use of electric lighting, heat, and ventilation. Even Plečnik, at first, had viewed the project favorably and included a model of Wagner's church in the 1905 exhibition of religious art. But Plečnik's turn in artistic philosophy brought a change in opinion toward his former master's design. Writing about the completed church in 1908, in the newly launched Czech architectural journal *Styl*, Plečnik criticized specific elements of the church, from the cupola down to the pews, for their disregard of principles of Catholic architecture. Overall, he charged, the structure gave the impression of a Protestant church or a concert hall. In no way was it a Catholic church.[31]

In his bitter rebuke, Plečnik excoriated not only Wagner's inappropriate design but also his former master's worldly life and outlook. According to Plečnik, the success that Wagner had enjoyed his entire life disqualified him from designing churches. "He has dismissed with a smile the eternal, universal laws; therefore, he has become unworthy of grace. He has lost contact with the people. He does not understand their spirit and their needs. He does not feel what is most sacred to people, in a word, God." In contrast, Plečnik offered a vision of how the artist should conduct himself—not with the haste of the moderns, but with the deliberation of the ancients, who saw everything as sacred. "Moderns work without conscience; yes, we work more quickly," he declared. "But I doubt that future generations will remember us with the respect that we, thank God, show to the ancients."[32] This complaint about the apparent hypocrisy of the worldly Wagner de-

---

31 [Plečnik], "Kronika," 115–16.
32 Ibid., 116.

signing a church was at the root of Plečnik's anger. An artist's creativity was a demonstration of integrity, Plečnik held; it was a manifestation of moral character. "A foolish person builds foolishly," he wrote to Kotěra in 1907, after viewing the exhibited projects of Wagner's students. "A reasonable one builds intelligently, a virtuous one nobly, a dissolute one badly."[33] Plečnik saw dissolution around him in art and architecture. Instead of reverence, there was hurriedness and a fixation on the contemporary; instead of morality, a disdain for virtue; instead of harmony, the dissonance of no fixed beliefs. Wagner's church was a representation of an age without conviction. In Plečnik's view, the structure demonstrated "a confession-less style, a belief in nothing definitive, changing daily with the mood." The result was a "genuine soufflé," he judged: the church was "a provocative crossbreed with the absence of firm convictions."[34]

The editors of *Styl* made clear that this appraisal of Wagner was Plečnik's alone, not the journal's. Wagner, after all, was an influential figure for early twentieth-century Czech design. His student Jan Kotěra, widely regarded as the founder of modern Czech architecture, promoted Wagner's principles of rationalism and social function in his own work as a designer and professor in Prague. Because we do not have Kotěra's letters to Plečnik, we do not know how he responded to the sharp rebuke of Wagner, or to Plečnik's general pronouncements on contemporary art and the immortality of society. Kotěra and Plečnik were an odd pair of friends. Plečnik could be both charismatic and withdrawn, tempestuous and morose, vacillating between debilitating self-doubt and single-minded self-confidence. Kotěra, on the other hand, was commonly viewed as outgoing, generous, and elegant.[35] Despite the differences in character, we can gather from Plečnik's letters that Kotěra was open in his correspondence to Plečnik, recounting his own personal triumphs and trials. Plečnik in turn clearly regarded Kotěra as an intimate, and his direct and constant use of religious language and exhortations to Kotěra suggest a sharing of beliefs. However, Kotěra's architectural work and his biography do not

---

33 Plečnik to Kotěra, 1907, letter 64 in *Kotěra/Plečnik: korespondence.*
34 [Plečnik], "Kronika," 116.
35 Vybíral, "Verba et Voces," 66–7.

indicate religious leanings. Early in their careers, Plečnik chided Kotěra for turning away from church architecture. "It will be the beginning of your decline," Plečnik warned.[36] But the Czech architect did not pay heed. In the first decade of the century, Kotěra took commissions for public meeting halls and private villas but not churches. Even the tombs and gravestones he designed displayed no religious symbolism.[37]

Whether he moved away from religious sentiments he had once shared with Plečnik or kept any spiritual affections private, Kotěra was more characteristic of, and comfortable in, the modern culture of the turn of the century. At the same time, Kotěra found something deeply compelling in Plečnik. Writing about his former classmate in 1902 in the Czech journal of modern art *Volné směry*, he acknowledged that Plečnik's monastic habits had alienated other students in Wagner's school. Yet Plečnik's unquestionable talent and unmatched creativity earned him respect. He was a true individual who was swayed neither by Wagner's teaching nor by artistic fashion. As Kotěra wrote, Plečnik "did not rejoice when the first waves of the new style broke through—nevertheless he was among the first of the moderns and thus a model to many."[38] The designer who adhered to the rationalist principles of the age, who came to be regarded as the father of twentieth-century Czech architecture, pointed to Plečnik—with his rejection of the world and talk of God—as the one who should be admired. Kotěra was not alone. Others who identified themselves as modern, and who did not share Plečnik's Catholic devotion, would find themselves drawn to the mercurial architect.

Caught between Prague, Vienna, and Ljubljana

Even though Plečnik had only a handful of realized designs to his name, Jan Kotěra promoted the Slovene's work to students and colleagues, and he initiated Plečnik's move to Prague in 1911. In January of that year, Plečnik arrived from Vienna to take a teaching position at

---

36 Prelovšek, "Kotěra's Viennese Period," 92–3.
37 Skálová, "Sepulchral Architecture," 318.
38 Kotěra, "Jože Plečník," 91.

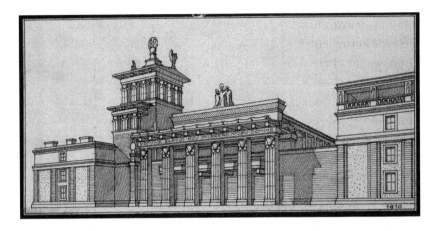

FIGURE 2.5. Plečnik, variant on the Church of the Holy Spirit, 1910.
Jože Plečnik Collection, Museums and Galleries of Ljubljana, Slovenia.

the School of Applied Industrial Arts, where Kotěra himself had taught. After Kotěra's appointment to Prague's Academy of Arts, he had recommended Plečnik for his former position and then invited (and pestered) his friend to accept the school's offer.[39] Plečnik was initially reluctant, but the offer came at a propitious moment, a time when he was facing professional obstacles and personal isolation in Vienna. Early in 1910 Plečnik had started work on a large-scale project: a new parish church to be built in the Ottakring district. But the design and construction of the church proved to be grueling. From the start, the architect had the support of the parish priest, Franz Unterhofer, but sponsors for the new church were hard to find, and the building committee constantly altered its demands. In the summer of 1910, the project appeared to turn a corner when the building committee found a wealthy donor: Sophie, Duchess of Hohenberg. The promise of capital allowed Plečnik to expand upon his earlier design. He held to the

---

39 Kotěra traveled to Vienna in July 1910 to tell his friend personally of the school's decision to offer him a professorship. Plečnik was reluctant to accept the offer. He did not know the Czech language, and he regarded the move to a school of decorative arts as a step backward for him professionally. But Kotěra was insistent, sending Plečnik the forms required for the move and even buying him a new coat for his interview with the Ministry of Culture. See Plečnik's letters to Kotěra of 22 July 1910, letter 80; 3 September 1910, letter 82; and 1 October 1910, letter 83 in *Plečnik-Kotěra: korespondence.*

original idea of a basilica, but he included choir lofts on each side, running the entire length of the sanctuary. The design was technically innovative: the choir lofts were to be constructed of reinforced concrete, supported only at the ends. The revision also broke with traditions of Catholic architecture. By adding the choir lofts, the clerestory windows were pushed outwards, and without supporting piers, there was no separation of the nave and the side aisles. Just as Plečnik had denounced the innovations in Wagner's church as violations of sacral architecture, so too did his design bring criticism from Catholic traditionalists.[40] Unfortunately for the architect, his main critic was Duchess Sophie's husband—Archduke Franz Ferdinand.

The heir to the imperial throne thought himself an expert in artistic matters, particularly those related to the Catholic Church, and he issued a stern rebuke of Plečnik's design. As the architect reported to Kotěra, Franz Ferdinand judged his church "a mishmash of a Russian bath + stables (instead of stables we might put hayloft) + a temple to Venus."[41] The Archduke's criticism did not scuttle the project (even the heir to the throne could not nullify contracts already signed with suppliers and builders), but his verdict did bring a steep drop in funding for the construction. The building committee members also sided with Franz Ferdinand, leading Plečnik to revise his plans again. The architect felt himself isolated and scorned. "They all flee from me as they would from the plague," he wrote to his brother. "If the Archduke hinders the completion of my plans, things will be bad for me overall."[42]

Things did get bad. "In the last year, I don't think I was outside on a single Sunday. I agonized over the church," he later wrote to Andrej.[43] The difficulties surrounding the Vienna project confirmed Plečnik's decision to leave the city. He described the job offer in Prague and

---

40 Despite his condemnation of Wagner's church design in the Czech journal *Styl*, Plečnik drew upon his former professor's ideas, particularly in regard to technical issues, in the design of his own church. See Prelovšek, *Jože Plečnik: Architectura perennis*, 78.

41 Plečnik to Kotěra, beginning 1911, letter 91 in *Kotěra/Plečnik: korespondence*.

42 Jože Plečnik to Anrdej Plečnik, 19 January 1911, quoted in Prelovšek, *Wiener Arbeiten*, 150. On the church project in Vienna, its difficulties, and Plečnik's changes in its design, see Prelovšek, *Jože Plečnik: Architectura perennis*, 78–86, and *Plečnikova sakralna umetnost*, 41–60.

43 Jože Plečnik to Andrej Plečnik, 1911, quoted in Prelovšek, *Josef Plečnik: Wiener Arbeiten*, 153.

Kotěra's good offices as providential.[44] But Plečnik also recognized that the political atmosphere in the capital made his move necessary. He saw the archduke's criticism and the committee's defection as evidence that the capital was not a hospitable place for a Slav. "I truly yearn to leave here," he wrote to Kotěra. He went on: "It is all a work of diabolical vengeance—and in the end there is no way to help it—you cannot change blood—i.e., nationality."[45] Plečnik could only hope that his situation would be better among the kindred Czechs.

Plečnik's connection to Prague lasted twenty-five years and resulted in his most notable work as an architect. At first, however, he found the city an ill fit. Like any visitor to Prague, Plečnik was enthralled by its mysterious beauty. The windows of his studio offered a view of the Vltava River, the Gothic and baroque structures of the Malá Strana district on the opposite side, and above those, Prague Castle. He described the old city's bending streets and hidden squares in letters to Andrej, his other brother Janez, and his sister Marija. The Vltava blanketed the city with fog, and in the narrow streets the fog was thickened with chimney smoke. But on spring mornings the city was cast in gold, and he enjoyed walking the streets, seeing the tradespeople, shopkeepers, and Jews (his studio was not far from the old Jewish quarter). "Everything is wrapped in a special Slavic atmosphere," he wrote.[46]

Plečnik compiled lists of the Czech words he was learning and their Slovene equivalents. He extoled the virtues of *knedlíky*, the bread dumplings that are a staple of the Czech diet. But Plečnik also came to realize that the Czechs were not the people he had expected. Yes, he esteemed the cultural works that had long impressed him, and he found people to be pleasant. But they were also, as he wrote to Andrej, "strange."[47] During his first years in Prague, Plečnik complained repeatedly to his family of isolation and loneliness. The promise of being reunited with Kotěra was dashed. Although Kotěra found Plečnik a place to stay in his own mother's house, there was little time for outings. His friend had work as a professor at the Art Academy and as the

---

44 Plečnik to Kotěra, 3 September 1910, letter 82. See also letter 97 in *Kotěra/Plečnik: korespondence*.

45 Plečnik to Kotěra, 18 January 1911, letter 92 in *Kotěra/Plečnik: korespondence*.

46 Jože Plečnik to Maria Plečnik, March 1911, PC MGL.

47 Jože Plečnik to Andrej Plečnik, 22 January 1912, PC MGL.

leading designer in Prague. And he had a young family. Meanwhile, Plečnik found little hospitality among his new colleagues. In his first months in the city, he spent hours alone in his studio and ate by himself at the pub. Even after a year in Prague, he spent his Sundays and holidays alone. "I wish I was away from here," he declared to Andrej on one day off work at the end of his first school year.[48] A year later, at the end of 1913, he still complained of his solitary life. "I sit and sit in Prague and go nowhere, just straight from home to school. I have no company at home."[49] The refrain was the same in the early months of 1914, after three years in the city: "I feel like a prisoner," he wrote to Andrej.[50]

One aspect of Prague culture that compounded Plečnik's sense of isolation was the absence of religiosity in the city. He bristled at the anticlericalism at the heart of Czech nationalism.[51] Beyond the political opposition to the Church, Plečnik saw an overall spiritual deadness. The size of the congregations for Sunday mass varied: some weeks there might be a hundred worshippers, other weeks fifteen, and still other weeks only a few people joining Plečnik at church. "From time to time, you see an elegant priest on the street, or at a concert." Plečnik wrote to his sister. "He glides silently and looks splendid. And silently they look at him. But they care nothing for him. They are all the worst kind of anticlericals."[52] Throughout the city he found beautiful, ancient churches, but they were, in his words, like old, wet tombs. "All faith is dead," he wrote to his sister only weeks after his arrival.[53]

Plečnik's sense of isolation in Prague, living among people who were fellow Slavs yet still alien to him, fueled an attachment to his native Slovenia. Was Plečnik a nationalist? That is difficult to say. In many ways, Plečnik eschewed a distinct nationalist identification. His

---

48 Jože Plečnik to Andrej Plečnik, June 1912; and Jože Plečnik to Andrej Plečnik, January 1912, PC MGL. See also Peter Krečič, *Jože Plečnik*, 82–3.
49 Jože Plečnik to Andrej Plečnik, 31 December 1913, PC MGL.
50 Jože Plečnik to Andrej Plečnik, early 1914, PC MGL.
51 For example, Plečnik derided the spring 1912 gathering of the Sokols, the nationalist gymnastics organization founded in the early 19th century, as little more than an opportunity to attack Catholics. Jože Plečnik to Andrej Plečnik, June 1912, PC MGL.
52 Jože Plečnik to Maria Plečnik, March 1911, PC MGL.
53 Ibid.

social circles in Vienna had been cosmopolitan, encompassing other students from Wagner's school, artists affiliated with the Secession, and Catholic patrons and artists. He was not a proponent of language rights. As late as 1912 and 1913 he still wrote entire letters to his brother in German. Unlike the Croatian sculptor Ivan Meštrović, Plečnik was not involved in the Yugoslav cause. When Meštrović proposed in 1913 that Plečnik lead the new Yugoslav Academy of Arts in Belgrade, the architect declined. And he reacted angrily when Meštrović and Serbian art critic Kosta Stranjić added his name to the advisory council of Yugoslav artists and academics, without Plečnik's knowledge. For all his disenchantment with decadent culture in Vienna and anti-Catholic liberalism in Prague, Plečnik understood that a move to Belgrade would have put him outside the orbit of modern European culture.[54] Plečnik was polite in replying to Meštrović's overture: he was too old for the demands of organizing a new school, and he did not have the required "bureaucratic spirit." But in a letter to Austrian officials, Plečnik adamantly disavowed any connection to the Yugoslav organization. At that same time, in 1913, Plečnik had been nominated to succeed Otto Wagner as professor of architecture in Vienna, and he knew that an association with any group in Belgrade would dash his chances. Plečnik had deep love for his Slovene homeland, but concern for his personal reputation and professional prospects outweighed any loyalty to the South Slavic political cause.

Plečnik never received the professorship in Vienna. The Academy of Arts faculty twice forwarded his name as Wagner's successor (with Wagner's endorsement), but the Ministry of Culture refused to confirm the nomination. Czech deputies in the imperial parliament offered to contest the appointment, but Plečnik refused. Although disappointed, he had instincts for neither self-promotion nor nationalist political agitation. Plečnik suspected that Archduke Franz Ferdinand had intervened to prevent his appointment, and evidence suggests that this was indeed the case.[55] But Plečnik also recognized that the situation in Vienna was becoming worse for Slavs. The two Balkan wars in

---

54 Prelovšek, *Jože Plečnik: Architectura perennis*, 115. See the copy of Plečnik's letter to Meštrović, 28 October 1913, enclosed in the letter to Andrej Plečnik, autumn 1913, PC MGL.

55 On Plečnik's nomination to succeed Wagner, see Prelovšek, *Jože Plečnik: Architectura perennis*, 115–17.

1912–13 and rising diplomatic tensions between Austria-Hungary and Serbia stirred animosity. "I've read so much hatred toward the Slavs here since the war started," he wrote to Andrej.[56] Plečnik saw the wars and the surrounding diplomatic crises as an episode of the German, Austrian, and Hungarian animus toward the Slavs. But his feelings of kinship over international events did not move him to active nationalism. Unlike Meštrović and Masaryk, Plečnik was not moved to stand in defense of the Slavs. Certainly, he proudly identified himself as a Slav and felt sympathy for the Serbs in their struggle against the Austrians, but he did not demonstrate affiliation to their cause.

Plečnik had felt himself a stranger in Vienna. But he was also a stranger in Prague. "This country can love only what was born in it," he wrote to his brother during a holiday that he spent alone.[57] Whatever attachment he had to a nation, it was felt most deeply as a simple connection to home. For Plečnik, nationality was an embrace of the familiar: the streets of his hometown, the weekly pattern set around going to church, the landscape that he had known since childhood. Plečnik returned home often, taking trips with his brothers in the Slovenian countryside and mountains. In solitary moments in his Prague studio he wrote of his desire to see the Karst lands and the Goriška region along the border with Italy.[58] He wrote enthusiastically to Andrej of finding a book in Prague that included a few lines from Slovene folk songs, albeit in German translation.[59] And Plečnik looked forward to the weekly appearance of the Ljubljana newspaper *Slovenec* in one of his regular cafés, not because he was invested in the politics of the nation but because its pages offered a connection to home.[60] To solidify these links to home, Plečnik made plans in the spring of 1914 to buy a house in Ljubljana with his younger brother, Janez. Then in his forties, Plečnik saw the house as a haven during the many trips to his home city. The prospect of his own house offered Plečnik a spark of hope in his lonely evenings and weekends in Prague. He even bought a map of

56 Jože Plečnik to Andrej Plečnik, autumn 1912, PC MGL.
57 Jože Plečnik to Andrej Plečnik, June 1912, PC MGL.
58 Ibid. See also Krečič, *Jože Plečnik*, 83.
59 Jože Plečnik to Andrej Plečnik, undated [early 1914], PC MGL.
60 Jože Plečnik to Andrej Plečnik, June 1912, PC MGL.

Ljubljana and studied past city plans. He set to work marking up the map, imagining how he would design the city's streets.[61] A decade later, when Ljubljana's municipal building office commissioned the architect to reconfigure the central thoroughfares and squares, Plečnik had the opportunity to realize his ideas about the city. The three bridges at the center, the terraced channel of the Ljubljanica River, the stairways and footbridges, the columned marketplace, the pyramids and pillars: all carry Plečnik's distinct signature. One of the architect's students suggested that many of these changes were inspired by Plečnik's own walks through the city. Indeed, one can identify his handiwork along the path from the house he bought in the Trnovo district, northward along Emona and Vega Streets into the center of the city, through the open space of Congress Square, which he designed, and to the nearby Ursuline Church of the Trinity, where he worshipped.[62]

The Professor as Spiritual Mentor

Despite his feelings of loneliness and isolation in Prague, Jože Plečnik was respected by the city's guild of architects. Years before his move, in 1906, the new architectural journal *Styl* had published an appreciative profile of Plečnik. The author of the unsigned piece was intimate with the architect's character and work habits, offering a nuanced and insightful portrait. "His relationship to contemporary life is full of misunderstanding and sorrow," the article explained. The key to Plečnik's character was his profound religious faith and ascetic rigor. The author went on: "Plečnik is a believer who measures his artistic production according to his faith. His artistic individuality comes out of an asceticism and directness of convictions; his faith demands of him an honesty to the end result and drives him to criticism of his own work."[63] As a designer, Plečnik worked slowly, methodically, even painfully. But the result, according to *Styl*, was the most distinct vision of the age. "An artist of such character and manner of work is never popular,"

---

61   Jože Plečnik to Andrej Plečnik, spring 1914, PC MGL.
62   Peter Krečič plots the various axes of Plecnik's likely walks and his interventions along each path in *Plecnik: The Complete Works*, 109–22.
63   A., "Jože Plečník," *Styl* 1 (1906): 129–30.

the piece concluded. His projects from that period, even his most extensive ones, were for the most part only in the form of sketches; never built, for all intents and purposes they had no influence on the development of architecture and public opinion in Austria. Nevertheless, the Czech author concluded, there were few artists of the modern school who were as original as Plečnik.

For all his severity and stiffness of character, Plečnik was capable of great charisma and generosity. These traits were particularly apparent in his teaching, and they inspired deep loyalty and fondness among his students. Plečnik had not taught before taking the position at Prague's School of Applied Industrial Arts, and he had been concerned that the move to a vocational school would be a step down professionally. But from the start, he devoted himself to the work of teaching and to his students. Plečnik's studio, overlooking the Vltava River, was a distinct space. In contrast to the absence of faith he found in the city, the professor's religiosity infused his classroom. Certainly, there were students who bristled. But others shared their teacher's ideas of architecture as a task done in faith and the artist as a servant of God.

We have little record, in Plečnik's own hand, of what he taught or hoped to convey to his students. He wrote to his brother Andrej only rarely about his teaching. In one letter, at the start of the 1913 term, he wrote about his students, their abilities and motivations: "This year I have eighteen18 lads. Most are new—a few of them have already been plagued with many years in workshops—they have clumsy hands—an imprisoned spirit, etc. And that is the work—to lead them in a direction, God knows which, at least in the direction that I know myself."[64] Plečnik's manner of teaching was individual. According to reminiscences of his students in Prague and later in Ljubljana, the architect moved around the studio, offering personal instruction at each student's drawing table. They quickly recognized that Plečnik's word in artistic matters was final. But they accepted his authority after watching what he could do with the pencil. "There was no resistance to the truth of the teacher, for he did not strive for it in words but with his

---

64 Jože Plečnik to Andrej Plečnik, undated letter [1913], quoted in Prelovšek, *Josef Plečnik: Wiener Arbeiten*, 161.

own work," wrote one former student, Josef Štěpánek, who became a prominent Czech architect. "And how could a student resist, when he saw how his teacher had the spirit for any kind of task?"[65]

Plečnik's lessons aimed first at developing the drawing skills of his students, both in terms of their technical ability and their care in observation. But even these drafting assignments showed a deeper intent. For one lesson, Plečnik set out Russian dolls for his students to use as inspiration for designs for crèches. "I told them that between the Christmas tree and the Nativity scene there must be something that is Slav—now let the seed germinate—something may come of it."[66] Plečnik also promoted an understanding of Slavic culture with class field trips to Moravian and Slovak villages; students then designed cottages and chapels in the style of rural wooden structures they had seen. At the same time, however, Plečnik also brought the students to Dresden, Leipzig, and Berlin in order to study urban architecture. The one negative bias in his teaching was against contemporary design. Plečnik emphasized study of classical architecture. Students hoping to learn about current trends in theory and design were disappointed; instead, most of their projects required drawing of capitals, urns, arched bridges, and columned façades decorated with friezes.

Despite these authoritarian tendencies, there was a collaborative environment in Plečnik's studio. When he later began work as architect of Prague Castle, Plečnik missed the engagement with students in the studio, a factor that led him to take the teaching position in Ljubljana.[67] Former students recalled their professor's openness, as he would tell them about his own life and ask about their backgrounds and interests. As Josef Štěpánek later wrote, students lingered in the classroom at the School for Arts and Crafts at the end of the day to continue their conversations, "wise conversations on every possible subject."[68] A published volume of the Prague students' projects shows

---

65   Štěpánek, "Plečnik, učitel a mistr." On Plečnik's approach to teaching, see Krečič, *Plečnik: The Complete Works*, 49–51.

66   Jože Plečnik to Andrej Plečnik, 21 November 1912, quoted in Prelovšek, *Jože Plečnik: Architectura perennis*, 117–18.

67   Report by Blažek, 12 Feburary 1924, AKPR, file T 49/23, folder Plečnik 2.

68   Štěpánek, "Plečnik, učitel a mistr," 60.

FIGURE 2.6. Otto Rothmayer, *Ceremonial Gate.*
In Plečnik, *Výběr prací školy pro dekorativní architekturu v Praze*, 115.

how interactions with their teacher carried over into their designs; there were details in student projects that had appeared in Plečnik's earlier drawings. In turn, Plečnik later used some elements from student designs in his own projects, such as Otto Rothmayer's tapered flagpoles, which clearly inspired the flagpoles Plečnik later placed at Prague Castle.[69]

The compilation of student drawings also shows the teacher's philosophy of architecture; there are churches, chapels, and classical

---

69 Plečnik, *Výběr prací školy pro dekorativní architekturu v Praze*. On Plečnik's borrowing of his students' ideas, see Krečič, *Jože Plečnik*, 90.

FIGURE 2.7. František Novák, *Bishop's Throne*, 1912.
In Plečnik, *Výběr prací školy pro dekorativní architekturu v Praze*, 49.

FIGURE 2.8. Antonín Moudrý, *Bell Tower*, 1912.
In Plečnik, *Výběr prací školy pro dekorativní architekturu v Praze*, 76.

structures, and the students' designs juxtapose styles of the past and present. For instance, a drawing of a bishop's throne by one of Plečnik's first students combines a range of elements: the hall has a basilica ceiling and neoclassical windows, the ciborium resembles an archaic temple with thick columns, and the throne and screen have geometric decoration that suggests art deco. Meanwhile, the two people approaching the throne are dressed in clothes of the early nineteenth century. Antonín Moudrý's bell tower from 1912 stacks together, from top to bottom, a Slavic roof and attic crowned with a two-dimensional icon; an art nouveau angel; arched Renaissance windows; three stories of arcades with cubist columns; an arrangement of geometric blocks recall-

FIGURE 2.9. Josef Fuchs, family house, 1919.
In Plečnik, *Výběr prací školy pro dekorativní architekturu v Praze*, 29.

ing the baroque palaces of Prague; and a base that resembles an ancient shrine. In contrast, Josef Fuch's 1919 design for a family house was much less cluttered, yet still eclectic in its sources. The ground level has a rational plan and unadorned exterior, with windows framed by geometric shutters and sills. But the façade of the upper floors is composed of stacked wooden beams, complete with protruding, interlocked ends, topped by the pitched roof of a rural cottage. The combination of elements in the student projects recalls a common appraisal made of Plečnik, that he was willing to adopt elements from all manner of architectural periods and styles.

A photograph of Plečnik from 1912, his first year of teaching, offers further visual evidence of the environment in his studio. He is shown in profile, facing his window that overlooked the Vltava. On an upper shelf is arranged a collection of knick-knacks: dried flowers tied with ribbons, bowls decorated with Slavic folk designs, a crucifix, and a statue of the Madonna and Child. The Catholic tone of the studio went beyond the symbols on the wall. Josef Štěpánek recalled how students entered a "spiritual bath" created by "an atmosphere of religios-

FIGURE 2.10. Plečnik in his Prague studio, 1912.
Jože Plečnik Collection, Museums and Galleries of Ljubljana, Slovenia.

ity, a fervently Catholic bias for crepuscular chapels and niches, a submission to mysticism and the typography of the Latin language."[70]
Despite the hint of impatience with Plečnik's religiosity, Štěpánek valued the relationship with his professor, even after he had established
his own reputation as an architect. In the first years after leaving
school, Štěpánek wrote warmly to Plečnik to report on his own work.
One greeting featured Štěpánek's drawing of a decorated Easter egg

---

70 Štěpánek, "Plečnik, učitel a mistr," 60.

that incorporated the initials of the Czechoslovak Republic into the intricate floral pattern, perhaps an acknowledgment of the kind of lessons he had gained in the master's studio.[71] Correspondence from Plečnik's other Czech students shows that they likewise remembered his lessons as well as his personal affections. His collected letters include dozens of postcards, sent years later by former students in their travels, depicting the exteriors and interiors of churches, religious statuary and icons, and classical structures and ruins. Whether or not they shared their professor's convictions, Plečnik's former students long remembered what he valued.

Many letters from Plečnik's students praised the teacher for his direction on their careers and for the example he had set. Some followed Plečnik into teaching, gaining positions at vocational and technical schools in the newly independent Czechoslovakia. After starting work at a vocational school in the north Bohemian city of Litomyšl, Alois Metelák regularly visited Plečnik whenever he was in Prague, seeking his professor's advice on teaching.[72] Bohumil Andrlík taught in a technical school in the remote Slovak town of Spišská Nová Ves and wrote to Plečnik of the challenge of undoing the influence of Hungarian rule there. He found his Slovak students to be woefully lacking in education, but he followed Plečnik's example and sat with each one at his drafting table, "wanting to induce in some of them a love for the task."[73] He even asked to bring his students to Prague to meet his former professor. Andrlík and Metelák also sought Plečnik's input on their own design projects. When Metelák entered a competition for a monument to the Czech Brethren and Jan Amos Komenský in 1922, he asked Plečnik's critique on his drafts and sent updates on the monument's construction after his proposal was selected. His letters indicate the great respect he retained for Plečnik, even after his own professional success. "As always, you showed us the better path to what is right."[74]

Along with statements of gratitude, letters from Plečnik's students also referred to the architect's beliefs and the religious environment of

71 Štěpánek to Plečnik, 14 April 1919; see also note dated 8 June, no year, PC MGL.
72 Letters of Metelák to Plečnik, and those of his other former students, are collected in PC MGL.
73 Andrlík to Plečnik, 5 June 1921, PC MGL.
74 Mezera to Plečnik, 16 November 1922, PC MGL.

his studio. Some of Plečnik's former students clearly shared the faith of their professor. One from his first group of students, Alois Mezera, wrote of the piety of the people in the Austrian Tyrol, where he lived in the early months of 1914. During the war, when Mezera was serving in the Austrian army, he sent postcards of Catholic chapels and monstrances.[75] Other students used broader religious language, avoiding specifically Catholic references. For example, Josef Stejskal wrote that he owed his position at a vocational school to Providence, "as you used to say."[76] His letters, like those of other students, had a tone of reverence for Plečnik. "Oftentimes I remember the school in which we gently nested under your protective wings," wrote one former student.[77] Stejskal wrote of the "greatness of your spirit," a term shared by František Oktávec. "I think of you every day," Oktávec wrote in July 1917, from an army garrison. "I cannot forget the time I spent in your school. Perhaps now I am especially brought to treasure the spirit of your school."[78]

This "spirit" that his students remembered was not the third person of the Trinity. It was the spirit of Plečnik. For these former students, the architect was indeed an instrument of the divine, and his studio had been a sacred space. While they might not have shared in the practice of his Catholic faith, they venerated Plečnik himself as someone on a different plane, as a representative of the spiritual in their lives. The architect cultivated this role in his students' lives. One of his later Slovene students recalled the first meeting with the professor, after Plečnik had taken a position in 1921 with the newly formed University of Ljubljana. The teacher struck a mysterious figure—lean and gaunt, in black coat and wide-brimmed hat, with pince-nez over his sharp nose and a gray, bristle-brush goatee. His new students were startled: "When the flock had calmed down, he stood before us like a Good Shepherd. He crossed his hands on his chest like a priest before the sermon, collecting his thoughts and relaxing himself. He lowered his head, allowing the well-groomed beard to touch his chest. He

---

75 Mezera to Plečnik, 14 March 1914, 19 March 1916, and 24 December 1916, PC MGL.

76 Josef Stejskal to Plečnik, 18 March 1921, PC MGL.

77 Eduard Olejšek to Plečnik, 14 March 1922, PC MGL.

78 František Oktávec to Plečnik, 3 July 1917, PC MGL.

closed his eyes, concentrated, and began in a calm, monotonous voice to greet us, who would henceforth be his faithful and unfaithful students."[79]

In his manners, asceticism, and mystical faith, Plečnik was a formidable character. In Ljubljana, as in Prague, sessions in Plečnik's studio were a mix of exacting master class and idiosyncratic indoctrination, all wrapped in the mystery of a sacred ritual. Still, students were drawn to him—to his personal charisma, to his skill as an artist, and to his demanding yet generous approach as a teacher. Certainly, there were students who did not share Plečnik's Catholic devotion. But just like Jan Kotěra in Vienna and, later, Tomáš Masaryk in Prague, Plečnik's students found something deeply compelling about the architect. Despite his overt religiosity, or perhaps because of it, they saw Plečnik as a person set apart, and they responded to him with reverence and loyalty.

Cubists and Monument Builders

Jože Plečnik was not as isolated in Prague as his letters suggest. He rented a room in the house of Kotěra's mother, not far from the architect's own villa in the city's upscale Vinohrady district. He found a friend in the cleaning lady at the college, a woman named Pepinka Kolářová. Kotěra sometimes gave gifts of wine to his Slovene friend, which Plečnik then shared with Pepi. Other Czech architects and artists also sought Plečnik's acquaintance and even invited him to contribute to projects. He helped architect Ladislav Skřivánek, a former Vienna classmate, on the design of an apartment building in Prague's Old Town, across the street from the City Hall, and he collaborated on unrealized projects with sculptor Stanislav Sucharda, one of the leading figures of the turn-of-the-century arts in Prague. Both men regarded Plečnik as a friend.[80]

---

79 Quoted in Krečič, *Plečnik: The Complete Works*, 72.
80 Both Sucharda and Skřivánek warmly addressed the architect as friend in their letters. In contrast, the few letters he received from sculptor František Bílek, with whom he was also acquainted in Prague, addressed Plečnik formally as professor.

One of the collaborations between Plečnik and Sucharda was for a major design competition in 1913 that involved many of Prague's leading architects and sculptors. The aim of the competition was to find a design for a monument to Jan Žižka, the Hussite commander who had led the successful defense of Bohemia against Catholic armies seeking to crush the reform movement. One of Žižka's greatest victories took place in 1420 on Vítkov Hill, at the time just east of Prague's old city walls. By the early twentieth century, the hill was surrounded by the growing industrial suburb of Žižkov, and civic leaders wanted to erect a monument to the great general for whom the city was named (Žižkov was incorporated into the city of Prague in 1922). The competition they announced brought more than fifty submissions, which were displayed in a public exhibition in early 1914 and then discussed in Prague's arts and cultural press. The summit of Vítkov Hill was a venue of epic scale, a site visible throughout Prague, and some design teams proposed grand projects. Owing to the organizing committee's limited funds, however, the most ambitious projects were rejected. Indeed, the competition guidelines had stipulated that the proposed designs could not use granite, marble, or any other stone. Instead, the monument to Jan Žižka was to be made of concrete.[81]

After rejecting projects due to cost, the jury still had difficulty in choosing a winner on artistic criteria. After extending the deliberation period, the judges recognized the most accomplished designs in the competition, awarding three second-place prizes and one third-place prize. But the first prize was not granted; the jury announced that none of the proposals merited construction.[82] One problem with the competition, which reviewers noted when the projects were put on public display, was that there was no clear sense of what Jan Žižka meant to the Czech nation and therefore what a monument to Žižka should communicate. Josef Chocol, one of the few leading young architects who did not enter the competition, argued in his review that the organizing committee had not offered artists a guiding vision of Žižka's person, his historical significance, and his relevance for the

---

81 The competition is detailed in Pencák, "Soutěž na pomník Jana Žižky."

82 Ibid., 75.

twentieth century. But Chocol's view of the Hussite general had little
to do with history either. Instead, he was a hero of the modern individual, motivated by ideals and animated by some spiritual force. The
sculpture of Žižka had to be "a monument of the iron energy and fullest exertion of the will of a man who was faithful to a definite idea
and an overpowering inspirer of the people to all-out resistance."[83]
The young writer Karel Čapek agreed that the competition revealed
the lack of a clear view of Žižka. "Few of the projects offered anything
more than Žižka standing or Žižka on a horse, Žižka with a sword or
Žižka with a mace." In Čapek's view, this confusion over the figure of
Zizka was a symptom of the deeper confusion in modern art. "There
were crumbs of modern sculpture, stirred into a bubbling eclecti-
cism," he wrote. "But there was almost nowhere a consistent and energetic approach, fully confident in the direction of traditionalism or
fully confident in the direction of the contemporary. Almost nowhere
was there restraint, but neither was there anything extreme. Compromise with tradition was contaminated by compromise with the new
and latest art."[84]

Uncertainty over how to represent Jan Žižka went beyond the sty-
listic unrest in early modernist art. The confusion in the design competition continued a pattern in Czech hero-making. The early twentieth century was a time of monument building in Prague and other
cities and towns across Bohemia and Moravia. Businessmen, politicians, and journalists launched campaigns to erect statues honoring
important figures of Czech history, in order to mark public spaces as
distinctly Czech.[85] Throughout these years, Josef Václav Myslbek
worked on his sculpture of St. Václav, which was placed at the top of
Wenceslaus Square in 1924. Plečnik's friend and sometime collaborator Stanislav Sucharda designed a large monument to nineteenth-century historian František Palacký, known as the "father of the nation,"
that was unveiled in 1912. Most popular were statues of Jan Hus.

---

83 Chocol, "Soutěž na Žižkův pamatník" [Competition for Žižka's Monument], *Prehled* (1914), quoted
    in Pencák, "Soutěž na pomník Jana Žižky," 78.
84 Čapek, "Soutěž na Žižkův pomník" [Competition for Žižka's Memorial], *Lumír*, 13 March 1914, in
    O umění a kultuře, 378.
85 See Wingfield, *Flag Wars and Stone Saints*.

Sucharda and Plečnik briefly collaborated on a proposal for a Hus monument, but the project never got further than sketches. Plečnik drew Hus at his moment of martyrdom, engulfed by flames.[86] Sculptor Ladislav Šaloun, designer of the statue now standing on Old Town Square, had also depicted Hus as a martyr in his first model, with hands bound, head bowed, and robe pulled off his shoulder—an embodiment of the suffering national soul. According to the sculptor, Hus in his moment of martyrdom represented the heights of the nation's powers, "as well as its nearly fatal fall."[87] This vision, however, ran afoul of the organizing committee. The Czech politicians and businessmen who were paying Šaloun, as well as the journalists and critics commenting on the whole process, did not want a defeated Hus. The true Hus, insisted one journal, was "the liberator of the nation's spirit and power."[88] The steering committee called for changes to Šaloun's original design: Hus's head was to be upturned, his figure separated from the surrounding groups of figures that Šaloun planned, and his presence in the sculpture magnified. In 1905, Šaloun went back to work—with a new contract and specific instructions from the committee. His revised sculpture, following these directions, was unveiled on Old Town Square in 1915, on the 500th anniversary of Hus's martyrdom.[89]

The statues of Czech national heroes—Hus, Žižka, and others—have been properly interpreted in many ways: as works of art, as markers on the cultural landscape, as objects in a struggle of competing national identities.[90] But these nationalist monuments are also sacred places. According to geographers David Atkinson and Denis Cosgrove, most public monuments, "especially those intended to encapsulate an imagined national spirit or identity, seek to materialize ideas of

---

86 In a note to Sucharda, Plečnik explained that the image he had sketched showed "the final, most gruesome and most noble moment" of the sacrifice. Plečnik, note on drawing, 2 October 1913, Archiv Národní galerie, Sucharda Collection, doc. 3040, IIIc.

87 Hojda and Pokorný, *Pomníky a zapomníky*, 80.

88 Quoted in Paces, *Prague Panoramas*, 44.

89 Paces discusses the criticism of Šaloun's models and the eventually unveiling of the monument during the war in chapter two of *Prague Panoramas*.

90 See Paces, *Prague Panoramas*, and chapter five of Wingfield, *Flag Wars and Stone Saints*.

the sacred, the mystical, and the transcendental."[91] In functioning as this kind of national-sacred site, the monument to Jan Hus on Old Town Square is uniquely Czech as an icon of Somethingism. Hus is not a sacrificial figure embodying the nation's difficult history, as Ladislav Šaloun had first intended. Nor is he, as Tomáš Masaryk insisted, the moral teacher and religious reformer calling the Czechs to conviction and action. Instead, with his head upturned, jaw fixed, looking ahead, the version of Hus unveiled on the square during the war was an encouraging symbol to the nation—a nation that was itself moral and even sacred, while at the same time modern in its resistance to Catholicism.[92] Anthropologist Ladislav Holy has argued that Czech nationalism, both in the past and today, is tacit rather than overt.[93] The invocation of great heroes from Czech history is enough to express the greatness of the nation. There is no need to explain what these historical figures did; the simple listing of their names evokes the nation's virtuous traditions. In Holy's words, these figures are "spiritual ancestors," and the attributes with which they are associated are transferred to subsequent generations. For example, because Jan Hus was a defender of truth, the Czechs, as the "nation of Hus," are defenders of truth.[94] The virtues are received, not demonstrated. In the same way, Somethingism confers a notion of rectitude that is passively gained— no active commitment or catechism required. Jan Hus fits well into the shrine of Czech Somethingism. As a man of letters, he represents education, freedom of intellect and conviction. But Jan Žižka—the leader of an army of radical peasants, swinging vicious flails in a bloody war of religion? Not so much.

One other problem for judges of the Žižka memorial competition was that many of the designs were in the cubist style. Even though the jury included a member of the cubist group, as well as representatives of other modern arts associations, the judges questioned whether the

---

91 Atkinson and Cosgrove, "Urban Rhetoric and Embodied Identities," 30. Martin Schulze Wessel puts the Hus cult in the broader context of the sacralization of nations in nineteenth-century Europe: "Die Konfessionalisierung der tschechischen Nation," 138–41.

92 Schulze Wessel, "Die Konfessionalisierung der tschechischen Nation," 141.

93 Holy, *The Little Czech and the Great Czech Nation*, 136.

94 Ibid., 130–32.

general public would accept a nationalist monument executed in a new, international style. Cubism had appeared in Czech art only three years earlier, with an exhibition by a handful of young painters and sculptors who called themselves simply the Group of Fine Artists. This first exhibition received mixed reviews, but the trend took hold. Jan Kotěra's submission to the Žižka contest, which he completed along with established sculptor Jan Štursa, adopted the style. Kotěra and Štursa depicted Žižka on horseback, a massive figure at the head of two lines of warriors carrying banners. Their use of cubism gave the figures a primitive, rugged look, and the judges acknowledged the project with one of the second-place awards. Although the monument was not built in the style, Czech cubism became an important moment in the cultural history of East Central Europe. Many of the leading artistic figures of interwar Czechoslovakia were among the cubists, including Karel Čapek and his brother Josef, a well-known artist and writer.[95] In contemporary Prague, cubism is a significant part of the city's cultural profile: tourists can find the works of cubist architecture and decorative art featured in postcards, coffee-table books, and even a dedicated museum. For the Czechs, the cubist movement has provided visual confirmation of the nation's Europeanness. The group's 1911 exhibition featured work of the Parisian cubists, including Pablo Picasso, thus linking the young Czechs to this new trend in European art.[96] Forward-looking, integrative, and cosmopolitan, cubism was an "art of confidence and optimism in the modern world."[97]

"The real *raison d'étre* of cubism," wrote art historian Edward Fry, "resided in its secularism, in its skepticism of tradition, and in the desire to criticize all conventions... It represented the aim of opening up to the larger world of Western Europe."[98] Indeed, one of the attractions of cubism for these young Czech artists was its rationality. Karel Čapek saw himself as a literary cubist. Cubism appealed to his pragmatic mindset, in that it provided an organizing frame to artistic expression, while at the same time offering something of a scientific ap-

---

95 On Karel Čapek as part of the cubist movement, see Ort, *Art and Life in Modernist Prague*, 46–59.
96 Liška, "Important Prague Exhibitions, 1911–1922."
97 Ort, *Art and Life in Modernist Prague*, 53.
98 Fry, "Czech Cubism in the European Context," 12.

proach. Čapek maintained that by following the principles of cubism a writer could look at a character or situation from multiple directions.[99] This rationalizing and harmonizing approach also appealed to the painter Bohumil Kubišta, who, like Čapek, had first encountered cubism as a student in Paris. Kubišta wrote in 1912 of the move from a God-centered to a human- and individual-centered art. "People no longer listen to or worship the representatives of divine power, who have lost almost all their influence," he wrote.[100] The atheistic current of the modern age governed all aspects of public life, as people turned to the authority of industrialists, inventors, political or class movements. The artist must therefore seek new forms, consistent with this move from theism to atheism.

For other artists, however, the appeal of cubism was not its rationality but its spirituality. The word "spiritual" (*duchovní*) appears repeatedly in statements of the Czech cubists. Derived from the word for "soul" or "spirit," *duchovní* has two principal meanings in these contexts. First, the word was used to refer to the inner, imaginative capacities of artists and the broad reach of the arts. As painter Emil Filla wrote: "There is no work of art that does not touch upon eternal questions and is not at the same time an answer to the meaning of life, that is, its purpose and value. The artist eschews the physical world and turns instead to the creative act, whose products are more certain and more permanent."[101] The second meaning of *duchovní* was more expansive: in this use, "spirit" was the immanent essence of the world that an artist could reveal. In influential essays of the cubist movement, sculptor Otto Gutfreund and architect Pavel Janák wrote of the artist's vision penetrating and suffusing a material object, allowing the object's spirit to be revealed.[102] Even Bohumil Kubišta, who called for an art reflecting the atheist outlook of the times, drew upon religious

99   Thomas Ort discusses Čapek's preference for cubism over the subjectivism of expressionism in *Art and Life in Modernist Prague*, 56–58.

100 Kubišta, "The Intellectual Basis of Modern Time," 101. Originally published as "O duchovém podkladu moderní doby" [On the spiritual foundation of modern times], *Česká kultura 1* (1912–1913).

101 Filla, "Život a dílo" [Life and works], *Umělecký měsíčník 1* (1911–1912), in *Práce oka*, 31.

102 Janák, "The Prism and the Pyramid." Originally published as "Hranol a pyramida," *Umělecký měsíčník 1* (1911). Gutfreund, "Surface and Space." Originally published as "Plocha a prostor," *Umělecký měsíčník 2* (1912).

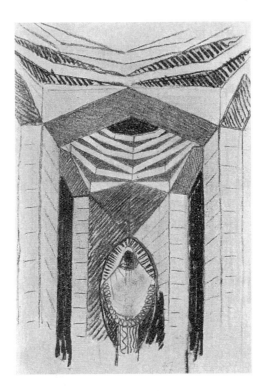

FIGURE 2.11. Plečnik, drawing of a chapel, 1907.
Jože Plečnik Collection, Museums and Galleries of Ljubljana, Slovenia.

principles in explaining the links among people and between humanity and the world. Yes, modern people had rebelled against God, but in the process they drew upon a "mysterious universal force," which he explained with reference to the universal soul of Hinduism, the *atman*.[103] The cubists saw themselves as atheists, or more appropriately, as anti-theists. But they were not materialists. They maintained belief in a spiritual reality, which provided harmony and unity to the universe. It was the creative task of the artist to access and manifest that "mysterious universal force."

Given the cubists' yearning for a spiritual art, it is no surprise that some of their number found inspiration in the work of Jože Plečnik. The

---

103 Kubišta, "The Intellectual Basis of Modern Time," 101.

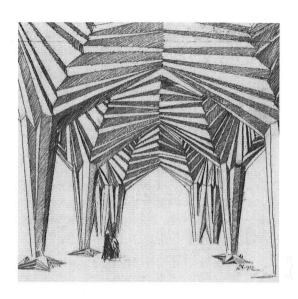

FIGURE 2.12. Pavel Janák, monumental interior, 1912.
In Švestka and Vlček, eds., *Czech Cubism, 1909–1925.*

leading architects of the cubist circle had trained in Vienna under Otto
Wagner or in Prague under Jan Kotěra, both of whom held that rationalism was the theoretical foundation of modern architecture. But in
1910, one of the leading lights in the circle, Pavel Janák, threw down the
gauntlet of aesthetic and generational challenge. In his essay "From
Modern Architecture to Architecture," a founding statement of the
Czech cubist movement, Janák argued that architecture had to demonstrate beauty and creativity, rather than fixing upon function, structure,
and social utility. Like the cubist painters and sculptors, Janák wrote of
artists using their creative energy to act upon—and within—physical
matter. A model figure for this kind of architecture, "true architecture,"
in Janák's words, was Plečnik.[104] Like the cubists, Plečnik was drawn to
the expressive possibilities and timeless nature of geometric shapes. In
his drawings from the first decade of the century, the architect played
with shapes. Seeking to break away from Secession-style ornamentation
and floral designs, Plečnik sketched façades broken into geometric

104 Janák, "Od moderní architektury do architektuře."

shapes and structural elements in tapering forms. Indeed, drawings by both Plečnik and Janák show that they thought in similar ways about the use of geometric forms in creating dynamic structures. As Plečnik's biographer Damjan Prelovšek points out, Janák's essay not only referred to the older artist by name, it also echoed some of his ideas, "confirming the view that the theoretical side of Czech cubism did in part derive from admiration for the Slovenian architect."[105]

The young architects of the cubist movement became Plečnik's greatest supporters in Prague (and even his friends). In turn, he adopted some elements of their designs in his own work, such as use of the pyramid. He did not, however, identify himself with cubism or any other architectural fashion.[106] One area, though, in which he did correspond with the cubists was his understanding of the task of the artist. More than a creator of images, sculptures, or structures, the artist was responsible for unlocking eternal truth. "Art is something great and deep," Plečnik told his students in Ljubljana in the 1920s. "The artist evokes an unusual respect, almost a fear... The artist is alone in the world. In him there is something divine, different than in an ordinary person."[107] In the case of architecture, this truth was found in the creative use of material. Both the Catholic Plečnik and the pantheistic cubists insisted that architecture had to aspire to something greater than function. They sought beauty, for it was beauty that revealed the spiritual. As Plečnik instructed his students, each person had a soul that longed for beauty. "Man is thirsty for beauty. He wants to be good and to look upon beauty."[108] Plečnik's words echoed those of Janák: "The sense of beauty is a proof, and a result of the connection between people. It is directly part of the human fabric, not just a property of individuals... The sense of beauty penetrates and springs from the human well through individual people—they are the conduits. The true reasons are far and deeply removed."[109]

---

105 Prelovšek, *Jože Plečnik: Architectura perennis*, 88–9.

106 Ibid.

107 Lenarčič, *Plečnik: Spomini na Plečnika*, 48.

108 Ibid., 92.

109 Janák, diary entry of 6 June 1912, reprinted in Žantovská-Murray, "Sources of Cubist Architecture in Bohemia," appendix.

The brief but influential cubist movement holds an imporant place in the history of Prague art and culture. In addition, Czech cubism is a telling moment in the history of Somethingism. The cubists saw themselves as living in an irreligious age. Still, these artists did not—or could not—accept a materialist understanding of the cosmos. They insisted on a spiritual element that was present in humanity, the natural world, and artistic creation, and they maintained that their search for this spiritual something set them apart as artists. But in adopting a new, West European style and a rational form for that striving, their spiritualized art took on a modern guise. The spirit of the cubists offered an antidote to the modern age in its promise of harmony, beauty, and deeper purpose, while at the same time it fulfilled the tenets of modernity in being the source of individual creativity and remaining unbound to any creed or institution. However, as with other adherents to Somethingism, some members of the Group of Fine Artists did not free themselves entirely from religious traditions. At the close of the First World War, designer Vlastislav Hofman completed a series of lithographs for the mystical Catholic writer and publisher Josef Florian, including a series of Biblical figures in the style of Ethiopian icons. Hofman wrote to Florian after a 1920 showing of his work that critics accused him of no longer being modern because he made images of Madonnas. "But I don't mind. Once in a while I throw it back at them and continue on my merry way."[110] Josef Čapek also collaborated with Florian, producing illustrations for some publications released by the Catholic writer's press. Years later, despite his refusal to subscribe to any creedal belief, Čapek had his daughter baptized in a Catholic church. "The church is able to give an appropriately large and significant expression to the important moments of life, like the entrance into marriage and death," he explained to his wife.[111] Another cubist, Josef Gočar, also brought his son for christening. The man who designed the most celebrated example of Czech cubist architecture, the House of the Black Madonna (home today to Prague's cubism museum), chose as the boy's godfather an artist he had long respected: Jože Plečnik.

---

110 Letter of Hofman to Florian, 22 April 1918, quoted in Nešlehová, "The Dostoyevsky Series and Hofman's Other Portfolios," 181.

111 Quoted in Čapoková, *Vzpomínky*, 177.

FIGURE 2.13. Plečnik, plan for Žižka monument, May 1913.
Jože Plečnik Collection, Museums and Galleries of Ljubljana, Slovenia.

Conclusion

Plečnik's part in the Žižka monument competition is still uncertain. His archive includes several draft sketches, finished plans, and photographs of the model of his design. He had planned to submit a proposal with Stanislav Sucharda, but in the end the architect entered the competition alone. He also entered under a false name, signing his work as A. Pail.[112] Most likely, the pseudonym was a response to the committee's call for projects from "Czechoslavic" (československé) artists—not the only time that Plečnik would face the exclusion of Czech nationalism.

Plečnik's project changed dramatically from the call for submissions in spring 1913 to the deadline in the following autumn. There are several drawings dated to May, only few weeks after the competition was announced. These first drafts worked at the idea of a victorious heroic figure, on horseback, set inside a monumental, inverted semidome. In an early sketch the semidome was set upon a single support,

---

112 Pencák, "Soutěž na pomník Jana Žižky na Vítkově," 82.

FIGURE 2.14. Plečnik, model submitted for Žižka monument competition, November 1913. Jože Plečnik Collection, Museums and Galleries of Ljubljana, Slovenia.

like the halved cup of a chalice. The chalice was the symbol of the Hussite movement, following from Jan Hus's insistence that lay churchgoers receive the wine as well as bread in communion. Other proposals later submitted to the competition also employed the symbol, but none used the chalice to such monumental effect as Plečnik's early designs.

These early projects were also unique in that they showed Žižka not as a rugged medieval hetman but as a classical hero, clean shaven and draped in robes. He carries a spear rather than the obligatory Hussite mace, and Plečnik's Žižka even lacked the distinctive eye patch (Žižka had lost an eye in battle). Another early drawing broke in a different direction from the standard Žižka imagery. The central figure in this monument is riding a leaping horse, sitting on what appears to be Roman horned saddle. His upper body is stripped bare, with a wide sash around his midriff, decorated in an archaic, zigzag pattern, and he wears a pointed cap. The figure is more akin to Byzantine-Slavic Southeastern Europe than German-Slavic Central Europe. This figure also carries no weapons. Instead, his arms are outstretched, with palms upturned. The pose is one of victory, as if he is summoning his followers forward, or giving praise to God.

These were Plečnik's ideas in May. By the November deadline his design for the project had changed. The basic plan remained: a hero on horseback inside a halved chalice, with figures stationed on the brim. But rather than a dynamic sculpture at the center, depicting a classical hero riding forward in victory, the submitted model featured a traditional and restrained portrait of Žižka. The general sits motionless on a stationary horse. He is bearded and wears a medieval cloak and helmet. Likewise, the watching figures on the chalice have been turned to Hussite soldiers, wearing tunics, helmets, and holding pavises. Before Žižka stand two guardians in medieval dress, one with a shield, the other with a chalice. The references are unambiguous, and the composition straightforward. Other than the monumental chalice, it is unremarkable. The design did not earn a prize, nor did it gain much notice from reviewers.

What brought this significant change in design? A possible explanation is found in Plečnik's letters to his brother. The architect did not discuss his plans for the Žižka competition with Andrej, nor did he mention the reasons for Sucharda's departure from the project. He did, however, write about events in the news. At the time that Plečnik was working on these designs, he was following reports of the conflict in the South Balkans.[113] In the autumn of 1912, an alliance of the small Balkan monarchies—Serbia, Montenegro, Greece, Bulgaria, and Romania—attacked the armies of the Ottoman Empire. By the following

---

113 He discussed the war in his letters to Andrej in 1912.

spring, Ottoman forces had been swept almost entirely from Europe, and the major powers were meeting in London to draw new boundaries in the liberated territory. The final treaty was signed on May 30. Within weeks, however, bloodshed resumed in Southeastern Europe, as the former allies turned against each other in a fight over the spoils. Plečnik followed the Second Balkan War in the newspapers during the summer and grieved over it. In letters to Andrej in 1913 and early 1914, he wrote of the violence of war, the suffering of the Slavs, and the enmity of the Austrians, Germans, and Hungarians. "How much pain there must be for every Slav in times as these," Plečnik wrote. "Maybe it's God's will that the Slav must pay in blood for every shred of rights."[114] Perhaps these events in Southeastern Europe had their expression in Plečnik's art, in the turn from a monument featuring a jubilant hero to one depicting a solemn scene of commander and watchmen.

The bigger question is why Plečnik even went forward with the Žižka project. Why did an insistently Catholic architect design a monument honoring a Hussite general and then, the following year, sketch a sculpture of Hus himself? Plečnik's biographers do not give a clear answer. Perhaps he had encouragement from Kotěra, or from his younger admirers, like Pavel Janák and Josef Gočár. Then again, maybe not—after all, Kotěra, Janák, and Gočár all submitted their own proposals to the Žižka competition.

Although the drawings for the Žižka and Hus monuments are minor moments in Plečnik's long creative career, they do reveal something significant about his personality, particularly relating to his beliefs. The writings of his contemporaries and biographers emphasize the strength of Plečnik's convictions. He could be rigid in his judgments, just as he was in his work habits. At the same time, however, people who did not share Plečnik's beliefs showed remarkable commitment to him. We see this with his students in Prague, with his friend Jan Kotěra, and with his teacher Otto Wagner, who insisted that Plečnik succeed him at the Academy in Vienna even after his former student had excoriated him as "unworthy of grace." What drew

---

114 Jože Plečnik to Andrej Plečnik, autumn 1912 (autumn 1913?). The letter is undated by Plečnik himself, but it is filed with other letters from autumn 1913, and its description of the Balkan Wars corresponds to the later date. PC MGL.

these people to Plečnik? Certainly, his talent and creativity were part of it. But perhaps people were also drawn to Plečnik because he was able to bend his convictions when necessary. Pavel Janák wrote in his diary of Plečnik's fervent nationalism, yet the older architect avoided any association with nationalist groups that might jeopardize his future prospects.[115] He was a devoted Catholic who decried the irreligion of Prague, yet he designed monuments to Czechs whom the Church regarded as heretics. Yes, Plečnik was a person of profound faith and strongly stated, often traditional ideas. But he was not doctrinaire or inflexible. He was a modern—in his art as well as his willingness to shape his beliefs depending on the circumstances.

Tomáš Masaryk was a modern believer who needed God as the source of truth, as the linchpin to his ontological and ethical thinking. Convinced that his ideas were founded in unchanging truth, he had no qualms about making declarations and challenging others. Jože Plečnik, in comparison, was just as austere as Masaryk in his personal habits, just as disciplined in his work, just as moralistic in his view of the world. He was, however, reluctant to assert himself with people other than his confidantes. The architect held to God not as the guarantor of truth but as personal anchor. With his swings from certainty to self-criticism and his constant loneliness, Plečnik's religiosity—its traditions, its rituals, its worship—served as a source of comfort. His letters would bounce from one topic to another in a jumble of clipped thoughts, and then, at places, he would rest with the declaration: "as God wills." This longing for contentment in God is evident in the architect's writing and his art. Throughout his collected drawings—everywhere from the backs of envelopes to sheets of drafting paper—one finds detailed renderings of cherubs, chalices, and chapels: their precise lines providing a moment's haven. In a few drawings, there is a figure tucked in a corner. Sometimes the resemblance is apparent, sometimes it is a rough doodle. Perhaps it is him—the architect finding a place for himself in the timeless world he has created.

---

115 Janák, diary entry of 17 June 1912, in Žantovská-Murray, "Sources of Cubist Architecture in Bohemia," appendix.

Chapter Three

The Social Worker Longing to Serve

After the creation of Czechoslovakia, two of Tomáš Masaryk's adult children gained high positions in the new state. His oldest child, Alice Garrigue Masaryková, became director of the newly formed Czechoslovak Red Cross organization, while her brother Jan, nine years her junior, became a diplomat in the Foreign Ministry. Jan Masaryk served first as *chargé d'affaires* at the embassy in Washington, DC, and then was appointed ambassador to London in 1925. At the start of the Second World War, he became foreign minister in the Czechoslovak government in exile, formed in London by his father's longtime accomplice, Edvard Beneš. When Beneš returned as president to the reconstituted Czechoslovakia after the war, Jan Masaryk remained foreign minister, and he continued in the post even after the Communist coup in 1948, the only member of the cabinet who was not a party member or fellow traveler. Two weeks after the formation of the Communist-led government, Masaryk was found dead below his apartment window at the Foreign Ministry building—perhaps a suicide or, as many have argued, the victim of Soviet agents. Whatever the cause, Masaryk's death was a shock in Britain and the United States, where he had been a popular representative of his country. The first casualty of the Cold War, Jan Masaryk gained a lasting place in the history books.

In the family history, however, Jan Masaryk was something of ne'er-do-well. Good with jokes, the life of a social gathering, Jan was partial to drink and not at all inclined to hard work. His habits as a young man worried his parents and frustrated his older sister, who resented having to pay his debts.[1] He left for the United States at age twenty, gaining a job through his father's long-standing connection with Charles Crane. After six years, his employers had enough and sent him home. The young man's moral nature, reported a company executive, was "dormant, undeveloped, remarkably so for one of John's inherited social position."[2] Even after the war, when he had entered the diplomatic service, Alice Masaryková was still wary of her brother's lack of seriousness. Only later, after he had quit drinking, did Jan Masaryk gain his sister's trust.[3]

Alice Masaryková was everything that Jan Masaryk was not—serious, disciplined, hardworking, unbending in her morals. She also believed resolutely in her parents' ideal of service for others. From a young age, Masaryková was determined to work for the improvement of society. The question was: how to do that? As a European woman at the turn of the century, she had new opportunities open to her, but also found her options limited by social pressures. An attempt to study medicine ended abruptly; she then continued studies in history and sociology—at each step, the only woman in her classes. Throughout her academic work, she yearned for a more direct involvement in the social problems of the day, especially the injustices faced by working-class women. The solution came with a year-long stay in Chicago. Masaryková worked alongside the pioneers of social work at the city's settlement houses. She learned the methods of social surveys, community organization, and educational and health programming. Furthermore, she saw the Protestant social gospel in action. When Masaryková returned to Prague, she was eager to launch the same kind of public welfare work she had done in America, with its roots in both social-scientific analysis and the conviction that religious faith must be manifest in good deeds.

---

1   Alice Masaryková discussed her parents' and her own problems with Jan in letters to her mother (18 October 1903) and her father (3 May 1906), MÚA AV ČR, TGM Collection, Korespondence III, box 60, folder 34, and box 54, folder 2.

2   Charlotte Masaryková relayed this assessment to her husband in a letter from New Jersey, 11 September 1913, MÚA AV ČR, TGM Collection, Korespondence III, box 54, folder 1.

3   Alice Masaryková expressed her concerns about Jan's "thoughtlessness and selfishness" in a letter to her father, 27 July 1921, MÚA AV ČR, TGM Collection, Korespondence III, box 54, folder 2. Her opinion had changed by 1930, when they were working together at international conferences: AGM to TGM, 1 October 1930, Korespondence III, box 54, folder 4.

Masaryková's understanding of her vocation coincided with a deepening—or even discovery—of her religiosity. Tomáš and Charlotte Masaryk did not take a direct hand in their children's religious upbringing. Alice Masaryková took up that task herself. Her beliefs developed from multiple sources and acquired a syncretistic, wholly individual character. She valued American Unitarianism, as demonstrated by her mother, and the Czech Protestant heritage, as interpreted by her father. But she also found comfort in the aesthetics and shared experience of worship. She sought her father's expertise on religious matters, but she also felt at home with the traditions of the Christian church. Unlike Masaryk, the modern believer who subjected religious ideas to his measure of rationality, Alice Masaryková weighed beliefs and practices according to her impulse to serve. As with her father, her assembled convictions did not fit within a specific church. They were wholly personal, grounded in tradition yet turned to the contemporary world.

Discovering Faith and Vocation

Tomáš Masaryk's opinions and activism brought him notoriety. They also brought a narrowing of his social circle. "When the century ended," wrote his longtime collaborator Jan Herben, "Professor Masaryk was the most isolated man in Czech public life."[4] Masaryk counted few lasting friendships in his life; instead, his consistent source of support was his family. Charlotte Masaryková's letters to her husband, when he was serving in parliament in Vienna in the 1890s, are poignant with affection, and their children's recollections brimmed with fond memories and respect. Masaryk was a devoted father who got down on the carpet to play with his children when they were young. Later photographs of the family show parents and children relaxed and playful in each other's presence, quite unlike the stiff portraits we are accustomed to seeing from the period. Tomáš and Charlotte Masaryk also practiced what would be called today "intentional parenting." They were not disciplinarians; instead, they followed a deter-

---

4   Herben, *T. G. Masaryk: Život a dílo Presidenta Osvoboditele*, 94.

FIGURE 3.1. Tomáš and Charlotte Masaryk with their children, 1905.
Masaryk Institute and Archive, Academy of Sciences, Czech Republic.

mined philosophy for the family, seeing it as a school to inculcate
virtues of work, altruism, and love.[5]

Charlotte Masaryková looked upon their oldest child with great
fondness and pride. "My Alice, a hero of the first class from the day she
was born," she wrote in her diary in 1920. "The dearest, strongest creature perhaps that the world has ever produced."[6] Born in 1879 in Vienna, Alice Garrigue Masaryková was the first of five children: Herbert followed in 1880, Jan in 1886, and Olga in 1891, while another

---

5 Skilling, *T. G. Masaryk: Against the Current*, 114–15.
6 Entry for 30 August 1920, black-bound diary, MÚA AV ČR, CGM Collection, box 2, folder 6.

daughter, Eleanor, died shortly after her birth in 1890. Part of Charlotte Masaryková's respect for her daughter might have stemmed from memories of Alice's second year, when Charlotte was bedridden with depression. Charlotte kept a diary from those months, in which she recorded admiring notes of the seemingly contented, intelligent toddler. "Everybody loves you, & you make all who look at you happy," the proud young mother wrote. The little girl was also forced to be independent, learning to walk on her own during her mother's illness. Charlotte observed distinct traits: her daughter was energetic, musical, determined. "Alice's character is very decided. You know what you want very well & it is not without tears that you do what is good for you in opposition to your desires."[7] The scenes from her childhood established a motif for Alice Masaryková's life. She would become a woman of determination and independence, but not without struggle against the expectations and prejudices of the times.

Alice Masaryková was part of the first generation of girls able to take advantage of new education opportunities in late nineteenth-century Prague. She studied at the Minerva School, the first gymnasium for girls in the Austrian Empire, and in 1898 she entered the Czech university in Prague to study medicine. Already as a gymnasium student Masaryková planned to be a physician, seeing that as the best vocation by which to serve society. Human physiology fascinated her, and she was amazed at her dissection of a cadaver. She recalled the experience years later: "I can clearly remember the complex working machine, enlivened by water, air, and the fruit of the earth, and controlled by the human will. What a precious tool that is given to us! How necessary it is to carefully protect the spirit in the flesh!"[8] But Masaryková's medical studies were short-lived. Problems with her eyesight made lab work difficult, and out of vanity's sake she refused to wear her glasses. She was the only woman among the fifty students in her class, and the male professors dismissed her knowledge and abilities. Perhaps more than the professor's slights, Masaryková was disturbed by their basic outlook. She found that her professors were fixed

7   Entry of 26 November 1880, in notebook titled "Alice," MÚA AV ČR, CGM Collection, box 2, folder 7d. See also earlier entries, dated 1 August and 1 September.

8   Masaryková, *Dětství a mládí*, 101.

on the body as machine, but they did not see the spirit within the machine. There were some who had a firm moral sense, she recalled, but there was no religious awareness.[9] In a reflection written decades later to a friend, Masaryková admitted that the materialism of her professors frightened her.[10] Moreover, as she later explained, she did not see how that approach could be the best way to serve people. "From my childhood I had been interested in medicine and had wanted to help people," she wrote. "But somehow I could not connect this desire with the actual study of medicine."[11] Masaryková's medical studies lasted only one year. She was so disappointed by leaving that she could not bear to walk near a hospital.

Another factor in Masaryková's decision to leave medical school was her expectation of marriage. At the time, Masaryková was not involved with anyone. In fact, there had not been any romantic relationship to that point in her life. But after years of attending a girls' gymnasium, she was surrounded by men for the first time in her life at the university. The experience triggered the feeling that marriage would come, and it would compel her to give up medicine. "The real revolt was that I thought marriage was my sure destiny," she wrote to a friend decades later. "I willed it."[12] At age nineteen, Masaryková showed the independence and strength of character to step alone into medical school, and after leaving medical school, she became the first woman to earn a doctorate in history at Prague's Charles University. But she still felt that the social expectation of what she should do as a woman outweighed what she wanted to do as a person.

Masaryková completed her degree in history at the same time as her father was involved in the Hilsner affair.[13] During this same period, in the first years of the new century, she began her own involvement in public affairs. Masaryková participated in the organization

---

9   Ibid., 102.
10 Alice Masaryková, letter to Ruth Crawford Mitchell, 1940, quoted in Mitchell, *Alice Garrigue Masaryk*, 41. On Masaryková's decision to leave medical school, see Skilling, *Mother and Daughter*, 77–8; and Lovčí, *Alice Garrigue Masaryková*, 47–8.
11 Mitchell, *Alice Garrigue Masaryk*, 40.
12 Ibid.
13 Masaryková had her father as a professor for courses in sociology and philosophy of history. Seznam přednášek, Alice Masaryk Collection, Lilly Library, box 1, folder 1.

Slavia, which pressed for suffrage and other women's issues, and she gave public lectures on women's rights in Bohemia. *Slavia* also organized discussion groups and lectures on social issues, fostering Masaryková's interest in the obstacles facing working-class women, abused women, and prostitutes. These social-welfare concerns led to an involvement in the temperance movement, an interest she shared with her father.[14] Alcohol abuse was a major problem in the empire, even among children, and in 1901 the imperial Ministry of Education sponsored a temperance conference in Vienna. Tomáš Masaryk spoke at the conference, and while there he met a young physician and temperance activist named Richard Fröhlich. Masaryk arranged for his daughter to visit Fröhlich, an ophthalmologist, for treatment of her eyesight problems. The meetings proved to be momentous. Masaryková was moved by Fröhlich's involvement in the antialcohol movement, particularly his promotion of temperance among Vienna's workers. Her own commitment to the movement intensified, and she remained a determined critic of alcohol consumption throughout her life. In addition, Masaryková was moved personally by the good doctor. She was impressed with him as a man of both culture and conviction, someone who put his beliefs into action. In her early twenties and finishing her university studies, she believed that she had found the man who was made for her.[15]

At the same time, though, Alice Masaryková was determined to continue her education. She spent the fall semester of 1901 at the University of Berlin, and in the spring of 1902 she traveled to London to research her dissertation, a study of the Magna Carta. Masaryková completed her doctorate in Prague in 1903 and decided to return to Germany for postgraduate work. She moved to Leipzig, the city where her parents had met, and enrolled in courses in history, sociology, and economics: an interdisciplinary program aimed at giving her a broad understanding of contemporary social problems. Masaryková was aware that she was among the few pathbreaking women in European universities. In one letter from Leipzig, she commented to her mother

14   On Masaryková's early civic engagement, see Skilling, *Mother and Daughter*, 78–9.
15   On the relationship, see Lovčí, *Alice Garrigue Masaryková*, 55–6; and Skilling, *Mother and Daughter*, 78–9.

that she was the only woman in classes at the university. "Just fancy!" she wrote.[16]

Masaryková occasionally thought of becoming a historian or writer, but she felt an uncontainable need to give of herself and contribute tangibly to the improvement of society. "I want to do my duty," she wrote to her father at the beginning of the term in Leipzig, "duty & a strong will are the motors of my life, which I don't mean to throw away."[17] Her studies were at once invigorating and despairing. Observing the effects of urban poverty, such as child labor and prostitution, and learning about social problems brought her only "headache & pain." She wrote to her mother, "It makes me mad to see women degraded in their & through their womanliness. It hurts me, it hurts me!"[18] From Leipzig, Masaryková wrote of exhaustion and desperation. She also reported the same debilitating headaches and bouts of depression that her mother suffered. Her antidote was to work, even though she felt inadequate to the work she sought to do. "I have to think about things no girl is fond of thinking," she wrote to her mother. "I often howl—howl like a little child—till I am tired & get to bed. But who looks at things as they are—cannot be quite happy. If I was an artist!! Something grand! I would write a poem or I should compose a sonata & those wretched feelings would fade away. But to give them away in commonplace actions, to feel the burden of the whole society on your weak shoulders... I am not even a boy that I might use a strong work which would make me feel better."[19]

While in Leipzig, in these months of personal struggle, Masaryková began to discover a religious longing. Although she later acknowledged the profound religious influence of her mother during her childhood, she did not consider herself religious before this time. "Though I am a nasty freethinker, there is more religion in my inmost soul than you

---

16 AGM to CGM, 30 October 1903, MÚA AV ČR, TGM Collection, Korespondence III, box 60, folder 34.

17 AGM to TGM, 12 September 1903, MÚA AV ČR, TGM Collection, Korespondence III, box 54, folder 2.

18 AGM to TGM, undated letter (fall 1903), MÚA AV ČR, TGM Collection, Korespondence III, box 60, folder 34.

19 AGM to CGM, 26 January 1904, MÚA AV ČR, TGM Collection, Korespondence III, box 60, folder 34.

would think," she wrote to Charlotte.[20] Her letters suggest not only surprise at these religious interests but also a defensiveness, a need to justify affections that her mother and father did not share. Masaryková recognized in herself, and confessed to her mother, a love for the ceremony and beauty of worship—music filling a church, the architecture, the processions and prayers of the faithful. As a break from her studies, she attended music programs at St. Thomas Church, the Lutheran church where Bach had served as cantor. "I <u>love</u> church music," she declared after one performance.[21] As Masaryková acknowledged throughout her life, she gained from her mother a love of poetry, music, and art. Charlotte Masaryková was a talented pianist, and Alice took refuge in the piano in her boarding house in Leipzig. In listening to Bach's "sweet prayers" and the *Requiem* of Berlioz, "a modern man who longs for wings," Masaryková understood artistic beauty as a glimpse to the eternal, a faint idea of what lies beyond the commonplace. She wrote for pages to her mother of these newfound sentiments. "You will laugh at this letter, won't you?" she closed. "Don't!"[22]

Masaryková's few letters to her father from Leipzig are quite different in tone. She relayed the contents of her professor's lectures, along with her own critiques. "I see that I'm an ass," she acknowledged in one letter, after expressing her disagreement with one professor. "But you already knew that!"[23] She asked for Masaryk's help with her homework, sending questions and seeking his insight into topics. "I am devoid of thoughts & ideas," she wrote.[24] Masaryková also raised questions of God and religion to her father. But unlike the letters to her mother, in which she framed her developing religious inclinations as the soul's longing for transcendence, to her father she wrote of her growing understanding of Christian principles. "I am not of this world," she wrote in one letter, not because of some mystic experience,

20   AGM to CGM, 22 November 1903, MÚA AV ČR, TGM Collection, Korespondence III, box 60, folder 34.
21   Ibid. Underlining in the original.
22   Ibid.
23   AGM to TGM, 5 December 1903, MÚA AV ČR, TGM Collection, Korespondence III, box 54, folder 2.
24   AGM to TGM, 28 November 1903, MÚA AV ČR, TGM Collection, Korespondence III, box 54, folder 2.

but out of an awareness of how Christian ethics applied to contemporary social problems. "It appears to me that I will have to defend Christian truth—that it is a profaning of this truth when people think that everything is in order in the world. That everything is in order? People here are so satisfied with the world and mainly with themselves that it's an absolute horror to me." Still, she was hesitant to assert her new convictions. Maybe those who thought that all was right in the world were, in fact, correct. It was not easy to resolve these questions with philosophy, she admitted to her father. [25]

Along with her growing religious awareness, Masaryková also began to realize in Leipzig that her life of service would not include marriage. When her mother wrote of a potential suitor in Prague, Masaryková was furious: "I have some inward rooms that are to be treated with respect, with care, gently. I cannot understand that You, who have so much fine feeling, did not notice this." Marriage to the unnamed suitor, whom Alice referred to as "Dr. Š.," would bring the end to her plans. "He knew that I would be a splendid Hausfrau—that's all—at least almost all," she declared. "But where my life begins, there sympathy ceased."[26] Her mother might disagree with her, Masaryková asserted, but she had to show some respect. "I don't think it is just an idiosyncrasy with me, I think it is one of my good qualities."[27]

Looking to America

Intent upon freeing herself from any attachments, whether to Dr. Š. or Dr. Fröhlich, Masaryková left for America after finishing her studies in Leipzig in 1904. She had received an invitation, passed from industrialist Charles Crane to her father, to visit Chicago in order to deepen her theoretical and practical knowledge of social work. Crane had sponsored Masaryk's lecture series in Chicago the previous summer,

---

25 Ibid.

26 "Dr. Š." was a different man than Dr. Fröhlich. The letter suggests that "Dr. Š." was a resident of Prague. Moreover, in a letter written to her mother the previous day, 10 December 1903, Masaryková speaks kindly of Fröhlich.

27 AGM to CGM, 11 December 1903, MÚA AV ČR, TGM Collection, Korespondence III, box 60, folder 34.

and he had spoken of Alice's interests to two women working with the urban poor and immigrants in the city: Jane Addams, the founder of Hull House, and Mary McDowell, who had worked at Hull House and later started a settlement house near the stockyards on the South Side.[28] Masaryková stayed only a short time at Hull House, although Addams made a great impression on her. Most of her work was with McDowell at the University of Chicago Settlement. The months in America, from 1904 to 1905, proved decisive in shaping Masaryková's view of the world and her sense of vocation. Her studies in Leipzig had given her an academic understanding of current social problems, but her work in Chicago's poor districts showed what she could do to address those problems. In Leipzig, she had been the only woman in her classes. In Chicago, she was among many women similar to herself—middle-class, educated, religiously motivated—who had moved to the city to remake it.[29] Women like Jane Addams and Mary McDowell gave her a model of the social gospel, of religious conviction applied for social change. They were uninterested in theology and doctrine. As Addams stated in an 1892 address, "Jesus had no set of truths labeled Religious. ...His teaching had no dogma to mark it off from truth and action in general."[30] Instead, they saw Christianity expressed in sharing the lives of the poor and working to solve real problems through practical means. To be effective, this work required research and analysis of local social problems. However, Addams and McDowell broke from male academics in sociology who insisted upon a detached, statistically driven approach modeled on the physical sciences. The founders of the settlement houses fixed their attention on specific conditions and the lived experiences of local residents. Above all, Addams and McDowell insisted that those who served at settlement houses had to act as neighbors, albeit the kind of neighbor who "gossips in statistics."[31]

---

28 Lovčí, *Alice Garrigue Masaryková*, 63–4.

29 See Spain, *How Women Saved the City*, 2–3, and especially chapter seven on women social reformers in Chicago.

30 Addams, "The Subjective Necessity for Social Settlements," reprinted in *Twenty Years at Hull House*, 73. On the theological views of Addams, see Dorrien, *Social Ethics in the Making*, 168–75.

31 Williams and MacLean, *Settlement Sociology*, 133. On the methodological approaches of Addams and McDowell, as distinct from academic sociologists of the time, see Williams and MacLean, 114–22 and 135–65.

Masaryková found the ruins of capitalism when she arrived on the South Side in 1904, and it disturbed her. "I hate to take money from a capitalist," Masaryková wrote to her father, presumably in reference to Crane, "but I cannot help it—if he wants to buy my work."[32] This was the jungle described by Upton Sinclair in his famous book:

> There were no pavements—there were mountains and valleys and rivers, gullies and ditches, and great hollows full of stinking green water. In these pools the children played, and rolled about in the mud of the streets; here and there one noticed them digging in it, after trophies which they had stumbled on. One wondered about this, as also about the swarms of flies which hung about the scene, literally blackening the air, and the strange, fetid odor which assailed one's nostrils, a ghastly odor, of all the dead things of the universe.[33]

Sinclair was at the University of Chicago Settlement House researching *The Jungle* at the same time that Masaryková was living and working there.[34] Mary McDowell had introduced Sinclair to the neighborhood, and she was an inspiration for one of the book's sympathetic characters, but she did not hold fond memories of the brash socialist and was upset with the exaggerations in his best-selling book. Nevertheless, Sinclair's descriptions of the stockyard neighborhoods matched her own. In her accounts of the South Side, McDowell wrote of two-story wooden houses surrounding the stockyards and slaughterhouses, which poured foul, black smoke into the air, and blood, guts, and manure into the water. A stream that ran north of the stockyards had become a stagnant cesspool, gaining the name "Bubbly Creek" for its expulsions of methane.[35] The South Side was also home to the city's garbage dumps. Every day, uncovered wagons crawled through the neighborhood, carrying trash from the wealthier streets along the lakeshore.[36] This was the source of the swarms of flies that

---

32 AGM to TGM, 1904, MÚA AV ČR, TGM Collection, Korespondence III, box 54, folder 2.
33 Sinclair, *The Jungle*, 28–9.
34 Mitchell, *Alice Garrigue Masaryk*, 45–6.
35 McDowell, "City Waste," in *Mary McDowell and Municipal Housekeeping*, 7.
36 Ibid., 2–3.

Sinclair described. McDowell later recalled that in the summer months the walls of houses were black with insects. Sinclair's book was notable for spurring immediate regulation of the meatpacking industry, but it brought little change in living conditions on the South Side. In McDowell's words, "The nation's stomach was disturbed but its conscience was left at ease."[37] McDowell appealed to city hall for another decade after *The Jungle*'s publication before garbage shipments through the neighborhood were shut down.

McDowell had been invited in 1894 to direct the settlement house by University of Chicago faculty members who sought to establish a "laboratory of social service." Like Masaryková, she had been deeply influenced by her own father, a devout Methodist who engaged in various religious and social initiatives. Following her father's teaching that religion must be expressed in the everyday actions of those who profess belief, McDowell worked for the Women's Christian Temperance Union and organized a kindergarten and women's club at Hull House. But as she later recalled, her faith and sense of purpose grew deeper after moving from her family's comfortable home in Evanston to the impoverished neighborhood near the South Side stockyards, among "those in the struggle for survival."[38] Although the new settlement house she headed was linked to the university, McDowell resisted having it serve as a field station for researchers in its first years. As one University of Chicago professor noted, McDowell "was so concerned with making herself a good neighbor that she steadfastly held off the university investigators."[39] Instead, the building on Gross Avenue (a street named today in honor of McDowell) housed English lessons and reading classes for adults, a kindergarten, game rooms, a gymnasium, and a skating rink in the winter. McDowell also became a neighborhood mediator, settling disputes among Poles, Lithuanians, and Ukrainians, Slavs and Italians, and the European immigrants and African Americans and Latinos who had moved to Chicago. During the settlement house's first decade, racial tensions simmered on the

37 McDowell, "How the Living Faith of One Social Worker Grew," 58.
38 Ibid., 60. For biographical sketchs of McDowell, see Curtis, *A Consuming Faith*, 159–61; and Williams and MacLean, *Settlement Sociology*, 132–5.
39 Percy Boynton, quoted in Williams and MacLean, *Settlement Sociology*, 137.

South Side. During both the Pullman strike of 1894 and the meat-packers' strike of 1904, companies had hired black workers to replace striking white workers, leading to violence in the streets. McDowell earned praise for her efforts to temper hostility and for her outreach to African American workers.[40]

McDowell also campaigned to improve conditions for women workers. Packing companies hired immigrant women for low-wage jobs, such as preparing meat for shipping in the freezers. This was the lowest rung in the plant, where women had to work while standing on boards set on iced-over floors.[41] McDowell helped organize the women's trade union to seek improvement of these working conditions. She also recognized how the grueling work affected women's lives outside the plants. A settlement house study of households with working mothers found that the women had been compelled to work in order to pay medical expenses for husbands who were sick with rheumatism, a common ailment among meatpackers who had to move between frigid and steaming rooms during the workday. These working mothers, in turn, became ill themselves, as they typically held night-shift jobs and then were unable to sleep during the day with children in the house.[42] In contrast, McDowell remarked on a different set of problems among young, unmarried women. The deadening monotony of packing work led to reckless behavior on weekends, and the mixing of unmarried men and women in overcrowded housing produced what McDowell saw as immoral conditions. Moral judgments aside, the consequences of the weekend behavior were real. McDowell watched as alcoholism, venereal disease, and unwanted pregnancies took their toll on young immigrant women from Eastern Europe.[43]

This linking of people's economic realities and their moral behavior became a fundamental part of Alice Masaryková's philosophy of social welfare. But Masaryková recognized another aspect to the grim experience of immigrant workers. As a young girl, she had regularly stayed

---

40 McDowell describes the neighborhood's racial conflicts in her essay "Prejudice," in *Mary McDowell and Municipal Housekeeping*, 28–33.

41 McDowell, "Our Proxies in Industry," in *Mary McDowell and Municipal Housekeeping*, 46.

42 Ibid., 48–9.

43 Ibid., 47.

with her grandparents in rural south Moravia, and when she was older, her family had taken their summer holidays in the village of Bystrička in central Slovakia. Tomáš Masaryk rented rooms in a farmhouse for their annual visits, and Alice took part in household and farm work alongside the farmer's children. Her family also joined the community suppers held in the village, usually followed with singing and games.[44] Masaryková cherished these summer visits throughout her life, remembering mountain meadows, cool streams, and welcoming villagers. She understood then what a shock it was for immigrants to move from rural Eastern Europe to industrial, urban America. Not only were these immigrants transplanted into the bleak and foul-smelling city, so different from the towns and villages they had left behind, but any skills they had learned in their youth now became irrelevant. As Mary McDowell recognized, men and women who had produced goods demanding great skill and care were now placed in industrial lines, required to produce quick and cheap results.[45] Even more damaging, in Masaryková's judgment, was the uprooting of the old social networks of the community. In her experience, mutual support and social control were woven into the fabric of village life. Individual behavior was curbed according to cycles of rural life and relationships between households. She knew from experience that life in a village was not idyllic, but in her view, it did promote social harmony. In the city, however, this source of social support and restraint was lost. In a 1939 speech, she recalled what she had discovered on Chicago's South Side:

The immigrant families, transported as they were, lost the social control which in the old village was given by the universal and simple rhythm of village life that goes on almost unchanged in each season, as well as the long established and therefore unquestioned forms of relationship between families, which influence the behavior of individuals.

In the stockyards' neighborhood, near neighbors were strangers to each other; there was little of mutual thoughtfulness and help.

---

44 Masaryková, *Dětství a mládí*, 21–4 and 44–54.

45 McDowell describes this debasing of immigrants' skills in her essay "The Foreign Born," in *Mary McDowell and Municipal Housekeeping*, 16.

Typical were the backyards and alleys of that part of town. They were piled with cans, all kinds of rubbish, a dead cat, and badly smelling remnants of food.[46]

This idea of the loss of community and order became central to Masaryková's understanding of social problems. In her view, problems such as alcoholism, prostitution, and poor living conditions were not simply products of material want. Instead, they were the result of an absence of relationships that provided people, especially women, with accountability and encouragement. Without longstanding neighborly relations, immigrants and other newcomers to the city—whether Chicago or Prague—felt no responsibility to others or to themselves. For Masaryková, as for her father, social issues were fundamentally issues of individual morality. But she set the individual moral agent more firmly within a social context. A person's surroundings, particularly the larger network of relationships, shaped her decisions and behavior. Certainly, moral will and spiritual awareness were important, but they were not always sufficient to overcome breaches in those surroundings. People also needed tangible help in order to make the right choices. In a letter to her father from Chicago, Masaryková commented on the failed approach of one group of people she observed there: the Unitarians. She judged them as overly dogmatic and intellectual, offering no help to people other than the assurance the God would deliver them from their trials.[47] During her months working alongside McDowell, Alice Masaryková saw that religious belief had to be expressed in action and that real assistance and community were needed to lift the poor.

For all she learned in Chicago, Masaryková still had difficulty adapting to the surroundings. "Alice was serious, sincere, and somewhat intense," Mary McDowell recalled years later. The head of the settlement house judged her as a typical recent university graduate—full of ideas and determined to assert her independence. Masaryková was also rigid in her morality. "She was most uncompromising—al-

---

46 Masaryková speech, 1939, quoted in Mitchell, *Alice Garrigue Masaryk*, 51.
47 AGM to TGM, 12 November 1904, MÚA AV ČR, TGM Collection, Korespondence III, box 54, folder 2.

most a puritan in her firmness," wrote McDowell.[48] Alice was particularly taken aback by the informality of American society, the American sense of humor, and especially the familiar interactions between men and women. Eventually, she settled into the new environment. "She became more at home," recalled McDowell, "less intense, played a bit with us."[49] These bumps aside, McDowell acknowledged that Masaryková was a tireless worker, who attracted people with her earnestness and openness. "When she spoke to the Bohemians, either to small or large audiences, she was glorious," McDowell remembered.[50]

During her time in Chicago, Masaryková was surrounded by Bohemians, as the Czechs were called at the time. The city was a magnet to immigrants from across Central and Eastern Europe: Czechs, Slovaks, Poles, Ukrainians, and Lithuanians. With her ability in Slavic languages (in addition to a native knowledge of Czech and Slovak, she had also studied Russian), Masaryková was a valuable liaison at the settlement house. Her particular interest was the Czechs. She sought to nurture the immigrants' links to their homeland, organizing Czech reading groups for women and a library for children, and writing articles for Czech-language publications. This work fostered her own interest in the homeland, which flowed in different directions. On the one hand, her academic training and literary interests spurred the idea of writing a history of the Bohemian Lands, and she even made research expeditions to Czech communities in Iowa, Nebraska, and Cleveland. On the other hand, Masaryková remained fixed on the goal of helping people in need. She told McDowell of her plans to start a nursing school back home, and a social welfare program. Just as when she had arrived, Masaryková was full of ideas and torn over what to do. Her feelings for Fröhlich still kindled, and she had to decide if the relationship had any future. And she was drawn to stay in America. A year after her return to Bohemia, she wrote to her mother of the Statue of Liberty and all it represented. The contrast with the Habsburg

---

48 Mary McDowell, letter to Ruth Crawford, 29 August 1920, in Mitchell Collection, Lilly Library. The letter is quoted in Mitchell, *Alice Garrigue Masaryk*, 48.
49 Mary McDowell, letter to Ruth Crawford, 1920, quoted in Mitchell, *Alice Garrigue Masaryk*, 46.
50 Ibid.

Empire was stark. "I shall work hard to be able to leave this jail Austria," she stated, "or to fight for more light for it."[51]

From Jan Hus to Clean Underwear

Masaryková arrived back in Prague in the summer of 1905. In the year after her return, she resumed her activity with a variety of social causes. She went back to work with the temperance movement, and she participated in meetings of the Brno-based women's organization, the Young Women's Academy (*Divcí akademie*), which advocated for educational opportunities and the right to vote. Her speeches and writings for these groups, typically to audiences of working-class women, brought her public recognition apart from being Professor Masaryk's daughter.[52] She was Dr. Masaryková—in a society that placed great weight upon titles, her doctorate was significant. But activism did not pay. The kind of work she felt most called to, the social work she had done in Chicago, did not yet exist in Habsburg Europe. Forced to find paying work, Masaryková took a position in the fall of 1906 at a girls' gymnasium in České Budějovice, roughly seventy-five miles south of Prague.

Like any young teacher, Alice Masaryková found her students a captive audience for her developing ideas of the world. Now twenty-six years old, Masaryková used her classroom as a laboratory for her nascent philosophy of social welfare, the tasks of women, and the health of the nation. Students adored her. "She astonished us," recalled one, writing years later. "She aroused our interest. She was so different from the rest of the professors."[53] The teenage girls in České Budějovice, and later in the Holešovice district of Prague, where Masaryková taught after 1907, saw their young teacher as a remarkable figure. She was tall and athletic, outgoing and energetic, informal yet purposeful. Decades later, her former students recalled her dynamic manner and "dark, shiny eyes" as well as what she had taught them. Upon arriving in České Budějovice,

---

51   AGM to CGM, 13 October 1906, MÚA AV ČR, TGM Collection, Korespondence III, box 60, folder 34.

52   Lovčí, *Alice Garrigue Masaryková*, 71.

53   Quoted in Mitchell, *Alice Garrigue Masaryk*, 53.

Figure 3.2. Alice Masarykova, 1913. Masaryk Institute and Archive, Academy of Sciences, Czech Republic.

Masaryková took the unheard-of step of asking her students what kind of history they would like to learn. The girls objected to lessons about "insignificant wars," so Masaryková offered instead a course on the broad cultural history of Europe, with ventures into sociology and moral lessons. The lectures were unlike anything the students had heard from their male teachers. As one Prague student recalled, "They were lectures to young women about our role in the future as women, clean in body and mind, well educated, cultivated, and productive... What a wonderful feeling to find somebody who saw in us future women instead of little schoolgirls!"[54] Masaryková also saw her students as confidantes with whom she could share her political opinions. She did not

54 Ibid., 60.

hide her disdain for the imperial court and aristocracy.[55] And she declared that her students, as young women, had value and purpose in their own right, not simply in relation to men. They were necessary for the future of the nation. One former student recalled: "Bohemia, she told us, was a small nation, and to have a chance to survive in the large world's competition, each one of us had to be a first-class human being. She said a nation was not an abstract word, a nation was every single one of us—even girls! Therefore, it was our duty to make ourselves decent and strong so that the whole nation would be strong."[56]

The influence of her father was apparent in Masaryková's teaching. Following Tomáš Masaryk, she insisted that the critical study of history would allow students to understand the nation's spiritual current as well as their own individual tasks in daily life.[57] But Masaryková also looked to other sources in forming her pedagogical approach. One inspiration was Horace Mann (1796–1859), a founder of American public education. As the head of the Massachusetts board of education, Mann had been a visionary proponent for universal public education, and many of the practices he instituted were later adopted in other states. Mann also advocated for equality in education. In 1852 he became president of the newly founded Antioch College in Ohio, one of the country's first coeducational schools, and he was responsible for hiring the first female professor in the United States to have the same rank and pay as her male colleagues. As an example of an enlightened Unitarian, inspiring teacher, and selfless public servant, the figure of Horace Mann resonated in the Masaryk household. Charlotte Masaryková, in particular, was drawn to Mann, and she kept a multivolume collection of his writings in her bedroom until the end of her life.

Alice Masaryková was familiar with these books. In her first year of teaching in České Budějovice, she translated a biographical essay from the collection of Mann's writings for the school's almanac. The essay discussed Mann's idea of education as building both the intellect and moral character of young people, at a time when the American republic was establishing itself. His description of the remnants

55 Lovčí, *Alice Garrigue Masaryková*, 84–86.
56 Quoted in Mitchell, *Alice Garrigue Masaryk*, 60.
57 Lovčí, *Alice Garrigue Masaryková*, 83.

of the colonial system in early nineteenth-century America would have sounded familiar to Czechs in the Austrian Empire. Past generations, raised in the colonies, held "respect for established authority, merely because it was established; of veneration for law, simply because it was law; and of deference both to secular and ecclesiastical rank, because it had been accustomed to rank."[58] As those values waned, two threats loomed: the rule of avarice and pride, and the rule of vice and false knowledge. In Mann's view, the antidote to both was a pedagogy that trained students to look to the greater interests of the community and to the immutable laws that govern the natural and moral world. Mann had left the Puritan faith of his upbringing, but he remained committed to practical morality rooted in Christian principles. Rather than repeating a catechism and tales of miraculous stories, a teacher should build students' individual consciences, inculcating them with a love of God, truth, and human welfare. The essay described Mann's philosophy "as a sort of compromise between modern science and the religious or Christian spirit."[59] Masaryková surely recognized her father in the description of Mann as someone who "believed in truth and its sovereign right," who shook off "all the slavish bonds of the church, of tradition, and of consecrated dogmas, to follow his conscience and reason." At the same time, the essay stated, Mann was like his Pilgrim ancestors in his devotion to truth. "Only, while they stopped at the Bible, he goes farther; and, without repudiating the Christian tradition, he associates with it the tradition of the human race and of science."[60]

The other source of Alice Masaryková's pedagogy was also American, but more contemporary and widely known: the writer Helen Keller. By the early twentieth century, Keller was already world famous. Masaryková had read Keller's autobiography as she was beginning postgraduate work in Leipzig.[61] The story so moved her that she wrote a biographical sketch for her father's journal *Naše doba*. The piece also highlighted the teaching methods of Annie Sullivan, which

---

58 Pécaut, "Horace Mann," 535.
59 Ibid., 537.
60 Ibid., 538.
61 Lovčí, *Alice Garrigue Masaryková*, 30.

Masaryková cited as a direct contrast to the education system of the Habsburg Empire.[62] The story of Keller and Sullivan stayed with Masaryková over the next decade. While teaching in Prague she expanded her article into a short biography based on Keller's various writings. The seventy-page book featured long, translated passages from Keller's memoirs and other writings along with passages from Sullivan's published diary. Masaryková presented Sullivan as a persistent teacher who demonstrated gentleness and love, guiding her student to gain an independent, conscious view of the world. Masaryková quoted Keller's own praise of Sullivan: "She used every appropriate moment to point out to me the beauty that is in everything, and she never stopped trying, in word, in deed, in example, to make my life useful."[63] Keller's original text had stated that her teacher sought to make her life "sweet and useful," but such sentiments did not fit into Masaryková's teaching philosophy. Nor would sweetness have resonated with the book's intended audience. The Helen Keller book was released by a socialist press, in a series intended for workers, and Masaryková published it under a male pen name: Jan Skála, the equivalent of John Bedrock.[64]

Writing under her rugged pseudonym, Masaryková presented Helen Keller as an example to be emulated. Her portrait showed an educated woman who read in English, French, and German; whose favorite books were the Bible, the *Iliad*, and works of Shakespeare; and who cited Plato and Leibniz. If someone of Keller's limitations was able to gain a university degree and become a published author, then couldn't anyone—man or woman, worker or peasant—rise above their station through education and work? To be sure, a wise and giving teacher had played an integral role in Keller's formation, but Keller herself was also determined to attain a useful life. In her book, Masaryková stressed this optimism, pointing to Keller's positive and hopeful outlook as essential to her accomplishments. This was a lesson not only for workers, but also for people of privileged background, for someone like Ma-

---

62 Ibid., 62–3.

63 Skála [Alice Masaryková], *Helena Kellerová*, 20–1.

64 Masaryková's book was published during the First World War, after her father had left Austria-Hungary to work against the government. By using her own name, the book would have likely been censored. The pen name thus allowed the book to appear without political entanglements.

saryková. After her return from Chicago, she raised this lesson in a speech to the educated young women of the *Dívčí akademie*. "We women are strong," she declared, citing Keller and Jane Addams as examples, as well as the ordinary woman engaged in quiet, unpretentious work. Masaryková warned, though, that this representative working-class woman was worn down and diminished. She wanted to improve herself and had the capacity for hard work. But she needed the help of others. "She is waiting on us women to lead her out of her degradation," Masaryková told her audience. "Offer her a hand, and she will gladly accept it."[65] Masaryková recognized the challenge that Keller posed to someone of her station and ability. "From her I realized the meaning of the words which had puzzled me," she wrote a decade later. "'He who has little, even that little shall be taken from him, and he who has much, unto him shall be given.' ...He who has a talent and uses it with all his heart, he will have more, and more will be given unto him."[66]

For Masaryková, Helen Keller was not only an example of the transformative power of education, optimism, and diligence; the American writer was also someone who deeply felt the inequalities of the world. In the short biography, Masaryková translated a long passage from Keller's memoir in which she described a visit to an American city:

Several times I have visited the narrow, dirty streets where the poor live, and I grow hot and indignant to think that good people should be content to live in fine houses and become strong and beautiful, while others are condemned to live in hideous, sunless tenements and grow ugly, withered, and cringing. The children who crowd these grimy alleys, half-clad and underfed, shrink away from your outstretched hand as if from a blow. Dear little creatures, they crouch in my heart and haunt me with a constant sense of pain. There are men and women, too, all gnarled and bent out of shape. I have felt their hard, rough hands and realized what an endless struggle their existence must be... Oh, that men would leave the city, its

---

65 Quoted in Lovčí, *Alice Garrigue Masaryková*, 73–74.
66 Masaryková to Rela Kotíková, 7 March 1916, in English-language manuscript, "Letters to Prison: To Women Workers," MÚA AV ČR, AGM Collection, box 1, folder 1.

splendor and its tumult and its gold, and return to wood and field and simple, honest living! Then would their children grow stately as noble trees, and their thoughts sweet and pure as wayside flowers.[67]

Keller's revulsion at the filth of poor neighborhoods corresponded with Masaryková's own association of uncleanliness with social decline. During her stay in Chicago, with its foul air and filthy streets, Masaryková recognized the importance of public hygiene to social welfare. At the same time as Mary McDowell was engaged in her campaign to close the garbage dump on the South Side, Masaryková organized neighborhood boys into cleaning crews that would fan throughout the streets and alleys, collecting trash.[68] As a teacher, she made personal cleanliness a constant lesson to her students in České Budějovice and Prague. She lectured her students on the importance of daily bathing, checked the girls' fingers and nails for dirt, and arranged for dental visits for girls from poorer families. For Masaryková's students, the fixation on cleanliness was a source of laughs. "We girls used to say that she started with Jan Hus and finished with clean underwear," recalled one.[69] To Masaryková, however, the connection between the reformer and underclothes was clear. Body and soul were inseparable; therefore, personal hygiene was integral to personal morality. In the same way, the physical and moral hygiene of the individual was integral to the health of the community and the nation.

The linking of personal habits to the greater good—even habits of eating and bathing—drew in part on the thinking of Masaryková's father. Tomáš Masaryk was known for his ascetic habits, and he held that such practices were part of the recipe for an ordered life. "Fresh air and sunshine; moderate food and drink; a moral life and a job involving muscles, heart, and brain; people to care for and a goal to strive for—that's the macrobiotic recipe for success," he declared in his later years.[70] But Alice Masaryková came to have a different understanding of the

---

67 Keller, *The Story of My Life*, 124–25. The passage is translated into Czech in Skála, *Helen Kellerová*, 33.

68 Mitchell, *Alice Garrigue Masaryk*, 51.

69 Milka Mráčková, "Ve škole a cestou do školy" [In School and the Path to School], quoted in Mitchell, *Alice Garrigue Masaryk*, 60.

70 Čapek, *Talks with T. G. Masaryk*, 236.

body, both that of the individual and the collective body of the nation. Tomáš Masaryk viewed the nation according to the Platonic dualism of body and soul, material and spiritual. The nation's body was its language, customs, politics, and economics, while the soul was evident in its religion,literature, philosophy, and classical music. Body and soul were integrated in that the material part—the organization of the state, society, and economy—should be an expression of the spiritual. But for Masaryk, following Plato, the soul always preceded the body. Alice Masaryková used the same language of body and soul in speaking of the nation, and like her father she saw the progress of the nation as a spiritual task, requiring education, cultivation of morals, and awareness of the divine. Yet Masaryková differed from her father in her awareness of the body, both metaphorical and literal. Her interests in social welfare and public health would lead her to conceive of body and soul in a mutual, rather than hierarchical, relationship. While her father, a true follower of Plato, saw the gaining of knowledge and the tending of the soul as the first steps to virtue, Masaryková would come to view care for the body as integral to the virtuous life. We see an example of this connection of the physical and material in her understanding of baptism. For Masaryková, the waters of baptism represented not a covenantal ritual or a sign of spiritual cleansing; instead, she connected New Testament passages about water baptism directly to physical cleansing, even swimming.[71] For her, cleanliness was not simply *next* to godliness; it was an essential part of the moral and spiritual life.

Alice Masaryková yearned for harmony: body and soul, the practical and the spiritual. This was a key part of the social gospel she learned from Mary McDowell in Chicago. "Is it not true that there is a unity of common life and that even common things have relation to spiritual values?" asked McDowell in stating her understanding of religion.[72] It was also a goal that Masaryková shared with her father. During her

---

71 On baptism and cleanliness, see Masaryková's short memoir "Kriminál" [Criminal], in *Drahá mama/ Dear Alice*, 187. The same connection of baptism to bathing is in her letter to Rela Kotíková, a young Czech woman who shared Masaryková's cell during her imprisonment. The letter, dated 8 June 1917, was translated into English and included in Masaryková's manuscript "Letters to Prison: To Women Workers" (1920), MÚA AV ČR, box 1, folder 7.

72 McDowell, "How the Living Faith of One Social Worker Grew," 42.

years as a teacher in České Budějovice, she sought her father's wisdom about belief, ideals, and her path in life. Isolated from the male teachers at the girls' gymnasium, who expected her to clean the faculty lounge while they hit on the students, Masaryková took long, solitary walks in the countryside, visiting old chapels and castles, all the time wondering about eternal life. What is it like? When does it begin? She recognized that her father still had not reached clarity in his views, that the worldview he desired was not yet clear. Still, she sought his direction. "If you have some concise creed, or some paper that could explain these mysteries to me, I will be grateful."[73] Another letter, from December 1906, offered an aspiring poet's account of her surroundings—dark castle towers outlined against gray clouds, grass blades breaking through a fresh snowfall, the coat of an old peasant, like a "symphony of pale lilac," hundreds of sparrows perched in trees like plump pears. Apprehensions of beauty and thoughts of the divine and the yearning to serve others swirled together in the letter, from one paragraph to another. "I thought I was agnostic, but I see I am not, but deeply religious," she declared.[74]

Masaryková saw that the theism of the philosophers, as her father endorsed, was beyond her reach. "How can I dare to reach with my limited brain—that what is not to be reached?" she asked. Like the women in the Chicago settlement houses who lived out their faith in service, Masaryková did not trouble herself with theological formulas or doctrinal boundaries (at different times in her life she wrote of worshipping at Reformed, Lutheran, and Catholic churches). Instead, she professed a religion that was manifest in action. "If I shall be true to myself I shall love mankind and live that religion which is expressed in creeds," she wrote.[75] She remained perplexed about life after death, but her religion was not aimed to personal salvation in the hereafter. Rather, she claimed to have found haven in this life: her "religious deeds" had led her to quiet, to blessing, to a sense of peace.

---

73 AGM to TGM, 6 December 1906, MÚA AV ČR, TGM Collection, Korespondence III, box 54, folder 2.

74 AGM to TGM, 20 December 1906, MÚA AV ČR, TGM Collection, Korespondence III, box 54, folder 2.

75 Ibid.

Building Her House on the Rocks

The years of the First World War were difficult for the Masaryk family. In December 1914, Tomáš Masaryk crossed the Austrian border into Switzerland, along with his youngest daughter, Olga, who was twenty-three at the time. For the next four years, Masaryk traveled from country to country, seeking Allied support for the dissolution of the Habsburg Empire. The story is often told in heroic terms, but for Masaryk the time abroad was trying. Based first in Switzerland and then in England after 1915, Masaryk's daily life was filled, as before, with a wide range of tasks: teaching at the University of London, writing articles and speaking on the political situation in East Central Europe, corresponding with his collaborators in the Czech and Slovak independence movement, and meeting with potential supporters of their cause. Masaryk later wrote in his postwar memoirs of the campaign for an independent Czechoslovakia as being guided by Providence. In letters to Charlotte during the war, he sometimes expressed this belief that he was part of a greater plan, a working of history toward some goal.[76] More often, however, he confided doubt and loneliness to his wife. He wrote in July 1915 from Switzerland, only days after delivering a speech that called for Czech independence: "When depressed (as to-day) I sit at home, working little, half asleep, thinking of you and our children. I feel it, what a sacrifice it was, to take this burden on my shoulders."[77] Masaryk wrote of wanting to hold his wife's hand. He even imagined sneaking back across the border to see her.[78] Before setting off from England to Russia in April 1917, Masaryk expressed to his wife what he would later tell his biographers: she had made him the man he was. "Charlie—I thank you for all you did for me and with me! I know and tell it to you, that I would not have

---

76 See Masaryk's English-language letters from London to Charlotte Masaryková, in Prague, 1 January 1916 and 15 April 1917, MÚA AV ČR, TGM Collection, Korespondence III, box 60, folder 33. Interestingly, Masaryk did not write of Providence in these letters; instead, he used the Greek philosophical concept of teleology.

77 TGM to CGM, 15 July 1915, MÚA AV ČR, TGM Collection, Korespondence III, box 60, folder 33. Masaryk's underlining.

78 TGM to CGM, 20 November 1915 and 21 July 1916, MÚA AV ČR, TGM Collection, Korespondence III, box 60, folder 33.

FIGURE 3.3. Charlotte and Alice Masaryková, 1916.
Masaryk Institute and Archive, Academy of Sciences, Czech Republic.

achieved what I achieved, without you and that I would not have developed as I developed." Perhaps wary of danger in Russia, just weeks after the fall of the tsar, Masaryk wrote with a tone of finality, but also with a measure of hope. "I will see you here," he closed, "not only in the life beyond."[79]

Masaryk's despair abroad was magnified by bad news from home. In March 1915 their oldest son, Herbert, died at age thirty-five from typhus. He had contracted the disease while serving as a volunteer at a refugee camp in Poland. After an unsuccessful attempt to emigrate to the United States, the younger son, Jan, was drafted into the Austri-

---

79 TGM to CGM, 15 April 1917, MÚA AV ČR, TGM Collection, Korespondence III, box 60, folder 33.

an army and eventually stationed on the front—"working for what we hate," Masaryk noted.[80] Charlotte's health worsened during this time, particularly after 1916. Alice cared for her mother at the family apartment in Prague's Malá Strana district. They received visits from Herbert's widow and two daughters as well as Masaryk's former students and associates.

But Charlotte also had to make frequent stays at a Prague sanatorium. Meanwhile, Alice was still teaching at the girls' gymnasium in Holešovice, and in the summer of 1915 she volunteered as a nurse at a military hospital in Pardubice.[81] She was also involved in social work projects. At the war's beginning, Alice Masaryková was working toward founding a school for social work, fulfilling a dream she had held since her time in Chicago. And she was active with an organization that she had helped to launch in 1911. Called the Sociological Section (*Sociologická sekce*), this initiative brought together university students, academics, and members of women's and workers' organizations. Their aim was to gather reliable data of social conditions in Prague's industrial districts and then implement practical measures to address problems facing the working poor.[82] But her work came to an abrupt end in the fall of 1915. On October 28, police brought her to a Prague jail for questioning about her father's activities. Two weeks later, she was transferred to a military prison in Vienna and charged with high treason.

News of Alice Masaryková's imprisonment quickly reached the United States. Tomáš Masaryk contacted his patron and friend Charles Crane, who raised Alice's case with his highly placed contacts in the media and government. Masaryk also enlisted the aid of Mary McDowell.[83] She in turn marshaled the support of leading figures in American social work and women's groups. By April 1916, the State Department was receiving appeals from immigrant organizations,

---

80   TGM to CGM, 13 February 1916, MÚA AV ČR, TGM Collection, Korespondence III, box 60, folder 33.

81   Skilling, *Mother and Daughter*, 90–1; and Lovčí, *Alice Garrigue Masaryková*, 147–48.

82   On the Sociological Section, see Lovčí, *Alice Garrigue Masaryková*, chapter eight.

83   The letters of both Tomáš and Olga Masaryk to Mary McDowell, from April 1916, are in the Tomáš Masaryk Collection, Lilly Library, box 1.

women's associations, pacifist groups, and trade unions. Stories about Masaryková appeared regularly in American newspapers. In the melodramatic language of the day, the *New York Times* described an impressive, attractive young woman unjustly imprisoned: "She was distinguished looking and beautiful when animated by an idea or when speaking in public. She was magnetic and forceful. All who know this gentle, sympathetic, and simply democratic young woman will believe her innocent of the charge of treason. She had a constructive mind and was no anarchist in word or deed. To take the life of, or to imprison one so young and so noble will be an atrocity that cannot be forgotten by American women."[84]

Masaryková's American supporters were fearful that she would lose her life, and in the last days of April mistaken reports of her execution hit front pages in the United States. But on the same day that the *New York Times* was reporting her death, Alice Masaryková was reading Tolstoy in her cell in Vienna and asking her mother to send some better pens. "Nothing new," she wrote. "Life here is always the same."[85]

At first, Masaryková was incredulous at her arrest. "Often I think to myself, what would Herbert think," she wrote to her mother two weeks after she was detained. "I think that he'd also see this as comic—me, Alice Masaryková, in prison!"[86] As the letter suggests, her imprisonment was not all that severe. She received gifts of chocolate and pastries, which she shared with her guards. They in turn allowed her to keep goldfish and finches in her cell. One day during her initial detention in Prague, the guards allowed her to go to a sanatorium outside the prison; on the return trip, she stopped at the fashionable Café Louvre. When she objected to a third-class seat for her transfer to Vienna, the guards moved her to second class, and they all had to take a taxi to the prison in order to accommodate her baggage.[87] In the memoir of her imprisonment, Masaryková cast herself as calm and dignified. She recounted how a guard at the Vienna prison told her

---

84 *New York Times*, 28 April 1916, quoted in Unterberger, "The Arrest of Alice Masaryk," 101–2.
85 AGM to CGM, 28 April 1916, letter 141 in *Drahá mama/Dear Alice*.
86 AGM to CGM, 16 November 1915, letter 3 in *Drahá mama/Dear Alice*.
87 Skilling, *Mother and Daughter*, 93–4.

that he had once heard her father give a lecture. "I arrest you in the name of the law," she joked. "How could you dare?"[88] In her own telling, this assured demeanor struck her jailers and fellow prisoners. "How is it that you're happy? Everyone comes here in tears," remarked a cellmate when Masaryková arrived. Masaryková jumped on her plank bed. "I'm not part of a gray jail," she assured herself. "I am myself, Alice Masaryková—no number, no register."[89]

Even in the Vienna prison, the conditions Masaryková faced were not harsh. There was occasional work, such as sewing blankets for soldiers. Most of the time, she busied herself with books sent by her mother; she recited passages of Shakespeare and Goethe, and studied books on social work and public health. Some of her cellmates were young Czechs also imprisoned on political charges, and she offered them lessons in English, German, and even art history.[90] Still, her time in prison was trying. She longed to be with her mother, whose health deteriorated during Alice's detention. Alone in Prague, Charlotte Masaryková questioned the path her life had taken. "My whole life has been so strange," she wrote to her daughter in prison. She went on: "I was not satisfied with my surroundings, even though I found many good and nice things around me."[91] Alice's own health also failed. Many days she suffered depression or headaches, and at night she was unable to sleep. In March 1916, she wrote to her mother of having a nervous breakdown (she used the English term in the letter). "I always wake up at night and I cannot remember where I am, and then I cannot recall why I'm here. My heart was pounding violently."[92] The letter

---

88 Masaryková, "Kriminál," in *Drahá mama/Dear Alice*, 202.

89 Skilling, *Mother and Daughter*, 95; and Masaryková, "Kriminál," in *Drahá mama/Dear Alice*, 205. One of the cellmates later confirmed Masaryková's account of her arrival. Rela Kotíková, who would become a lifelong friend of Masaryková, recalled of her arrival: "When the cot was ready, she sat down on it, resting her chin between the palms of her hands, the elbows on her knees. She looked cheerfully around. Nobody had ever entered the cell with such an expression! It was so unusual that even those who did not exactly welcome the newcomer sat up and watched her in surprise." Mitchell, *Alice Garrigue Masaryk*, 76.

90 Masaryková, "Kriminál," in *Drahá mama/Dear Alice*, 204.

91 CGM to AGM, 16 April 1916, letter 130 in *Drahá mama/Dear Alice*. The translation is from an English version of Charlotte's letters that Alice prepared for publication in the 1960s. The manuscript is deposited in her collected papers, Lilly Library, box 1.

92 AGM to CGM, 21 March 1916, letter 104 in *Drahá mama/Dear Alice*. Underlining in original.

shows that her turns in health were linked to insecurity and anxiety about her purpose in life. Her state of mind changed dramatically, even in the course of a day. One morning in December 1915, she was deep in depression. "At noon a sudden change," she reported: "a will for life, for love, for truth."[93] At one low moment, Masaryková even expressed a shade of anger toward her father:

> I would like to write to father, to tell him that I'm here, that I've been banished on account of his political writings, that I have not been informed of his political work, that he must, must, speak loudly and free me. I smile in front of people, I appear well when I see freedom a long way off, but then I'm devastated here. And his scientific papers! Great God almighty, what do we say after 50 years. I don't know his work, but I recognize its quality, whether ... on whatever: trends, fashion, anything goes, he maintains correct and independent thinking. He thinks independently. Imagination?! God, I know what a nothing I am, only a person yearning to do social work, who has had a hard life and a firm faith. But if my weakness is to be condemned, it must be also understood.[94]

Through the doubt and loneliness, Masaryková's experience in the Vienna prison was formative. As she later told people, prison life moved her "to build her house on the rocks."[95] Just as Charlotte had done in her depression, Alice scorned her own failing health and pressed on in her work, studying the books she had received. "The person who wants to do good is not able to bend to weakness," she wrote after a struggle

---

93 AGM to CGM, 12 December 1915, letter 13 in *Drahá mama/Dear Alice*.

94 AGM to CGM, 22 May 1916, letter 162 in *Drahá mama/Dear Alice*. Underlining in original. Shortly after the war, Alice translated the letters into English and prepared them for publication. This letter was not included in the collection. See manuscript in Alice Masaryk Collection, Lilly Library, box 4, writings.

95 Mitchell, *Alice Garrigue Masaryk*, 103. Masaryková revisited her prison experience throughout her life, by editing, translating, and publishing her prison memoirs, her letters to her mother, her mother's letters to her, and the letters she sent after her release to prisoner Rela Kotíková. The letters to Kotíková were published in 1920 as a small volume, that fits into the palm of the hand, by the Czechoslovak Red Cross. A selection of her own letters were published in *The Atlantic Monthly* as "From an Austrian Prison," November 1920, 577–86; and "The Prison House," December 1920, 770–79. Her mother's letters were published in 1948 as *Listy do vězení*. Masaryková worked on translations of her mothers' letters into English until her death. See manuscript in Alice Masaryk Collection, Lilly Library, box 1.

with depression.[96] The cell Masaryková shared with eleven other women—some political prisoners as well as women accused of prostitution and theft—became the crucible in which she forged her life's philosophy and sense of mission. At the foundation was the principle she had gained from her father: life must be lived *sub specie aeternitatis*. Her actions were not simply subject to the judgment of God; instead, each moment of her life was imbued with the eternal.[97]

At the same time, though, Masaryková's letters expressed a conception of the divine and religion much different than that of her father. Whereas her father's articles and lectures discussed God and eternity as necessities of moral philosophy, Alice Masaryková wrote in her letters—often with bolts of lyricism—of moments of awe, when the apprehension of beauty struck her as a glimpse of the eternal. Oftentimes, in relating these moments of fulfillment to her mother, Masaryková connected her perception of this divine beauty to a place of worship— the sight of a young cellmate's dark eyes sparked a longing to attend Good Friday services; dreams of swans on a lake and spring leaves led to the memory of a mountain chapel lit with villagers' candles; the thought of walks in Prague's Royal Gardens revived a scene from her childhood, a school visit to St. Vitus Cathedral.[98] Glimpses of natural beauty brought her to thoughts of God, and thoughts of God brought her to what she had read or heard or studied or seen in her travels. In her letters, she turned in the space of a sentence from God to Goethe or Shakespeare or the Czech author Božena Němcová.[99] A letter to her mother from January 1916 is characteristic: "I do not know why, but my old friend Michelangelo comes very close to me again. If I close my eyes, I see the Sistine Chapel. Can you imagine the grand sweep? It's like the music of Haydn—stirring, powerful—the world. No compromises. God—darkness. A lie is certainly darkness, and the truth is light. The person who lives the truth is active—positive."[100]

---

96   AGM to CGM, 12 December 1915, letter 13 in *Drahá mama/Dear Alice*.
97   AGM to CGM, 14 December 1915, letter 14; and 12 January 1916, letter 39 in *Drahá mama/Dear Alice*.
98   AGM to CGM, 15 April 1916, letter 129; 24 March 1916, letter 109; and 11 April 1916, letter 124 in *Drahá mama/Dear Alice*.
99   AGM to CGM, 15 April 1916, letter 129; and 25 April 1916, letter 138 in *Drahá mama/Dear Alice*.
100 AGM to CGM, 12 January 1916, letter 39 in *Drahá mama/Dear Alice*.

As her declaration of a positive, active life indicates, Masaryková's thoughts of beauty and the divine did not lead her into a contemplative withdrawal. Her recollection of the cathedral visit, for instance, brought the longing for work. "The world is beautiful," she wrote. "God help me to get back soon to the world that I so love, and back to work. It is my food!"[101] The breeze over a mountain lake, springtime flowers decorating an altar, a crafted piece of ancient marble, a young girl suffering from tuberculosis in a dirty room near the Chicago stockyards—episodes of her life, scenes of beauty and misery, all were juxtaposed into what she saw as an irresistible call to service. Masaryková did not feel compelled to action out of obligation to an eternal, moral imperative. Instead, she understood her life as one of devotion and offering. As she wrote to her mother: "My life, as it is given to me, shall become an active prayer."[102]

Conclusion

Although she could not have imagined while in the prison the direction her life would take after 1918, Alice Masaryková did expect that the end of the war would open the door for dramatic social change in Europe. "Ah, how beautiful is a land of justice!" she wrote in prison. "Heaven—everything. After the war, this will be life! Full of vitality! The new age will bring something new."[103] She shared this expectation with her father, who saw the war's end as a victory of democracy over premodern theocracy. Plečnik was more circumspect. Already by December 1918, still living in Prague, he was wary of the new rulers of the republic, grousing to a friend that "government is government." As for the new president, Plečnik was unimpressed after his inaugural speech. The architect took a scoffing tone in a letter to his brother: "Masaryk stated ex cathedra—no, declared—that all political power is from the people!"[104] He would come to change his opinion.

---

101 AGM to CGM, 11 April 1916, letter 124 in *Drahá mama/Dear Alice*.
102 AGM to CGM, 24 March 1916, letter 109 in *Drahá mama/Dear Alice*.
103 AGM to CGM, 1 February 1916, letter 58 in *Drahá mama/Dear Alice*.
104 Jože Plečnik to Andrej Plečnik, 24 December 1918, PC MGL.

Plečnik did allow some enthusiasm for the new state to enter his studio. The professor had his students design monuments to the fallen and triumphal arches—of course, in the classical style. In the artistic philosophy he had impressed on his students, Plečnik corresponded with Tomáš Masaryk the philosopher-turned-president and Alice Masaryková the social worker, revealing a foundation for their future collaboration. For all three, a constant watchword was harmony. They saw the solution to contemporary problems in time-honored sources. All three were far-reaching—and seemingly contradictory at times—in choosing their sources. But they were confident that varied ideas could be integrated within a harmonious whole. This harmony—of the classical and modern, the scientific and religious, the particular and universal—was the formula for positive change in the new age that opened after the war.

In the years before the war, the philosopher, the architect, and the social worker had sought to find sure footing, a reliable outlook based on their personal convictions. Certainly, experience and internal reflection contributed to their pledges of conviction, but correspondence with friends and family shows that their thinking was also in response to external trends: for Plečnik, changes in modern art; for Masaryková, urban poverty and social dislocation; and for her father, the civilizational upheaval of an age that had lost its sense of God. Angered by the trends of the times, all three found assurance in the religious ideals they defined. Personal assurance in a spiritual sense—what we might call salvation—was not the goal of their religious beliefs. For each of these modern believers, religion was not restricted to the individual relationship with God. At the core of their respective religious convictions was the sense that they were an instrument of God, that they were being used by God for a greater purpose that served others. They did not seek the kingdom of God in any ecclesiastical sense. Instead, their goal was human flourishing, the transformation of individuals and communities. This flourishing was not the end in itself—it was an opening to transcendence, a way of living and organizing life that reached beyond "this life."[105]

---

105 Taylor, *A Secular Age*, 20.

Part Two

Czechoslovakia under the Perspective of Eternity

Chapter Four

The House of Masaryk and the Moral Republic

"O Czech people, the government of your affairs will return to you!" These words, stated originally by Jan Amos Komenský and repeated by Tomáš Masaryk in his first address as president, have lasting resonance in modern Czech history. Seven decades after Masaryk's speech, Václav Havel repeated the phrase in his first address after the 1989 revolution, and visitors such as Bill Clinton, Margaret Thatcher, and George W. Bush recited the line in saluting the former political prisoner turned president. As Prime Minister Thatcher stated in Prague in 1990, only months after the fall of communism, the declaration summed up "everything that has been achieved in Eastern Europe."

But Masaryk's citation of Komenský in 1918 went beyond a pithy endorsement of democracy. The quotation read, in full: "I still trust God that, after the gales of wrath brought upon us by our sins have passed, O Czech people, the government of your affairs will return to you. And it is in this hope that I appoint you heirs of all that I have inherited from my ancestors and have sheltered through hard and difficult times. And whatever good I have gained, through the work of my sons and God's abundant blessing, all that I leave to you."[1]

The words of Komenský, like an invocation, indicated Masaryk's understanding of events. The new president announced that the prophecy and prayer of the bishop of the Czech Brethren, written after

---

[1] Masaryk, address to the National Assembly, 22 December 1918, in *Cesta demokracie I*, 24. Translation by Ludmila Tydlitátová.

the Habsburg rulers had sent Czech Protestants into exile, had been "fulfilled to the letter." The events of 1918—the Allied victory in the World War, the collapse of the Austro-Hungarian Empire, and the founding of the Czechoslovak Republic—were the culmination of the inevitable current of history that Masaryk had mapped over the previous decades. Democracy had defeated the forces of medieval theocracy. A state built on moral foundations was replacing a government rooted in mystical claims to divine grace. "Spirit has triumphed over the material," he announced, "rights over force, truth over cunning."[2]

Tomáš Masaryk was not unique in seeing Europe after the First World War as the stage for a new, brighter age of history. Activists, intellectuals, and politicians across Europe—both men and women, secular and religious in outlook—understood the four years of destruction as the prelude to new institutions that would repair broken societies, help the needy, and maintain the peace. This was Masaryk's expectation for the Czechoslovak Republic. As one of the new states in Europe, Czechoslovakia was at the vanguard of a dawning historical era, in which the advance of democracy would bring a new politics. But Masaryk's vision went beyond politics. Building upon decades of thinking on nationhood, history, morality, and religion, he conceived of an all-encompassing "world revolution": an epochal change that would transform not only the structures of the state but also the mindset of individuals. In the words of one of his interpreters, Masaryk saw the state not as an end in itself; instead, it was "the means to a higher end: cultural-social life; the liberation of the human spirit; the Kingdom of God."[3] This final end was the highest, in Masaryk's own view. As he explained to Karel Čapek in a conversation that was not included in the published volumes of his biography: "I saw in politics an instrument. The aim for me was religious and moral. Still today I do not say that the state will be the fulfillment of a cultural mission. Instead, we must work toward the building of the City of God."[4]

Masaryk rarely used the terms "City of God" or "Kingdom of God" in his rhetoric. Instead, he wrote and spoke publicly of *humanita* as

---

2   Ibid.
3   Van den Beld, *Humanity*, 68.
4   Čapek, unpublished manuscript, appendix to *Hovory s T. G. Masarykem* (1990), 517.

the purpose of the Czech nation's development, of *sub specie aeternitatis* as the guiding principle of its political life, and of the ideals embodied by figures like Jan Hus and Jan Amos Komenský. Masaryk believed determinedly in all of these ideas. They were his religion. They were true. At the same time, they were useful. Ever the admirer of his wife's homeland, Masaryk agreed with Alexis de Tocqueville's analysis that the American republic and its active citizenry were "made possible by a great respect for religion and for morality."[5] He insisted that Czechoslovakia likewise required a common religious and moral conviction. His second annual address to the National Assembly, on October 28, 1919, made clear the need for such shared convictions. Notably, he did not mention God in the speech. Instead, he pointed to Something as the source of national strength:

> Without morals, without individuals of character, without healthy families, without faithful friendships, without loyalty to the various social organizations of which we are members, without responsibility in all of our activities, the republic cannot be strong. Without the recognition of moral authority, the authority of fundamental principles and capable figures, democracy is impossible. We have attained an independent republic because we ardently believed in our national ideals. We recognized and felt at our core something sacred (*něco svatého*). We had trust in other people and in the people. In the same way, we will maintain our republic and democracy, if we believe in our ideals, if we recognize that which is sacred, and if we have trust in each other.[6]

Although he did not use the term, and neither did Tocqueville in his analysis of American democracy, President Masaryk promoted a civil religion to the people of Czechoslovakia.[7] Rather than a legitimation of government authority or a reminder of history, this civil religion would

---

5   Masaryk, address to the National Assembly, 28 October 1919, in *Cesta demokracie I*, 173.
6   Ibid., 172–73.
7   Roman Szporluk suggested this connection of Masaryk's political ideas to civil religion well before Robert Bellah made the term famous in his 1967 essay. See Szporluk, "Masaryk's Idea of Democracy," 49n85. Jan Patočka stresses Masaryk's understanding of American democracy through the lens of Tocqueville in his essay "An Attempt at a Czech National Philosophy and Its Failure," 12–3.

forge solidarity among the republic's citizens, instill the discipline necessary for democratic freedom, and motivate them in building the new state and society. Robert Bellah famously—and controversially—described an American civil religion that has asserted a higher, universal purpose for the United States from its beginnings. A main theme of this American civil religion, as expressed by leaders of the early republic, is that even though the government derives its authority from the people, the workings of the state and the actions of its citizens are measured by a transcendent authority.[8] Masaryk promoted a similar, religious conception of Czechoslovakia's purpose and meaning. In his rhetoric as president, Masaryk repeatedly pointed to the Czech nation's religious identity and moral purpose as the foundation of the state. Masaryk's daughter Alice, in her role as the founding director of the Czechoslovak Red Cross, joined him in promoting this civil religion. But Masaryková went even further, putting the rhetoric into practice. In leading an organization that encompassed thousands of volunteers, she understood the Red Cross as a means of implementing her father's political program, not only by bringing improvements in public health and welfare but also by encouraging a new spirit of civic engagement. Based on their experiences in the United States, both father and daughter admired the virtue of civic participation in American democracy. They believed that shared religious convictions would inspire a similar engagement in Czechoslovakia.

Civil religion is promoted in words as well as in symbols, rituals, and monuments. As scholars have noted, Masaryk was well aware of the value of symbols. Indeed, the president himself became an important symbol in the Czechoslovak Republic, the central figure in a cult of the leader.[9] But Masaryk saw ceremony and symbols as important not simply for establishing the authority of his office, or the legitimacy of the republic, or the validity of his political program. Symbols had an educational value. They served to build culture, which in turn

---

8   Bellah's idea of an American civil religion, first presented in his 1967 *Dædalus* essay "Civil Religion in America," has been subject to much debate over the last four decades. Recently, the notion of civil religion in American history has been revived with the work of Harry S. Stout and George C. Rable on the Civil War, and Raymond J. Haberski and Andrew Bacevich on the contemporary military actions of the United States.

9   On Masaryk's leader cult, see Orzoff, *Battle for the Castle*, 119–32.

would shape the outlook and behavior of citizens. For Masaryk, the most important symbol in the republic was the presidential seat, Prague Castle. Historians of architecture have seized upon his charge that the castle would become "a symbol of our national democratic ideals," and most interpretations of Jože Plečnik's work as the castle architect have emphasized this democratic intent. But one must clarify that the national, democratic ideals Masaryk claimed as ours, as belonging to the Czechs, were actually his. At the root of these ideals was his personal religious philosophy. The personal beliefs of Plečnik and Alice Masaryková differed in many respects from those of Tomáš Masaryk, but there was agreement among them that the renovation of Prague Castle had significance beyond politics. The president, his daughter, and their architect understood that the castle was to be a sacred site for the new republic—a physical manifestation of democracy practiced under the aspect of eternity.

The Philosopher as President

When independent Czechoslovakia was declared in October 1918, the founders agreed that the only structure for the state was a republic and the only man to act as its president was Tomáš Masaryk. As leader of the Czechoslovak movement overseas during the war, Masaryk had gained unequalled stature. The provisional assembly, composed largely of Czechs involved in prewar political groups, elected the new president by acclamation on November 14, while Masaryk himself was still in Washington, DC. When the new president arrived in Prague on December 21, thousands cheered as he was driven through the streets and squares of the capital, across the river and up the hill to the castle. He went immediately to the nearby sanatorium where his wife Charlotte had been staying for months. His first night at the castle passed with little sleep.[10] The next day, he delivered his first address to the National Assembly, opening with the words of Komenský. And then the work began.

President Masaryk acknowledged the practical tasks of establishing a new state in his first speeches in the winter of 1918–19. He spoke

---

10 Ludwig, *Defender of Democracy,* 53.

of purging the pernicious influence of the Habsburgs from state offices, of furthering relations with the Western Allies, and of guarding against the rising threat of Bolshevism. But Masaryk also insisted in his early statements that building the Czechoslovak republic was not limited to political institutions and material demands. "Our democratic republic," he declared, "which has overthrown the old political authorities, which has toppled monarchism and militarism, will rest firmly only on an all-encompassing morality."[11] When speaking of the state's moral foundation, Masaryk typically linked it to religion. Even when calling for the separation of church and state in the new republic, the president insisted on a deep reverence for religion. "The state, as a truly cultural implementation of politics, cannot be biased against religion," he stated in a memorandum on the separation of church and state. "On the contrary, it must regard religion in the same way it regards science, the arts, and all other cultural strengths and components of society."[12] A religious sensibility was necessary for a genuine civic morality, for the humanitarian democracy he had envisioned for years. The republic would be built upon the work, sacrifice, and mutual responsibility of its citizens, at the core of which was an awareness of the eternal. As he said in his 1920 address to the National Assembly, "The sense of eternity makes us humble, strengthening the sense of moral responsibility and leading to the recognition of a general harmony."[13]

Masaryk offered his most complete interpretation of the war and his vision for the Czechoslovak Republic in his memoirs, published in 1925. The book's title, *Světová revoluce* (The World Revolution), made clear Masaryk's understanding of the conflict and the resulting creation of the Czech and Slovak state. Following ideas he had presented in his book on Russia, Masaryk stated that the war had been a struggle for freedom and democracy against the forces of theocratic absolutism. The Allied victory, the founding of the republic, and the advance of democracy had ushered in a new era, not only for European politics

---

11 Masaryk, address to the National Assembly, 28 October 1919, in *Cesta demokracie I*, 172–73.

12 Masaryk, "Memorandum o zádách odluky církve a státu" [Memorandum on the separation of Church and State], 2 November 1919, in *Cesta demokracie I*, 186.

13 Masaryk, address to the National Assembly, 7 March 1920, in *Cesta demokracie I*, 234.

but for all of human history. The democratic revolution required "new people, a new human, a new Adam."[14] Masaryk's reference to the "first man" signaled his understanding of the postwar transformation as far more than a political or social change; it would bring a change in people's outlook, their relations with others, and their motivations in daily life. "Democracy emerges from an entire perspective of the world and of life, a new point of view, a new method," Masaryk wrote in his memoirs. "The acknowledgement and implementation of the equality of all citizens, the avowal of freedom to all citizens, the humanitarian foundation of brotherhood inside and out—this is something quite new, not only politically but also morally."[15] The new Adam, as citizen of a new state and a new Europe, would embody the bold inquisitiveness of the modern sciences, the egalitarian outlook of the democratic ethic, and the active service of humanitarian ideals.[16]

In Masaryk's telling, the political and human development of the postwar period was the next stage in a historical progress that extended back to the founding of the first theocracies in Egypt, Israel, Greece, and Rome. The millennia-long rule of priests and emperors was decisively ended, breaking the hold of institutional religion over politics, society, and culture. Masaryk expected, as he had written for decades, that this removal of church authority (*odcírkevnování*) would also extend to religion, thus allowing the democratic citizen to comprehend its true substance: love, sympathy, and compassion.[17] With this clearer religious conviction, harmonious with reason and with individual autonomy, people would act toward their fellow citizens out of a consciousness of eternity. Masaryk cited Tocqueville in arguing for a religious basis to civic life. The French author had recognized a shared religious and moral sense at the core of the American republic, the president wrote. The Czechoslovak republic needed the same: a religious foundation for all areas of political and social life. From Toc-

---

14   Masaryk, *Světová revoluce*, 365.

15   Ibid.

16   For thorough examinations of Masaryk's political thought as presented in his memoirs and other presidential statements, see chapter seven of Szporluk, *The Political Thought of Thomas G. Masaryk*, and chapter five of Van den Beld, *Humanity*. A philosophical critique is offered by Scruton in "Masaryk, Kant, and the Czech Experience," 44–59.

17   Masaryk, *Světová revoluce*, 370.

queville, the president turned to the Apostle Paul, referring to 2 Corinthians 4:1–2: "Therefore, having this ministry by the mercy of God, we do not lose heart. We have renounced disgraceful, underhanded ways; we refuse to practice cunning or to tamper with God's word, but by the open statement of the truth we would commend ourselves to every man's conscience in the sight of God." This, Masaryk declared, "is the program of the republic and democracy *sub specie aeternitatis.*"[18]

In this sense, Masaryk acknowledged, the new democratic state upheld one legacy of the old theocracies: the recognition of a God-ordained moral order remained necessary to the fabric of society. The republic would take up the functions of the theocratic state related to the moral conduct of society, such as education and social welfare. But there was a vital difference between Masaryk's theocracy and that of the bishops and nobles he had worked to dethrone: in a democratic society, religious authorities would not legitimize the power of the state, and the state, in turn, would not use religion as an instrument of coercion. Moreover, the religious foundation of the state would take a more advanced form. As the president explained in the closing chapters of his memoirs: "Spiritual absolutism, the various forms of caesaropapism and worldly absolutism, all of which exploit religion, will be overcome by a higher, more humane morality and a higher religion, freely directing all of public life—Jesus, not Caesar. I say this, in that our aim is to realize the religion and ethic of Jesus, his pure and spotless humanitarian religion. In love to God and to others, Jesus understood the whole law and the prophets, the essence of religion and morality. Everything else is incidental."[19]

Masaryk often repeated this motto, "Jesus, not Caesar." What did he mean? To understand Masaryk's statement, we must keep in mind his idea of a new religion. As president, he no longer used the term "new religion" explicitly. Instead, he spoke of this "higher religion" or "humanitarian religion." But the substance was the same as the new religion he had proclaimed at the turn of the century. Jesus was the highest human example of living in truth, acting in love for one's

---

18 Ibid., 374.
19 Ibid., 372.

neighbor, and freely choosing a life of service. Caesar, on the other hand, represented not just state power, but state power exercised over religion and in collusion with religion. He pointed out in his memoirs that "theocracy" should be "the rule of God." In practice, however, from the empire of Caesar to that of the kaiser, theocracy had been the rule of priests and nobles using theology to justify their power and suppress their subjects. The democratic state would not use such coercion, but this did not mean that religion would be absent. "The modern person wants religion that is in agreement with reason and religion that is free and individual," Masaryk wrote.[20] In coming to conviction freely, without the compulsion of state or church, people would live out the moral qualities of true religion: love, sympathy, *humanita*. Masaryk explained: "*Humanita* is the newer word for the old idea of love for one's neighbor."[21] The democratic state would flourish as citizens served each other in love, with the awareness that they were anchored in eternity. Likewise, in the overall direction of the republic, the practical would be subject to the measure of the true and moral, the immediate to the measure of the eternal. "I conceive of the state and politics, just as I do of all of life, *sub specie aeterni*," Masaryk stated in one of his later interviews with Karel Čapek. "In this sense, I am a theocrat. Consistent *humanita*, metaphysically speaking, is nothing other than theocracy."[22]

The House of Masaryk and Managed Democracy

Masaryk's charge to the citizens of democratic Czechoslovakia was grand in its aim and formidable in scope. Shake off the remnants of Austrian rule, with its unprincipled bureaucrats serving church and throne. Turn away from the amorality of political liberalism and the stupor of nominal Catholicism. Recognize that you are individuals whose acts have eternal consequence. And join fellow citizens—and God—in the building of a wholly new political association, founded

---

20 Ibid., 371.
21 Ibid., 374.
22 Čapek, "Politik a filosof" [Politician and philosopher], appendix to *Hovory s T. G. Masarykem* (1990), 517.

upon the principle of love for one's neighbor. The rhetoric was lofty. But how would Masaryk, as president, translate this vision of a moral republic into practical governance?

Masaryk spoke of religion as necessary for democracy. But like his thinking on religion, his vision of a democratic system of government was unsystematic—and unorthodox. Scholars have shown that Masaryk had little concern for the structure of a democratic state.[23] Andrea Orzoff applies the term "managed democracy" to the president's approach to governing and politics.[24] On matters of institutions and popular sovereignty, Masaryk wrote little more than generalities. Instead, he described democracy as administration "by the people, for the people." Participation of the citizenry was not a matter of holding office or even voting. According to the president's vision of democracy, citizens would participate actively as workers, as volunteers committed to the benefit of society and the state. Through this process, the divide between government and people would be erased. Citizens and the organs of the state would work together seamlessly, united by a shared ethic and purpose.[25]

Masaryk's devotion to Plato was evident in his idea of who would govern the state.[26] He maintained that positions of leadership would be held by people with both the expertise and the intellectual and moral resources to make wise decisions. As he said in his 1919 address to the National Assembly, moral authority in a democracy was established by both "fundamental principles and capable figures." Masaryk and his close associate Edvard Beneš were such capable figures. Party politicians were not. Masaryk judged party leaders as too narrow in attention to truly represent and serve the nation. For that matter, he did not hold the "masses" in high regard either. In his first months in office, Masaryk deliberated ruling as dictator in order to establish the necessary foundations of the republic. One army officer who longed for Ma-

---

23 On Masaryk's notions of democracy, see Bugge, "Czech Democracy," 17–22; Klimek, *Boj o Hrad*, 1:84–9; Szporluk, *The Political Thought of Thomas G. Masaryk*, 45–46; and Van den Beld, *Humanity*, 108–112

24 Orzoff, *Battle for the Castle*, 59.

25 See Sporluk, *The Political Thought of Thomas G. Masaryk*, 71–73; and Bugge, "Czech Democracy," 20–3.

26 Eva Schmidt-Hartmann sees the Platonic sources of Masaryk's political thought already in one of his early essays. See *Thomas G. Masaryk's Realism*, 77–79.

saryk to take this step, to rule as an enlightened dictator, was disappointed that he did not. As the officer later recalled, "More than a statesman, more than a philosopher, Masaryk the Prophet rejected it."[27] Masaryk himself recalled years later in a private conversation that he had been uncertain at the start of his presidency about how to establish a unified state, a true democracy, out of the disparate elements that comprised Czechoslovakia. "Democracy is a terribly difficult thing," he told Alice during an evening chat. "True democracy is the autonomy of small units, connected by a unifying idea. For us, having different nations, different faiths, different cultures, this is difficult to create. In addition, we leaders did not know what to do. We had to learn—and we are learning—everything. I myself did not know what a president is—I was prepared theoretically, but the practice was entirely new. From the start, I was greatly concerned about the republic."[28]

In devoting attention to the foundations of the unified republic, Masaryk pressed for an expansion of presidential authority within the emerging parliamentary system. The constitution ratified in February 1920 decreed a bicameral parliament, a prime minister serving as the head of government, and a president, elected by parliament for seven-year terms, as head of state. According to the constitution, the president's powers were somewhere between the strong executive of the American system and the weaker heads of state in European parliamentary democracies. However, Masaryk's political leverage far exceeded his constitutional powers, owing to his unmatched personal authority. The president's chancellery functioned in Czechoslovak politics as a governing institution parallel to the prime minister and cabinet, with Masaryk's staff pressing his agenda in the ministries and parliament. Masaryk himself was deeply invested in political disputes of the day, even writing op-ed pieces under assumed names in defense of or opposition to certain policies or politicians.[29] Yet as the enlightened leader, in the tradition of Komenský, Masaryk's concern extended beyond administrative measures or political decision-making. His aim was the moral improvement of the citizens. As he had declared in

---

27   Quoted in Klimek, *Boj o Hrad*, 1:33. See also Bugge, "Czech Democracy," 8.
28   Gašparíková-Horáková, diary entry of 27 May 1929, in *U Masarykovcov*, 31.
29   See Orzoff, *Battle for the Castle*, 66–9.

his first address: "Man and nation do not live by bread alone. We all have realized that we need reeducation."[30]

As president, Masaryk sought to use the authority of his office—constitutional and extra-constitutional—to spur this reeducation. He directed particular attention to three institutions that had been coercive instruments of the monarchy but would be vital to the new moral environment of the republic: schools, the police, and the military. The president entrusted these institutions to longtime associates, giving the charge that reform had to extend beyond organizational structures to the mindsets of the people who occupied them.[31] Masaryk also supported the development of new or existing organizations outside the government, furthering what we now call civil society. Organizations for women and veterans, welfare and health associations, periodicals, academic institutes, and Protestant clubs such as the YMCA gained the president's support in the 1920s. Masaryk's aid for these groups went beyond words: throughout his presidency, he made financial gifts from money left over from the wartime contributions by Czechs and Slovaks in the United States. From this Fund for Humanitarian and Social Purposes, which opened with some 5.3 million crowns (equivalent to $157,000 at the time), the president gave gifts to, among others, theatre groups in Olomouc and České Budějovice, a hospital for the disabled in Prague, a music school in Bratislava, exiles from Ukraine and Russia, the Czechoslovak hockey association and Olympic committee, and a village mayor in rural Slovakia who used the money for student scholarships. Even individuals, such as composer Bohuslav Martinů, linguist Roman Jakobson, and former Russian leader Aleksandr Kerensky, received support from the president.[32] Masaryk's gifts furthered his image as the *tatínek* (daddy) of the nation, a leader both stately and kind.[33] It also set an example of moral

---

30 Masaryk, address to the National Assembly, 22 December 1918, in *Cesta demokracie I*, 32.

31 Soubignon, *Tomáš Garrigue Masaryk*, 240–44.

32 The gifts are recorded in a ledger book in MÚA AV ČR, TGM Collection, Republika, box 535, folder 22. As the president's gifts became known, his office received frequent requests for support, prompting a more regularized process of disbursement. Whereas gifts had been made in an ad hoc fashion at first, in 1925 Masaryk adopted the practice of giving dozens of donations at Christmastime, providing a few hundred or few thousand crowns each to local churches, veterans groups, and cultural organizations.

33 Soubignon, *Tomáš Garrigue Masaryk*, 280–82.

FIGURE 4.1. Tomáš and Charlotte Masaryk leaving the polling place after voting, 1920. Masaryk Institute and Archive, Academy of Sciences, Czech Republic.

action, the kind of generosity and encouragement of good work that he saw as necessary for a democratic society.

Masaryk's benevolence, along with the idea of a managed democracy, arose out of the moral elitism of his household. Masaryk and his family consistently identified themselves as democrats. In one letter to his wife during the war, Masaryk eschewed the suggestion that he was a chosen instrument of God in his leadership of the national movement. "I do not feel like an instrument of the Lord, not at all, because everyman is the same instrument," he wrote to Charlotte in English. "There is democracy in my metaphysics."[34] At the same time, however, Masaryk and his family described themselves on occasion as aristocrats. "I am an aristocrat myself," Masaryk once declared in a public lecture, indicating that his position as a professor set him apart from others.[35] Alice Masaryková acknowledged her own "aristocratic"

---

34 TGM to CGM, 1 January 1916, MÚA AV ČR, TGM Collection, Korespondence III, box 60, folder 33.

35 Szporluk, *Political Thought of Thomas G. Masaryk*, 47. Robert Pynsent describes Masaryk as a "moral aristocratist" in his essay "Masaryk and Decadence."

moral views. "I should love to be among refined people all the time, I have such a craving for that," she wrote to her mother during her teaching stint in provincial České Budějovice. "But in the meantime I meet few people who are my equals."[36] Later, when she was Red Cross director, Alice Masaryková conceived of an "aristocratic democracy" as necessary for Czechoslovakia's progress.[37] In order to establish the republic's foundations, Masaryková and her father held that people of cultivation were needed in positions of leadership—an aristocracy not of blood, but of talent, religious awareness, and moral conviction. Of course, President Masaryk met that description. Alice Masaryková believed that she did as well. In her role as Red Cross director, she projected herself as someone cultured, wise, and devoted to faithful and selfless service—a fitting associate to her father.[38]

Within the Masaryk family, the model of aristocratic comportment was not the president, but his wife. One friend of the family, who associated with noble families of the old empire, had said of Charlotte that she was the most aristocratic person he had known, "in her bearing, in her every movement."[39] By the end of the war, though, this impressive person was fading. Afflicted by mental illness throughout her life, Charlotte Masaryková was also diagnosed with heart disease and confined to a sanatorium in Prague's Veleslavín district (site of today's Canadian Medical Clinic). Masaryk came to her bedside immediately after his triumphant return in December 1918. On occasion over the next few years she was able to leave the hospital, to join her family at the castle or at the president's country retreat. She went on car rides with her husband (she noted that Masaryk even drove), and read the manuscript of his memoirs.[40] And she made a special note in her diary on April 18, 1920, when she voted for the first time in her life. But

36 AGM to CGM, 27 October 1906, MÚA AV ČR, TGM Collection, Korespondence III, box 60, folder 34. See also AGM to TGM, 20 December 1906, Korespondence III, box 54, folder 2.

37 AGM to Mrs. Krčméyrová, 5 October 1932, MÚA AV ČR, AGM Collection, folder 20.

38 Masaryková's understanding of her character and role in Czechoslovakia are shown in her letters from prison published in *The Atlantic Monthly*. She selected the letters herself and translated them in a dramatic, erudite style. See "From an Austrian Prison" and "The Prison House," both published in 1920.

39 Čapek, *Talks with T. G. Masaryk*, 116.

40 Masaryková made sporadic entries in different diaries in 1920 and 1921. MÚA AV ČR, CGM Collection, box 2, folder 6.

she grew weaker in the summer of 1922, while her husband and Alice were away in Italy on holiday. Her few letters to Masaryk during these months are written in an unsteady, childlike script.[41] There are no surviving writings from her after that. In spring 1923, she suffered a heart attack and then a stroke. Although she had been ill for years, her death on May 13 was still a crushing blow to the family. Tomáš Masaryk knelt by her deathbed and wept. After she was taken away, he had his iron cot moved into her room and slept there, among her books and photographs. In the days before her burial, their son Jan, then thirty-six years old, brought his blanket and pillow to the room where her casket lay. He curled up on the floor and slept outside his mother's door.[42]

Alice Masaryková had sat with her mother in those final days and received what she took to be her charge. "Alice, you work with father, and when he is gone you will work alone," Charlotte told her daughter. "Father will do a great thing, the greatest thing he has yet done."[43] Alice subsequently took it upon herself to remind Tomáš Masaryk of his task, to hold his attention to the example and expectation that his wife had held. Even before Charlotte's death, Masaryková had chided her father for lagging. She wrote that he was sealing himself away, working himself too hard, and enjoying too much of Jan's amusements. Alice was unimpressed by her brother, and she tried to warn her father of Jan's "selfishness and thoughtlessness."[44] Masaryková continued the exhortations after her mother's death. Shortly after Charlotte's passing, she retreated to the spa at Františkový Lázně, bringing along her mother's diaries and letters. She wrote a stream of notes and letters to her father, reminding him of Charlotte's example of faith and her religious vision. Her mother's great goal had been to have people rise above their pettiness and become holy. At the same time, however, Charlotte had asked herself: Are people even able to do that? Can people rise above their own strength? "I think in every direction it is nec-

41   CGM to TGM, 6 June, 28 June, and 19 July 1922, MÚA AV ČR, TGM Collection, Korespondence III, box 54, folder 1.
42   Mitchell, *Alice Garrigue Masaryk*, 134–35.
43   Ibid.
44   AGM to TGM, 27 July 1921, MÚA AV ČR, TGM Collection, Korespondence III, box 54, folder 2.

essary to answer this question," Alice wrote to her father.[45] Masaryková recalled memories of her mother to encourage her father, even correct him. "You say of God that it's impossible to love him, since you don't know him," she wrote. But there was the possibility of progress in knowing God, Masaryková insisted. "It is certainly true that we perceive only a fraction, but we do 'progress.' And this is a direct glimpse of the Principle that is far higher than humanity and human ability." It was her responsibility—and her father's—to aid people in that ultimate, spiritual awareness. "Clearly, infinite progress is not completed in the body," she wrote. "We have the possibility and obligation to help in this development."[46]

Helping people was Alice Masaryková's purpose in life. But she saw herself and her father as helping people *up*, to the position of refinement and moral conviction that they already occupied. She wrote a line of Shakespeare to Masaryk as a summary of their task: "Treat everybody according to <u>your own honors & dignity</u>."[47] This was not simply the noble work of a man of learning and cultivation. As Masaryková often reminded her father, his good and beautiful work—the work of building a democracy that would cultivate morality among its citizens—was the work of God. "Papa, I know that the Lord God is watching over us," she said one night. "I'm always bolstered in the belief that he chose us to bring the ideal of true democracy to reality in our state."[48]

The managed democracy of Masaryk's republic was true democracy, just as it was a moral democracy, because its leader was a moral man guided by God. In the same way, the work of those around him—his family and his closest associates—was true and blameless, because

---

45 AGM to TGM, 10 June 1923, MÚA AV ČR, TGM Collection, Korespondence III, box 54, folder 2.

46 AGM to TGM, 6 June 1923, MÚA AV ČR, TGM Collection, Korespondence III, box 54, folder 2.

47 AGM to TGM, 9 October 1926, MÚA AV ČR, TGM Collection, Korespondence III, box 54, folder 2. Alice underlined the key words. The line from *Hamlet*, act 2, scene 2, line 493, actually reads, "Use them after your own honor and dignity." But Masaryková got the meaning right. Hamlet makes the statement in response to Polonius, who advises treating people as they deserve. Hamlet replies:

> God's bodykins, man, much better. Use every man
> after his desert, and who should 'scape whipping?
> Use them after your own honor and dignity. The
> less they deserve, the more merit is in your
> bounty. Take them in.

48 Gašparíková-Horáková, diary entry of 27 May 1929, in *U Masarykovcov*, 32.

they also understood and acted according to truth. Masaryk's belief in his moral rightness, and the convergence of his purposes and the republic's, provided the justification for actions that others might have judged as less than upright. For example, Masaryk often used the Fund for Humanitarian and Social Purposes to secure political backing and support his allies. Masaryk directed cash gifts to various publications that supported his policies.[49] Large, regular payments also went to Edvard Beneš in support of his various "propaganda outlays." As foreign minister, Beneš directed the state's public relations and information-gathering bureaus, both housed within his ministry, and he was a constant presence at the League of Nations and international conferences. This work was funded to a large extent from the account that Masaryk controlled.[50]

Other than the money directed to Beneš, the most frequent and sizeable payments from Masaryk's humanitarian fund were to members of his own family. The president himself, who took pride in his spartan existence, often deposited money *into* the benevolence fund, and his only personal withdrawals were to purchase books. Meanwhile, Alice Masaryková received funds only to support her travels to international Red Cross meetings. The younger children, however, drew repeatedly from the account. In 1925–26, his first year as Czechoslovak envoy in London, Jan Masaryk received regular payments of £200. Even greater were the sums that went to his sister Olga, who was living in Geneva with her husband, a Swiss physician, and their two young sons. The account ledger lists monthly disbursements to Geneva, from 10,000 up to 75,000 Swiss francs, along with supplementary transfers of tens of thousands of crowns. These funds ostensibly supported, according to an entry note, "national affairs." In total, Olga Masaryková-Revilliod received in 1926 alone over 1.4 million crowns (roughly $42,000 at the time), which amounted to fifteen percent of the year's

---

49 Most notable of these politically motivated donations was a one-million-crown donation to support the founding of a new, centrist party and an associated political journal, *Přítomnost* (The Present). Orzoff, *Battle for the Castle*, 98.

50 For example, in May 1923 Beneš received two payments totaling more than 878,000 Czechoslovak crowns. At the exchange rate of roughly thirty-three crowns to the US dollar at the time, this equaled more than $26,600.

outlays from the fund.[51] Clearly, this would qualify as corruption by today's definition: a president using funds originally given as political donations to maintain his daughter's life in Switzerland. But Tomáš Masaryk was incorruptible, as were his children and closest associates. Just as Masaryk's ideals were those of the nation, the purposes of the house of Masaryk were synonymous with the purposes of the republic.[52]

The President's Conscience

On rare occasion, Alice Masaryková expressed—privately—the differences between herself and her father. "You don't believe in nurture," she wrote to Tomáš Masaryk in 1921. "I don't believe in politics. Here it is necessary to understand each other, to complement each other. Nurture is my main gift, and I have great results."[53] The passage reveals not so much a difference in philosophies as a distinction in how to put those philosophies into practice. Masaryk was an idealist like his daughter, but that idealism was tempered by attention to the practical. Historians have made clear that, once in power, Masaryk did not refrain from contravening his own principles. "Masaryk's plans and high ideals sometimes seemed to be built on sand," wrote Antonín Klimek, one of the first Czech scholars to conduct research in Masaryk's archives. "Fortunately, Masaryk as president did not hold rigidly in practice to his many ideal schemes. As he himself said, his head was in the clouds, but his feet were firmly on the ground."[54] In contrast, Alice Masaryková believed without hesitation in her father's ideals—as well as her own—and held those ideals as applicable to practical problems. From the turn of the century, when she had studied in

---

51 For disbursements in 1926, see the account book *Fond pro účely sociální a humanní v Živostenské Bance* (*Disposiční fond*) [Fund for Social and Humanitarian Purposes in the Živostenská Bank], pages 120–75 of the account ledger. MÚA AV ČR, TGM Collection, Republika, box 535, folder 22.

52 Peter Bugge's essential article on the politics of the First Republic, drawing upon the extensive archival material presented in Antonín Klimek's book *Boj o Hrad*, emphasizes the outright bribes that Masaryk and Beneš would pay for the support of politicians and newspaper editors. Bugge states that the president and his foreign minister "used the whole system of bribery and spying not for personal profit, but for the good of the state, with which both men unconditionally identified their own position." Bugge, "Czech Democracy," 19.

53 AGM to TGM, 27 July 1921, MÚA AV ČR, TGM Collection, Korespondence III, box 54, folder 2.

54 Klimek, *Boj o Hrad*, 1:87.

Germany and then served in Chicago, Alice Masaryková had been committed to a life of service. Now, with the founding of the Czechoslovak state and the Red Cross, she saw herself as working alongside her father to fulfill her life's work and his vision for the nation.

After her mother's death, Alice Masaryková became her father's constant companion and trusted adviser. She stepped into the role of first lady of the republic, hosting ceremonial events at Prague Castle. In evening conversations, Alice and her father engaged in discussions of his writings, of literature, philosophy, and religion, and despite her professed dislike, politics. By the late 1920s, she wrote notes nearly every day, offering prayers, sometimes raising questions about his views, and always expressing her admiration and love. "Dearest father, my best friend," she wrote in one note.[55] "Alice, you are my conscience," Masaryk acknowledged.[56]

In addition to her roles as companion and confidante, Masaryková also held official duties as director of the Red Cross. The Red Cross had operated in the Austro-Hungarian Empire, but mainly to provide medical aid to soldiers. Shortly after the founding of the independent republic, President Masaryk announced the formation of a Czechoslovak chapter of the organization. With the backing of Prague civic officials and leaders of health organizations, he named Alice its first director in February 1919.[57] The president understood improved health care as an important task of the republic. "Health—a healthy spirit and a healthy body—are in the end the aim of all politics and administration," he declared in his 1919 New Year's address.[58] But in the early months of 1919, public health was not simply an ideal of the state. It was imperative for the stability of the republic. Like the other new states of East Central Europe, Czechoslovakia faced a public health catastrophe in the wake of the First World War.[59] The Allied blockade

---

55 AGM to TGM, 10 November 1926, MÚA AV ČR, TGM Collection, Korespondence III, box 54, folder 3.

56 Gašparíková-Horáková, diary entry of 3 October 1931, in *U Masarykovcov*, 125.

57 Lovčí, *Alice Garrigue Masaryková*, 245–47.

58 Masaryk, New Year's address to the National Assembly, 1 January 1919, in *Cesta demokracie I*, 60. See also "Poselství prezidenta republiky," 22 December 1918, in *Cesta demokracie I*, 32.

59 Stepanek, "Social and Economic Problems." On overall conditions in the Czech Lands during the last years of the war, see Šedivý, *Češi, české země, a velká válka*, 318–26 and 340–44.

of Austria-Hungary had brought severe deprivations to the civilian population of the Czech Lands and Slovakia in the last years of the war, and agricultural production dropped by more than half from pre-war levels. Rates of tuberculosis and infant mortality had climbed during the war.[60] Even more menacing were health threats from the East: cholera and trachoma spread in the newly acquired regions of Slovakia and Subcarpathian Ruthenia, while a typhus epidemic loomed in Poland and Ukraine. And like the rest of Europe, the entire country had to contend with the influenza epidemic in late 1918 and 1919. In Prague alone, 1,064 people died from the Spanish flu in the autumn months of 1918.[61]

In her role as Red Cross director, Alice Masaryková worked on two fronts to address the public health crisis. First, she turned to the Allies for assistance. At the same time as Edvard Beneš negotiated in Paris to secure Czechoslovakia's frontiers, Masaryková moved in other circles in the French capital, as well as in London and Geneva, appealing to aid organizations and private donors. The donations she gained—medicines and medical equipment, clothes and blankets, volunteer nurses and physicians to staff clinics and teach training courses—proved essential to the founding of the Czechoslovak Red Cross.[62] Foreign assistance was also indispensable in meeting the overall needs in postwar Czechoslovakia. The country received more than 98,000 tons of relief supplies from France, Italy, and Britain during 1919. Meanwhile, the American Relief Administration delivered an additional 270,000 tons of foodstuffs to Czechoslovakia.[63] Masaryková was a key figure in securing this aid, meeting with administrators of the French, British, Canadian, and American Red Cross societies,

---

60 League of Nations Health Organization, *The Official Vital Statistics of the Republic of Czechoslovakia*, 62–63; and Pelc, *Organization of the Public Health Services in Czechoslovakia*, 52–53.

61 Although severe, this number did not approach the mortality rates in Western Europe, where in France (166,000 deaths), Britain (229,000), and Germany (225,000) the flu was particularly devastating. Šedivý, *Češi, české země, a velká válka*, 341–42.

62 Švejnoha, "Alice Masaryková a mezinárodní hnutí Červeného kříže"; and Pelc, *Organization of the Public Health Services in Czechoslovakia*, 38–39.

63 "Agreement between the Czechoslovak National Republic and the American Relief Administration," 24 February 1919, and "Report to the President of the Supreme Council on Relief Operations," 3 September 1919, in Bane and Lutz, eds., *Organization of American Relief in Europe*, 293–96 and 714. See also Surface and Bland, *American Food in the World War and Reconstruction Period*, 32–37.

along with the director of the American Relief Administration, Herbert Hoover. She also took a leading role in coordinating delivery of the supplies. Complementing her duties with the Red Cross, she directed a second nongovernmental agency, simply called Care for Children (*Pečé o děti*), that handled the distribution of supplies in cooperation with ARA officials. In December 1919, Care for Children was feeding more than 465,000 children across Czechoslovakia. By the end of 1921 it had provided more than 15,000 tons of clothing and blankets, cocoa, powdered milk, and cooked meals.[64]

Masaryková's second strategy in leading the new Red Cross was to set the foundation of a broad-based organization that would promote improved public health and welfare. Like her father, she sought to import American models. Even before becoming Red Cross director, she contacted Mary McDowell in Chicago and asked her former mentor to send a team of trained social workers to Prague. In order to gain a firm understanding of the city's social problems and root out Habsburg influences in welfare offices, Masaryková wanted these American social workers to conduct a survey of the city, similar to what social welfare groups in the United States had been doing for decades. The initial group of three young women, eventually growing to five Americans and twelve Czechs, spent the year 1919 cataloging existing welfare agencies in Prague and researching health problems, sanitation conditions, and facilities for children. Their final report, including Masaryková's introduction, made repeated reference to social work practices in the United States.[65] The team of American women also worked in the summer of 1919 to train twenty-six Czechs in social welfare practices, with the aim that they would become the first social workers for the new state. But Alice Masaryková wanted to adopt not only American methods in the republic; she also hoped that the Red Cross would give an example of the engaged, democratic citizen, one who

---

64 Surface and Bland, *American Food in the World War and Reconstruction Period*, 169–71.

65 One of these young American social workers was Ruth Crawford (later Mitchell). She described the group's work in Prague in a 1921 article in the social welfare journal *The Survey*. See Crawford, "Pathfinding in Prague." A copy of the final report, in published and manuscript form, is in her collected papers at the Lilly Library. Also in the collection are Mitchell's letters to her parents from Prague in 1919–20, her diary, and her reports to the Overseas Committee, War Work Council of the YWCA. Mitchell Collection, Lilly Library, box 1, correspondence.

FIGURE 4.2. Tomáš and Alice Masaryk visiting a sanatorium, undated. Literary Archive, Museum of [Czech] National Literature.

contributes to civic life and works to improve the general welfare. She saw the organization as a vehicle for instilling the virtues of responsible, moral citizenship in the people of Czechoslovakia. In fact, she hoped that every citizen would one day become a member of the Red Cross.[66] For Masaryková, this wish was more than a grand fantasy for the organization she led; it was a practical strategy for the success of the new state. The involvement of all citizens in volunteer service would not only improve the health and welfare of the country, it would also fulfill the ideals of the republic, as described by her father.

In her statements at Red Cross meetings, Masaryková connected her father's notions of service and moral responsibility to the work of volunteers in reviving the nation's health. They were models of active citizens contributing to the building of a harmonious, just society. In

---

66   Masaryková, "Dobrý soused" [The good neighbor], undated manuscript (1922?) addressed to members of local Red Cross chapters, LA PNP, AGM Collection, box 1.

Masaryková's words, Red Cross members offered their talents to their communities, the republic, and all of humanity, motivated by "a spiritual strength and a spiritual foundation in uncertain, hectic conditions." This was, she insisted, "the essence of democracy."[67] Masaryková's vision of the Red Cross's work also followed her father's idea of democracy as administration, a system in which morally enlightened experts led while everyone else contributed their service. In explaining the organization's tasks in speeches and writings, Masaryková often repeated themes from an early manuscript titled "Dobrý soused" (The Good Neighbor), which offered the small, rural village as a model of neighborly relations and mutual support.[68] The vision was romantic: the "wise manciple" kept order, while the villagers practiced neighborliness. Yet as she observed in Chicago and Prague, this ideal community did not survive the villagers' migration to the city. Masaryková wrote of poverty in the cities, poor living conditions, and disease, but of greater concern to her were the social and moral effects of urban living. Life in the city was not "harmonious," as it was in the village. Instead, relations were shallow and fleeting, and the absence of love among neighbors was stark.

According to Masaryková, this social dislocation was especially trying for women. Women were isolated in cities, and they received no encouragement in the daily work of managing a household. Masaryková wrote hypothetically of a woman living in the city, a new arrival from the countryside, who at first cleans her flat with care, puts flowers in the window, and attentively selects food at the market. But with illness and unemployment and the social distance of the city, she loses energy for this work. Without the stability of a well-managed home and the support of neighbors, she spirals into alcoholism and addiction, neglect of her children, and even prostitution. Masaryková used the term "slavery" to describe this condition, but she did not associate it with industrial labor or urban poverty. The enslaved were people whose moral integrity had been worn down by their surround-

---

67 Ibid.
68 Several of Masaryková's speeches and articles, in typescript and manuscript form, are collected in LA PNP, AGM Collection, boxes 1 and 2. Masaryková's secretary, Iva Šmakalová, collected many of these writings into a published booklet: Masaryková, *Československý Červený kříž*.

ings. She used the evolutionary image of humans and beasts, with the suggestion that both social conditioning and individual moral lapses caused people to fall to the level of animals. "Modern society is on the threshold between the human and the animal," she wrote. "Many people have lost the healthy instincts of the animal, yet they still have not evolved to a higher humanity. Instead, they revert to the breed of domestic animals, with obtuse, blunted instincts."[69] The Red Cross could lift these people up. More important than the tangible support the organization provided was the opportunity to serve. Volunteer service in the Red Cross opened an escape from a debased condition toward a more moral way of life. As individuals evolved to this higher humanity through their service, the result would be a harmonious, supportive community, like that of the village.

As with the president, Alice Masaryková saw the establishment of democratic Czechoslovakia as the opening of a new era in political and social organization. "We are participants in a great rebirth of humanity," she declared to Red Cross volunteers, her rhetoric echoing Masaryk's talk of a "world revolution" and a "new Adam."[70] The Red Cross was essential to the creation of the moral republic. Individual volunteers would recognize where to offer their own expertise and where to serve humbly, motivated by goodwill for their neighbors and an awareness of the eternal. Masaryková, like her father, saw a religious outlook as necessary for this kind of service. "To be involved in the Red Cross means to have a spiritual strength and a spiritual foundation in uncertain, hectic conditions," she wrote. "I am convinced that only the person who lives with a conscious religiosity can be worker in the Red Cross in the true sense of the word."[71] In their work for the community, these spiritually motivated volunteers would partner with state offices in the processes of legislation and administration. Masaryková expected that the partnership of state agents and Red Cross volunteers would erase the differences between politics and religion, between, on the one side, the data of statistical bureaus and pol-

---

69 Masaryková, "Mezinárodnost a červený kříž" [Internationalism and the Red Cross], undated address to the Red Cross in Lány, LA PNP, AGM Collection, box 2.

70 Masaryková, *Československý Červený kříž*, 73; and "Dobrý soused," 7.

71 Masaryková, *Československý Červený kříž*, 73.

icies of government officials and, on the other, the selfless altruism of believers.[72] "We stand at the threshold of a new age," she told one gathering of Red Cross volunteers, "an ensouled culture for our nation and humanity. In this culture, art and science will not be in conflict with religion. And wherever this conflict is absent, everyday life will always have fervor."[73]

Alice Masaryková's utopian visions were not unusual in Europe of the 1920s. In the wake of the Great War, activists, philanthropists, and politicians across the ideological terrain proposed ideas for far-reaching solutions to Europe's social and political problems. Like many of these postwar idealists, Masaryková melded a longing for premodern patterns of life with an appreciation of modern advances. In her own life, Masaryková embodied the feminist principles that her father and mother had advocated in the nineteenth century. Yet she was also a traditionalist, as we see in her concerns about the lax housekeeping of urban women, her appreciation for the neighborliness of the rural village, and her attention to the moral decline of the urban poor. Like Jane Addams and Mary McDowell in Chicago, she insisted upon the necessity of research and education in advancing social welfare. At the same time, she emphasized the religious sensibilities of volunteers. Masaryková's desire to bridge the modern and traditional was evident in her understanding of the Red Cross's insignia. Like her father, Masaryková often used Christian imagery and language in public statements, but turned in different directions. For example, she pointed to the Red Cross's symbol as representative of the new democratic society, but not for its Christian meaning. Instead, the vertical axis symbolized the connection of heaven and earth, of principles and action, an awareness of the eternal and a commitment to the immediate. The horizontal axis, in turn, symbolized the union of East and West, the traditional and the modern, the harmony of the rural village and the advances of a new age—just like Czechoslovakia on the map of Europe.[74]

72 Masaryková, "Dobrý soused," 3.
73 Masaryková, "Kříž" [The Cross], undated address, LA PNP, AGM Collection, box 1.
74 Ibid.

A Fortress of the Mighty God

True democracy, according to Alice Masaryková and her father, required work, the cooperation of people and government. It required a critical perspective and a spiritual awareness on the part of citizens. It required moral responsibility. And true democracy required beauty. Democracy must be harmonious, with the words, rituals, and symbols of the state offering inspiration to the citizenry. As admirers of Plato, father and daughter saw aesthetics, ethics, and politics as being integrally connected: the Beautiful was an expression of the Good.[75] For the president, the building of a moral republic required a symphony: parliamentary rhetoric and administrative regulations, the state's symbols and ceremonies, and even the person of the president. "Without imagination," he wrote in his memoirs, "magnanimous and creative politics in the world is impossible."[76]

In one of his turn-of-the-century lectures, Masaryk had discussed the role of art in the education of the nation, citing the example of John Ruskin. According to Masaryk, the English artist and intellectual showed "how all art in its foundation is of ethical origin, how it can lead to ethical goals, and how it aids learning." He admired Ruskin's belief that not only individual dwellings should be beautiful models of artistry, but also entire cities, particularly public buildings. "By such aesthetic work, premeditated to the last detail," Masaryk commented, "the whole nation might be elevated aesthetically and morally, and general education might spread.[77] Masaryk later suggested in his book *Russia and Europe* that there is such a thing as a "democratic aesthetics." Years later, the president elaborated in his memoirs: "Democracy is not crudeness and vulgarity, but it calls for a conversation of simple and natural forms; these develop only where there are people who are honest to themselves and independent. Democracy has its own elegance."[78] More than simply expressing beauty, the external

---

75   On the Platonic roots of Masaryk's understanding of art and the function of Prague Castle as a monument, see Güllendi-Cimprichová, "Architekt Josip Plečnik und seine Unternehmungen in Prag," 99–101.
76   Masaryk, *Světová revoluce*, 563.
77   Masaryk, "How to Work," in *The Ideals of Humanity and How to Work*, 168.
78   Masaryk, *Světová revoluce*, 379.

FIGURE 4.3. Prague Castle, third courtyard, 1918. Archive of Prague Castle.

forms of democracy would have an enlightening influence on the citizens. In the new republic, the primary symbol in this aesthetic promotion of democracy was to be the seat of the president, the ancient castle overlooking the city of Prague. According to Masaryk's view of art, the castle would serve both as tangible sign of the nation's history and reminder of its ideals.[79]

Masaryk was not alone in pressing for the renovation of Prague Castle. From a practical standpoint, the complex of palaces, chapels, and battlements was ill equipped to serve as the center of government

---

79 On Masaryk's idea of the castle as monument, see Güllendi-Cimprichová, "Architekt Josip Plečnik und seine Unternehmungen in Prag," 94–8 and 104–7.

for a modern state. By 1918, it was a shadow of its former glory. The castle was home to merchants and residents (including Franz Kafka for a brief time during the war). It was open to traffic, and the cobblestoned courtyards and lanes were busy with automobiles. Already in spring 1919, tour groups started trooping through the citadel: workers groups, architecture students, Russian émigré artists, and German technical students. Meanwhile, the interior halls and staterooms were crowded with officials and office seekers. In the first weeks of the republic's existence a swarm of politicians and clerks staked claims to different rooms on behalf of the prime minister, the Ministry of Defense, and the Foreign Ministry. Following the officials came the suppliants, who loitered in the halls, smoking and whittling. In the commotion, furniture scraped across parquet floors and Asian carpets served as doormats. As one observer remarked, it was a good thing that the castle was open to the public, but that did not mean allowing "wantonness and an orgy of crudity."[80] These complaints about the mistreatment of historic artifacts were countered by the observation that there was not much of value left. Indeed, the castle had suffered from neglect in the last decades of Habsburg rule. For one of the first state dinners, the staff had to haul china and silver across town from Prague's Municipal House.[81]

Beyond the need to update the castle buildings, planners and preservationists alike recognized that the ancient citadel demanded restoration as a landmark. Prague Castle does not look much like a castle, if we are thinking of a fortress with walls, crenellations, and turrets. It began as a hilltop fortress for the dukes of Bohemia, and some of its ancient walls and towers are still present, integrated with—and even enveloped within—the buildings we see today. Over the centuries, an amalgamation of structures was built within and around the fortress, in a variety of architectural styles, from the medieval Romanesque and Gothic, through the Renaissance and baroque, to the neoclassical. It is a unique architectural monument, something that Czech histori-

---

80 Karel Herain, "Světla a stína" [Light and shadow], *České slovo*, 30 December 1919, collected in clippings file, APH KPR, SV, box 12, folder 370.

81 The various mistreatments of the Prague Castle, including supposed acts of vandalism, are discussed in the Presidential Office Memorandum of 20 February 1920, APH KPR, SV, box 12, folder 370.

ans and preservationists stressed in their discussions about its future.[82] Even more than that, the castle was a captivating presence above the capital. As one commentator wrote in the daily *České slovo*:

> The castle does not consist solely of the courtyards and surrounding district. It is not only the presidential seat. The entire mass rises from the silence, from the smoking chimneys. Its windows, opening toward the morning sun and glimmering in the evening haze above the Vltava, reflect the daily lives of the people. Breathing with ordinary life, housing the work of the first citizen of the republic, Hradčany has ceased to be a myth, a fable. It is pleasure to look at the castle early in the morning, when it is rousing to life, its chimneys puffing greetings to Prague like a neighbor, and know that once again, inside, the feelings and fears of the people, their joys and concerns, are being considered, that work is being done, and that a democratic, governing care for the state and nation is flowing.[83]

Given the castle's symbolic importance, restoration work required connecting the citadel's past to its new role as the focal point of the republic. As one art historian stated in a meeting about the castle's future: "Its building is complete. There is only adaptation left to do in the future. But for this future, Prague Castle is the cornerstone, not only in terms of construction, but also in terms of philosophy, culture, and politics." Therefore, the work on the castle had to be conducted with diligence and careful attention. "It is the task of our times that [the castle] be watched over, guarded, with a sharp eye, mindful of both the distant past and the future, which will again be—God willing—bright and glorious."[84]

---

82 On the condition of Prague Castle at the time of independence, debates surrounding its renovation, and the appointment of Plečnik, see Malá, "The Castle Architect," 123–31. Güllendi-Cimprichová discusses renovation work at the castle before and after 1918 and the appointment of Plečnik in "Architekt Josip Plečnik und seine Unternehmungen in Prag," 70–9 and 120–25.

83 Herain, "Světla a stína."

84 Opening remarks by Prof. Dr. Karel Chytil, from the meeting of 5 December 1919, in memorandum presented by the Kruh pro pěstování dějin umění to the President's Office, 19 February 1920, APH KPR, SV, box 20, folder 175.

Although they agreed on the need for renovations, Czech architects, preservationists, and government officials had to find a common approach as to how to carry them out. Initially, in the first months of independence, different architects worked on different parts of the castle. For instance, Jan Kotěra, now respected as Prague's foremost architect, was commissioned to design the presidential apartments. By the end of 1919, however, it was apparent that this use of multiple designers would not work. At a meeting of architects, academics, and preservationists in December 1919, the suggestion that a single person take responsibility for the renovation project was met with applause. "The castle, in itself, is a significant whole, and for that reason it is necessary that one person oversee it," declared one architect, to general approval. In the following weeks, deputations of architects, artists, and academy professors brought this suggestion to the president's office. And they all proposed one man capable of the task: Jože Plečnik.[85]

Plečnik had spent the war years in Prague, despite his nagging discontentment and loneliness. He still had students at the School of Industrial Arts, although some were drafted into military service. The war had not been productive for Plečnik as an architect. His only steady work was designing chalices for Catholic priests. Nevertheless, his reputation continued to grow. Immediately after the war, he was invited to submit a design for a major new church in Prague. Meanwhile, the founders of the University of Ljubljana, opened in 1919, attempted to lure him to the new school's department of architecture. Rumors arose that Plečnik would leave Prague to join the faculty. The first group of architecture students in Ljubljana made a direct, dramatic appeal to the respected architect: "A small number of us have gathered in anticipation of a master to show us the correct path, since our spirits thirst for art and for a strong will to lead us." The students

---

85　The president's chief of staff, Přemysl Šamal, also claimed a hand in finding Plečnik. Writing in recognition of Plečnik's birthday, he wrote how he heard of the architect from a former classmate who was teaching at the School of Industrial Arts. Šamal, note of 23 January 1932, attached to newspaper clippings on Plečnik's birthday, AKPR folder T 49/23. Plečnik's involvement in the castle project is described in depth in the two biographies of the architect: Prelovšek, *Jože Plečnik: Architectura perennis*, chapter four; and Krečič, *Jože Plečnik*, 94–131. Essays in the catalog to a 1996 Prague exhibition on Plečnik's architecture are also valuable, particularly Prelovšek, "Ideological Substratum in Plečnik's Work," and Malá, "The Castle Architect and the Castle Building Project."

FIGURE 4.4. Jože Plečnik, 1925. Jože Plečnik Collection,
Museums and Galleries of Ljubljana, Slovenia.

played to Plečnik's sense of patriotism, writing that they would have to
go abroad, to schools outside of Slovenia, if he did not come to be their
teacher. "We ask you, Professor, be our master here at home."[86] The
appeal worked. Even though he recognized that his artistic horizons
would be limited in Ljubljana, with its population of roughly 60,000
people, Plečnik was devoted to his homeland. In addition, he had personal reasons for wanting a move: Plečnik had stumbled into a ro-
mance with a woman in Prague, and he saw the job in another country
as a convenient escape. He accepted the offer from Ljubljana and gave
his first lectures at the new university in fall 1921.[87]

---

86 Letter of students of the Architectural School of Ljubljana, written by Dragotin Fatur to Plečnik, 18
    July 1920, PC MGL.
87 Krečič, *Jože Plečnik*, 95–7.

FIGURE 4.5. Alice Masaryková, 1921. Jože Plečnik Collection,
Museums and Galleries of Ljubljana, Slovenia.

At the same time, however, Plečnik was drawn to the commission
from President Masaryk. In the months of drawn-out negotiations
with the University of Ljubljana, Plečnik completed his first project for
the president. In the spring of 1920 he was commissioned to direct the
repair and updating of the estate at Lány. The government had purchased the chateau in this town some twenty miles west of Prague to
serve as a country retreat for the president.[88] The architect's work in
renovating the chateau and its gardens impressed Masaryk. Arriving
there in August 1921, after a summer holiday in Capri, the president
immediately felt at home, and he resolved that Plečnik would be entrusted with the entire castle project.[89] Ostensibly, Plečnik was to

---

88 Krajčí, "Lány."
89 See letters of Alice Masaryková to Plečnik, 14 August 1921, 1 December 1921, 11 May 1922, and 22
    December 1922, PC MGL.

present his designs to an oversight committee, composed of the castle's physical plant administration, art historians, and other designers. In practice, though, Plečnik was responsible only to Masaryk and to the president's personal liaison, his daughter Alice.

Alice Masaryková was initially wary of this relatively unknown professor. In her first letters to the architect, mistakenly addressed to "Jan Plečnik," she sounded out his views and acknowledged her own apprehensions. She admitted to accepting rumors that he was some advocate of the neo-Gothic style—in other words, a low-talent historicist. But the pace of the letters quickened in spring 1921. While we do not have copies of Plečnik's replies, or any record of their conversations in the castle's hallways or at the construction site, we see from her surviving letters that Masaryková found in Plečnik a master artist and a man of profound spirituality. Already in her first letters of 1921, she plotted out a shared faith, writing out favorite passages of scripture, assuring him of her prayers, and thanking him for his "sincere and unsentimental, strong friendship."[90]

Masaryková's letters did address the mundane matters of a major reconstruction project: the position of the toilet in the presidential water closet, the design of wallpaper and color of paint, the disposition of the servants' quarters. But as with Masaryk's view of the republic and Masaryková's vision for the Red Cross, the practical was always connected to the ideal. Instructions about specific details in the building turned promptly to lofty pronouncements on art and religion, to the grand importance of the castle project in the building of Czechoslovakia and the reshaping of Europe. Masaryková often drew parallels between her responsibility for the castle and her leadership of the Red Cross. Her work in social welfare and public health had the potential to improve people's physical and moral health. Likewise, she claimed, the castle would have transformative power, breaking people from their "small-spiritedness."[91] She saw Plečnik's work at the castle as vital to the reshaping of the Czechs, indeed all Slavs of East Central Europe, into a democratic people. The citadel had to demonstrate a uni-

---

90 Masaryková to Plečnik, 23 May 1921, PC MGL. Translation by Wilma Iggers.
91 Masaryková to Plečnik, May 1921 and May 1922, PC MGL.

fying ideal, a harmonious order that modeled the organization of the state. Of course, this ideal was Masaryk's vision of democracy, of a citizenry working together in reciprocal love and awareness of the eternal. The president's daughter saw the castle as a physical representation of those principles. It was necessary, she wrote to Plečnik, to have "the spirit of the founder of the Czechoslovak Republic speak in stone."[92] The architect would shape the stones of the castle according to his artistic vision, and those stones then would shape people.[93]

Alice Masaryková saw the castle through a prism of truth and beauty, self-sacrifice and love, just as she had assessed her life while in prison during the war and as she understood her tasks with the Red Cross. Essential to this perspective was a sense of the eternal. In her letters to Plečnik, Masaryková insisted upon the sacredness of the castle and the architect's duty to God. From the start of their correspondence, Masaryková described the castle as a project of sacral architecture. The castle was, in her words, a "holy Acropolis," a "sacred precinct," and the "Fortress of the mighty God."[94] As a sacred space, like the hilltop citadels of the ancient world, the castle was a site of communication between the earthly realm—politics, art, social work—and the eternal realm. In part, the aesthetic accomplishment of Plečnik's architecture offered this link to the divine. "Beauty is a manifestation of genuine truthfulness and love to God and man," Masaryková wrote. "Everywhere God touches—is Beauty."[95] Even the material Plečnik used for the construction had spiritual quality. Masaryková shared with the architect a belief in the invisible connected to the visible, the eternal and spiritual present in the immediate and material. Both humanity *and* the matter of the earth existed in God.

In encouraging Plečnik toward his task, the building of a sacred acropolis, Alice Masaryková enclosed with her letters a variety of inspirational materials: postcards of the classical ruins of the Mediterranean

---

92 Masaryková to Plečnik, May 1922, PC MGL.

93 Masaryková to Plečnik, 1 October 1922, PC MGL. See also Masaryková's letters dated 11 November 1921, 25 May 1922, 7 March 1923, 25 March 1923, and 9 April 1923.

94 Masaryková to Plečnik, 22 August 1922, 28 September 1924, and 12 December 1925, PC MGL. See the discussion of Masaryková's religious beliefs as an influence on her views of the castle, in Žantovská-Murray, "'Our Slav Acropolis,'" 179.

95 Masaryková to Plečnik, 31 December 1931, PC MGL.

and the wooden churches of Slovakia, devotional poems, her mother's letters, pages of Augustine's *Confessions*, and passages of scripture, from an entire volume of Mark's Gospel to quotations of the prophets. Enclosed with one letter, posted in February 1923, were several pages torn from a Czech-language pocket Bible: Psalms 120–134, the Psalms of Ascents. The verses that Masaryková underlined indicated her understanding of the castle project as a work of spiritual meaning, even associating the Prague citadel with Jerusalem. Her red pencil pointed to the ultimate goal of the architect: "Unless the Lord builds the house, those who build it labor in vain. Unless the Lord watches over the city, the watchman stays awake in vain."[96] Masaryková maintained that only with awareness of the eternal would the president's house, the city below, and the republic be brought into order. And just as independent Czechoslovakia was the central point in the new, postwar Europe, so too did Prague Castle have far-reaching significance. In 1922, after the first fruits of Plečnik's work were evident, Masaryková wrote to the architect of the project's true scope. As she wandered through the castle and its gardens, she felt "a closeness to God." She looked at the castle and thought of Prague. "And as I think of Prague, I can see in a flash a tiny village in the Carpathian Mountains and I remember the Republic— and as I think of the Republic, I suddenly understand how we carry ourselves through the cosmos—and I hear the words of Genesis: 'Let there be lights in the firmament of the heavens to separate the day from the night; and let them be for signs and for seasons and for days and years.'"[97]

For Masaryková, Plečnik was more than a master architect: he was a spiritual confidante (and, most likely, the object of romantic affection).[98] But the question arises: why did Tomáš Masaryk, an inveterate critic of the Roman Catholic Church who had few active Catholics in his close circle, rely upon this devout Catholic architect to complete the renovations of Prague Castle? Although Masaryk indicated no personal relationship with Plečnik, it is likely that he, like his

---

96 The underlined passage is Psalm 127:1. Enclosure with Masaryková to Plečnik, 11 February 1923, PC MGL.

97 The quotation is from Genesis 1:14. Masaryková to Plečnik, 1 October 1922, PC MGL. English translation in Žantovská-Murray, "Our Slav Acropolis,'" 213.

98 Dagmar Hájková, the leading Czech scholar of the Masaryk family, gleans from Masaryková's correspondence that they shared a kiss—once.

daughter, recognized in Plečnik something of a kindred spirit. "He understands you with the experienced wisdom of his age and with the immediacy of a boy from Moravian Slovakia," Alice Masaryková confided to the architect. Like Masaryk, Plečnik had a deep reverence for the ancients. Both men sought a synthesis of contemporary solutions and timeless truths as a remedy to the tumult of the age. Perhaps most importantly, Masaryk recognized Plečnik as a man of incorruptible morals, of asceticism and discipline, of unshakeable morality. As the president expressed to his daughter, Plečnik was qualified to be the castle architect not only in terms of his technical and organizational abilities, but "in character, too."[99]

Above all, Masaryk was convinced that Plečnik was an architect of unique talent and the only person capable of directing the castle renovations. The president demonstrated this faith in his repeated interventions to remove bureaucratic obstacles from Plečnik's work and to prevent him from leaving for good to Ljubljana. After Plečnik took the professorship in Slovenia in 1921, he moved into the house that he had purchased there years earlier. He returned to Prague only during school holidays—a few weeks in the fall and winter, and a month or so in the summer. Many of these visits ended with his abrupt departure. Plečnik was a man of firm convictions, especially in regard to art, but he was averse to any confrontation. His typical means of coping with obstacles and stress was to flee. Meetings with the advisory committee, to which Plečnik was supposedly responsible, left the architect "very irritable" and "embittered," in the words of one castle official.[100] On one occasion Plečnik fumed when the construction supervisor altered his plans. But Plečnik did not want to imperil the man's job, so he simply packed his bags and returned to Ljubljana.[101] In another instance he left in a huff when asked to pick furniture for the estate at Lány.[102] Plečnik's assistant at the castle, a former student named Otto

---

99 Masaryková to Plečnik, 11 June 1922, PC MGL. Translation by Wilma Iggers.

100 František Blažek, note of 30 March 1922, to memorandum of 21 March 1922, MÚA AV ČR, TGM Collection, Republika, box 370, folder 10.

101 Přemysl Šámal, memorandum of 12 January 1923, AKPR, folder T 49/23.

102 František Blažek, notes of 27 August 1922, MÚA AV ČR, TGM Collection, Republika, box 370, envelope 10.

Rothmayer, was often responsible for ferreting out the reasons for the master's departures. In one instance, Rothmayer found Plečnik packing his bags in his simple room in the castle. "When will you be back?" Rothmayer asked. "I don't know," Plečnik replied. "Maybe in a month—or who knows when."[103]

On all of these occasions Masaryk called upon his staff to lure the touchy architect back to Prague. There were people at the castle "prepared to fulfill every wish that you imagine," declared the president's chief of staff in one letter to Plečnik. "The entire project must be yours, all of it yours!"[104] Masaryk repeatedly confirmed Plečnik's full authority over the project. "I insist that no one, for any reason, will disrupt Prof. Plečnik in his work during his stay here," he ordered his office.[105] The president himself appealed to Plečnik. The work at the castle was historic, he wrote to the architect. "If some castle bureaucrat inconveniences you with his shortsightedness and lack of understanding, don't pass over it as if it does not matter," Masaryk instructed. "You have my full trust and gratitude."[106] Along with that trust and gratitude Masaryk also offered Plečnik a rank within the civil service, the freedom to bring his best students from Ljubljana to work alongside him, and a generous honorarium, paid from the humanitarian fund. He even pressed the Academy of Arts in Prague to offer the Slovene a full professorship. When the faculty stalled, saying that they had to follow the proper appointment channels, the president instructed his chief of staff to visit the academy and expedite the process. Tell "those stupid babblers," Masaryk instructed, that Plečnik "is a master and the usual bureaucratic formulas ... do not apply."[107]

Plečnik did not accept the professorship or the money. He even refused to accept his salary. Still, he returned to Prague year after year. For all his threats to leave, the architect was captivated. First of all, he had great respect for Masaryk. Plečnik was aware of Masaryk's unorth-

103 František Blažek, memorandum of 6 September 1924, AKPR, folder T 49/23.

104 Přemysl Šámal, memorandum of 12 January 1923, AKPR, folder T 49/23.

105 Přemysl Šámal, record of meeting with TGM, 14 February 1925, AKPR, folder T 49/23.

106 Masaryk to Plečnik, 29 March 1923, AKPR, folder T 3917/32.

107 Confidential note, written by Kučera, on memorandum of Šámal to Masaryk, 9 June 1923, AKPR, folder T 49/23.

odox religious ideas. Nevertheless, he regarded the president as "a great, profound philosopher."[108] He described Masaryk to his students in Ljubljana as someone who was on higher plane, an aristocrat. "We cannot live without an aristocracy," he said. "I'm not thinking of dukes and barons, but an aristocracy of the spirit."[109] As for the work itself, Plečnik welcomed an assignment that required "big ideas."[110] The castle project was varied and challenging, and the architect was absorbed. He researched the buildings and grounds, then drew and redrew and drew again. The autonomy that Masaryk granted him suited a man of Plečnik's conviction and disposition. He was, on the one hand, certain of his own artistic vision. At the same time, he was wholly aware of the historic significance of the castle complex. The ancient citadel demanded profound respect and deliberation. His measured pace frustrated officials and construction supervisors, but the architect insisted on its necessity. In April 1923 the director of the castle's administration asked Plečnik for his estimate of the following year's budget. In previous years, the construction office had budgeted five million crowns for the work (roughly $147,000 at the time). The director wondered if they should request more, maybe seven or even ten million crowns. No, Plečnik replied, five million was enough. He then gave his reasons:

> The castle is not an American skyscraper, or a tenement house, or the villa of some industrialist. Therefore, the architect must decide on the execution of individual adaptations, not to mention the artistic details, very cautiously and after due consideration. Certainly, we could use ten million crowns, if necessary. But how? The matter would not be thought through. It would not be appreciated. It would not be refined. We would not commit our work to the castle. And so, not only would we not benefit the castle, we would outright ruin it. We cannot forget that we are not building things at the castle for the needs of the next two or five years. We are building for the distant future, in a place that is uniquely prominent, and historically and

108 Lenarčič, *Plečnik: Spomini na Plečnika*, 22–3.
109 Grabrijan, *Plečnik in njegova šola*, 83.
110 Memo of conversation with Otto Rothmayer (unsigned, presumably written by Blažek), 30 August 1922, MÚA AV ČR, TGM Collection, Republika, box 370, folder 10.

architecturally dear to everyone. If I can advise you then: Please, do not rush these renovations. Please, leave me and the others enough time. Only then will it be possible to accomplish a good work.[111]

Conclusion

"He has enough savvy to understand what's at stake," Tomáš Masaryk said of Plečnik, in a conversation with his daughter. "We don't have to explain it to him."[112] For Masaryk father and daughter, there was a great deal at stake at the castle. The renovation was more than a public-works project: the castle reborn was to be a lasting legacy of Masaryk's presidency. In addresses to parliament and his memoirs, the president declared his vision for the castle. And in his testament, signed in April 1925, Masaryk declared his wish for Plečnik to complete the renovations of the castle, its gardens, and the surrounding district after his death. He even instructed that Plečnik would design his tomb. "The nation views the castle as a national matter," he wrote. "Therefore, the transformation of a castle conceived and established under a monarchy to a democratic castle must have the attention not only of presidents but also of the government."[113] But the castle was more than a symbol of democracy. It was an artistic, material expression of the republic's founding principles. In its harmony, its evocation of the classical, the contemporary and the sacred, the castle was to be a physical statement of Masaryk's philosophy, of *humanita* and *sub specie aeternitatis*. The castle, the republic, and the president were linked. As Alice Masaryková reassured her father: "Our house will be in such order as you wish to have for the whole republic."[114]

Czechoslovakia was a beacon of democracy in the new Europe that emerged after the Great War. Or so went the official line. Historians have shown that the picture of interwar Czechoslovakia as a model democracy was deliberately conceived by the government in Prague and

---

111 František Blažek, record of conversation with Plečnik, 20 April 1923, AKPR, folder T 23/21, part II, box 19.

112 Masaryková to Plečnik, 9 April 1923, PC MGL. Translation by Wilma Iggers.

113 Testament of President Masaryk, 20 April 1925, copy in PC MGL.

114 AGM to TGM, 8 October 1925, MÚA AV ČR, TGM Collection, Republika, box 371, folder 11.

promoted at home and abroad. This rhetoric covered a number of blemishes in the emerging state: constraints imposed by managed democracy, the chauvinism of Czech nationalism, even the artifice of Masaryk's leadership cult. But for Masaryk himself and his daughter Alice, the ideals of the Czechoslovak Republic were not simply a political slogan. As Robert Bellah wrote of the American founders and the beliefs and symbols that they shaped, "The civil religion expressed what those who set the precedents felt was appropriate under the circumstances. It reflected their private as well as public views."[115] Likewise, Tomáš and Alice Masaryk believed that their work fulfilled the purposes of Providence. Czechoslovakia would be a new kind of political association, one that would open a new era in human history. And the seat of the republic's authority, Prague Castle, would be an aesthetic expression of those God-ordained ideals. Like the acropolis of classical Athens or Jerusalem of the Psalms, the castle would be a meeting point of the sacred and earthly, the religious and the political, the wisdom of the republic's founder and the measure of eternity. The castle would inspire and instruct the republic's citizens and, beyond that, the people of Europe.

It is easy to scoff at the idealism of the Masaryks, with their talk of a "new Adam" and a "fortress of the mighty God." At the least, we can file the president and his daughter among the dreamers of the early twentieth century who conjured far-reaching schemes of political and social renewal. But the Masaryks did act on their beliefs, in ways that contributed to the real improvement of people's lives in Czechoslovakia. For example, we can acknowledge the positive effects that Masaryk's humanitarian gifts produced. Yes, a lot of money from the president's fund went to political allies or family and friends. Nonetheless, these spurious gifts do not erase the fact that a sitting president gave leftover political donations to children's hospitals, homes for the disabled, local cultural groups, and even professors seeking book subventions. Even more impressive was the work of the Red Cross under Alice Masaryková. Already in 1920, more than 200,000 people were serving as Red Cross volunteers. In its first three years of operation, the Red Cross administered more than 14,000 smallpox vaccina-

---

115 Bellah, "Civil Religion in America," 8.

tions in the Těšín region on the Czech-Polish border, provided for some 2,500 children suffering from tuberculosis to recover at sanitaria in Switzerland, and opened thirty-one child welfare centers in Slovakia and Ruthenia. The Red Cross also steered the efforts of volunteers to problems outside the country, establishing the new state's reputation as a contributor to the international aid community. In one campaign, students in more than 2,000 schools across the country collected food and money for children suffering from famine conditions in Soviet Russia.[116] The efforts of the Red Cross also contributed to advances in public health and welfare in Czechoslovakia. By the early 1930s, marked improvements were shown in rates of infant mortality and tuberculosis infection, and the overall death rate declined, with a corresponding rise in the average life expectancy.[117]

For decades, historians have criticized the high ideals of the Masarykian republic as illusory. The first Czechoslovakia is widely described as deeply flawed, even as a failed state.[118] More recently, our view of Tomáš Masaryk has also been revised. We now know that the president exercised cunning just as often as conviction in leading the republic. But we should not confuse political tactics with cynical politics. Masaryk believed fully in the ideals he expressed for the Czechoslovak state and the role that the republic was to play in Europe. This vision was entrenched in his personal religious philosophy. Alice Masaryková likewise held earnestly to her father's ideals, and she helped bring real benefit to people's lives by putting those ideals into practice with the Red Cross. And we can say that Jože Plečnik also believed in Masaryk's vision and the mission of Czechoslovakia in Europe. Slovenia was his home, but the architect professed greater admiration and loyalty to the noble man in the Prague Castle than to the Yugoslav king in Belgrade.

---

116 Lovči, *Alice Garrigue Masaryková*, 293–97. Masaryková's advocacy for the Russian and Ukrainian populations, including appeals for support at international conferences, earned her criticism from the conservative press in Czechoslovakia.

117 For a summary of the public health situation through 1926, see League of Nations Health Organization, *Official Vital Statistics of the Republic of Czechoslovakia*, 62–3. On the progress made by the early 1930s, see Klimek, *Velké dějiny zemí Koruny české*, 14:89–90.

118 Mary Heimann's synthetic history of twentieth-century Czechoslovakia makes this latter judgment in its title: *Czechoslovakia: The State that Failed.*

Masaryk's ideals did prompt people outside the castle to act, to set themselves to the kind of work for others that he always regarded as the essence of democracy. One of these was a young man who visited Prague Castle in 1920, as part of a group of university students. The president spoke to the students and other visitors about his wish that people of every walk of life would commit themselves, in cooperation, to the development of the state. He explained the ideals of *sub specie aeternitatis*, of eternity as a guide and measure for the work of building a democratic society, and of a republic founded upon morality. The young man returned to his dormitory, his head full of ideas and plans. He talked with friends about the president's charge. Quickly, a circle of like-minded students grew, from universities and gymnasia throughout Prague, both young men and women. They called themselves the Student Revival Movement. They held meetings in dormitories, organized conferences in cities and towns across the Czech Lands, and with support from the government, the group's leaders attended international student meetings in Europe and even the United States. The young man who sparked the movement, named Václav Maria Havel, later became one of the most successful entrepreneurs in interwar Prague, but he remained committed to working with students. Writing decades later, the father of the future Czech president described this activity with young people as his contribution to furthering the ideals of the first president. In his memoirs, the elder Havel recalled a speech he gave to fellow students in a small Moravian town. With his training in engineering, Havel's speech brimmed with construction metaphors. But at its core was Masaryk's vision, which he had adopted as his own after that audience at the castle: "We are constructing a building. We are constructing a better future... We want our nation as well as all of humanity to be made better. We want the world to recognize Love. We want a magnanimous spirit to govern the world. We want the true kingdom of God on earth. And for this we want to fight!"[119]

---

119 Havel, *Mé vzpomínky*, 135–36. On Havel's audience at the castle and the beginnings of the Student Revival Movement, see 128–31.

Chapter Five

The Moral Republic and Its Discontents

Masaryk's vision of Czechoslovakia as a moral republic earned accolades abroad. The philosopher-turned-president became a symbol of the transformation of Europe, much like the playwright and dissident Václav Havel did decades later after becoming president in 1989. Already in 1921, for instance, a *New York Times* editorial spoke highly of the benefits of Masaryk's "wise guidance," which had brought a measure of development and "righteous living comparable with that of our most highly developed States."[1] Masaryk and his trusted accomplice Edvard Beneš were adept in promoting this image of the president as a wise leader and the republic as a developed and democratic state. But behind the rhetoric were deep political divisions in the new state. After each of the First Republic's four parliamentary elections, there were fifteen or sixteen different parties holding seats in the assembly. The Communist Party was consistently among the top parties in gaining votes (usually gaining ten percent of the vote), even though it stood for overthrow of the republic; a smaller fascist party, led by a former general, opposed the state from the Right and launched a failed coup in 1933. Meanwhile, nationalist parties demanding autonomy for the country's Slovaks and Germans also held seats in the assembly. In order to maintain stable government, the president and a small group of political elites, nearly all Czech, managed the administration of the state under the guise of democracy. The leaders of the leading parties (excluding the Communists, Germans, and Slovaks)

---

1   *New York Times*, editorial, 1 November 1921.

worked together as the Five (*Pětka*) to direct the agenda of parliament, while the president and his supporters sought to influence the cabinet and assembly—or circumvent them. As these internal maneuvers played out, Beneš orchestrated a foreign policy that brought a tenuous promise of security and long-term survival—a promise that proved to be illusory.

Czechoslovakia did not survive. In autumn 1938, the republic's borderlands were sheared off by the Munich Agreement and the Vienna Award, and the state came to an end a few months later, in March 1939, with the German occupation of the Czech Lands and the declaration of independent Slovakia. Historians now attribute the First Republic's demise as much to its fractious domestic politics as to the menacing external forces that emerged in 1930s Europe.[2] As some scholars have pointed out, a key factor in this internal dissonance was an ambiguous definition of democracy in the Czechoslovak state and a wariness of democratic practices. Peter Bugge observes that the mainly Czech political elites in the republic saw to it that "democracy did not come to mean popular rule in any literal sense," at the national and the local levels.[3] Of course, Masaryk's practice as president—his preference for a managed democracy led by moral and intellectual elites—contributed to this weakening of the state's institutions. But we must also ask how Masaryk's ideas, his moral and religious program, played into the uncertain function of democracy in Czechoslovakia and the frailty of the interwar state. As we have seen, from the start of his presidency Masaryk intended the republic to be about more than politics—Czechoslovakia was founded, in his view, on moral principles. Yet, however noble these ideals were, the revolution that Masaryk proclaimed did not take place. Why not?

One cause for the failure of Masaryk's program for the republic is that his ideas—*humanita* and *sub specie aeternitatis* and "Jesus, not Caesar" and a "new Adam"—were simply too far-flung. Historian Roman Szporluk and philosopher Roger Scruton both argue that Masaryk failed to translate his universalist moral and religious philosophy into a

---

2   The title of Mary Heimann's chapter on the First Republic is telling: "A Troubled Democracy." Heimann, *Czechoslovakia: The State that Failed.*

3   Bugge, "Czech Democracy," 26.

functioning program for a particular nation-state.[4] Whether due to lack of patience or ability, Masaryk the moral and political thinker did not write plans for lasting institutions. At the same time, the president's supporters who engaged in the day-to-day work of building the republic promoted incomplete variations on his philosophy. Certainly, there were young Czechs like Václav Havel's father who committed themselves to Masaryk's vision for their state. But the president's vision was ambiguous. Even in the network of his closest supporters, his mix of moral, religious, and political ideals was subject to a range of interpretations.

Masaryk's political-moral philosophy also had its critics. The two most prominent Protestant thinkers of the time, philosopher Emanuel Rádl and theologian Josef Lukl Hromádka, counted themselves as solid followers of Masaryk. They blamed the president's liberal supporters for failing to understand and adhere to his ideas for the state. At the same time, however, they pointed out flaws in those ideas. In their view, this faithful yet critical respect for Masaryk's philosophy was the correct approach, in contrast to the empty slogans and distortions they saw in Czech political life. On the other hand, intellectuals who identified with the Catholic Church found it hard to embrace the ideas of a man who had been a notorious critic of their faith. One Catholic writer in particular, novelist and essayist Jaroslav Durych, raised the banner of opposition against a republic he saw as an intractable foe to the Church. Although Durych also condemned Czech Protestantism, he judged Czechoslovakia from a similar position as Rádl and Hromádka: for them, the failings of the state were matters of faith, truth, and a turning away from God.

Critics of Masaryk, whether Catholic or communist, had to be careful. Czechoslovak law treated attacks on the president as treason, and Masaryk's unique stature wrapped him in a special layer of protection. Critiques had to be disguised or indirect. One object associated with the president that critics used as a proxy target was the renovation of Prague Castle. Today, Jože Plečnik's work at the castle is cele-

---

4   Scruton, "Masaryk, Kant, and the Czech Experience," 56–7; and Szporluk, *Political Thought of Thomas Masaryk*, 156–57 and 160–61.

brated as an integral part of Prague's landscape. At the time of the construction, however, Plečnik's plans were met with attacks from the political Right and Left, nationalists who objected to a foreigner working on the symbol of Czech independence, and preservationists who saw the architect as defiling a historical landmark. With the president himself sealed from attack, the castle became a representative of his power and the secular, liberal democracy he endorsed. Alice Masaryková was correct in imagining the castle as the architectural expression of her father's ideals. What she did not expect was that many Czechs would oppose those ideals and their embodiment in the castle.

Dissonant Voices in the Castle

In the years that work crews occupied Hradčany, bringing Jože Plečnik's plans into form, another castle spread its shadow over Prague and the Czechoslovak Republic. In the 1920s the term "Castle" (*Hrad*) was used to describe the network of supporters who promoted President Masaryk's political agenda. Contemporary observers (typically the president's opponents) and historians of the interwar republic recognized this wide-reaching association—officials in the ministries, members of parliament, bankers and industrialists, publishers and editors, writers and academics—as a powerful network of political influence.[5] Its members courted new allies, isolated foes, gathered information, and wrote books and articles that promoted the president and his policies.

Much attention on this network has focused on its influence on political issues of the day, on domestic and foreign policies, the composition of cabinets, and the question of Masaryk's successor as president. But the Castle cannot be viewed simply as a political alliance. Given Masaryk's own preoccupation with matters of culture, it is appropriate to view the Castle also as an intellectual network, an association that conducted its business in ideas, not just political maneuvering. Only recently have we come to understand the Castle's part in advancing the cult of Masaryk and enshrining his interpretation of Czech histo-

---

5 On the Castle, its personnel, and its functions, see Orzoff, *Battle for the Castle*, chapter two; and Klimek, *Boj o Hrad*, vol. 1, chapter ten.

ry as the official national narrative.[6] Indeed, this was the mortar that held the Castle together. The Castle had a big roof, incorporating people of different professions and political persuasions. But these men were not linked by a common institutional structure, formal meetings, or membership requirements.[7] To be sure, religious adherence also had no role in connecting them.[8] What held them together was reverence for the man at its center—or actually, for his image as the wise and stately ruler, the philosopher who liberated his nation. We can ask then: If the members of the Castle were linked by a shared belief in Masaryk, did they also accept *his* beliefs? Did the intellectuals, officials, and businessmen of the Castle share Masaryk's concern with developing the morality of a democratic people? Did they accept his conviction that attention to religion was necessary for building the republic? And if the castle standing above Prague was to be an architectural embodiment of Masaryk's moral and political philosophy, how then did the metaphorical Castle, as network of political and cultural elites, comprehend and communicate his ideas?

The Castle included men who had long been disciples of Professor Masaryk, who fully accepted and followed his teachings on religion and the ethical life. Among these was Vasil Kaprálek Škrach, the president's librarian and literary secretary. Škrach had studied philosophy under Masaryk in the years just before the war and was involved in causes endorsed by his professor, such as the student antialcohol organization and the Sociological Section led by Alice Masaryková. The university student became a frequent guest in the Masaryk home, and during the war he often visited Charlotte Masaryková. When he married, he followed Masaryk's example in adopting his wife's family name as his own middle name. Given his connections to the family and his fidelity to Masaryk's ideas, Škrach was a logical choice to serve as guardian of the president's vast body of writings. Working from

---

6   See Orzoff, *Battle for the Castle*, especially chapter three on the Castle's work on defining a standard historical narrative for the nation and the republic. The view of the Castle as an intellectual network or circle also draws from Kadushin, "Networks and Circles in the Production of Culture."

7   For a collective sketch of the Castle's members, see Bachstein, "Die soziologische Struktur der 'Burg.'" See also Bosl, "Der Burgkreis."

8   Firt, "Die 'Burg' aus der Sicht eines Zeitgenossen," 1:98–99. See also Huber, "Die 'Burg' und der Kirchen."

Masaryk's manuscripts, Škrach finished a third volume of *Russia and Europe*, and he edited the journal *Masarykův sborník* (Masaryk's anthology), launched in 1924, which featured commentaries and studies of Masaryk's thought. He also prepared new editions of Masaryk's older books. The order in which they appeared is notable: Masaryk's book on Jan Hus was republished in 1923, his doctoral dissertation on suicide in 1926, and the turn-of-the-century book on the principles of *humanita* in 1930. Škrach's task, as the person responsible for publishing the president's writings, was to ensure that his ideas were communicated to the people of Czechoslovakia. Few people were as familiar with those ideas as was Škrach. Indeed, we can point to him as the Castle's most knowledgeable adherent to Masaryk's philosophy, as well as one of its most committed.[9]

Few of the Castle's intellectuals and politicians, however, shared Škrach's understanding of and adherence to Masaryk's thought. Take for example the central figure of the Castle, apart from the president himself: Masaryk's closest ally overseas during the war, his constant foreign minister, and his eventual successor as head of state, Edvard Beneš. Like Masaryk, Beneš was a man of humble origins who gained advanced education and experience abroad, rising to attain standing as an academic, intellectual, and statesman. Also like Masaryk, Beneš's rationality and moralism led him to a serious, ascetic life. But Beneš differed from Masaryk in that this sober and analytical manner was not leavened with approachability or any sense of common touch. Needless to say, Beneš did not share Masaryk's popularity, among the public or with other politicians. The president's son Jan, who served under Beneš in the diplomatic corps, was characteristically blunt in explaining the lack of goodwill toward the foreign minister and eventual president. "He is such a professor—the disputatious type that has twenty-seven reasons for every fart," Masaryk confided to an assistant. "And he talks through his nose too much."[10]

Beneš also did not share Masaryk's religious convictions. A former Catholic, he had left the Church as a student and adopted a notion of an

---

9   See "Vasil Kaprálek Škrach," in Broklová, *Mám jen knihy a skripta, cenná práce životní*, 76–79.

10   Fischl, *Hovory s Janem Masarykem*, 102.

immanent divinity. He did speak of Providence, which guided human progress, and he understood himself as its instrument. But otherwise, he did not reveal his opinion on religion, perhaps due to the fact that his opinion differed from that of his wife, who held that religion was need-ed for a full, meaningful life.[11] Some read Beneš's silence, coupled with his determined trust in science, as a sign of unbelief. "It is a paradox," one intellectual of the Castle circle remarked, "but it appears to me that Masaryk believes in God while Beneš believes in Masaryk." Or, as one Czech historian observed, "Beneš believed, above all, only in himself."[12]

Although not an explicit atheist, Beneš's view of politics was whol-ly materialist and mechanistic, much different than Masaryk's politi-cal philosophy. Rather than seeing the eternal as the ultimate measure of statecraft, Beneš maintained that matters of policy and administra-tion could be understood scientifically. As foreign minister, Beneš prided himself on his supposedly peerless analytic ability. His ex-changes with other diplomats and politicians, whether in Prague, Par-is, or Geneva, where he was an active participant in the League of Na-tions, were less negotiations than lectures. Masaryk was well aware of this steely, pedantic approach, and he confided to an assistant his wish that Beneš would balance rationalism with poetry.[13] But Beneš could not do poetry. In his hands, Masaryk's vision of a humanitarian poli-tics reads like a cold directive. For example, Beneš offered this expla-nation of his work for Czech independence during the war:

I did not fulfill my national and human duty in the struggle for na-tional independence because I regarded the collective entity of the nation as a factor which is self-sufficing and constitutes an end in itself. I fulfilled this duty simply because I regarded it as a dictate of humanity for every individual just as every collective entity to live without unnecessary restrictions and to develop a national culture. For him who believes in the ideals of humanity, every step, every act, every sentiment is a service to humanity, to the nation, and to the progress of his own individuality at the same time. Such service and

11   Mišovič, *Víra v dějinách zemí koruny české*, 82n10.
12   Klimek, *Boj o Hrad*, 1:94.
13   Gašparíková-Horáková, diary entry of 3 October 1931, in *U Masarykovcov*, 126.

such labour do not await nor demand recognition or reward. They are an end in themselves, giving the individual the maximum of satisfaction and the maximum range for expressing his personality.[14]

In this passage of his memoirs, Beneš did grant some part for religious belief in this merging of humanitarianism and self-actualization. But contrary to Masaryk, he did not hold to belief as the necessary impulse for civic morality. Instead, the foreign minister noted, service to the nation and community was "regularly accompanied and sanctified by religious faith."[15] In other words, religious belief provided additional meaning—for some people—to work for the greater good.

Looking beyond the president's inner circle to the outer wings of the Castle, we see a similar reinterpretation of, or even ambivalence toward, the moral-religious philosophy at the core of Masaryk's politics. Among the broader network of intellectuals, two figures most often identified with the Castle, by both contemporary observers and historians, were journalist Ferdinand Peroutka and writer Karel Čapek. By the early 1920s Čapek had matured from the young writer of the prewar cubists to the foremost literary figure of the new Czechoslovakia. In the 1920s, his dramas were performed in Berlin, London, and New York, and his novels and short stories were translated into several languages. He maintained links with writers and intellectuals across Europe, while at home he enjoyed wide popularity as a prolific contributor to the daily *Lidové noviny* (People's News). Čapek also wrote for the weekly *Přítomnost* (The Present), the influential journal of political and cultural criticism edited by Peroutka. Originally a journalist with the daily *Tribuna*, Peroutka's work brought him to the attention of Masaryk, who invited the twenty-nine-year-old writer to edit the new journal. With a donation of one million crowns from the president's personal fund, *Přítomnost* launched in 1924, becoming the principal herald of Masaryk's politics. Observers of the time recognized Peroutka and Čapek as integral members of the Castle, and both writers supported the president's program. They viewed Masaryk's po-

---

14   Beneš, *My War Memoirs*, 494–95.

15   Ibid.

litical ideas and his stature as the means of establishing a peaceful, progressive, ordered republic, secure from the threats of political extremism.[16] Čapek wrote already in 1920, before he had entered the president's personal circle, that Masaryk's "optimistic faith in human progress and development ... will keep the ship of our young state safe from jolts from the right and the left."[17]

Čapek's support of the president also arose from his concern for civility in a modern, democratic society. Čapek was a moralist, in some ways a conservative. He expressed unease about the boorish, self-centered behavior he observed, not only in politics but also on city streets. He insisted upon "decency" (*slušnost*) as the highest virtue for himself and others. Service to others, trust, respect, cooperation, "ordinary and innate human kindness": these practical, everyday actions offered the solution to contemporary incivility.[18] Čapek valued Masaryk's political philosophy, with its emphasis on small work for the community, as a practical antidote to the pettiness, greed, and selfishness that darkened people's hearts. Yet even though Čapek expressed appreciation for the moral dimension of Masaryk's political philosophy, he did not repeat the president's mantra of democracy as practiced *sub specie aeternitatis*. Čapek did not write of love for one's neighbor, nor did he point to some transcendent truth as the measure of one's actions. As a committed adherent to the Anglo-American philosophy of pragmatism, he rejected any faith, ideology, or philosophy that made claims to universal truth, a position that shaped his journalism as well as his literature.

Čapek took pride in identifying himself as a relativist. His 1920 vignette "Pilate's Creed" best expresses the writer's own creed that claims to absolute truth were not valid in a complex and wonderfully diverse world.[19] The story was part of a series, later collected in the volume titled *Apocryphal Tales*, in which Čapek turned familiar stories from the Bible, classical literature, or history in different directions, perhaps adding a

---

16 On the role of Čapek and Peroutka as Castle intellectuals, see Orzoff, *Battle for the Castle*, 77–82 and 86–8.

17 Čapek, "Víra" [Faith], first published in *Národní listy*, 7 March 1920, appendix to *Hovory s T. G. Masarykem* (1990), 370.

18 For an example of Čapek's indictment of people's internal moral failings, see "O našich špatnostech," first published in *Lidové noviny*, 7 November 1926, republished in *Od člověka k člověku II*, 88–9.

19 Klíma, *Karel Čapek: Life and Work*, 45–6.

coda or looking at a character on the margin. First published in periodicals, many of the stories were commentaries on current events or statements of Čapek's own philosophical positions. In "Pilate's Creed," the writer expanded upon the question Pontius Pilate poses to Jesus in the Gospel of John: What is truth? (18:38). Imagining the meeting of Pilate and Joseph of Arimathea on the evening of Good Friday, Čapek cast the Roman governor in a positive light as he again raises the question of truth to the follower of the crucified Jesus. In response to Joseph's statement that there is "only one truth for all things," Pilate gently maintains that such is the view of a child whose understanding of the world is limited only to what he sees. "The world is a large place, Joseph," Pilate states, "and there is room in it for many things. I think that there is actually room for many truths." As a foreigner, Pilate knows that he cannot judge this land, or any land, as wrong. In the same way, he admits that he cannot judge the teachings of Jesus as wrong. "All countries are right," he states; therefore, "the world has to be terribly wide in order for them all to fit in next to each other." So it is with truths. Pilate explains:

> The world would have to be immensely vast, spacious, and free for each and every actual truth to fit into it. And I think it is, Joseph. When you climb to the top of the high mountains, you see that things somehow blend together and level out into a single plain. Even truths blend together from a certain height. Of course, man does not and cannot live on a mountaintop; it's enough for him if he sees his home or his field close by, both of them filled with truths and such things. There is his true place and sphere of action. But now and then he can look at a mountain or the sky and say to himself that from there his truths and such things still exist and nothing has been stolen from him; rather, they have blended together with something far more free and unbounded that is no longer his property alone.[20]

Joseph is unconvinced, and he charges that Pilate is neither hot nor cold, but lukewarm. Pilate answers that he believes, ardently, that

---

20 Čapek, "Pilate's Creed," *Apocryphal Tales*, 91. Čapek's "Pilátovo krédo" was first published in *Ruch filozofický*, December 1920.

there is truth and that people can recognize it. Not certain people, not he *or* Joseph, but every person has a share of truth. "I believe. Absolutely and unquestionably, I believe," Pilate affirms at the story's end. "But," he asks, "what is truth?"[21]

Čapek identified himself with Pilate in uttering the question, "What is truth?"[22] His skepticism was respectful and healthy, open to a belief in truth. He allowed people the freedom to believe their own truths, as long as those beliefs brought positive results and they were not imposed on others. In contrast, Ferdinand Peroutka tended toward a more provocative skepticism. Peroutka established his reputation as a journalist in the early 1920s with a series of critical articles on Czech culture and identity, later published as a book, *Jací jsme* (What we are like, 1924). Peroutka targeted many of the myths—and mythmakers—at the heart of Czech nationalism. His jabs were piercing. The ideals of Czech patriotism were shallow, with little grounding in reality, he charged. The works of Czech poets, painters, and writers were, for the most part, masterly knockoffs of foreign sources. And the Czechs were not so much descendants of the heroic Hussite warriors as the children of Franz Joseph's dutiful subjects. But the essay's most sustained critique came against the "meaning of Czech history" as defined by Tomáš Masaryk and his supporters. According to Peroutka, this view of Czech history was inaccurate, an example of how Masaryk's tendencies toward "prophet and preacher" could hinder his instincts as a scholar. In touting the legacies of the Czech religious reformers and his Protestant notion of *humanita* as the driving force of Czech development, Masaryk showed himself as more a mystic and romantic than a critic and realist. [23]

According to Peroutka, more important than the Bohemian reformation for the development of modern Czech culture was the influence of Catholicism. "We are a nation," he wrote, "in which there is often displayed a greater dose of sensual growth and verdancy than in Prot-

---

21 Čapek, "Pilate's Creed," 92.

22 See the studies of Čapek's relativism as a feature of his literary writing: Steiner, "Radical Liberalism: *Apocryphal Stories* by Karel Čapek," in *The Deserts of Bohemia*, 69–93; and Thomas, "Humanism and Relativism in Karel Čapek's *Kniha apokryfů*," in *The Labyrinth of the Word*, 116–31.

23 Peroutka, *Jací jsme*, 53–4.

estant nations... It is quite clear that if we have anything to thank for the rejuvenation and stimulation of creativity in this land in the nineteenth century, it is Catholicism."[24] Despite the anticlerical current of the nineteenth-century nationalist movement, its leaders continued to show an intellectual debt to Catholicism. According to Peroutka, even the fiercest critic of the Church in the 1800s, journalist Karel Havlíček, had been a "Catholic atheist." Peroutka charged that Masaryk was misguided in stressing the importance of Czech Protestantism—and religion in general—in contemporary society. "If the tradition of the Czech Brethren was truly alive today in the country, then Masaryk and the nation would be much more similar than they in fact are," he wrote. "Masaryk is only a representative of a resilient minority." In describing how the Czechs were, rather than how Masaryk imagined them to be, Peroutka pointed out that the average Czech knew very little of Hus as a religious thinker. Instead, Hus was a misty figure of the distant past. The Czechs' adherence to Hussitism was "nothing more than a masquerade."[25] Peroutka argued, though, that this religious indifference among the Czechs is what made Masaryk such an extraordinary figure. The president had declared his intent to transform hearts and souls, something that would have been unnecessary amidst an already religious nation. "The religious person represents a revolution and raises an uproar only among a nation that is apathetic, indifferent, uncreative, and inert in its religious instincts," Peroutka observed.[26] As leader of the faithless Czechs, Masaryk was indeed a revolutionary figure.

Given Peroutka's criticism of Masaryk's interpretation of Czech history and culture, his entrance into the president's close circle was remarkable. Peroutka was one of very few journalists to enjoy open access to the president.[27] Like Čapek, he held Masaryk in high esteem, regarding the president as an ideal figure, a man of deeds. At the same time, Peroutka acknowledged that he did not agree with the president on all matters.[28] Identifying himself as part of a new, modern genera-

---

24 Ibid., 57.
25 Ibid., 60.
26 Ibid., 64.
27 Kosatík, *Ferdinand Peroutka*, 87–9.
28 Ibid., 90–1.

tion of Czechs, Peroutka saw Masaryk as the last of the nineteenth-century builders. Whereas Masaryk was fixed upon how things *should* be, Peroutka and his generation sought to assess how things were. Yet for all of Masaryk's idealism, Peroutka saw that the president's ideas and actions were directed toward practical ends. In the eyes of both Peroutka and Čapek, this was Masaryk's great contribution: his attention to daily life, to real problems, to practical solutions. "We recognized that more than beautiful ideas are necessary," Peroutka wrote of his generation, "that our ideas have to be applicable to the person and the state in practice."[29] Masaryk's philosophy and personal example were valuable in their application, with their emphasis on the committed work of the individual citizen in building democracy. The principles at the foundation of his philosophy—consideration of God, the eternal, or the teachings of Jesus—were incidental. What mattered was the practice. "What is religion with Masaryk?" Peroutka asked in a *Přítomnost* essay. "Certainly, it is not like the old religious type. It is not looking upward in adoration and contemplation. It is something else: it provides him the assurance that a man of action needs."[30]

This was a difficult trick for the Castle's intellectuals—to distinguish reverence for Masaryk the exemplary leader from a selective reading of his ideas, to parse the practical thrust of his philosophy from its religious foundations. The selective, even equivocal approach that Peroutka, Čapek, and other Castle intellectuals took toward the president's philosophy was evident in their view of Masaryk's daughter. While members of the Castle revered Tomáš Masaryk, they barely tolerated Alice Masaryková. One of Čapek and Peroutka's literary associates described in his memoirs how Čapek had to suffer the interventions of Masaryk's "puritanical daughter" in his relations with the president. When Čapek began work on his biography of the president in the late 1920s, Masaryková's overprotective devotion to her father prompted repeated (and much-resented) interventions in the writing, aimed at removing anything that would "lower the president from the pedestal upon which she wanted to keep him—at any cost."[31] To oth-

---

29　Quoted in ibid., 91.
30　Peroutka, "Masarykova osobnost III," 225.
31　Firt, *Knihy a Osudy*, 263.

er figures within the president's network of supporters, Masaryková was a naïve idealist, a political meddler with no serious ideas. Although she constantly interfered in matters of the state, both domestic and external, she had, in the judgment of one of Masaryk's staffers, "no ability for any kind of political activity."[32]

Certainly, Alice Masaryková did idolize her father, and she was an idealist—but so was Tomáš Masaryk. Both believed that convictions must be demonstrated in deeds. However, Alice Masaryková's deeds and her practical abilities did not gain the esteem of the Castle's members. The building of the state, as Peroutka titled his later account of the republic's first years, was a story of coalitions and negotiations conducted by Czech politicians, not clinics, immunizations, and health surveys carried out by foreign nurses. The political commentators of the time—like later historians—devoted relatively little attention to issues of public health, social welfare, and international aid in interwar Czechoslovakia. As they fixed on the domestic and international politics of the new state, led by the practical statesman Masaryk, observers neglected and derided the idealism of his daughter. In the view of one official in the presidential chancellery, her invitations for advisers from international organizations "cost us loads of money and served us as well as a square peg in a round hole."[33]

But Alice Masaryková saw any attempt to separate ideals and practice as mistaken. She viewed the Castle's writers with suspicion, not because they threatened to knock her father from his pedestal but because they did not comprehend his ideals. During one meeting at the president's country estate, for example, Masaryková implored Čapek to keep "filth" out of his political writing. In reply, the writer insisted on his loyalty to the president. Masaryková's concern, though, was not political positions. She was mindful of an overarching moral standard. Čapek did not understand this, observed Masaryk's archivist, who witnessed the conversation. Instead, he maintained that his good intentions and literary skill could soothe the wounds from any political sparring. "The decent word of Karel Čapek can have a good echo

---

32 Antonín Schenk, quoted in Klimek, *Boj o Hrad*, 2:232; see also Klimek, *Velké dějiny zemí Koruny české*, 13:239, and 14:25.

33 Jiri Guth-Jarkovsky, quoted in Klimek, *Boj o Hrad*, 1:176.

among the public," he declared.[34] For Alice Masaryková, however, the moral republic demanded more than decency. She understood this as her father's belief as well.

Catholic Intellectuals and the "Culture War"

Throughout his academic and political career prior to the war, Tomáš Masaryk had been a relentless critic of the Roman Catholic Church. Then he became president of a state with an overwhelmingly Catholic population. The first census of the republic, conducted in 1921, found that eighty-two percent of the population in the Czech Lands identified themselves as Catholic. Of course, census figures did not indicate how many of these Catholics practiced their religion, or how deeply they identified with the faith. Many observers of the time, both Catholic and non-Catholic, observed that most Czechs—as opposed to the republic's Germans and Slovaks—had only a nominal affiliation with the Church.[35] The word often used to describe the average Czech's religiosity was "indifferent."

But this generalization of Czech irreligion obscured the fact that Catholic participation was quite strong in regions of Moravia and southeastern Bohemia. The Czech Lands also had an active Catholic literary and intellectual culture. During the interwar decades, there were cultural and devotional journals, newspapers, translations of European Catholic writers, and prose and poetry of varying quality written by clergy and laypeople.[36] From the first days of the new republic, many of these Catholic writers and intellectuals felt themselves thrust into a "culture war," in which they had to defend their rightful place in the nation. On November 3, 1918, only six days after the declaration of independent Czechoslovakia, a troop of firemen from the working-class Žižkov district pulled down a column honoring the Virgin Mary

---

34 Gašparíková-Horáková, diary entry of 27 September 1929, in *U Masarykovcov*, 38.

35 For an overview of religion in Czech society at the start of the republic, see Miškovič, *Víra v dějinách zemí koruny české*, 78–83. See also Šebek, "Die katholische Kirche in der Gesellschaft."

36 Martin Putna's history of Czech Catholic literature during the interwar republic, *Česká katolická litk eratura v kontextech, 1918–1945*, offers a comprehensive account of this large body of writing, from the work of notable authors to small, regional publications.

on Prague's Old Town Square. For the firemen and the crowd that cheered them on, the sixteen-meter baroque column, which had been erected in 1650 to celebrate the defeat of Bohemian Protestants, was a symbol of Habsburg domination. But for Catholic writers and journalists, the toppled column became a defining symbol of the republic: its destruction revealed the depth of anti-Catholic hostility among Czech nationalists, and it was a signal that committed Catholics would be marginalized in their own country. Moreover, the fact that state authorities were powerless to stop this act of vandalism and other anti-Catholic demonstrations showed that the new government would not represent those who identified themselves as both Czech and Catholic.[37] The leaders of the mob went unpunished. One even had parliamentary immunity. He was among many vocal opponents of the Church in the provisional National Assembly and municipal government of Prague in the first years of the new state.

In the view of many Catholic intellectuals, the greatest threat of all was that the government was led by a notorious critic of the church. After taking office, President Masaryk did not speak against Catholicism with the same vehemence as Professor Masaryk had done at the turn of the century. At the same time, though, he did not seek to build bridges. In his first months as president, Masaryk advocated the separation of church and state, and the government took steps to limit Catholic influence in education. Masaryk's interpretation of Czech history, with the Hussite movement and the Unity of the Brethren as high points, now gained official sanction. The Hussite slogan *Pravda vítězí* (The truth prevails) was emblazoned on the presidential flag, and in 1925 the anniversary of Hus's execution, July 6, was established as a national holiday. Masaryk's participation that year in ceremonies marking the first official Jan Hus Day led the papal nuncio in Prague to leave the country in protest, opening a diplomatic breech between Czechoslovakia and the Vatican.[38] For committed Czech Catholics,

---

37 On the toppling of the Marian column and the broader "culture war" (*kulturní boj*) in the early months of the republic, see Paces, *Prague Panoramas*, 87–96; and Putna, *Česká katolická literatura v kontextech, 1918–1945*, 172–84.

38 The diplomatic conflict between the new government in Prague and the Vatican is discussed in Paces, *Prague Panoramas*, 116–28; and Marek, "Das Verhältnis zwischen Staat und Kirchen."

there seemed to be little about the new president and the new republic to secure their approval—except for the fact that he had led the liberation of the nation and the creation of an independent state. Thus they found themselves in a bind: how could they reconcile love of their nation, respect for their leader, and loyalty to their church?[39]

Among Czech Catholic political groups, views of the president ranged from sharply critical to warily accepting. Conservative Catholics, known derisively as "clericals," regularly attacked Masaryk and the secularizing trends of the republic in the pages of their newspaper *Čech*. But they were a small fringe group with little political significance. Larger and more influential was the Czechoslovak People's Party, descendent of the late nineteenth-century Christian Socialist movement in Moravia. Led by the Moravian priest Jan Šrámek, the People's Party took a moderate stance toward the republic: it declared support for Masaryk as president but opposed the separation of church and state and restrictions on the Catholic Church's public activities. The People's Party did not rank among the top parties in terms of voter support (the party's share of the vote dropped from 11 percent in 1920, to 10 percent in 1925, and then 8.4 percent in 1929), but it was able to rally opposition to government measures against the Church. The People's Party was consistently represented in the cabinets of the interwar years. Moreover, Šrámek held a spot in "The Five," the leaders of the main Czech parties who together guided parliament's agenda.[40]

Czech Catholic intellectuals were likewise divided over Masaryk's leadership. The nation's independence was cause for celebration, but they knew well that Masaryk had been a vehement critic of the Church. What would be the place of Czech Catholics in a republic led by Tomáš Masaryk, they asked? Would Czech independence, even in a state opposed to the Church, be beneficial to Catholic citizens? And with national culture dominated by the likes of Čapek and Peroutka—not to

---

39   Martin Schulze Wessel examines loyalty and disloyalty among Czech and German Catholics by looking at the cases of people, including priests, who were charged under the law for "protection of the state," which covered a range of political statements. He finds that among Czech Catholics there was a range of views of the republic, from emphatic approval to moderate opposition. See Schulze Wessel, "Katholik und Staatsbürger?"

40   Putna, *Česká katolická literatura v kontextech, 1918–1945*, 185–92; and Trapl, *Political Catholicism and the Czechoslovak People's Party in Czechoslovakia*, 49–51.

mention Jaroslav Hašek, who mocked Catholicism in his popular novel *The Good Soldier Švejk*—they wondered what their role would be as Czech intellectuals. Would Catholic writers and thinkers contribute in any meaningful way to the culture of the new republic, or would they be consigned to the margins as curiosities and dissidents?[41]

The most prominent and influential Czech Catholic writer of the interwar period took up these questions, and answered them with biting and brilliant criticism of the republic. Jaroslav Durych was a physician and officer in the Czechoslovak army. He was also a prolific and masterly writer of novels, stories, poems, and essays. Even critics who deplored Durych's fervent Catholicism acknowledged that he was among the most accomplished stylists and original voices in Czech letters. He produced literary works that earned wide acclaim and readership, and he penned critical essays that scourged the culture and politics of the day.

From the very founding of Czechoslovakia, Durych was an objector.[42] The toppling of the Marian column stung him throughout the republic's two decades. He held a personal grudge against the military authorities for dispatching him to Užhorod, at the far eastern end of the state, and not allowing his wife and children to join him. And he rejected the ideology of the republic. While serving in the remote, ethnically mixed region of Subcarpathian Ruthenia, sandwiched among Hungary, Romania, and Soviet Ukraine, Durych recognized the civilizing potential of an independent Czech-led state. He even coined a new name for the republic: the "Czech Empire." But Durych had little enthusiasm for promoting Masarykian morals to the citizenry. He delighted in not preaching lessons mandated by the Czechoslovak Red Cross, such as abstinence from alcohol.[43] Instead, he longed for an

---

41   Putna discusses the reaction of various Catholic intellectuals in his two-volume history of Czech
       Catholic literature. Views ranged from the strong opposition of influential lay writer and publisher Josef Florian to the more positive view of priest and poet Jakub Deml in the 1920s, a stance rooted in his
       Czech nationalism. See *Česká katolická literatura v evropském kontextu, 1845–1918*, 413–14 and 457–
       65. On Catholic intellectuals' opposition to the conciliatory approach of the People's Party, see *Česká
       katolická literatura v kontextech, 1918–1945*, 192–95.

42   Durych's son Václav uses the term "dissident" to describe his father's political stance to the Czechoslovak Republic. Durych, "Jaroslav Durych (stručný životopis)" [Jaroslav Durych (Brief biography)], in
       Jaroslav Durych: život, ohlasy, soupis díla a literatury o něm, 13.

43   Durych to Jakub Deml, 19 March 1921, LA PNP, Deml Collection.

empire that would take up the heritage of St. Vojtěch (also known as Adalbert) of Prague, the tenth-century bishop who had carried the gospel to Hungary, Poland, and Prussia. Rather than Masaryk's republic of bland civility and humanitarianism, Durych envisioned a Catholic realm that would bring spiritual revival to the East.[44]

Durych was mired in despair during his time in Ruthenia.[45] He felt banished in Užhorod, far from his family and from the empire's center. The newspapers and journals from Prague only stoked his anger. It was at this time, in his isolation and rage, that Jaroslav Durych the writer began to emerge. The literary talent had been evident in his first volumes of verse and stories published during the war, but in the early 1920s Durych adopted a deliberately provocative stance, a voice of scorching indignation. In his personal bitterness and growing anger against the government, Durych claimed that this new approach was necessary in order to reveal the corruption of the age. "All the stories and terrible events are absurd and comical," he wrote of the news of the day to a fellow Catholic writer. "They're like a chaos of broken pottery. One shard throws its reflection and color on the others and the image emerges of some cosmic witches' Sabbath. I smile when I read that twenty-five million people somewhere are dying of hunger. I am horrified when I read about the Hoover aid mission for Czechoslovakia. The laughter of little children depresses me. The look of a beautiful young woman nauseates me."[46] Durych's remarks indicated the tone his writing would take in the decade ahead: sarcastic, ironic, aimed to shock his readers. He declared the aim of his writing: "I want to give the republic an enema."[47]

Durych was transferred to Prague—and reunited with his family—in 1923. While continuing to work at a military clinic, he published collections of poetry, short stories, and novels.[48] He also became a regular contributor for the newspaper *Lidové listy* (The people's pages), the her-

---

44 See Putna, *Česká katolická literatura v kontextech, 1918–1945*, 377–79.

45 See especially Durych's letters to Jakub Deml of 17 February 1922 and 4 May 1922, in which he bemoans his dead-end situation. LA PNP, Deml Collection.

46 Durych to Jakub Deml, 28 March 1920, LA PNP, Deml Collection. Translated by Ludmila Tydlitátová.

47 Durych to Jakub Deml, 19 March 1921, LA PNP, Deml Collection.

48 See the summary of reviews of Durych's books, compiled by Jan Šulc, Jiří Kudrnáč, and Karel Komárek, in *Jaroslav Durych: Život, ohlasy, soupis, díla a literatury o něm*, 539–45.

ald of the Czechoslovak People's Party, the moderate Catholic party. It was here that he began to apply the enema—an approach that did not sit well with his editors. Durych fired volleys of sharp words and sarcastic images, upsetting those at the paper who wanted to maintain the favor of the ministers and politicians whom the writer skewered. The final straw came in June 1923, when Durych threw a bomb. In his essay "Staroměstský ryňk" (Old Town Square), the writer jabbed the secular nationalists and their reverence of Jan Hus. His description of the cult of Hus as a religion without God echoed what Ferdinand Peroutka had written in his book about Czech culture. But the provocative Durych went further, deriding the statue of the reformer on Old Town Square as "a bad monument of a bad preacher by a bad sculptor."[49] The slur sparked outrage. Polemics against the writer appeared in periodicals large and small, and a mob even marched on Durych's apartment and smashed the windows (the writer, his wife, and three young daughters were spending a Sunday afternoon at the park at the time of the attack). The military responded to the scandal by moving Durych out of the capital, assigning him to a military hospital in Olomouc. Meanwhile, the editors of *Lidové listy* and the People's Party distanced themselves from the writer. The party leaders claimed to have known nothing about the article before it was published, and they had no interest in re-igniting the culture war. The paper still published Durych's writing, but his pay was cut.[50] Recognizing his dim prospects with the daily and now disdainful of the People's Party, the writer set off on his own.

Durych joined with other Catholic dissidents to launch an independent journal of political and cultural criticism in the autumn of 1923.[51] Titled *Rozmach* (Breakthrough), the quarterly became required reading in Czech literary circles. Even those on the political Left, who disagreed with Durych's Catholicism, recognized the brilliance of his satire.[52] Durych's targets were varied, and his positions

---

49 Durych, "Staroměstský ryňk," *Lidové listy*, 10 June 1923, reprinted in *Jaroslav Durych—Publicista*, 253.

50 Durych, *Vzpomínky na mého otce*, 213–14. On the response to Durych's essay, see Putna, *Česká katolická literatura, 1918–1945*, 381–82.

51 Durych operated *Rozmach* from the cafés of Olomouc, where he was assigned in 1923. His presence in the capital became untenable after the publication of "Old Town Square," leading to his transfer. Durych, *Vzpomínky na mého otce*, 215–16.

52 Durych, *Vzpomínky na mého otce*, 221.

difficult to pigeonhole. He attacked supporters of Masaryk *and* the president's clerical opponents. He condemned the influence of assimilated Jews in the state bureaucracy, *and* he spoke directly and honestly against antisemitism. From Durych's standpoint, all were manifestations of the grotesque, the cheap, the empty—what he called "the plaster things of the world." Durych insisted, however, that he did not reject the world. If someone loved God, then that person must also love the world.[53] But Durych placed greater value on the eternal and the invisible. Reminiscent of G. K. Chesterton, Durych argued that true liberty was found only within the Church. "Only a Catholic stands on the ladder of freedom," he maintained. "Catholic discipline is the most valuable gift that can be given to the human spirit."[54]

Durych was still an officer in the army, and his scathing criticisms of the republic's political leaders, particularly Edvard Beneš, regularly brought him trouble with military authorities. But the writer had a stalwart and well-connected defender in Karel Čapek. Durych's distinctive Catholic voice was welcome in Czech letters, Čapek judged. "I am glad to read you again," he wrote to Durych in 1921, "and that from you, a Christian, I can get the words to indict the sinful injustices."[55] At the same time, Durych's opinions sometimes bewildered Čapek. For instance, Čapek and Peroutka invited Durych, along with other prominent writers of the day, to submit an essay for a special issue of *Přítomnost* in 1924 on the topic: "Why I am not a Communist." Durych's submission turned the prompt on its head, giving approval to the Communists' violent extremism as work that needed to be done. Čapek and Peroutka left the essay unpublished.[56] "You're determined to make yourself a martyr to your irony," Čapek chided. "I fear that this time you are going to alienate yourself from people more than you can bear."[57]

Still, Čapek recognized Durych as unrivaled literary talent, and he tried to draw him into the circle of Czech literary and political elites.

53 Durych, "O úpadku závisti" [On the degeneracy of envy], *Tvar*, February 1928, reprinted in *Jaroslav Durych—Publicista*, 271–72.

54 Durych, "Žebřík svobody" [The ladder of freedom], *Rozmach*, 15 September 1925, reprinted in *Jaroslav Durych—Publicista*, 270.

55 Čapek to Durych, 1921, in Dandová, ed., "Korespondence Karla Čapka," 79.

56 The essay, "Proč nejsem komunistou," is reprinted in *Jaroslav Durych—Publicista*, 188–90.

57 Čapek to Durych, December 1924, in "Korespondence Karla Čapka," 93–94.

By the mid-1920s, Čapek's domestic and international literary success had earned him standing as Czechoslovakia's most prominent public intellectual, while his membership in the Castle network put him in regular contact with the president and other leading politicians. Taking advantage of these connections, Čapek organized regular Friday-afternoon gatherings of writers and politicians, beginning in 1926. The meetings of the "Friday Men" (*Pátečníci*) at Čapek's home have become legendary in Czech cultural history, bringing together figures like Čapek's brother Josef and other artists, Ferdinand Peroutka, and even, on occasion, Edvard Beneš and Tomáš Masaryk. Čapek sought to create something of an intellectual salon, a civil forum for an exchange of views on politics, literature, and culture.[58] Keeping with his pragmatic philosophy, Čapek wanted people of varied perspectives to participate in the gatherings, even the talented, opinionated, and controversial Catholic writer Jaroslav Durych.

But Durych rejected—in harsh terms—Čapek's invitation to a meeting in April 1926. Having published attacks on many of Čapek's other guests, Durych feared being seen at the gathering as a "bumpkin idiot and Catholic ass."[59] Moreover, he suspected some secret agenda on Čapek's part, that the popular writer with inside connections was trying to buy him off in some way. The charge was an affront to Čapek. There was no hidden motive, he insisted: "I am nothing more and nothing better than an ordinary, decent man."[60] Here, in this personal letter, was a summation of Karel Čapek's moral frame—to be an ordinary, decent man; to be sensible and civil; to bring together men who shared an interest in literature and politics, without pretense or prejudice to their different stations and opinions. Čapek, as man and writer, embodied the pragmatic ethics of Masarykian democracy: the morality of small work and everyday kindness, of tolerance and civility. But to Jaroslav Durych, this "apparent gentlemanliness" was alien and condemnable. Durych insisted upon principles that were grounded in, as he believed, a conviction of the Absolute. Čapek's pragma-

---

58 On the meetings of the Friday Men, see Orzoff, *Battle for the Castle*, 88–92.
59 Durych to Čapek, 18 April 1926, in "Korespondence Karla Čapka," 105. On this spat between Čapek and Durych, see Durych, *Vzpomínky na mého otce*, 262–67.
60 Čapek to Durych, 14 April 1926, in "Korespondence Karla Čapka," 104–5.

tism, in contrast, was insipid and gutless. More galling to Durych was that this so-called philosophy had become the doctrine of the state. As a believer in Truth rather than truths, in dogma rather than "democracy as discussion," Durych could not abide the mindset that Čapek represented, no matter how well intentioned it might have been.

Durych spelled out his dilemma—and that of other Catholics, he claimed—in an open letter to Čapek, published a few months later in *Rozmach*. What should be the stance of a believing Catholic toward the state, he asked, toward a state that views Catholics with animosity? Catholics had been told that all segments of the nation should work together, "that it is necessary to usher in a general harmony." Yet despite their willingness to contribute to this harmony, Czech Catholics remained ostracized. "Perhaps, in the eyes of the builders [of the state]," Durych ventured, "we are dolts, hypocrites, double-crossers, incompetents, and crooks."[61] When the state is founded upon the "ephemeral phenomenon" of Protestant atheism, where does the Catholic place his loyalty? Catholics saw the world differently, he declared: "For we [Catholics] are dogmatists. Even in matters that do not directly relate to the Tridentine catechism, we want to have definite and binding formulations. We do not want to profess loyalty to the nation, to the state, and to the authorities only with our mouths or with some stylized words. We want to trust faithfully and unbendingly, to work for it, to exist for it, and even, if necessary, to give our lives and blood."[62]

Durych posed this question to Čapek, the "popular, influential, and celebrated" writer. Whereas Catholics sought to live according to Truth, Čapek was a man with connections but no convictions. "Loyalty is easy for you," Durych jabbed. "You don't have any clash of morals. For you it's nothing more than sitting down and writing a few lines."[63] In Durych's view, Čapek was the embodiment of the republic: erudite, internationally fashionable, and with a veneer of spirituality. With decency and benevolence, writing sentences like a virtuoso, Čapek led people who believe in God to accept instead a natural, rational view of

---

61 Durych, "List Karlu Čapkovi o loajalitě" [A letter to Karel Čapek about loyalty], *Rozmach*, 15 August 1926, reprinted in *Jaroslav Durych—Publicista*," 204.

62 Ibid., 208.

63 Ibid.

the world. For those few people unable to surrender their faith, Čapek lovingly sets aside God for them, like a seeing-eye dog for the blind. Čapek even convinces God to capitulate. The God who was allowed to exist in Karel Čapek's world had to conform himself to the national purpose, clarity of reason, and the Czech sense of humor. With the congeniality of a diplomat, wrote Durych, Čapek gave God a proper exit; he did not gloat, judge, or seize his property. In this way, Čapek was the model of the "atheist-gentleman."[64]

Masaryk's Message Is Our Message

Protestants comprised a small minority of the population in the Czech Lands: only four percent according to the 1921 census. Most Czech Protestants were therefore encouraged by Masaryk's rise to the presidency. Clergy, theologians, and university professors regarded the president as one of their own. They endorsed Masaryk's religious ideas, particularly his view of the Czechs' Protestant history as the core of the national heritage, and they supported his program for a moral politics founded on reverence to God.[65] Some Protestant intellectuals, however, recognized the challenges facing Masaryk. Although they shared his ideas about the nation's history and the necessity of religious conviction, they understood that the vast majority of Czechs did not. The question they raised was: Why not? Why did the Czechs—the nation of Hus, Komenský, and now Masaryk—not embrace the president's religious philosophy? Was it a deep-rooted aversion to faith within the national culture? Was it a matter of their own failure, as Protestant leaders? Or was there a flaw in Masaryk's ideas?

The two Protestant intellectuals who regularly asked these questions were among Masaryk's greatest supporters and his most perceptive critics. Emanuel Rádl was a professor in the Philosophical Facul-

---

64 Durych, "Svět Karla Čapka" [The world of Karel Čapek], in *Ejhle člověk!*, 55.

65 Among the figures I count here are writer, critic, and literary historian Jan Blahoslav Čapek, Protestant minister and theologian Josef Bohumil Souček, religious historian František Linhart, philosopher Jan Blahoslav Kozák, and journalist and editor Jaroslav Šimsa. The one Catholic intellectual associated with Masaryk was the Jewish convert and priest Alfred Fuchs. According to Masaryk, Fuchs had "a Protestant view, he accepts the doctrine of grace." Gašparíková-Horáková, diary entry of 15 February 1931, in *U Masarykovcov*, 100.

ty of Charles University. Trained as a biologist, his research and writing turned to the history and philosophy of science, and his work in those fields had been translated into other languages—a mark of prestige for a Czech academic. His younger colleague Josef Lukl Hromádka taught at the newly established Hus Protestant Theological Faculty, the seminary that was opened in Prague for the Czech Protestant Church. Friends and collaborators, Rádl and Hromádka shared a sense of mission for bringing ideas out of the classroom to the general public; they were active as public speakers, contributed regularly to periodicals, and authored books and pamphlets that addressed the current social, cultural, and political situation in Czechoslovakia. Both men also had longstanding connections to the Masaryk family. Rádl had academic ties with Masaryk before the war and had written admiringly of his philosophy.[66] During the war, Rádl was held in suspicion at the university for his connections to Masaryk; still, he made regular visits to Charlotte and Alice Masaryková. After independence, he served as principal editor of the new Czech encyclopedia that was compiled with the president's support and bore his name, *Masarykův slovnik naučny* (Masaryk's encyclopedia). Hromádka contributed regularly to *Masarykův sborník* (Masaryk's anthology), the journal edited by Vasil Škrach, the president's librarian and literary secretary. An ordained Lutheran minister who had studied in Basel, Heidelberg, and Aberdeen, Hromádka had published his first articles before the war in *Čas* (Time), the journal that Masaryk himself had edited. And he had worked with Alice Masaryková in a Bible study circle that aimed to apply the teachings of scripture to contemporary social problems.[67]

As Protestants whose religious thought drew deeply from the Bohemian reformation, Rádl and Hromádka were favorable to Masaryk's interpretation of Czech history. They agreed that the early modern

---

66 On Rádl's personal and intellectual links to Masaryk, see Lochman, "Emanuel Rádl," 83–95.

67 On the life and work of Rádl, see Löwenstein, *Emanuel Rádl: Philosoph und Moralist*. The collection of conference papers edited by Tomáš Hermann and Anton Markoš looks at various facets of Rádl's scientific, philosophical, religious, and political writing: *Emanuel Rádl: vědec a filosof*. On Hromádka, see Neumärker, *Josef L. Hromádka: Theologie und Politik im Kontext des Zeitgeschehens*; and Nishitani, *Niebuhr, Hromadka, Troeltsch, and Barth*.

protest against the Catholic Church had been a decisive moment in Czech history, endowing the nation with a rich corpus of moral and social thought. Masaryk, they judged, had been correct in looking to these ideas as the foundations of the national community. The emphases on the freedom and responsibility of the individual citizen and on the spiritual and moral as foundations of politics were ideas, according to Hromádka, "that are quite dear to us," as Protestants.[68] Rádl agreed. He was a vigorous defender of Masaryk's theory of Czech history, not so much for its Protestant content but for its emphasis on individual autonomy and agency as opposed to deterministic understandings of social forces or national character. Nationhood was not an instinct, Rádl charged, and national history could not be reduced to a zoological process. The philosopher held that Masaryk's accomplishment had been to refute ideas of the nation as some organic community and to stress instead the actions, beliefs, and ideals of individual people. The meaning of Czech history was not an inherent tendency driving the nation but a set of ideals that should inspire people to action. Masaryk's vision of Czech history thus was a challenge to Czechs of the present. "The meaning of Czech history," Rádl wrote, "has to be the meaning of life for each of us."[69]

Both Rádl and Hromádka praised Masaryk's theory of Czech history for its emphasis on the actions of individuals and the spiritual content of the nation's past, and they held Masaryk's ideas as sources of inspiration for the nation. At the same time, though, they recognized that Masaryk's views on history were being misread, unappreciated, or simply neglected. While Masaryk had founded the republic upon the religious and humanitarian ideals he saw revealed in Czech history, the Czech people had lost sight of those ideals. According to Hromádka, "the Czech soul fundamentally changed" after 1918. Therefore, "our message," the message implicit in Masaryk's view of history, "was incomprehensible to them."[70]

---

68 Hromádka, *Cesty českých evangelíků*, 53.

69 Rádl, "O smysl našich dějin" [On the meaning of our history], in *Spor o smysl českých dějin*, 469. Hromádka summarizes Rádl's opinion of Masaryk's theory in his biography, *Don Quijote české filosofie*, 113–18. See also Löwenstein, *Emanuel Rádl: Philosoph und Moralist*, 133–36.

70 Hromádka, *Cesty českých evangelíků*, 14.

In part, the disregard of Masaryk's religious ideas was a symptom of modernity. Hromádka, the pastor and theologian, wrote that Europe's Christian civilization was coming to an end in the twentieth century. The unified culture upon which Europe had been built—an amalgam of classical learning and Christian faith that dated to the age of Constantine and Augustine—was in the process of disintegration. The sciences, arts, education, and politics had all gained autonomy from their religious foundations.[71] Rádl likewise asserted that Europe had lost its overarching ideals and sense of purpose, resulting in an atomized society and a debased culture. No longer did people reflect upon the past. No longer did people struggle with fundamental ideas. Instead, the modern European was fixed only upon the present, upon immediate material conditions.[72] Ironically, even though modern society suffered from an increase of "selfishness," the identity and autonomy of the individual had been swallowed by larger forces: society, nation, race, class, economics. Rádl the scientist argued that, owing to this fixation on material forces and technological progress, individuals no longer attended to the internal life, to their unique, spiritual identities. Moral convictions, let alone the individual's relationship with the divine, amounted to nothing in the calculus of modern life. "People today do not believe in God," he wrote, "in immortality, in morality, because people do not believe in themselves alone."[73] In the specific case of the Czechs, nationalists had stripped the Bohemian reformation of its true meaning and substance, offering instead political slogans. People claimed Hus, Žižka, and Komenský as national heroes, yet they were unmoved by—or wholly unaware of—the religious convictions of these historical figures. In the words of Hromádka, Czech nationalism had become "a religion without God."[74]

In addition to these broader and long-term movements, Hromádka and Rádl also saw the secularization of the Czech Lands as the result of unique historical and political circumstances. In the late 1920s they asked why the republic that Tomáš Masaryk led as president was so dif-

---

71   Nishitani, *Niebuhr, Hromadka, Troeltsch, and Barth*, 86–93.
72   Rádl, *Válka čechů s němci*, 7; and "O nehistoričnosti naší doby."
73   Rádl, *Válka čechů s němci*, 115–16. See also Kohák, *The Embers and the Stars*, 13–19.
74   Hromádka, *Cesty českých evangelíků*, 11.

ferent from the vision he had expressed at its founding. Hromádka and Rádl credited Masaryk with attempting to turn Czechs' attention to the ideals of Hus and Komenský. Czechs of the 20th century, however, particularly after the founding of the republic, had become even more distant from the reformers. They lamented that in the whirlwind of political disputes and economic problems, there was little consideration of the state's ideals or the challenge Masaryk had issued to Czechoslovakia's citizens. Hromádka blamed the quarrelsome campaigns of discontented groups within the republic: the national minorities, Catholics, members of the conservative Agrarian Party, Communists, and right-wing Czech nationalists.[75] Rádl, on the other hand, looked not to those who opposed Masaryk's republic but to its builders. Instead of ideals, those who claimed to follow Masaryk adhered only to politics; all aspects of life were politicized, and the individual's loyalties were owed wholly to the state and to the nation conceived as an organic community. Rádl pointed to Czech schools as one area where this degradation was apparent. Before the war, political influence on schools had been restrained. When politically conscious Czechs had shaped the curriculum, they sought to emphasize Hus and Komenský as figures of universal importance. After the war, however, the schools became centers of political indoctrination, places where children were inculcated with the opinions of the "governing generation." The results were already apparent after the republic's first decade: "The great euphoria of patriotism settled on the schools after the war. The newness of the state and the sudden freedom brought with it a reverence of national heroes, and teachers helped establish the state by instilling into the heads of students Czech identity, politics, patriotism, Czech history, and resistance to German identity."[76]

Rádl proved to be a sharp critic of the Czechoslovak Republic. As an internationally recognized scholar, he had unique standing in Czech letters. He was also a longtime colleague and supporter of Tomáš Masaryk. And his approach was not ideological, but philosophical. For these reasons, his 1928 book *Válka Cechů s Němci* (The

---

75 Ibid., 58–9.
76 Rádl, *Válka čechů s němci*, 195.

Czechs' War with the Germans) was a significant analysis of Czech nationalism and the political culture of the interwar state. In assessing Czechoslovakia's first decade, Rádl found the very foundations of the republic to be flawed. He faulted the politicians who had exercised power at the republic's foundation for creating a state built upon exclusivist nationalism. "Germans, Hungarians, and the Catholic Church were considered enemies of the state," he wrote, "and thus it was necessary to use state power against them."[77] The state had been established in the name of the "Czechoslovak nation." Rádl found both parts of this formulation to be incorrect: there was no such thing as a Czechoslovak nation, and the republic's operative definition of nation was misguided. Here he turned his criticism toward Masaryk. In Rádl's judgment, Masaryk's view of the Czech nation and its history was founded upon the flawed philosophies of Johann Gottfried Herder and the nineteenth-century German romantics, who maintained that the nation was an organic community.[78] Rádl disputed the president's unfortunate belief that Czech identity has been defined in the nation's struggle against the Germans; he criticized sharply, for example, Masaryk's remarks in 1918 that the Germans of Bohemia and Moravia were "emigrants and colonists." This phrase had proven deleterious to the republic, in that it gave sanction to politicians, journalists, school administrators, and local officials who acted on the conviction that Czechoslovakia was a national state of the Slovaks and Czechs, with the minorities reduced to lower status. Even more galling to Rádl was the subordination of the individual to the nation. Although Masaryk had sought to articulate a conception of the nation that would promote individual agency, he undermined that autonomy by investing too greatly in the ideal of the nation as living entity.[79]

Ultimately, Rádl's critique was grounded in his convictions as a believing Protestant. Rádl's fundamental objection to what he saw as Masaryk's positivistic conception of Czech history and identity was

---

77 Ibid., 125.
78 Ibid., 176. Rádl argued that Masaryk had attempted to offset this nineteenth-century idealist vision of the nation with a strong measure of skepticism when he was a professor and critic. As president, however, Masaryk had adopted the German romantics' conception of the nation.
79 Ibid., 117–28 and 267–68.

not its determinism or the subordination of the individual to the organic collective. Instead, he was principally distressed by the anthropocentrism of Masaryk's program. In other words, Rádl felt that Masaryk's humanitarian program was "too worldly." Because the nation had been established as the foundation and aim of the republic, the activities of the state and its citizenry were focused upon furthering the political standing of the collective, rather than enhancing the freedom and responsibility of the individual. "The specific collective (the nationality) is for him the main aim of the state, in no way the freedom of the individual and the freedom of the collectives," Rádl concluded. "This especially is the aim that political and moral striving seeks in this world, a world that in the end is material."[80] Rather than resembling Anglo-American democracy, Czechoslovakia looked more like Bolshevik Russia—in Rádl's view. Fulfilling Masaryk's mandate of "Jesus, not Caesar" was not a matter of the republic's organization. Instead, it was a matter of freeing the individual from the constraints of race, nation, and state: the gods of the modern age. This struggle against the powers of the age was the same as that of the early Christians with the Roman Empire, and the English Nonconformists with the established churches. This had been the struggle of Masaryk the philosopher and critic, Rádl claimed. The implication was that it was not the struggle of Masaryk the president. Still, Rádl insisted, this remained the central issue facing Czechoslovakia. The solution to this problem would determine the future not only of the republic but also of the rest of East Central Europe.

Mysterious Stones at the Castle

By 1922, the first results of Jože Plečnik's work were coming into view. Besides the initial renovations of the president's retreat at Lány, workers at Prague Castle were shoring up and leveling the gardens beneath the southern walls of the palace, and they were completing the paving of the first courtyard. As work progressed, the accolades came in. Plečnik, however, was unmoved. Indeed, he was annoyed with the

---

80   Ibid., 268.

FIGURE 5.1. One of Plečnik's first completed projects at the Prague Castle: the paved first courtyard and the tapered flagpoles. Jože Plečnik Collection, Museums and Galleries of Ljubljana, Slovenia.

constant requests to lead other architects, government officials, and various dignitaries on guided tours of the construction site. He again bolted to Ljubljana in January 1925, prompting Masaryk to declare that the architect was not to be bothered at all. Plečnik did return, and with Masaryk's unqualified backing and few financial limits (on occasion, he even refused the president's and Alice Masaryková's requests for meetings) he was free to pursue grand visions for the castle. His drawings from the late 1920s included a monumental staircase and

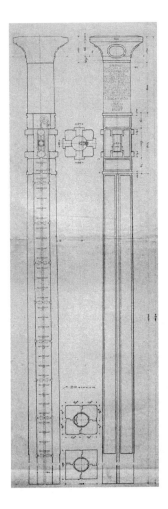

FIGURE 5.2. Plečnik, early plan for the monolith, with the opening at the top for the eternal flame, 1921. Jože Plečnik Collection, Museums and Galleries of Ljubljana, Slovenia.

columned portal leading to the castle gardens; a four-story-high, pillared entrance hall between the first and second courtyards; and the paving of the cobblestoned third courtyard with large slabs of granite—a project unprecedented at the time.

Alice Masaryková continued to encourage Plečnik in the project with letters of support and suggestions on details. She was drawn espe-

FIGURE 5.3. Plečnik, drawing of the monolith standing outside the castle walls, on the monumental stairs leading to the Paradise Garden, 1921. Jože Plečnik Collection, Museums and Galleries of Ljubljana, Slovenia.

cially to Plečnik's plan for a stone obelisk that would stand on the monumental staircase leading from Hradčany Square down to the Paradise Garden below the castle walls. Plečnik had suggested the monument, intended to honor soldiers in the Czechoslovak Legions who had died in service during the World War, in his first meeting with Tomáš Masaryk. The president was delighted with the idea, even composing the inscription for the stone.[81] Plečnik drew several versions of the pillar. The original idea was for a simple, unadorned stone, but this model gave way to versions with varying styles or ornamentation, some topped with a sculpture of the Czech lion and Slovak cross. A common element in the early drawings was the inclusion of an eternal light at the top of the monument. Plečnik devised an unusual and challenging scheme:

81   Gabrijan, *Plečnik in njegova šola*, 76.

FIGURE 5.4. Workers with the granite bowl to be placed in the Paradise Garden, 1924. Jože Plečnik Collection, Museums and Galleries of Ljubljana, Slovenia.

place the flame *within* the obelisk, near the top, with portals in the stone that would allow the light to shine in each direction. Imagine the sight: an enormous, freestanding stone pillar, rising sixty feet or more outside the castle's southern walls, reaching to the full height of the façade, and shining a light that could be seen through the city below. Alice Masaryková was thrilled. Even the stones of the castle would "praise God—with us people," she wrote to Plečnik.[82]

The project was challenging from the start. The original slab of granite, measuring thirty-four meters, cracked in its bed. Quarriers were able to remove a second stone, nineteen meters long, and began moving it from Mrakotín, in southwest Moravia. But in a comedy of mismanagement, the military detachment handling the transport allowed the stone to slip down an embankment and crack in two. A third attempt to lift a stone from the quarry, in September 1924, also ended

---

82   Masaryková to Plečnik, 9 April 1923, PC MGL.

with a break. The remaining fragment of this stone, however, measuring sixteen meters long, was deemed satisfactory. It made the trip to Prague in late summer 1925 and eventually reached the castle courtyard in March 1926.[83] In the meantime, the Paradise Garden below the castle walls had been completed, with the enormous granite bowl that was to have been the obelisk's mate set at the base of the monumental stairs—by itself. Plečnik looked elsewhere for a site for the monolith, ultimately deciding on the third courtyard. Unadorned, without inscription, sculpture, or eternal light, this stone was finally erected here in 1928.

The six-year drama of the obelisk was a topic of great interest and controversy. In late summer 1923, the hewing of the second, nineteen-meter obelisk, as well as the successful trip of the enormous granite bowl, were, in the words of one newspaper, "the sensation of the countryside."[84] A flurry of articles in the Prague dailies, in Czech and German, recounted the stone's quarrying and travels, with various speculative numbers thrown out regarding its length and weight—18 meters, 19.3 meters, 20 meters, 70 tons, 90 tons. The flurry of press coverage swelled to a blizzard after the quarried granite slid down the embankment and broke. Reactions to the mishap reflected the ideological divides of the republic: the left-wing papers *Rudé právo* (Red Justice) and *Ceské slovo* (The Czech Word) saw the broken monolith as evidence of bureaucratic corruption and the failure of the military to accept civilian control.[85] The Catholic paper *Lidové listy*, in contrast, pointed out that the break of the "column" ("like the Marian column, pulled down at Old Town Square," the paper pointed out) happened—not coincidentally—on the feast of St. Mary's birth. *Pražský večernik* (Prague Evening News) commented on the symbolism of the monolith, noting that it distinguished the Czechs from other contemporary nations. "England, America, and other Western states are again building cathedrals. Our republic, however, prefers a pagan column." Instead of following the progress of this monolith, the evening daily

---

83 On the quarrying and transport of the various stones, see Malá, "History of the Obelisk"; and Prelovšek, *Jože Plečnik*, 128.

84 *Venkov*, 19 August 1923. Collected in APH KPR, SV, Inv. no. 212, box 495.

85 *Rudé právo*, 18 October 1923; and *Ceské slovo*, 30 October 1923. Collected in APH KPR, SV, box 495.

urged, attention should be turned to St. Vitus Cathedral as a monument of Bohemia's long history. The Gothic cathedral, "speaking in stone, reminds us of that for which we were famous in the past and that which caused our fall."[86]

The press rose again in August and September 1925, with the extraction of the new stone. For the people of Mrakotín, where the quarry was located, the stone was an object of great pride; wreaths and banners draped the obelisk and the train carrying it, while local Sokol groups and schoolchildren saluted the carriage as it made its slow progress to Prague.[87] To *Rudé právo*, however, the obelisk was symbolic of the republic's failures, bringing to mind "the long finger" of a thief, stealing from the working class.[88] When Egyptian pharaohs built their pyramids, the communist paper observed, they also did not care whether the people had enough to eat. The stone's winter stay at the Dejvice train station brought further scorn from the *Rudé právo*, which noted the symbolism of an inert stone waiting beside the tracks for some direction as to where to go. All of the high ideals of the democratic state were embodied in this homeless, purposeless rock. "The monolith resembles all the noble and virtuous ideals of democracy, which are adrift in the clouds above the republic. Every eye is upon them, every mouth invokes them, but they are never received down here below. And if they finally do [come down], will there be a place for them?"[89] On the opposite end of the ideological scale, the conservative Catholic paper *Čech* also seized upon the indecision and delays. Assurances from the government that Masaryk himself was paying for the monolith brought no relief. What of the transportation costs? And the workers? And how could Masaryk, as a private citizen rather than president, decide himself to place this monument within the castle? "How is it that in Prague one can put whatever 'private' gift he wants wherever he wants?"[90] The editors of *Čech* insisted that they had great esteem for the political ideals of Czechoslovakia's founding, and they

---

86 *Pražský Večerník*, 11 September 1923. Collected in APH KPR, SV, box 495.
87 *Narodni politika*, 5 December 1925. Collected in APH KPR, SV, box 495.
88 *Rudé Právo*, 4 December 1925. Collected in APH KPR, SV, box 495.
89 *Rudé Právo*, 22 December 1925. Collected in APH KPR, SV, box 495.
90 *Čech*, 22 January 1926. Collected in APH KPR, SV, box 495.

looked forward to the end of the monolith's delay at the station, when it would stand next to St. Vitus Cathedral. "Perhaps it will even have some symbolic significance," the paper jeered.[91] For the editors of *Rudé právo*, in contrast, the significance of "this symbol of the Czechoslovak ideals" was perfectly clear. The obelisk "symbolizes nothing more than dead illusions."[92]

The uncertain journey of the obelisk was not the only cause for complaint regarding the castle project. Throughout the 1920s, critics rejected specifics of the project. The cultural critic for the conservative newspaper *Národní listy* rejected Plečnik's proposed renovation of the castle's third courtyard, the large area adjacent to St. Vitus Cathedral. The capital's leading preservationist organization, the Club for Old Prague, objected that the foreigner Plečnik apparently showed little regard for the castle's heritage. One popular journal, meanwhile, lamented that the renovations of the castle gardens would bring the closing of a favorite pub in the Malá Strana neighborhood below Hradčany Hill.[93]

Plečnik's supporters moved to defend the architect against his critics. Like Jan Kotěra's introduction of Plečnik to a Czech audience in 1902, these apologies portrayed the artist as a man of profound morality and wisdom, someone who was at once modern and deliberative, pragmatic and moral. For example, a leading proponent of historical preservation in Prague, architect Karel Guth, insisted that Plečnik indeed had great respect for architectural tradition. Writing in *Lidové noviny*, the daily newspaper closely linked to the Castle, he described Plečnik in terms that would hopefully appeal to the Castle's conservative Catholic opponents: "calm, humble, an abjurer of society, the descendant of the anonymous builders of medieval cathedrals, obedient to their mystical work."[94] Guth insisted that the architect took care to preserve the castle's historic monuments, that he was deliberate and

---

91 *Čech*, 8 April 1926. Collected in APH, KPR, SV, box 495.

92 *Rudé Právo*, 22 December 1925. Collected in APH KPR, SV, box 495.

93 *Pražský illust. zpravodej*, 1925. Collected in APH KPR, SV, box 495. On criticism of Plečnik's renovations, particularly the paving of the third courtyard, see Güllendi-Cimprichová, "Památková hodnota, religiozita."

94 Karel Guth, "Architekt Plečník na pražském hradě" [The architect Plečník at Prague Castle], *Lidové noviny*, 24 December 1929. Collected in APH KPR, SV, box 495.

respectful in the formulation of plans. Even though at first glance his designs appeared unusual and new, the observer could be assured of Plečnik's devotion to history. The architect "has not disappointed those who have placed trust in him," Guth declared, referring indirectly to Masaryk. "His art rises above all doubts... And just as it is not possible to doubt Plečnik's art, so is it necessary to trust in his love for and reverence to historical monuments."[95]

As *Lidové noviny* published defenses of Plečnik aimed at conservative Catholics and nationalist Czechs, one of the architect's longtime advocates in Prague came to his defense against young modernists. Architectural styles had changed since Pavel Janák first hailed Plečnik in his manifesto of cubist architecture. Janák and his fellow cubists were now the leading designers in Prague, although they had left cubism behind. Meanwhile, the younger generation of Czech architects issued their own challenge to the establishment, arguing for international modernism and functionalism as the guiding styles for contemporary design. In the view of Karel Teige, the leading theorist of the 1920s avant-garde, Plečnik's influence as a designer and teacher was "basically negative and counter to the new healthy tendencies of today's architecture."[96] In the art journal *Volné směry*, Janák defended Plečnik against such charges. He also targeted a riposte against the architectural trends of the times, represented by Teige. Janák charged that contemporary architects searched for a single, binding theory of design; they were consumed with rational justifications and necessities. Unlike these designers in the studios and offices of Prague, the artist at the castle, "full of enthusiasm," deliberated on the dimension of columns. "Down below we hear of itemization, activity, organization, calculation, usefulness, profitability," Janák wrote. "Here [at the castle] we find an art of pure humility and sincere devotion to the task."[97] In no way was Plečnik a historicist or romantic, someone mired in the past. Instead, he was a man of his times, who used columns, cornices, and other elements in completely new ways. "Before

---

95   Ibid.

96   Teige, "Moderní architektura v Ceskoslovensku," *Mezinarodni soudoba architektura* 2 (1930), reprinted as "Modern Architecture in Czechoslovakia," in *Modern Architecture and Other Writings*, 112.

97   Janák, "Josef Plečnik v Praze," 97.

FIGURE 5.5. Granite bowl in the Paradise Garden. Jože Plečnik Collection,
Museums and Galleries of Ljubljana, Slovenia.

all of his works we say to ourselves: Here is a plan without precedent!"[98]
Indeed, in his profound originality as well as his understanding of materials and the social function of architecture, Plečnik was among the
most modern of artists.

Janák's praise of his friend and mentor echoed his theoretical essays of the previous decade. Then, as the leading theorist of the cubists, he had spoken of the need to animate matter with spirit. Just as he
had seen Plečnik's early drawings as a model of the new architecture
he proposed in 1910, now he saw the architect's project at Prague Castle as the realization of that architecture. But Janák's defense of Plečnik
was not simply a restatement of an artistic ideal. By the end of the
1920s, Janák was himself a man of the republic, an artist of the generation of Karel Čapek, struggling against a new generation of artists
radicalized by socialism. Led by the artist and critic Teige, the Czech
architectural avant-garde embraced the designs and ideas of Le Cor-

---

98   Ibid.

busier, Adolf Loos, and Walter Gropius. According to Teige, the designs of Janák and the cubists were just as obsolete as Plečnik's, based upon an "almost absurd misunderstanding of the fundamental and specific postulates of architecture" and creating a "diversion from the evolution of modern functional architecture; ... a cul-de-sac dominated by the priests of the romantic imagination."[99]

Janák and others of his generation, however, saw their artistic ideals not as romantic withdrawal but as engagement, as the freeing of the individual to create something new and dynamic for the benefit of the community.[100] Plečnik epitomized this individual creator, someone who was fundamentally modern in his disregard of normative definitions and conventions. Other architects, those "down below" from the castle, had become prisoners of rationalist demands, whether of capitalist efficiency or collectivist idealism. But in Plečnik's work, Janák wrote, "one feels a glimpse of spirit." Amidst the demands of function, architecture had to preserve attention to the spirit, to the heart, to the essence and nature of materials. Plečnik's work was the best example of this kind of architecture. At Prague Castle was a master who studied his materials "with the eyes of a man of the twentieth century." At the same time, Janák insisted, "Plečnik also is a soul who sees differently, better and more broadly, how material only comes to life through the human spirit—and thus understands that material can be good and truthful only insofar as it is used by a good, truthful, and worthy person."[101]

Conclusion

Pavel Janák's defense of Plečnik's work at Prague Castle echoed the language used by members of the metaphorical Castle in praising Masaryk. For example, playwright and critic František Götz, a member of Karel Čapek's circle of intellectuals, wrote a review in 1926 of a new

---

99 Teige, "Modern Architecture in Czechoslovakia," 142.
100 As Thomas Ort explains, Karel Čapek, Pavel Janák, and other Czech artists of their generation saw modernist creativity as a positive engagement not as a retreat into subjectivity. See *Art and Life in Modernist Prague*, especially the first chapter, "Prague 1911: The Cubist City."
101 Janák, "Josef Plečnik v Praze," 98–9.

edition of Masaryk's turn-of-the-century volume of lectures, *How to Work*. Götz praised the president for his depth of thought, his perceptive understanding of life, and his ideas of practical, determined work that served to build trust and cooperation among people. In picking up this book, Götz wrote, readers will see how Masaryk addressed questions with such a "new, expansive, and deeply absorbed and methodologically organized manner—an ethical genius. This thinker is an exacting, rigorous, and noble intellect." Masaryk's body of ideas, he concluded, "is full of direct, dispassionate light, but with much loving humanism. Alongside all of his rigor, directness, and objectivity, this ethical genius is also very humane. He knows how to anoint every day as a holy day. He knows how to amplify human trust and strength."[102] Like Plečnik in his work at the castle, Masaryk was a man of extraordinary insight and wisdom who comprehended truth in ways that others did not. The philosopher-president and his architect were praised with abstract, exalting terms—they were men of noble ideals, which should be accepted for their beauty, their harmony, their depth.

But there were Czechs who did not accept the ideals of President Masaryk: people like Jaroslav Durych, who objected to them outright or saw them as morally thin. And there were others, people who were the president's supporters, who adapted Masaryk's ideas according to their own viewpoints. Czech Protestants like Emanuel Rádl and Josef Hromádka saw the president's principles as being close to their own, as did secular liberals. Within the walls of the metaphorical Castle, the network of Masaryk's supporters, there were varying degrees of enthusiasm and ambivalence toward his ideas. Their point of agreement was devotion simply to Masaryk. As president, Masaryk sought to promote a civil religion for Czechoslovakia, a shared set of beliefs that would motivate the republic's citizens in cooperative, altruistic work. However, the civil religion proved to be more like a cult, with Masaryk himself the object of veneration.

Certainly, the American civil religion—which Masaryk held as a model—had its own cultish elements. In the early years of the repub-

---

102 Götz, "Etický genius" [Ethical genius], review of T. G. Masaryk, *Jak pracovat* (1926), in *Národní osvobození*, 12 September 1926, in clippings file, LA PNP, TGM Collection.

lic, the image of George Washington was everywhere. But Washington had a figure like James Madison, who codified the ideals of the new country in the Constitution and Bill of Rights. Masaryk did not have a Madison. As one of his foremost Czech interpreters put it, in philosophical terms Masaryk was like Socrates, the charismatic teacher and critic. What he lacked was a Plato, someone able to "conceptually and systematically formulate what is most important in his ideas, who indicates his overall lines and gradients, pointing out especially that throughout his entire life he acted not as a systematic thinker but as a critic of modern times."[103] Instead, Masaryk had promoters like František Götz and Karel Čapek, who praised the corpus of his thought and the character of the man himself as shining ideals. He had a political right-hand man in Edvard Beneš who was unfailingly loyal to Masaryk, but who trusted more in his own analytical skills than in God, eternity, or moral principles. He had a daughter who expressed his ideas in service with the Red Cross, and an architect who expressed his ideas in stone. If Masaryk had proponents who interpreted his work systematically, they were Rádl and Hromádka. But their approach, both critical and Christian, met with opposition from those within the Castle. Throughout the twenty years of the First Republic, the correct meaning of Masaryk's character and ideas was subject of debate among the different wings of his supporters. Meanwhile, outside the castle walls, the president's opponents attacked those ideas. As Czechoslovakia entered the 1930s, and economic and political turmoil struck the state, these opponents would find new strength in their resistance.

---

103 Machovec, *Tomáš G. Masaryk*, 49.

Chapter Six

Building Cathedrals in Modern Prague

In November 1928, a few days after the tenth anniversary of Czechoslovakia's founding, the marble obelisk finally took its place in the third courtyard of Prague Castle. By this time, many of Jože Plečnik's plans had been realized at Hradčany. The first courtyard, on the castle's eastern entrance, now had its towering oak flagpoles, flanking the baroque Matthias Gate. The large third courtyard was being paved with massive granite slabs. A staircase of marble and granite now led from that courtyard, through one of the castle's wings, down below to the Paradise Garden. The garden itself was a masterpiece, with its geometric green spaces and paths leading to columned porticos that overlooked the city. And inside the castle walls, the presidential apartments, salons, and library had been completed. Artist and academy professor Max Švabinský marveled at Plečnik's designs. "In his work is an unfathomable emotion and nobility, done in new master strokes, along with a complete reverence in his sense for the built architecture, for the trees, for the view of the old castle," he wrote to the castle administration. "No one could have done it better than him."[1]

At the same time, another major building project inside the castle was coming to a close. Since the mid-1800s, generations of masons, stonecutters, carpenters, and glaziers had worked to "finish" a structure started some five centuries earlier: the Cathedral of St. Vitus. For much of its history, the cathedral was a truncated structure. The Gothic choir and apse were built in the fourteenth century, along with sur-

---

1   Max Švabinský to the president's chancellery, 31 October 1928, APH KPR, SV, box 35.

FIGURE 6.1. The monolith standing on the paved third courtyard, 1928.
Jože Plečnik Collection, Museums and Galleries of Ljubljana, Slovenia.

rounding chapels, a short transept, and an open-sided tower, but construction was brought to a halt by the Hussite wars of the fifteenth century. Over the next two centuries, monarchs of Bohemia commissioned additions to the cathedral: for example, the trunk of the bell

FIGURE 6.2. Garden on the Ramparts. Jože Plečnik Collection, Museums and
Galleries of Ljubljana, Slovenia.

tower is in the Renaissance style, while the spire was built later in the
Baroque. Finally, in the mid-1800s, the canon of St. Vitus presented a
new project for the completion of the cathedral, with financial support
coming from high clergy and the nobility, including Emperor Franz
Joseph. By the end of the nineteenth century the cathedral had gained
the dramatic profile that towers over Prague today—the two spires rising above the western portal and the roofline of the long nave connecting to the older bell tower. Renovations of the interior, though, continued into the decades of the republic. By 1929, enough of this work was
finished to reopen the cathedral—in time for the millennial jubilee of
St. Václav's martyrdom.[2]

---

2   For an overview of the renovation project, see Kostílková, "Katedrála v 19. a 20. století. Jednota pro
     dostavení chrámu svatého Víta"; Petrasová, "Dostavba katedrály"; and Peval Zahradník, "Novodobá
     dostavba katedrály," in Zahradník and Líbal, eds., *Katedrála svatého Víta na pražském Hradě.*

The physical proximity of St. Vitus Cathedral and Prague Castle was symbolic of church-state relations in the Czechoslovak Republic. The cathedral, housing the remains of St. Václav and his successors as sovereigns of Bohemia, was under the authority of the archbishop of Prague. But the cathedral stands in the very middle of the citadel, surrounded by palaces and courtyards under the authority of the president. In the first years of the republic, this closeness of church and state power, sacred and secular space, led to nudges of discomfort and occasional sharp elbows of disagreement. The president's office, claiming ownership over the cathedral tower, tried to put a surveillance post in the belfry, while the archbishop's office repeatedly asked for floral decorations for the altar on feast days, requests that Masaryk's officials met reluctantly. The president's office denied permission for open-air mass in the courtyard on the Feast of Corpus Christi, but it allowed the castle gates to remain open for worshippers attending midnight Christmas services. As construction expanded on the renovations of the castle, the chancellery prohibited processions—some five hundred people at a time—on the feast days of Saints Václav and John of Nepomuk, Corpus Christi, and Easter. But why then, the archbishop's office asked, were socialist and workers' groups allowed to march through the courtyards for the national holiday and Masaryk's birthday? Throughout the 1920s, requests were made and denied. Appeals were lodged, and exceptions granted.[3]

The grumbling over their shared space indicated the deeper, ideological contest between the castle and the church in the Czechoslovak Republic.[4] On becoming president, Tomáš Masaryk was determined to have a separation of church and state, what he called the "depoliticization of the church" and the "de-ecclesiasticization of the state." Again looking to his wife's homeland, Masaryk hoped to import the American model of church-state relations. He cited this model in a let-

---

3   See the president's office exchanges on the various requests, in APH KPR, SV, box 18, sign. 3573/46; and box 46, sign. 3554/47 and sign. 1494/33.

4   On the tensions between the Catholic Church and the Czechoslovak government, see Paces, *Prague Panoramas*, 115–38; Trapl, *Political Catholicism*, 49–56; Marek, "Das Verhältnis zwischen Staat und Kirchen," 9–31; Schulze Wessel, "Konfessionelle Konflikte in der Ersten Tschechoslowakischen Republik"; and Šebek, "Der Tschechishe Katholizismus."

ter to the archbishop of Olomouc in 1919, insisting that his aim was beneficial: a "free church in a free republic."[5] But Masaryk's understanding of church-state relations was shaped by more than the American practice of freedom of religion; it also followed from his own religious biography and his idea of the new religion. In his lectures and articles at the turn of the century as well as his prewar book *Russia and Europe*, Masaryk had envisioned a religion without institutions. People would be free in the new religion to act upon their convictions outside the restrictions of doctrine, rituals, and church authority. Upon becoming president, he linked this religious freedom to the freedom brought by the republic: people would work for the benefit of others, in cooperation with a state that sought to establish the kingdom of God. Masaryk's expectation was that religion would become secularized in its liberation from churches, while the state would be sacralized through its citizens and leaders working in concert with each other and with God. Masaryk saw no role for the Catholic Church—or any other church, for that matter. Unlike the American civil religion, which its founders did not intend as a substitute for Christianity, the civil religion of Czechoslovakia was the next phase in the evolution of Christianity.

There were church leaders who supported Masaryk's ideas of religion. Liberal Protestants identified strongly with the president, as did a group of reformist priests who broke away from the Catholic Church in 1919. But of course, there was also resistance. The Catholic hierarchy opposed the separation of church and state, particularly the limiting of its role in education, while Protestant theologian Josef Hromádka argued that Masaryk misunderstood the function of churches. Even a secular modernist like Karel Čapek recognized the value of churches. He could not accept any church's claim to truth, but he recognized the meaning that people found in shared worship and rituals, and he lamented the loss of the meaning in the modern age.

This was the question: what was the role of churches in modern society? Would they wither away, becoming increasingly irrelevant to

---

5   Masaryk, "Prezident republiky o poměru církve k státu" and accompanying letter to Archbishop Leo Škrbenský, 2 November 1919, in *Cesta demokracie*, 1:188.

the realities of contemporary life? Could they be a source of comfort and guidance in an age of technology and dislocation, as Čapek suggested in some of his essays? Or was there a new way to communicate the message of the Christian Church, a way that would gain people's attention in modern Prague? The cultural history of the city in the interwar decades typically focuses on Čapek and his circle of liberal modernists, or the communist-leaning avant-garde. But Protestant intellectuals and Catholic artists were also active in this period, insisting that their faith remained relevant and could even be complementary to the modern age.

Religious Institutions and Masaryk's Civil Religion

The toppling of the Marian column on Prague's Old Town Square in November 1918 opened a turbulent chapter for the Catholic Church in the Czech Lands. In the first months of the republic a fierce storm hit the Church, dissolving its political influence in the new state, diluting its role in Czech society, and driving men and women from parishes. Taking their cue from the iconoclasts in Prague, vandals throughout the country tore down statues of the Virgin Mary and St. John of Nepomuk, denouncing them as despised relics of Catholic Habsburg domination.[6] While the new Czech political leaders distanced themselves from the hooligans, the anti-Catholic mood of the streets was matched in the provisional government and parliament. The dominant parties in the interim assembly—the Agrarians and National Democrats on the Right, the Czechoslovak Socialists and Social Democrats on the Left—acted on their anticlerical positions and passed legislation that limited the Church's authority or challenged Catholic teaching. New laws forbade political messages from the pulpit, decreed land reform aimed at the Church's holdings, and allowed for cremations. Meanwhile, the minister of education abolished compulsory religious education and allowed teachers to remove crosses from their classrooms.[7]

---

6   Paces, *Prague Panoramas*, 98. On the toppling of statues in the first days of the republic, see also Wingfield, *Flag Wars and Stone Saints*, 144–51 and 156–69

7   See Peroutka, *Budování státu*, 1:209–11; Trapl, *Political Catholicism*, 50–2; Marek, "Das Verhältnis zwischen Staat und Kirchen," 9–13; and Němec, "The Czech Jednota," 83.

The attacks in parliament and on the streets came at the same time as a struggle within the Church. Immediately after independence, Czech clerics sought to wrest control of the Church from German-speaking hierarchs and show that they were just as patriotic as secular nationalists. In the final weeks of October 1918, the German archbishop of Prague, Paul de Huyn, recognized the turn of events and fled to Rome. Czech priests took advantage of the archbishop's departure to form an organization called the Union of Czechoslovak Clergy (*Jednota československého duchovenstva*).[8] Meeting days after the declaration of independence, the Union declared its loyalty to the republic and to Rome. Its members responded quickly to the anti-Catholic atmosphere of Czechoslovakia's first weeks by offering its own slate of reforms. In December, the Union proposed greater autonomy from Rome and democratization of Church governance, the use of Czech rather than Latin for the Mass, an end to the celibacy obligation for priests, and a reassessment of the Church's judgment against Jan Hus. Czech priests in Bohemia overwhelmingly accepted the proposals, although Moravian and Slovak priests were less enthusiastic, indicating the regional differences within the Church.[9] Eventually, the Union did agree to the proposals, and in July a delegation of Czech and Slovak priests brought their requests to Rome. Needless to say, Pope Benedict XV did not approve.[10]

For most Czech priests, the quashed reform proposal was sufficient proof of their loyalty to the nation and republic. A minority of Union members, however, refused to surrender. Over the autumn and winter months of 1919–20, these priests took progressively radical steps: one married a woman in a civil ceremony; another wore secular clothes to an audience with the new archbishop and refused to kiss his ring. Later that year the reformers called all Czech priests to celebrate Christmas Mass in Czech. The new archbishop of Prague, a Czech university

---

8   There had been a Union of Czech Clergy formed at the turn of the century, but it had been dissolved in 1907 in the Catholic Church's crackdown on modernist theology.

9   Meanwhile, German priests had created their own organization. This group benefited from the proposals of the Czechs in that it allowed the Germans greater autonomy with their own parishioners and thus tightened connections between German communities and their priests. Němec, "Czech Jednota," 85.

10   Ibid., 84–7.

professor named František Kordáč, called for dialogue on questions of reform, but the radicals saw the Church as intransigent. They proposed that the only way forward was secession. On January 8, 1920, this fringe group of Catholic priests voted to leave the Roman Catholic Church entirely. The Czechoslovak Church was founded.[11]

There were two driving impulses in the creation of this new church. First, there was a desire to create a national, "Czechoslovak" institution, one that would be autonomous and democratic in its governance, that would employ the vernacular in sacred services, and that would be grounded in the teachings of the great figures of Czech church history: Cyril and Methodius, Jan Hus, and Jan Amos Komenský and the Brethren Church. The other impulse was to establish a modern church, to make Christianity more accessible to people by dissolving differences between clergy and laity and reevaluating doctrines and dogmas. These two impulses did not necessarily move in a common direction. In the first months of the new church, its founders proposed a smorgasbord of reforms for liturgy, ecclesiastical structures, and relations with other churches. They also moved toward further schism, as an even smaller faction of the breakaway clergy protested the new church's modernist turn and attached themselves to the Serbian Orthodox Church.

Despite its fractious and sometimes comic origins, the Czechoslovak Church did become a significant institution in the religious history of the interwar republic. Czechoslovakia's first census, conducted in 1921, counted over 525,000 adherents to the Czechoslovak Church, a remarkable figure for a body that had been in existence for only a year (the total population of Bohemia and Moravia at the time was just over ten million).[12] This tally was also a great leap from the church's own count of its members, just one month earlier, at 193,665. One historian

---

11   On the founding of the Czechoslovak Church, Czech-American émigré Němec takes a distinctly pro-Catholic approach, as indicated in the title of his long article "The Czechoslovak Heresy and Schism: The Emergence of a National Czechoslovak Church." See also the older surveys by Czech-American religion scholar Matthew Spinka: "Religious Movements in Czechoslovakia" and "The Religious Situation in Czechoslovakia." More recent studies by Czech scholars are: Frýdl, *Reformní náboženské hnutí v počátcích československé republiky*; and Marek, *České schisma*. Martin Schulze Wessel views the church's creation within the broader political and cultural context in his essay "Konfessionelle Konflikte in der Ersten Tschechoslowakischen Republik."

12   Brotánková, "Religiozita v okresech ČR v období 1921–2001," 24.

has asserted that the difference in numbers can be attributed to state-funded propaganda against the Catholic Church prior to the census.[13] More likely, the larger number in the census indicates that there were many Czechs who preferred nominal affiliation to the Czechoslovak Church over nominal affiliation to the Catholic Church. Since they were not active participants in the new church, they had not appeared on its member rolls. Nevertheless, whether nominal or practicing, true converts or people who simply checked a census box, these half-million adherents represented a serious blow to the Catholic Church. Taking into account both those who joined other denominations and those who left the organized churches entirely, the number of Catholics in Bohemia and Moravia dropped by 1.4 million in the eleven years since the last imperial Austrian census.

As the same time as the reformist priests were breaking from the Catholic Church, Czech Protestants—also motivated by a spirit of nationalism—moved toward ecclesiastical unity. The commemoration of Jan Hus's martyrdom in 1915 had been the catalyst for discussions of a union of Lutheran and Reformed Churches in the Czech Lands. As a speaker at one event that year had declared: "Our reformer is not Luther or Calvin, but Hus. And because we are Hussites, it is necessary under the circumstances to adopt another name."[14] Talks among clergy and elders continued during the war and moved to completion immediately after its end. On December 17, 1918, leaders of the Lutheran and Reformed Churches agreed to the creation of a unified body, the Protestant Church of the Czech Brethren. The church made immedi-

---

13 Němec's pro-Catholic stance is particularly apparent in this charge. He writes, for example, that the anti-Catholic press carried out "poisonous attacks and created a fearfully tense atmosphere for the weaker Catholics. Intimidation, scandal, sarcasm, and slander were not infrequently used." He does cite one example of such attacks, published in the newsletter of the Czechoslovak Church's West Bohemian diocese: "The time approaches when it becomes necessary for the Czech nation to judge and condemn Rome according to the words of President T.G. Masaryk. The forthcoming census must prove that our republic is not Roman anymore... We appeal to all Czechs to leave the Roman Catholic Church before the census and join the church of their choice and conviction." Němec, "Czechoslovak Heresy and Schism," 34.

14 Hrejsa, *Dějiny české evanjelické církve v Praze a ve středních Čechách v posledních 250 letech*, 408. On the formation of the unified Czech Protestant Church, see Matějka, "Die tschechischen protestantischen Kirchen." Ferdinand Peroutka criticized the Protestant unification as motivated more by politics than religion. *Budování státu*, 1: 273–74.

ate gains after the state's founding. Over 55,000 new members joined in 1921–22, bringing the total membership to 160,000. By 1927, the church's membership rolls had risen to more than 255,000.[15] The new church also enjoyed political favor. In 1919, parliament created a state-funded seminary as part of Charles University. That same year, the Catholic Church asked the assembly to establish a theological faculty at the university in Olomouc. The request was rejected.[16]

Like the politicians in the assembly, Tomáš Masaryk insisted on the separation of church and state in Czechoslovakia, which meant limiting the role of the Catholic Church. In a 1919 letter to Masaryk, the archbishop of Olomouc, Cardinal Leo Škrbenský, appealed for cooperation between the Church and government in moral education. Masaryk's rebuttal jabbed at the Church that had disappointed him in his youth: "Indeed, it is possible to teach the catechism, church history, etc.," he wrote to Škrbenský, "but religion as spiritual and moral strength cannot be simply learned, it must be instilled by example, it must be—in a word—lived."[17] The Catholic Church had failed to set that example for Masaryk when he was a student in Brno; therefore, he saw little need for its help now as president. In contrast, he viewed the revival of Protestantism favorably. In the final chapter of his memoirs, dedicated to religious life in Czechoslovakia, he presented data from the 1921 census showing the rise in membership of the various Protestant denominations: "almost one million," he pointed out, after adding together Protestants in the Czech Lands and Slovakia. Masaryk insisted that the numbers were proof of the continued importance of religion in Czech life. "Those who do not believe that the religious question is very important to our nation must change their conclusions," he declared.[18] But even if the number of Protestants had reached one million, they were still far outnumbered by Catholics. Despite its loss of members, including desertions to the

---

15   Spinka, "The Religious Situation in Czechoslovakia," 298–99.

16   Podivinský, "Kirche, Staat und religiöses Leben der Tschechen in der Ersten Republik," 230–31.

17   Masaryk, "Prezident republiky o poměru cirkve k státu" and accompanying letter to Škrbenský, 2 November 1919, in *Cesta demokracie*, 1:188. See also his address to parliament on the first anniversary of indepedence, 28 October 1919, in the same volume, p. 173.

18   Masaryk, *Světová revoluce*, 404.

new Czechoslovak Church, the Roman Catholic Church remained the largest in the republic—by far—with more than ten million adherents. Yet in Masaryk's view, at least according to his memoirs, it had no place in the religious life of the nation. He did not mention the Catholic Church at all.

For that matter, Masaryk did not say much in his memoirs about the Protestant or Czechoslovak Churches. Leaders of both new churches claimed allegiance to the president's ideas on religion, but Masaryk did not grant official blessing to either one. In private, he was outright dismissive of the breakaway Czechoslovak Church. "A new religion cannot arise because a few hundred priests decide to renounce celibacy," he told a visiting English Jesuit.[19] In his memoirs, Masaryk referred to the membership tallies of both churches as evidence of religious sentiment within the population, yet he offered no suggestion as to what role the people behind those numbers—the communities of believers—could play in fulfilling the religious and political principles he set. He had nothing to say on how the churches might contribute to the building of the moral, spiritual republic. "Jesus, not Caesar," he wrote at the conclusion of that chapter on religion, reiterating his motto with the emphasis of a pastor closing a sermon. "I repeat, this is the meaning of our history and democracy."[20] In Masaryk's view, however, the democratic state and the nation would take up the functions of the churches, the work of Jesus. The Czech nation would fulfill its religious heritage in building a sovereign republic, in which the state would take responsibility for social welfare, education, and the cultivation of citizens.[21] Of course, religious conviction was essential in this development, but it was a conviction of the individual, liberated from institutions. Masaryk anticipated "de-ecclesiasticization" [*odcirkevňování*] in every sphere of social life, ultimately even in religion."[22] The participation of churches in the moral republic was unwelcome, because churches were unnecessary. Religion would be

---

19   Firt, "Die 'Burg' aus der Sicht eines Zeitgenossen," 98–9.
20   Masaryk, *Světová revoluce*, 406.
21   Ibid., 373.
22   Ibid., 370.

secularized, while the nation-state would be made sacred.[23] According to Masaryk, the people and leaders of the republic would establish the kingdom of God, fulfilling their duties under the perspective of eternity.

Although he proposed no active role for churches in the Czechoslovak state, Masaryk did endorse organizations founded upon religious principles and promoting religious ideas. In particular, Masaryk supported the work of the Young Men's Christian Association (YMCA). Czechs and Slovaks had first encountered the YMCA in Russia during the war. A few hundred American YMCA staffers and volunteers worked in wartime Russia, providing aid to prisoners from the German and Austro-Hungarian armies and then to those Czech and Slovak prisoners who volunteered to fight on the Allied side. Masaryk himself met the head of the American YMCA, John R. Mott, when both men were in Petrograd in 1917. After the Bolsheviks came to power that November, American YMCA workers traveled with the Czechoslovak legions as they moved eastward across the Trans-Siberian Railway. At each major stop in Siberia and the Russian Far East, the YMCA set up canteens for Czech and Slovak soldiers, distributing tons of supplies sent from the United States.[24] These biscuits, chocolates, and cigarettes opened the door for the YMCA after the war in independent Czechoslovakia.

The YMCA continued to provide supplies and services at military garrisons in the new state, but its activities soon expanded to include university students, young workers, and children. Alice Masaryková and Emanuel Rádl worked together on the founding of the Czechoslovak chapter of the organization. As with her efforts in launching the Red Cross, Masaryková traveled to Geneva for the international conference of the YMCA in order to secure outside support.[25] Representatives of the American YMCA were present in the first meetings of the executive board in 1921, and American money helped the Czecho-

---

23 Unfortunately, Hartmut Lehmann does not directly address the case of Masaryk's Czechoslovakia in his essay "Die Säkularisierung der Religion und die Sakralisierung der Nation im 20. Jahrhundert."

24 Davis and Trani, "The American YMCA and the Russian Revolution," 483–85.

25 Šiklová, "Akademická YMCA v Československu a její příspěvek k formování studenstva a inteligence," 71.

slovak organization in its early years. Within only two years, its calendar was crowded with more than 11,000 events across the country, and more than 230,000 men and boys were participating. Beyond the efforts of Masaryková and Rádl, Ymka, as the organization was known in Czech (and pronounced as "eem-kah"), had well-connected leaders. The founding president was Professor František Drtina, a longtime supporter of Masaryk, and Apollo Růžička, director of the bank that held Masaryk's accounts, was an active member of the committee. Vasil Škrach was often involved in YMCA events, and even Edvard Beneš gave lectures for the organization. The leading figure among students was the young man who had been moved by Masaryk's speech at the castle in 1920: Václav Maria Havel. Son of a notable property developer, Havel came from a family of means, and in the early 1920s he was a man on the rise. As he finished his university education and stepped into the family business (his father died in 1921), Havel was also involved in all facets of the YMCA leadership and made several trips abroad for YMCA and Christian youth conferences.[26]

Thanks to these well-placed leaders and, especially, its links to the American organization, the YMCA quickly established a physical presence in cities across Czechoslovakia. Gifts of several hundred thousand dollars from the United States allowed for construction of a YMCA building in Prague. By 1928, the facility was hosting some 300 guests per night in its dormitory, serving meals to thousands in its cafeteria, and hosting a range of activities, from music lessons, Bible studies, and English classes to volleyball and basketball games. Additional YMCA centers in Brno, Hradec Králové, and Bratislava likewise provided meals to several hundred people each day.[27]

The Young Women's Christian Association in Czechoslovakia also had a direct connection to the house of Masaryk. During her stay in Chicago, Alice Masaryková had become familiar with the work of the YWCA, and when she invited American social workers to Prague in 1919, they came under the organization's auspices. Three of these young American women were present at the first meetings of the

---

26   Havel discusses his involvement with the YMCA in his memoir: *Mé vzpomínky*, 139–43 and 200–206.

27   Report on the social and education activites for 1928, Národní Archiv, YMCA Collection, box 1, folder 1. See also the booklet "Co je a co chce YMCA v Československu" (n.d., after 1931).

Czechoslovak YWCA, held at Prague Castle in November 1919. Alice was acknowledged as the initiator of the organizing committee, while her younger sister, Olga, was the chair. [28] Olga Masaryková's involvement was short lived, however, as she soon moved to Switzerland. The organizing committee started again the following spring. The new director was Marie Záhořová-Němcová, granddaughter of the beloved nineteenth-century writer Božena Němcová, while Alice Masaryková's personal secretary also served on the committee. In its first few years, the YWCA organized events similar to the men's association: summer camps, foreign language classes, Bible studies, swimming and sports. There were also programs not seen in the men's buildings: cooking, sewing, and home economics. In 1923, the YWCA moved into a new building in the center of Prague, financed by a loan secured by Hana Benešová, wife of Foreign Minister Beneš. The aim of the facility and others planned for Czech and Slovak cities was to provide shelter, meals, and educational opportunities for young working women. A booklet published on the building's opening began with a greeting from the president: "Our nation, whose strength is not in numbers, must strive to have women who are moral, physically strong, and capable of the great challenges of the mothers of future generations."[29]

Leaders of both the YWCA and YMCA claimed to follow the principles of Masaryk. Moral and physical development, education, and religious awareness were oft-repeated tasks of the organizations, all directed toward the practical needs of the nation. "The aim of the YMCA," stated an informational booklet, "is a genuine Christian conception of the practical life. All of our attention is directed to education toward practice, for real life."[30] The YWCA likewise stated that the purpose of its religious programs was to "build something positive

---

28 Crawford described the origins of the YWCA in a report to the Overseas Committee, War Work Council, YWCA, August 15–October 15, 1919. In her telling, the young Czech women who had been trained in the social work summer school were interested in their American teachers starting a chapter of the YWCA. Lilly Library, Mitchell Collection, box 1.

29 "První dívčí dům" [The first Young Women's House] 1923, Národní Archiv, YWCA Collection, box 6, folder 4.

30 "Co je a co chce YMCA v Československu" [What the YMCA is in Czechoslovakia and what it wants].

and practical for the life of our young women, to make them strong beings. Therefore, we put an emphasis on morality."[31] YMCA and YWCA publications declared their aim to promote a "conscious" Christianity, as opposed to the "religious indifference" of Czech public life. Ostensibly, the organizations did not promote any church, and they welcomed young people of any background. But the organizations did affiliate themselves with various Protestant youth groups, and in statements both public and private, their leaders targeted Catholicism. The source of Czech antipathy to religion, they held, was the conservatism of the Catholic Church and its links to the Habsburg Monarchy. Therefore, young Czechs had to learn that Christianity could be positive, that it could be a fulfilling conviction in their lives. This conviction was held individually, as Masaryk himself had modeled. The YMCA's account of its first decade stated: "Religious revival can come only through a new concept of Christianity, with fewer polemics, less verbosity, whether sacramental or political, and more of an expression of life, service, and a practical program. The call for Christian renewal in this sense has a great bulwark in the example of President Masaryk, who rejected disbelief and positivism. Through his influence many intellectuals have renounced 'clericalism,' but they remained faithful to religion."[32]

If the Czechoslovak Red Cross was the service arm of Tomáš Masaryk's new religion, then the YMCA and YWCA were its institutions of education. Their mission was to form young people according to the principles of a practical, positive, individualized religion.[33] Masaryk gave his blessing to the organizations in the form of substantial gifts from his personal account. During the 1920s, the YWCA received 150,000 crowns (about $4,400 at the time) from the president and the YMCA received 200,000 ($5,900). In comparison, the account book shows a one-time gift of 30,000 crowns for a conference of Czech Prot-

31   "Referát o náboženské práci v období 1921–25" [Report on religious work in 1921–25], Národní Archiv, YWCA Collection, box 6, folder 4.

32   "YMCA v prvním desítiletí 1921–1931" [The YMCA in its first decade 1921–1931] Národní Archiv, YMCA Collection, box 1, folder 1.

33   On the aims of the YMCA, see Šiklová, "Akademická YMCA v Československu," especially 77–80 and 83–85.

estants and no donations to the Czechoslovak Church.[34] Although these churches identified themselves with Masaryk's religious philosophy and Masaryk continued to identify himself as a Protestant, he kept his distance. The YMCA, YWCA, and Red Cross met Masaryk's idea of true religion: people gaining knowledge and being motivated to service. No worship. No sacraments. No doctrine.

The statement above about the YMCA's first decade went on to say that the intellectuals who had remained faithful under Masaryk's influence adhered to religious beliefs that were "more or less vaguely formulated" (*více méně nejasně formulovali*). To be sure, the guiding principles of these organizations were not always clear. They were opposed to Catholicism—that much was certain. After learning that a local chapter was cooperating with the town parish, the YMCA board decided that it had to approve all questions of "clear ideology" (Václav Havel chaired the ideology subcommittee).[35] But apart from its anti-Catholicism, the tent was broad. For more than a decade, the YMCA board included both Havel, a millionaire property developer who attended no church and was involved in Freemasonry, and Josef Hromádka, an ordained minister and neo-orthodox theologian with socialist leanings. At times, there was disagreement and even division. In 1926, an affiliated student organization broke along lines of belief, with students who wanted to maintain the group's religious principles integrating fully with the YMCA, and secular students forming the Ethical Movement of Czechoslovak Students. Both claimed to follow the ideas of Masaryk. The founders of YWCA, on the other hand, had difficulty clarifying the organization's mission at the very start. When Olga Masaryková chaired the organizing committee in 1919, the committee even debated removing the word "Christian" from the name, out of concern that Czechs would think it was a "clerical association."[36]

---

34 The ledger book for the account for social and humanitarian causes shows gifts to the YMCA and YWCA in 1923, 1924, and 1926, MÚA AV ČR, TGM Collection, Republika, box 535, folder 22.

35 Minutes, YMCA board meeting of 22 January 1922, Národní Archiv, YMCA Collection, box 1.

36 Minutes of the first YWCA committee meetings, 18 and 21 November 1919, are contained in Národní Archiv, YWCA Collection, box 6. See also Ruth Crawford's report, for August–October 1919, to the Overseas Committee, War Work Council, YWCA, Mitchell Collection, Lilly Library, box 1, correspondence.

When the organization's history was later written, this uncertain start was edited out. Publications of the Czechoslovak YWCA credited Alice Masaryková and the young American social workers with its inspiration and dated its founding to 1920. Olga Masaryková's brief leadership was not even mentioned.[37]

Faith, Truth, and the Culture of the Republic

The Czechoslovak Red Cross, YMCA, and YWCA were institutions of Tomáš Masaryk's civil religion. The president endorsed each with money and words of support, and his daughter Alice had a direct hand in the founding of all three. Another institution created at Masaryk's urging to further his aims for the republic was the weekly journal *Přítomnost* (The Present). The periodical had roughly the same size constituency as the YMCA and YWCA: *Přítomnost* had 4,500 subscribers in 1929, while the two organizations each had about 5,000 members.[38] But the influence of these institutions was much larger than the numbers suggest. Prominent intellectuals such as historian Jan Havránek and sociologist Jiřina Šiklová pointed to the publications, lectures, and discussion groups of the YMCA as a significant part of the cultural environment of interwar Prague, particularly for university students.[39] *Přítomnost*, meanwhile, features prominently in any account of the politics and culture of the First Republic. The contributors to the journal, like the organizers of the YMCA and YWCA, identified themselves as supporters of Masaryk and saw their efforts as following upon his aims for the republic. Clearly, however, there were significant differences. While people like Rádl, Hromádka, and even Václav M. Havel saw Masaryk's religious ideas are central to the mission of the YMCA and the republic, the leading men of *Přítomnost* adhered to the practical and political ideas in the presi-

---

37 Minutes of the YWCA committee meetings, 18 and 21 November 1919, Národní Archiv, YWCA Collection, box 6. See also the reports of 1920 and 1936 in box 7.

38 Orzoff, *Battle for the Castle*, 270n78; "První dívčí dům," Národní Archiv, YWCA Collection, box 6, folder 4; and Zpráva o programové sociálně výchovné činnosti Ymky v ČSR v roce 1928, Národní Archiv, YMCA Collection, box 1, folder 4.

39 Šiklová, "Akademická YMCA v Československu," 89; and Havránek, "Akademická mládež mezi křesťanstvím a atheismem a Rádlova profesura na universitě."

dent's message, steering away from his concerns with religion and history. The editor of *Přítomnost*, Ferdinand Peroutka, was sometimes sharp in his criticism of churches and religion. Yet his remarks about religion's present and future in modern society were not far removed from Masaryk's ideas, particularly those of the turn of the century. And in his personal thinking about God, Peroutka—like his collaborator Karel Čapek—saw his ideas as following from those of Masaryk and pointing in the direction of Something.

Ferdinand Peroutka was unique among the intellectuals of the Castle, in that he declared himself an atheist. Despite the antagonism toward the Catholic Church among Masaryk's supporters, few openly denied belief in God. Even Edvard Beneš, who took pride in his scientific approach to political and social questions, spoke regularly of Providence (he even gave a lecture on prayer at a YMCA meeting). Peroutka, however, stated in his book on Czech culture and identity that religion would continue to decline and eventually become extinct. The modern age had reordered people's daily lives and patterns of thinking, he observed, making the old religion obsolete. "We modern people are savvy... In the place of Genesis, we have the books of Darwin and the faith that we evolved from apes; in place of the Mass, we have the telegraph; in place of the surplice, the coat with tails; in place of St. Francis, the newspapers; in place of church, the gym; in place of the altar, the exercise bars." A person of the old religion, he wrote, "would be horrified of a religion comprised of the state, doctors, schools, hospitals, social laws, wage arbitration judges, living modern languages, health, work, democracy, simplicity, and just persuasion." The organizers of this new religion, that of modern life, were cleaning away the foul-smelling old religion, doing it so thoroughly that "there is no place for a god to rest, unless it is a creature so hazy, woeful, metaphorical, and fictional as the pantheistic god, dwelling in everything." There was no hope in seeking to preserve the old religion against science, democratic politics, and modern state administration. "We will not rescue the Czech's religion in this way."[40] Peroutka saw little future for the churches, whether Catholic, Protestant, or Czecho-

---

40 Peroutka, "Národ náboženský?," in *Jácí jsme*, 69.

slovak. Their mutual conflicts and criticisms were "of little interest to us," he wrote later in *Přítomnost*, "since in a while both confessions will be lying next to each other in the grave."[41]

Yet despite his atheism and predictions of religion's decline, Peroutka was also unusual among Masaryk's supporters in his explicit appreciation of the Catholic Church in Czech history and culture. If there was any goodness in the nation, he wrote in *Jácí jsme*, "you will still find that it is an inheritance from Catholicism." This Catholic legacy would be difficult to erase, he insisted. Moreover, Peroutka granted, there were plenty of upstanding Czechs who were also practicing Catholics. At the same time, many nonpracticing Czechs were actually Catholic in thinking, in moral perspective, and in commitment to truth. Even those Czechs who were atheists, Peroutka held (perhaps thinking of himself), were "Catholic atheists."[42]

Peroutka's appreciation for Catholicism as cultural practice and moral wellspring overlapped with an admiration for the English writer G. K. Chesterton. At first glance, the attraction seems odd: what drew the atheist political journalist, who prided himself on his hard realism, to the cantankerous Catholic writer, who wrote some of the most famous apologies for Catholic Christianity in the twentieth century? On a literary level, Peroutka was drawn to Chesterton's style and rhetorical approach. But beyond that, the journalist appreciated the joyful wonder, the sense of gratitude and optimism that Chesterton's writing exuded. Of course, Peroutka differed from Chesterton in insisting that this attitude of wonder did not depend on belief in the omnipresence of God. Rather than seeing the presence of God everywhere in the world, Peroutka believed that a full awareness of existence was sufficient to inspire fascination.[43] Peroutka still held to a rigorous skepticism, a rejection of dogma and metaphysics, and a trust in his own judgments. Yet, as his biographer Pavel Kosatík suggests, Peroutka's esteem for Chesterton indicates a deeper ambivalence, or uncertainty, toward matters of faith. Just as Peroutka was unable to decide

41 Peroutka, "Je pokrok ohrožen?," 97. Peroutka repeated this assessment in his later book *Budování státu*, 1: 275–76.
42 Peroutka, "Národ náboženský?," in *Jácí jsme*, 57.
43 Kosatík, *Ferdinand Peroutka*, 191–94.

between socialism and liberalism, "the need for 'God' never fully released him."[44]

Peroutka himself acknowledged this uncertainty in his memoirs, written in exile in the United States after the Communist takeover of Czechoslovakia. He recalled conversations with Masaryk about the existence of God. When the president asked him about his beliefs, Peroutka stated directly, "Yes, I am an atheist." He then added: "Unfortunately, an atheist." Peroutka held to this admission that his atheism was unfortunate. He claimed not to enjoy his absence of belief. "I knew how faith can be a positive strength, that religious feeling and awareness brought great happiness to many people, that it integrated them, and that without religion they would feel lost."[45] At the same time, however, he could not bring himself to faith, because he had never known proof of God's existence. He wrote of "proof" (*důkaz*) not as verifiable evidence or logical exercise; instead, he meant the subjective experience of God. "I recognize that there must be people who have had—or feel that they have had—a personal experience where they have seen proof of God's existence. But as for me, personally, no."[46]

In contrast, Peroutka found Masaryk to be someone with a psychological need for religion. The president was admirable—and unique—in his seamless integration of rationality and faith, and the grounded, practical direction of his belief. Masaryk, Peroutka wrote in *Přítomnost*, "was not a man crushed down by the greatness of God and controlled by religion; on the contrary, this is a man who controls his own religion; this is a religion not of dreams and musings, but of living vitality."[47] This was a religion unbounded by church or theology, a religion that Peroutka was able to extol, even endorse. Drawing from his conversations with the president, Peroutka described Masaryk's beliefs to his readers:

Religion as a historical system, religion as the church, is completely diminished in Masaryk by his rationality; but religion as an in-

---

44 Ibid.195.
45 Peroutka, "Ze vzpomínek zaznamenaných pro vysílání Svobodné Evropy" [From reminiscences recorded for Radio Free Europe Broadcast] in *Deníky, dopisy, vzpomínky*, 154.
46 Ibid.
47 Peroutka, "Masarykova osobnost II," 194.

stinct is ineradicable in him. He testifies to the strength, in no way the weakness, of this instinct that dispenses with definitive ideas about God. A weak faith needs precise formulations. However, the one who is full of faith can simply believe only in *something*. Privately, Masaryk has even spoken about religion without God. God is a transcendental matter, but in Masaryk's religion these transcendental elements are excluded by some dynamic strength.[48]

Questions of faith and the existence of God were more common in the essays and fiction of Karel Čapek. Unlike Peroutka, Čapek did not write of the eventual extinction of churches in the modern age. The writer was true to his pragmatic relativism. A professing Catholic or Protestant had just as much right to his religious convictions as Čapek had to his own philosophy. When a mother wrote a letter to *Lidové noviny*, asking whether she should send her daughter to religious classes, Čapek argued that it was preferable to have educated believers—or nonbelievers—than ignorant atheists. Proper religious education, he clarified, had to impart a sense of tolerance, contrary to the views of both intolerant clericals and communists. Toward that end, an ideal curriculum for religious education would include Komenský and Confucius, Tolstoy and Masaryk, John Stuart Mill and the Buddha. From these sources, students would come to understand the moral instincts that were, according to Čapek, common to all people: "honesty, truthfulness, good will to one's neighbors, defense of the weak."[49]

Čapek also recognized that churches offered something more than moral instruction. Traditional religious practice, he recognized, provided a sense of meaning and connectedness that had been lost in the modern age. In a 1922 vignette, Čapek described a visit to a church in rural Slovakia. With a gentle, observant touch, he wrote of the villagers' arrival in the churchyard, their prayers at the cemetery, and the separation of men and women, boys and girls, as they entered the sanc-

---

48 Ibid., 189.

49 Čapek, "Ještě k té náboženské výchově" [Again on religious education], *Lidové noviny*, 6 October 1923. See also "Náboženská výchova" [Religious education], *Lidové noviny*, 2 October 1923, and "Mravní výchova" [Moral education], *Lidové noviny*, 26 October 1923, in *Od člověka k člověku I*, 316–17, 311–13, and 318–21.

tuary. There was a primitiveness to the "nicely pagan-like" rituals. But there was also something enriching in their timelessness, in the solemnity of the ceremony. Unlike modern, "civilized" life, with its formlessness and chaos, the "primitive life" he witnessed in the village evoked both continuity and community. There was a symbolic unity, not only among the villagers, but between the villagers and their dead ancestors. Čapek appreciated the underlying message of the rituals, even as he acknowledged the distance between the villagers and urban moderns like himself: "Even though we do not have the same and do not live the same, we are the same before God and the community."[50] In comparison, Čapek found the life he knew in Prague to be lacking. "*Our* life—our modern, big-city, cosmopolitan life—has one key element that is common everywhere and in everything: the melting away, the splintering, the breakdown of all forms of life." Perhaps it was the result of a collapse in morality, Čapek mused, or a lack of neighborliness, or of a shared sense of social ethic. In any case, he lamented, his fellow moderns had become "jumbled, faceless, forsaken."[51]

Čapek measured religious belief and church rites according to pragmatic criteria: if they were beneficial to the health of the community, as he saw in Slovakia, and if people found individual meaning in them, then he granted his approval. His concern, however, was that churches and religious individuals often insisted too firmly on their understanding of truth. In several of his fictional works, Čapek scorned those who devoted themselves to possession of absolute truth. His early novel *Tovarno na Absolutu* (Factory of the Absolute), serialized in *Lidové noviny* in 1920 and published in book form the next year, treated the theme with a mix of science fiction and comedy. The novel describes the invention in Prague of the "Karburator," a machine that produces limitless power by crushing atoms. The twist, which Čapek devised from his readings of pantheist thinkers, was that as matter is crushed in the Karburator, the spiritual essence present in all things is released. Thus as each Karburator produced atomic ener-

---

50   Čapek, "Formy," *Lidové Noviny*, 10 September 1922, in *Od člověka k člověku I*, 230. Thomas Ort discusses Čapek's observations of this village church service in "Men without Qualities: Karel Čapek and His Generation," 282–83.

51   Čapek, "Formy," 230. Emphasis in original.

gy, the waste product was not radioactive material but the spirit of God, the Absolute. In the novel, this release of the divine spurs conversions and ecstasies, with hardened atheists drawn to devotion at the machines. Soon the Catholic Church intervenes, sending a bishop to claim control over the device in the interest of rationing its emissions and reconciling them with Church doctrine. "In the name of Heaven, do not imagine that the Church brings God into the world," the bishop declares to the Karburator's inventors. "The Church merely confines Him and controls Him."[52] The fat prelate is not the only one to insist on ownership of the Absolute. As Karburators are manufactured and distributed throughout the world, the overflow of the Absolute leads to an increase in religious and nationalist division. The competing claimants to the Absolute eventually plunge the world into "the greatest war," with the Chinese pushing the Russians into Africa, and the Japanese conquering Asia and North America. At the novel's close, in the year 1953, the world has been left in ruins by humanity's struggle to possess the Absolute.

Čapek is often credited for his prescience in the novel, for his warnings of technology run amok, bitter ideological strife, and authoritarianism and worldwide conflict. But the young writer's attention was more immediate. Writing after the Great War and in the midst of external and domestic struggles surrounding Czechoslovakia's founding, as well as the unfolding schism in the Catholic Church, Čapek warned his readers against clinging too strongly to their own definition of "Truth." In the next two decades, much of Čapek's literary output expressed this caution: beware Absolute Truth, with its fanaticism and titanic delusions, as opposed to the simple life, content with ordinary things and sown with humility and skepticism. Čapek insisted that his wariness of the Absolute—or rather, human abuse of the Absolute—did not translate to a dismissal of religion or God. After Jaroslav Durych described Čapek as the model of the "gentleman atheist," Čapek published his rebuttal in Durych's own journal *Rozmach*. Matters of religion and God were deeply serious to him, he

---

52   Čapek, *The Absolute at Large*, 43. On Čapek's novel as a critic of the various "faiths" and dogmas of the age, see Ort, *Art and Life in Modernist Prague*, 132–34.

wrote. Contrary to Durych's charge that his literary work elevated man over God, or even belittled God, Čapek protested that he called attention to God in his writing. God did not reveal himself in heavenly glory, he insisted, but in the form of the simple, fragile people that he depicted. This revelation of God in other people was by no means perfect, Čapek admitted. The voice of the divine in others could be childlike, but it could also be blustering. For this reason, the smallness of people, we must be leery of the Absolute. To refuse the Absolute was not to deny God. Instead, it meant being aware of the failings of all people, of the tendency to cast God in our own image and holding that image over others.[53]

In part, this circumspection toward people prevented Čapek the humanist from accepting any formulation of the divine. Despite his sympathy for the rites of the faithful, despite his belief that serving others was a service to God, he could not bring himself to accept any creedal or theological statement. Part of this reluctance was due to simple doubt. "Karel would have liked to believe," wrote his niece, Helena Koželuhová, "but he did not know how and in what to believe." Koželuhová wrote in her memoirs of conversations on free will, theodicy, and divine judgment that Čapek had with her husband, Adolf Procházka, a legal scholar and committed Catholic. Despite his curiosity, his inclination to belief, Čapek could not accept with any certainty the existence of the supernatural. Unlike Peroutka, Čapek was not an atheist by intellectual conviction. Instead, according to Koželuhová, he sincerely could not decide whether or not God existed. Moreover, he held that it was beyond human intellect to even grasp the matter. Both Karel and Josef Čapek did feel, their niece wrote, "that somewhere there must be something higher (*něco vyššího*). Something that gives order and laws to nature." This "something" was not a personal God, certainly not the God defined by priests and theologians, but closer to a pantheistic divinity. The brothers imagined, wrote Koželuhová, "that if there is some God, it must be sufficient when they are grateful for all the beauty in the world and when they glorify it

---

53 Čapek, "List Jaroslavu Durychovi" [A Letter to Jaroslav Durych], *Rozmach* 1 March 1927, in *O Umění a kultuře III*, 83–84.

with their whole work. If you honor your work, you honor the creator with it. And that's just what they did."[54]

"Those were their ideas," concluded the Čapeks' niece, "but they did not declare them. They did not assertively proclaim them." These ideas, however, are not absent from their work. Karel Čapek, in particular, pointed regularly at "something higher." We see it in his wartime story "Crossroads," in which two travelers encounter a mysterious set of footprints on a snow-covered road. The trail of the footprints suddenly disappears into undisturbed snow, leaving the two men grasping for, and failing to find, a rational explanation. Likewise, we see Čapek's Somethingism in his breakthrough play *R.U.R.*, at the end of which the Christian character Alquist witnesses the metamorphosis of robots into loving humans, and in his mature novels of the 1930s, which deliberate the human potential for evil. Even Jaroslav Durych recognized this metaphysical thread in Čapek's work, as have later commentators.[55]

In this stealthy manner of expressing his views, and in the views he expressed, Čapek was a characteristic member of the Castle. The representative intellectuals and politicians in Masaryk's circle did not echo the president's explicit emphasis on religious conviction as necessary for good citizenship, nor did they speak of God or Jesus. But they did hint at the spiritual, even the divine. Whether the Providence of Edvard Beneš or the pantheistic divinity of the Čapeks, there was Something up there. Even Peroutka, although a declared atheist, acknowledged the strength of religious belief and was compelled by what he regarded as Masaryk's "religion without God." Peroutka acknowledged, though, that this religion did not correspond to any church. The president was looking for church, he wrote, "which, strictly speaking, would not be a church."[56] In his own views on religion, Peroutka kept with the religious message of the Castle: benign, traditional religiosity was valid, even welcome, as was a benign, distant divinity. They might provide some sense of meaning for individuals and, even better, some measure of stability of society. But as for any larger role

---

54 Koželuhová, *Čapci očima rodiny*, 105.
55 Durych, "Svět Karla Čapka," in *Ejhle člověk!*, 40–2; and Putna, *Česká katolická literatura v kontextech, 1918–1945*, 231–32.
56 Peroutka, "Masarykova osobnost II," 192.

for institutional churches in the republic, the members of the Castle and the president were in agreement. Because clerics and theologians lay claim to the Absolute, they had no place in a modern democracy.

The Blasphemies of Jaroslav Durych

Jaroslav Durych is "our only genuine Catholic poet." So wrote Karel Čapek in 1920.[57]

At the time, Durych was still an emerging writer, looking for his voice and his audience. He was an officer and physician in a back-woods garrison, a husband and father separated from his family, and (he believed) an exile and dissident, resentful of his government and doubtful of his path in the world. A decade later, Durych would receive the State Prize for Literature and earn acclaim as one of the nation's best writers. He would also gain notoriety as one of the most controversial figures in Czech letters, not least of all for the feuds with his former admirer Čapek. The dispute between Čapek and Durych was about far more than literary matters. It was, as both men understood, about the fundamental meaning of the republic. As a biting critic of the culture and politics of interwar Czechoslovakia and a vigorous advocate of Catholicism, Durych earned enemies who saw him as, in the words of one critic, "a sworn enemy of our democracy."[58] Nevertheless, Durych gained critical acclaim and readers during the 1920s. His fame as writer, his infamy as a provocateur, and his boldness in taking on Čapek and even Masaryk offer evidence of Catholicism's revival in Czech culture. After the crisis of the republic's early years, by 1930 young Catholic writers were poised to establish themselves as significant contributors to the nation's literature. Their model was Durych—the novelist, poet, and essayist who wrote with brilliant style and moved in his own unapologetic direction.

---

57 The quotation in full stated that Durych, "along with Jakub Deml," was the Czechs' only Catholic poet. Deml discovered Čapek's appraisal in the newspaper *Narodni listy* and relayed the statement to Durych, who was serving with the Czechoslovak army in the distant forests of Ruthenia.

58 "Kdo má dostat Nobelovou cenu?" [Who must receive the Nobel Prize?], *Havlíček* (Prague) 19, no. 2 (24 January 1930), quoted in Durych et al., *Jaroslav Durych: Život, ohlasy, soupis díla a literatury o něm*, 584. As the title of the article indicates, this comment arose during the debate over whether Durych should be nominated for the Nobel Prize for Literature.

Although staunchly Catholic in outlook, Durych was not a dutiful follower of Catholic leaders. He was devoted to the Church, in its abstract form, and to the pope as its leader, but he was critical of the Church's human members: bishops, priests, and parishioners. Durych was a believer in the Absolute as the single measure of all things, including the Church and the republic. In the first issue of *Rozmach*, Durych declared that the journal's critical judgements would be based on principles " in no way civil or popular, but absolute," with attention to the fact that "the rise of the Czech Empire will come to be understood as a gesture of God."[59] This notion of the Czech Empire as the bringer of salvation to Europe's East emerged from his allegiance to the Church Invisible, Absolute, and Universal, and to the nation whose greatest heroes were not Hus and Komenský but the medieval saints.[60] He expected others to share his devotion, his understanding of the world in terms of good and evil. Therefore, he could not abide people who hedged on loyalty, faith, and conviction, whether out of political expedience or shallow philosophy.

Or religious complacency. While serving in Ruthenia, in his moment of anger and uncertainty, Durych saw the "witches' Sabbath" not only in society and politics, but also within the Church. Czech Catholics needed to be jarred awake. "It will be necessary to utter blasphemies that Voltaire couldn't imagine," he wrote.[61] These blasphemies would confront Catholics, imploring them to defend their convictions, unlike the so-called pragmatists and realists who stood for nothing. In his early essays for the newspaper *Lidové listy*, herald of the People's Party, Durych prodded Catholic readers with questions. Why had there been no reaction to the anti-Catholic displays of 1918? Why had Czech Catholics just been willing to go back to business in the wake of such outrages?[62] His scandalous 1923 essay "Old Town Square" was part of this campaign to jolt Czech Catholics. While his phrasing was provocative, the description of the cult of Hus as a religion without God only

---

59 Durych, "Uvod," 2.

60 Durych, "Český nacionalismus" [Czech nationalism], in *Jaroslav Durych—publicista*, 128–29. See Putna, *Česká katolická literatura v kontextech, 1918–1945*, 537–38.

61 Durych to Jakub Deml, 28 March 1921, LA PNP, Deml Collection.

62 Václav Durych, *Vzpomínky na mého otce*, 185 and 213–14.

affirmed what the atheist Peroutka and Protestant Rádl also recognized. Yes, Durych lifted the finger to the Hussite nationalists, but his main purpose was to give a fillip to the Catholic readers of *Lidové listy*.[63] "Catholics would be confronted with their own indifference to the destruction of the Marian column," observed Václav Durych in his biography of his father. "Someone from their own ranks had to make himself heard."[64] The elder Durych's statement in the essay, that all Czechs would be Catholic, has been read as example of the writer's ironic provocations and as a serious declaration of the nation's true identity.[65] According to the writer's son, Durych did not regard the essay as a joking matter.[66] But neither was it a counter-argument to the Hussite-Protestant narrative of Czech nationhood. Durych was not simply making a claim that the Czech nation would return to its Catholic faith. Instead, he was urging Czech Catholics to make it happen.

The 1920s were a period of remarkable productivity for Durych. Not only did he serve as editor and principal writer for *Rozmach*, which appeared biweekly, but he also published collections of poems, essays, and stories—some three or four volumes per year, while still holding his day job as a military doctor.[67] In 1929 alone, he published seven titles, including his most acclaimed and popular work: the historical novel *Bloudění* (Wandering). Still regarded as one of the finest works of twentieth-century Czech literature, *Wandering* is an epic novel, rich in detail, in vivid imagery and metaphor, and in the probing depiction of its characters, whether historical figures or the fictional principals who wander through seventeenth-century Europe.[68]

---

63 Ibid.

64 Ibid., 214.

65 The former reading is offered in Putna, *Jaroslav Durych*, 32; the latter in Paces, *Prague Panoramas*, 104–7.

66 The younger Durych records that his mother warned her husband against publishing the essay, but that Jaroslav Durych was compelled by the need to make the strong statement. Václav Durych, *Vzpomínky na mého otce*, 214.

67 Putna, *Česká katolická literatura v kontextech, 1918–1945*, 355–57. Putna devotes an entire chapter of his history of Czech Catholic literature and thought—a chapter totaling over one hundred pages—to Durych's writing and influence in interwar Czechoslovakia.

68 According to a 1998 poll in *Týden*, the leading Czech news magazine, literary critics chose *Bloudění* as the twelfth best Czech novel of the twentieth century (*The Good Soldier Švejk* was ranked first). Two other novels by Durych, *Boží duka* (1955) and *Rekviem* (1930), were also included in the top 35.

The novel centers on Bohemia during the Thirty Years War, opening in 1621 with the executions in Prague of twenty-seven leaders of the anti-Habsburg revolt and closing with the assassination of imperial general Albrecht of Wallenstein in 1634. In between, Durych sets chapters throughout Central Europe, the Netherlands, Spain, and even South America, drawing in characters such as Habsburg Emperor Ferdinand II, Cardinal Richelieu, and Swedish King Gustavus Adolphus. Appearing intermittently in these scenes are Durych's main characters: the Spanish maiden Angela and her two Czech suitors, the Catholic adventurer Kajetan and Wallenstein's attendant Jiří, who comes from a Protestant family but has little regard for God. It is Jiří who ultimately wins Angela's love—and earns her sharpest words. One of the novel's most famous passages is Angela's rebuke to him: "You hate God, ceaselessly, because He created you, and you did not create Him. You hate yourself for the fact that God made you, and you hate me only for the fact that God created me. And so you are afraid of me, that is why you blush in front of me, as if I'm some insult that your enemy has put before you to humiliate you. Surely, you also hate your father and your mother and scorn the devil only because God made them."[69]

Only a few pages later, at the novel's end, Jiří recognizes Angela's wisdom and is reconciled to God on his deathbed. Despite the clichéd ending, Durych's novel is not the typical tale of Catholic redemption. In places Durych adopted the tone of historical texts to make blunt statements against Catholicism's enemies. The first chapter describes Prague's St. Vitus Cathedral, recently reclaimed by the Catholics after the defeat of the Protestant rebellion, as "the former dwelling place of Hell," a place where Satan had once triumphed.[70] Protestants are cast as barbarians, desecrators of sacred places who in one scene nail a dog to a crucifix. But Catholics are by no means heroic. The novel's opening chapter describes a sordid meeting of Church leaders plotting the seizure of formerly Protestant property, and the next chapter presents the executions of the Czech Protestants as a gruesome and gratuitous

---

69 Durych, *Bloudění*, 585–86. An English-language translation of the novel was published in the mid-1930s in the United Kingdom and the United States under the title *Descent of the Idol*.

70 Durych, *Bloudění*, 15.

massacre. Most surprising is the road to redemption that Durych sets for Jiří. The character's skepticism is broken by a book Angela gives him: Jan Amos Komenský's masterpiece of devotional literature, *The Labyrinth of the World and the Paradise of the Heart* (1631). "He set to reading the book and his heart began to flame," Durych wrote. "Perhaps only twice in his reading did he hear the voice of the bishop of the Czech Brethren, otherwise he saw only the picture of a soul, clean and clear like the most beautiful face in a mirror of eternal morning."[71] Jiří is moved by the wisdom of Komenský's words, by the realization that Angela grasps this wisdom, and by his speculation that the words of this Protestant and of the Catholics are not so far apart. "Heretics and Catholics have had some of the same ideas," he muses.[72] Yet even though Durych granted approval to Komenský, Jiří's conversion in the end is to the Catholic faith. Having been injured in the assassination attack on Wallenstein, he prays to St. James and receives communion from a priest—and is joined in marriage to Angela. The device was common in Durych's fiction and poetry: the beautiful, devout, merciful young woman acting as the instrument of salvation and the embodiment of paradise.[73]

Wandering was a sensation. A few critics dismissed the book out of hand, given its subject matter and the provocative Catholicism of its author. But others who opposed the author's religiosity had to admit that Durych had created an extraordinary piece of literature. "Certainly, we must not agree with his conception [of Czech history]," wrote one critic, "but we have to recognize that a great poet wrote *Wandering*."[74] Reviewers described the book as lyrical and epic, transcendental and impressionistic; it was a "beautiful mosaic joined and melded into a single, splendid whole."[75] Critics also saw *Wandering* as an outstanding work of modern fiction, perhaps even a model of the contemporary novel. One reviewer compared Durych's approach, with

---

71 Ibid., 576.
72 Ibid., 575.
73 Putna, *Jaroslav Durych*, 47–50.
74 Josef Hora, "Waldšteinský roman J. Durycha," *Literární noviny*, 9 January 1930, reprinted in Durych et al., *Jaroslav Durych: Život, ohlasy*, 583.
75 R. Stilly, "Durychovo 'Bloudění,'" *Den* (Brno), 29 March 1930, reprinted in Durych et al., *Jaroslav Durych: Život, ohlasy*, 587.

its expressive visuals, to that of a film director, while another suggested that the novelist was like a journalist who unflinchingly depicts the horror of the times. But the term that was applied most often to the work was "baroque." Like the baroque artist, Durych created sprawling, vivid scenes, dense with images of sensuality and violence that revealed dramas of light and darkness, the sublime and the vile. "The greatest baroque painter is Rembrandt," wrote the revered critic F. X. Šalda. "I thought of Rembrandt throughout my reading of Durych's novel, how in its climactic places it was as if Durych translated Rembrandt into words."[76] Along the same lines, Durych's German translator compared the author to a cathedral builder, someone whose "impassioned spiritualism and the integrity of his spiritual vision, as well as his heroic individuality" produces a work of "architecture that begins on the earth and shoots up to the clouds."[77]

In addition to being an art of sweeping harmony and powerful drama, the baroque was also a form of propaganda: visual advertising for Counter-Reformation Catholicism. If *Wandering* was a masterpiece of the modern baroque, then what was *its* message? What did readers find in the novel? Reviewers recognized that there was something deeper in the story, that the lives of the characters and the events that surrounded them were connected to a supernatural order. A number of critics for secular periodicals wrote with familiarity of spiritual matters and spoke appreciatively of Durych's attention to the "Czech soul." For months after the book's publication, its religious theme was a consistent topic in the literary pages, as critics and reviewers wrote of the grace of God and the relationship between the spiritual and the physical. But Durych's aim was not simply to generate discussion of religion.[78] He sought to plumb deeper questions and prompt serious reflection. With his fictional characters Angela, Jiří, and Kajetan, Durych crafted a picture of wandering in the labyrinth, a world of pov-

---

76 F. X. Šalda, "In margine Durychova 'Bloudění,'" *Šaldův zápisník* 2, no. 6 (January 1930), reprinted in Durych et al., *Jaroslav Durych: Život, ohlasy*, 127.

77 Pavel Eisner, "Jaroslav Durych," lecture of 25 February 1931, reprinted in Durych et al., *Jaroslav Durych: Život, ohlasy*, 141. On Durych and the Baroque, see Putna, *Česká katolická literatura v kontextech, 1918–1945*, 403–17.

78 Durych wrote about the inspiration for the novel in the essay "Genese 'Bloudění.'"

erty, cruelty, avarice, and false religion. Was there hope in this labyrinth? The leaders of the Church are corrupt and dishonorable, while the hero Wallenstein, a man of nobility and wisdom, is killed just after he decides to challenge the emperor. Hope is found only in God's grace, in the paradise of the heart. Here was the endpoint of Jiří's wandering and the source of Angela's serenity and strength.

Although a historical novel, Durych's book was attentive to the present. In taking up the style of the baroque as well as setting his novel in the period, Durych challenged the prevalent culture of 1920s Czechoslovakia. The baroque was an age of extremes, in its history as well as its art. The dramatic, eccentric, and expressionistic aspects of the baroque offered a contrast to the art of the middle path: the pragmatic art of Karel Čapek and the smug liberalism of Ferdinand Peroutka. With the character Jiří, a man of Protestant upbringing who has little interest in God and takes prides in his rebellion, Durych presented a representative of contemporary Czech nationalism. And by placing Jiří in the seventeenth century, Durych held up a mirror image of contemporary civilization.[79] The story of *Wandering* came to him during his time in Ruthenia, with his own personal struggle and his fury against the republic coalescing into the idea of an epic novel. He began to read histories of the Thirty Years War and plot characters and scenes while walking in the forests near Užhorod. Although historical, the novel would reveal the absurdities and idolatry and horror of the world he read about in the newspapers from Prague. Albrecht of Wallenstein "also saw the world in this kaleidoscope," he wrote in the first months of the project. "The world was (and is) only a mirrored labyrinth," its glass reflecting a fearful, satanic landscape.[80] To Durych, the Czechoslovakia of Masaryk, of anti-Catholic iconoclasts who toppled statues, and of Čapek's gentlemanly atheism was this labyrinth. The novel he was writing, he recognized, was at its core not about the wanderings of the Spanish maiden Angela or Albrecht of Wallenstein, "but the agonizing Wanderings of Jaroslav Durych."[81]

---

79 Putna, *Česká katolická literatura v kontextech, 1918–1945*, 408–11.
80 Durych to Jakub Deml, 28 March 1921, LA PNP, Deml Collection.
81 Durych to Jakub Deml, 22 January 1921, LA PNP, Deml Collection.

In his own wandering, Durych brought Catholic writing to the main stage of Czech letters. His name even came up in Czech literary journals as a possible candidate for the Nobel Prize in Literature. Anti-Catholic critics shot down the idea, and Durych was not nominated. However, a Catholic writer did win the Nobel Prize in 1929: Norwegian novelist Sigrid Undset. The new literary journal that Durych had launched the previous year, titled *Akord*, featured translations of her work along with that of other European Catholic writers, such as G. K. Chesterton, Jacques Maritain, Paul Claudel, and Georges Bernanos. Jaroslav Durych thus was part of a trend that reached across Europe. In the decades after the Great War, Catholic writers and intellectuals gained prominence, earning the attention of non-Catholic readers and critics. In the Czech literary environment of the 1920s, with its multitude of small journals representing various styles, schools, and ideologies, Durych's rise was a case of singular talent and staggering production winning deserved attention. His success inspired younger Catholic writers. As an editor, first of the journal *Rozmach* and then of *Akord*, he gave many of those writers their first opportunities at publication. The challenge he had set down in his essay "Old Town Square" became their guide. "It falls on Catholics to make Czech culture Catholic," wrote one of his young collaborators in *Akord*.[82] This would be accomplished not through formulaic works or baptized versions of modernist styles, but through quality writing that moved readers. The writer's collaborators shared his outlook on literature as well as his antipathy toward Masaryk's republic. An important difference is that while Durych eschewed any political program, his associates did not. His first journal, *Rozmach*, had come to an end in 1927 when two of his collaborators turned toward fascism. To avoid such political entanglements, his second journal, *Akord*, was to be dedicated wholly to literary and cultural matters. But Jaroslav Durych could not resist political jibes. And as the new decade brought economic trouble at home and political turmoil in neighboring countries, his young colleagues could not resist the antidemocratic Right.

---

82 Putna, *Česká katolická literatura v kontextech, 1918–1945*, 561.

A Cathedral for the Modern Nation

Jaroslav Durych was distressed that Czech Catholics had not risen up in anger after the toppling of the Marian column, and his provocative writing was intended just as much to rouse Catholics as to rile secular nationalists. Yet even in the dark months of 1918–1919, as mobs vandalized statues and clergy plotted schism, there were signs of resilience. Catholic delegates in the provisional assembly, backed by public demonstrations of churchgoers in Moravia, were able to block passage of a bill mandating civil marriages. Representatives of the Czechoslovak People's Party thwarted passage of an education bill they saw as antireligious. Even the education minister's decree on religious decorations in classrooms conceded to Catholic opinion, as the order allowed headmasters and teachers the option to remove or keep objects on display.[83] The Catholic deputies' success in opposing legislation aimed against the Church was notable, given their small presence in the assembly and the anticlerical bent of the major parties. However, these results can be attributed less to their political skill than to the awareness by the assembly's leading politicians that more assertive measures would alienate Catholics in Slovakia and Moravia, a division that would play into the hands of the minority Germans and Hungarians. Indeed, Czechoslovakia's first parliamentary elections in 1920 showed a backlash against the early anti-Catholic policies. The People's Party gained the largest share of votes in Moravia and had surprisingly strong showings in the Bohemian cities of Pardubice, Hradec Králové, and České Budějovice.[84]

The resilience of Catholicism was also evident in the building of new churches in Czechoslovakia's capital. Eight new parish churches were built in Prague in the interwar period, mainly in newly developed, outlying districts.[85] In the design and construction of these new churches, Catholicism's political and social roles in the city intersected

---

83 Trapl, *Political Catholicism*, 49–51.

84 Ibid., 54.

85 In 1922, the municipal boundaries of Prague were expanded to their present extent, incorporating developed suburbs such as Smíchov, Žižkov, and Vinohrady, as well as districts further out that were still largely rural communities.

with the artistic and theological expression of the faith. A new church building not only drew upon the talents of architects and artists to create a meaningful space, it also required the generosity of donors, the approval of planning officials, and of course the commitment of churchgoers. For more than a decade these various players participated in a drama surrounding the planning and construction of Prague's largest and most prominent new church: the Church of the Most Sacred Heart of Jesus. Part of the church's notoriety, then as now, was that its architect was Jože Plečnik. Today, the building is regarded as one of Plečnik's most notable works and a defining example of twentieth-century church architecture.[86] What is missed in the numerous studies of the church, however, is that Plečnik's design had to fit the needs of a parish within a political environment frequently hostile to the Catholic Church. The planning of the church in the 1920s was beset with obstacles and wrapped in controversy. But parish leaders saw the new house of worship as vital for establishing the Catholic Church's standing in the capital of the republic. They held that the monumental structure, with Plečnik's bold design, would demonstrate Catholicism's importance to the democratic and culturally advanced nation.

The Church of the Sacred Heart stands in the Kralovský Vinohrady district of Prague, a stretch of land just east of the city center that had been for centuries the royal vineyards. By the late nineteenth century, urban sprawl had turned this area into a fast-growing, prosperous neighborhood. The district expanded from only 15,000 residents in 1880 to 51,000 in 1910 and more than 83,000 in 1921. This was an upscale area. Architect Jan Kotěra lived here, and Karel and Josef Čapek hosted the Friday meetings of intellectuals at their Vinohrady villa. There were several new residential and commercial buildings con-

---

86　The Church of the Sacred Heart has been the subject of much scholarly attention. Prelovšek discusses the church's design in *Jože Plečnik, 1872–1957*, 223–29; *Plečnikova sakralna umetnost*, 71–3 and 116–36; and "The Church of the Most Sacred Heart of Our Lord in Prague." Architectural historian Ivan Margolius devotes a book to the church's design: *Church of the Sacred Heart: Jože Plečnik*. Ákos Moravánszky discusses the church design in the context of modern Central European architecture in *Competing Visions*, 392–99. Cynthia Paces places the church in the context of Czech Catholicism and debates over national identity, *Prague Panoramas*, 140–48. A collection of essays by Prelovšek, Moravánszky, and others looks at various facets of Plečnik's design for the Prague church and its place in the context of early twentieth-century sacral architecture: *Josip Plečnik a česká sakrální architektura první poloviny 20. století*.

structed just before the war and then again in the early 1920s. These typically followed the latest architectural styles: cubism before the war, constructivism and art deco in the early 1920s.[87] In the midst of the boom, Catholic leaders insisted that the district needed a new church. Already at the turn of the century, they claimed that the number of Catholic residents in Vinohrady far exceeded the capacity of its only church, the neo-Gothic Church of St. Ludmila at present-day Náměstí miru. After years of appeals, in 1908 the city government granted land at King George Square (present-day Náměstí Jiřího z Poděbrad) for a new church in honor of Emperor Franz Joseph's sixtieth jubilee. In 1914 the archbishop of Prague formed a new parish for Vinohrady, appointing a priest and chaplain who held services in a small chapel on the square. Right away, a committee of parishioners began raising funds for a larger building. The onset of war stalled the project, but the committee resumed its work immediately after the close of fighting in 1918.[88] The following year, the building committee announced a design competition for a new "cathedral" (*chrám*) for Prague, a "house of God to commemorate the enthronement of Czech freedom and state independence."[89]

The 1919 design contest, as Czechoslovakia's first open architectural competition, was a major cultural event in the new state, a preview of the possible directions of independent Czech design. Coming at the same time as reformist clergy were breaking from the Catholic Church, the contest was also a cultural statement. The competition jury included representatives of the Church (parish priest František Škarda and Bishop Antonín Podlaha, dean of St. Vitus Cathedral), the respected director of the renovations at St. Vitus (architect Kamil Hilbert), and the most prominent Czech architect (Jan Kotěra). Their call for submissions placed few limitations on the design proposals, stating only that the projects must have "artistic merit."[90] A later statement in the

---

87   See Lukeš, "Architektura."

88   The early history of the parish is recounted in *Farní věstník* 1, no. 2 (1 May 1924), collected in AHMP, Church of the Sacred Heart Collection.

89   "Podmínky ideový soutěže o náčrty pro chrám" [Guidelines for the competition for Cathedral proposals] September 1919, AHMP, Church of the Sacred Heart Collection.

90   Ibid.

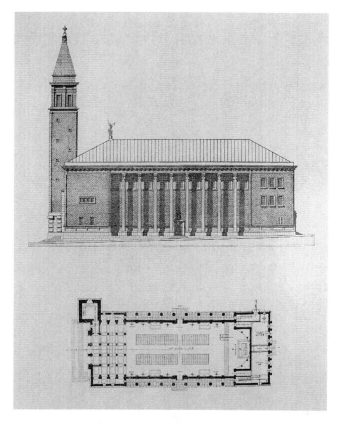

FIGURE 6.3. Alois Mezera, plan for Catholic church, 1920.
Archive of the City of Prague.

professional journal *Styl* explained that while recent churches had
been built according to conservative thinking, the new church, honoring the independence of the Czechs, could not be a "quaint pseudo-ca-
thedral" or "clad in a pseudo-stylistic garb."[91] The church in Vinohrady
would be a cultural monument, emblematic of the times and the cultural development of the nation.[92] To young artists and architects,

---

91 "Soutěž na druhý katolický kostel na Král. Vinohradech" [Competition for the second Catholic
church in Královské Vinohrady] in *Soutěž na druhý katolický kostel na Král*, n.p.. AHMP, Church of
the Sacred Heart Collection.

92 "Příznivcům domu Božího" [To patrons of the House of God], in *Soutěž na druhý katolický kostel na
Král*, n.p.

Figure 6.4. Jindřich Merganc, plan for Catholic church, 1920.
Archive of the City of Prague.

the committee offered a message: the Catholic Church was again a vital partner in the arts, as it had been in the past. Still, the jurors acknowledged, the young generation of artists would have to "tear down
many prejudices."[93]

The results of the contest generated much attention, as many of the
thirty-one designs broke dramatically from traditional church archi-

---

93 Ibid.

tecture. The first and second prizes went to two students of Jože Plečnik: Jindřich Merganc and Alois Mezera. Their designs were clearly inspired by the classical spirit of their professor's studio. Both projects followed the basilica design that Plečnik had used for the Church of the Holy Spirit in Vienna, with additional borrowings from the Gothic and Renaissance styles as well as vernacular architecture.

Yet even though members of the jury celebrated Merganc's and Mezera's designs and the overall results of the competition, they did not endorse a single design for the new church. Rather than entrusting the project to one of Plečnik's students, they hoped for the master himself to design the church. Likewise, Plečnik's admirers in the fraternity of Prague architects hoped he would take up the project. Even while the competition was underway, the Association of Czech Architects made a plea to Plečnik, signed by Merganc and Mezera along with the cubist designers Josef Gočár, Pavel Janák, and Vlastislav Hofman. "We have long been hoping that Prague would one day be enriched by a work of your hands, a work that we are certain would constitute one of its greatest jewels."[94]

Plečnik initially demurred. When the parish priest, František Škarda, first contacted him directly about the project in the autumn of 1918, Plečnik expressed concern about the "spirit of the people of Prague in religious matters."[95] But Plečnik was surprised by the attention the design competition received. Not only did he appreciate the designs, but he was also struck by the number of architects, of the "unbelieving Czechs" that participated in the competition. "So much deep emotion and meaning," he judged.[96] Plečnik eventually relented to the appeals and submitted his own design in 1922. This first proposal conceived of the church in the style of a classical temple, with an adjacent bell tower resembling a Venetian campanile. The building committee welcomed the design and sought to have the plans published in hopes of gaining favor for the project.[97] Whereas he had once been

94 Quoted in Margolius, *Church of the Sacred Heart*, 9.
95 Plečnik to Škarda, 25 October 1918, letter 2 in *Nejměmujte me nikdy*.
96 Plečnik to Titl, 26 March 1924, letter 13 in *Nejměmujte me nikdy*.
97 Titl to Plečnik, 24 March 1924, with copied letter of Podlaha to Titl, 23 March 1924, in PC MGL. See Plečnik's reply, Plečnik to Titl, 26 March 1923, letter 13 in *Nejměmujte me nikdy*.

wary of Prague's anti-Catholic sentiment, Plečnik was now committed to the project. Writing to Škarda's associate priest, Alexander Titl, the architect recognized that the path to completing the church would be difficult. It would be necessary to put the plans before the public, in journals and special publications. Plečnik urged Titl to convince people with his words. "Write like Augustine," he implored, "write in a fiery way, in a great way... I'm relying on it!"[98]

Despite Plečnik's enthusiasm, by 1924 the project was in jeopardy. The city planning commission requested changes in the project for the square, in order to correspond with the planned widening of adjacent streets. Neighbors of the square objected to plans for a school and library alongside the church building. The Czechoslovak Church appealed for a place on King George Square for its own building. And in the city council, Communist and Social Democratic politicians repeatedly raised challenges to the 1908 gift of land to the Catholic Church, claiming that the capital city of independent Czechoslovakia could not allow a transaction made in honor of a Habsburg emperor.[99] At the same time, the building committee had to contend with a chronic lack of funds. In 1924, the building committee had available only a half million crowns in cash, far below what was needed to construct any kind of church.

Mindful of the limited finances, Plečnik offered a wholly new plan in 1925. Gone were the classical and Venetian elements. In their place, the façade was decorated with interlocking arches and circular decorations. Dominating this second design was an attached belfry: a solid, towering structure that would house a multistory rectory. Plečnik preserved a basilica plan for the interior, with one adaptation both tectonic and symbolic: four concrete pillars arranged at the corners of the nave, with a fifth in the very center, representing Christ surrounded by the four Gospel writers. The central column was a favorite motif of Plečnik.[100] First, it was a defiant statement against functionalism: a column in the middle of a portal or, even worse, in the middle of a

---

98 Plečnik to Titl, 26 March 1924, letter 13 in *Nejměmujte me nikdy.*
99 Records of the church building committee, meeting minutes, 6 April 1924, 6 September 1925, and 14 June 1925, AHMP, Church of the Sacred Heart Collection.
100 Discussed in Margolius, *Church of the Sacred Heart,* 12.

FIGURE 6.5. Plečnik, variant for the Vinohrady church, 1922.
Jože Plečnik Collection, Museums and Galleries of Ljubljana, Slovenia.

church nave was ridiculous from a practical standpoint. But having the prime structural support at the center had great meaning for the architect. As a symbol of the divine, a central column could not be ignored. One had to move in relation to it. Yet even though this second design was certainly original and had the support of the building committee, the price tag of seven million crowns was well beyond available funds. Plečnik went back to the drawing board.

Plečnik agreed to submit a new design that would cost three million crowns (and pledged to complete all of his design work without charge). The building committee, meanwhile, launched a broad fundraising campaign. Over the next three years, the committee organized benefit concerts, a door-to-door collection in Vinohrady, and a second-hand sale—all of this along with special collections at other parishes in Prague.[101] The church committee continued to receive individual donations, some thirty-five to fifty contributions per month in 1926 and 1927. But with these gifts amounting only to hundreds, fifties, and tens, the parishioners' generosity was not enough to get the shovels digging.

---

101 Financial statement, records of the church building committee, 1 July 1930, AHMP, Church of the Sacred Heart Collection.

In their appeals for donations, the parish priests had to answer the same question that opponents of the church asked: Why was the new building necessary? As the committee recognized, even parishioners who lived near the square in Vinohrady were not keen on the new building, claiming that they would be willing to make the trip to St. Ludmila's. But as the parish priests, Škarda and Titl knew that without a church nearby, attendance of Catholics around King George Square would lag. "Today everybody wants things close at hand," the committee minutes noted, "and Catholics do not want to walk too far to church."[102] Committee members recognized, however, that they could not base a call for money on the fact that people were lazy. They had to convince parishioners that the church building was necessary not only for Vinohrady's Catholics but also for Prague as a whole, even for the nation. In the first issue of a new parish newsletter, the priests argued that the new church would be a testament to the Czechs' "high degree of cultural maturity." The construction project would also put people to work, laborers as well as artists, helping to revive the economy. As for the spiritual needs of the parish, Father Škarda wrote, "I consider it unnecessary to mention the religious significance of the cathedral for individuals, families, communities, the nation and state."[103]

In fact, Škarda and Titl did see it necessary to mention the reasons the church was valuable to the lives of individuals, families, and the larger society. In issue after issue of the parish newsletter, the two priests made the case vigorously for the local church and the Catholic Church. They warned against secular notions of morality, which set practicality and opinion over lasting, universal authority. They lamented Catholics who went to "worldly offices" to enter civil marriages and reminded parishioners of the church's firm directive against cremation. Parents were urged—repeatedly—to send their children to religious education and to have a Bible in the home. "But don't buy the Bibles that various Bible societies and Methodists offer you!" they

102 Records of the church building committee, meeting minutes, 19 November 1925, AHMP, Church of the Sacred Heart Collection.

103 "Zprávy z farnosti u sv. Aloise" [Report from the St. Alois Parish], *Farní věstník*, 1 May 1924, p. 2, AHMP, Church of the Sacred Heart Collection.

warned.[104] Škarda and Titl insisted that the Roman Catholic Church was *the* universal church founded by Christ.

At the same time, despite their rejection of ecumenism and criticism of contemporary society, the two priests also insisted that Catholicism was compatible with life in a modern, democratic state. Newsletter articles mentioned the strength of the Catholic Church in West European nations and in the United States. Škarda and Titl cited (in bold print) statements of American presidents George Washington and Theodore Roosevelt on the importance of faith for democratic citizenship, even though neither was Catholic. Following the same strategy of citing non-Catholics as authorities, the priests also referred to icons of Czech nationalism. Remember the words of František Palacký, the newsletter urged, referring to the nineteenth-century Protestant historian: "Human character has never been worsened by full commitment to God."[105] Likewise, they pointed out that Jan Hus had appealed to Czechs to serve God, to listen and obey his word.[106] But the priests also insisted upon Catholic practice, rather than endorsing faith in general. They called on parishioners to live their Catholic religion for the sake of responsible citizenship, contentment of character, generosity to the poor, and loyalty to the original faith of the nation. Go to Mass. Receive communion. Fulfill your obligations. To do so was not "unprogressive," the priests urged. "Drawing near to God brings a person at the same time nearer to genuine character," declared the parish newsletter. "Where you do not have this, there is not genuine progress, for genuine progress does not consist only in the perfection of machines, but also in the perfection of our human essence."[107]

According to the priests, clear evidence of the progressive nature of the faith was the planned church building in Vinohrady. Responding to criticism of the church in the conservative newspaper *Čech*, the parish priests insisted that Plečnik, as an artist of genuine religious devo-

---

104 Quotation is from *Farní věstník*, 1 July 1925. See also the issues of 1 August 1924 and 1 March 1925, AHMP, Church of the Sacred Heart Collection.

105 *Farní věstník*, 1 February 1925, AHMP, Church of the Sacred Heart Collection.

106 While citing Hus, the newsletter clarified that state-sanctioned celebrations of the reforming priest profaned rather than honored this legacy. *Farní věstník*, 1 July 1925, AHMP, Church of the Sacred Heart Collection.

107 *Farní věstník*, 1 February 1925, AHMP, Church of the Sacred Heart Collection.

tion, had offered a project that would integrate current design principles with traditional elements of sacral architecture. "Just as people fight every new development in part out of backwardness, and in part because they are professionally unqualified, so is it the case with our church," the parish newsletter declared. Plečnik's design had the approval of the priests and the consistory. It was modern, but also reflected a genuine piety. "The new structure will be characteristic of the religious culture and the forward thinking of our time."[108] Plečnik agreed. He wrote to Titl of his vision for the church:

> We are in a new, a wholly new age, but unfortunately the church of this age has not yet been invented. It's said that nuns prepare the ground for priests with quiet, good work. I would like to know how to accomplish a similar work—i.e., to finish a church in which every soul would find its nook. A glorious cathedral, a great forum— as is alive in all of us—I look forward to this for modern, contemporary people. I have a far-reaching dream, but I cannot get anywhere. I don't know how to bring it to life... You have an opportunity—study, ponder everything you see, so that you will be able to give the most you can to the design of your new church—a church which will be a church, only a church, truly a church and nothing more—and nothing less.[109]

In 1927 the protracted political and legal maneuvers that had blocked the church finally broke open—with the intervention of Plečnik's other patron in Prague. On the recommendation of a "special presidential council," the city assembly referred the question of the land grant to advisers at the Charles University Faculty of Law. The professors determined that the square indeed belonged to the Catholic Church. Foes again raised their voices. In public meetings and newspaper editorials, members of the socialist parties and the Freethinkers Association condemned approval of the land grant, arguing that the government must defend democracy against reactionary cler-

---

108 *Farní věstník*, 1 October 1928, AHMP, Church of the Sacred Heart Collection.
109 Plečnik to Titl, 16 November 1926, letter 23 in *Nejměmujte me nikdy*.

icals.[110] Over this opposition, the city council affirmed the law professors' finding and approved construction of the new church building in June 1928.[111]

At the same time, the Church of the Sacred Heart received a gift from above, or at least from a wealthy donor: a bequest of land that brought nearly four million crowns in sale. The construction estimate for Plečnik's third design came to roughly five million crowns, just over the amount of working cash available to the committee. Nevertheless, with the legal challenges averted and city approval gained, the parish leaders decided to go forward, "with God's help." On October 28, 1928, the tenth anniversary of the republic's founding, the cornerstone was set. Banners flew, music played, and children marched in their Sunday best on the warm autumn day. The intent was clear in choosing that day for the dedication: the church was to be a monument to Czech national independence. "This future cathedral will be built in memory of that great day when we gained independence," the parish priests declared. "This cathedral has to express our nation's gratitude to God for the gift of freedom. In this cathedral our prayers for our beloved land will be lifted to God."[112] Even though Fathers Škarda and Titl railed against the social and cultural changes since independence, they maintained that Catholic faith and practice were harmonious with citizenship in the democratic state. The new church would be proof.

The building committee and parish priests continued to make appeals for support as the new church's foundation was laid and its walls were raised.[113] Records of the fundraising campaign show that a large number of people, mainly from Vinohrady but also from other parts of Prague and the Czech Lands, contributed consistently to the building of the new church. In one three-week period in November 1930, for example, over ninety different donors gave money for the church, with amounts ranging from the two crowns given by a construction worker

110 Clippings from *Právo lidu*, 15 March 1928, and *České slovo*, 15 March 1928, in AHMP, Church of the Sacred Heart Collection.

111 Records of church building committee, meeting minutes, 27 June 1927 and 10 June 1928, AHMP, Church of the Sacred Heart Collection.

112 *Farní věstník*, 1 December 1928, AHMP, Church of the Sacred Heart Collection.

113 Records of the fundraising efforts are collected in the documents of the church building committee, AHMP, Church of the Sacred Heart Collection, box 3.

FIGURE 6.6 AND 6.7. Plečnik, design for the Vinohrady church, 1928. Archive of the City of Prague.

to 9,000 crowns left in a parishioner's will.[114] As the Great Depression slowed the Czechoslovak economy, however, donations for the new church dwindled and the project was on the verge of being halted in summer 1931. Titl and Škarda made a more pointed appeal. An article in the July issue of the parish newsletter commented on the number of millionaires who lived in Vinohrady. The article remarked that, unfortunately, the building committee was at the point of having to stop construction and increasing the ranks of unemployed, even though so many residents of the district were still living well. "How can it be that the rich do not know sacrifice while those without property make extra sacrifices?" the priests asked. "The rich think that the Lord God does not need anything, that they have their abundance and do not need to sacrifice anything for the Lord God. Their faith is like a small spark, which threatens to be extinguished at any moment."[115] The millionaires—and others—got the message. Whether the priests' reprimand was the inspiration, or the sight of the church itself taking shape on the square, donations climbed in the second half of 1931 and the years that followed.

As the building took shape on King George Square, another problem that the parish priests faced, along with the financial challenge, was persistent opposition to the unusual design. Plečnik's final plan before the groundbreaking in 1928 offered a bold vision of a modern church. He maintained the basilica structure from the earlier variants, but the church tower was a remarkable departure: a broad tower on the east end, nearly as wide as the sanctuary, with a circular window in its center and four towers, like royal maces, surrounding it.

The new design met with sharp criticism from conservative Catholics. However, Titl and Škarda used the protests for their own purposes. In the parish newsletter, they wrote of the complaints as evidence of the new church's suitability to modern Prague. The building in Vinohrady was proof that the broader Church was able to look forward. This view, that traditional convictions could be merged with modern design, corresponded to that of Plečnik. In his designs for the

---

114 *Farní věstník*, 1 January 1931, AHMP, Church of the Sacred Heart Collection.
115 "Bohaté Kral. Vinohrady?" [Wealthy Kralovské Vinohrady?], *Farní věstník*, 1 July 1931, AHMP, Church of the Sacred Heart Collection.

church in Prague as well as projects in Vienna and Slovenia, Plečnik held to the model of the Roman basilica because it represented what he saw as the democratic structure of the early Christian churches.[116] Plečnik sought a physical closeness of priest and worshippers in the space of the basilica, following his understanding of the early Christian service. At the same time, he had a Christocentric approach to worship, drawn from Byzantine and baroque churches. Bringing the altar closer to the congregation established Christ as the focal point of the church service and the church building (similar to the symbolic pillar in the center of the sanctuary in one of his early designs for the Vinohrady church).[117] Plečnik was adamant: Christ was Lord; he was not some democrat.[118] The church, therefore, was not a place for comfort. Plečnik refused any suggestion of modern upgrades to the Vinohrady church, such as central heating. "Such modern garbage does not belong in a Catholic cathedral of the Lord," the architect wrote to Titl. "A Catholic church is not a cinema, or a bar or a theater—it's Calvary."[119]

Even with this defense of traditional Catholic architecture, Plečnik saw his design for the Vinohrady church as a step forward. "No one, from the ancients to the moderns, has been able to build halls like these," he told his students in Ljubljana; "this is progress."[120] An essay in the parish newsletter echoed this assessment. Written by Josef Cibulka, a priest and Vienna-trained expert on Catholic art and architecture, the piece was intended to silence complaints that Plečnik's design was too modern, too provocative. Every age seeks the beauty of God, wrote the respected professor, and every new generation of artists mixes colors revealed by the light of God. Cibulka declared complaints about the church's modern design as unjustifiable. "There is no such thing as a *modern* Catholic church. It does not exist—there is only a Catholic church."[121] There would be prayer in the new sanctuary, there

---

116 Quoted in Prelovšek, *Jože Plečnik: Architectura perennis*, 77.

117 Krečič, *Jože Plečnik*, 66.

118 Plečnik to Titl, 7 January 1933, letter 87 in *Jejměnujte me nikdy*, 51.

119 Plečnik to Titl, 22 May 1932, letter 74 in *Jejměnujte me nikdy*, 44.

120 Quoted in Prelovšek, *Jože Plečnik: Architectura perennis*, 229.

121 Josef Cibulka, "Pějme Pánu píseň novou" [Let us sing a new song to the Lord], *Farní věstník*, 1 December 1928, AHMP, Church of the Sacred Heart Collection.

would be peace, there would be inspiration and jubilation. The church on King George Square would be a gate to heaven, wrote Cibulka at the start of construction. "We will sing a new song to the Lord."[122]

Conclusion

In December 1931 Tomáš Masaryk went to church—at least for a visit. He recorded his thoughts in a letter to a longtime collaborator and friend of the household:

> I want to say a few words about my visit to your church in Vinohrady. The question and problems of churches have long held my attention: how does a church's form and interior arrangement convey the main idea of religion? ... In our republic we have two main churches, the Catholic and Protestant. Catholicism is essentially mystical and mysterious, sacramental, therefore the ritual, especially the Mass, necessitates above all an altar. The sermon is secondary. Therefore, the placement of the pulpit is a difficult task, especially in Gothic cathedrals, but also in the Romanesque. Protestants put emphasis on the sermon. Again they have the problem, how and where to place the pulpit? Because a majority are second-hand Catholic cathedrals, they have not reached a general solution. And new churches conform to old, accepted models.
> I envision Christianity according to Jesus and thus I would have the cathedral mimic the Sermon on the Mount: in a spacious (not Gothic!) place an elevated pulpit would be the Mount and the preacher would speak from there. And he would have to be seen and heard from the sides...
> Your church is spacious; I like that; the only thing I do not understand is why you have two pulpits, as I was informed by the priest. Did you think about the relationship between pulpit and altar? Of course you did, maybe without much deliberation.
> I am only speaking about the inside of the church; the outside is a purposeful, interesting experiment.

---

122 Ibid.

I would like to add that I prefer Romanesque buildings; the cupola reflects the sphere of heaven, as we see it. The Gothic (architecture, not sculpture) is an expression of medieval scholasticism. It oppresses me, I do not feel well in it. This may be a personal view and up to a point unsubstantiated.

I do not wish to wear out the problem: there are still so many questions (there are more altars in Catholic churches—how to arrange them?, etc.), of decoration in particular—we could discuss this for a long time. And there is literature on the subject anyway.

I hope all is well. Stay healthy![123]

After receiving the letter, Jože Plečnik forwarded a copy to the chaplain of the Vinohrady parish. Alexander Titl was not impressed. "Someone can be an excellent statesman, perhaps even a 'philosopher,'" the priest remarked in reply to Plečnik, "but art is quite unfamiliar to him." Titl responded sharply to Masaryk's misunderstanding of a Catholic sanctuary, especially the president's suggestion that the interior should resemble the scene of the Sermon on the Mount. "Jesus also preached from a boat pulled to the shore," he pointed out. The letter showed that Titl's negative view went beyond the president's opinion of the church building. Indeed, he wrote with the tone of someone who had tired of Masaryk's criticisms of Catholicism over the years. He did not think highly of Masaryk's "iron logic," remarking that "scattered philosophy leads to similar judgments." Then he stopped himself. "Excuse me, dear professor," Titl closed, "but it is not possible to write everything."[124]

In halting his letter, Titl was likely mindful of Plečnik's relationship with Masaryk—and perhaps he remembered that this relationship had cleared obstacles for the church's construction. But the priest's reaction illustrates the difficulties that the Czech Catholic Church had with Masaryk. Titl recognized that the president commanded great respect, but Masaryk had also been a notorious opponent of the Church. He had brought independence to the Czechs, but

---

123 Masaryk to Plečnik, 23 January 1932, copy in Archiv KPR, number 675, file D 3917/32. Partial English translation in Prelovšek, "The Church of the Most Sacred Heart of Our Lord in Prague," 575–76.
124 Titl to Plečnik, 6 February 1932, PC MGL.

FIGURES 6.8 AND 6.9. The Church of the Sacred Heart on King George Square. Jože Plečnik Collection, Museums and Galleries of Ljubljana, Slovenia.

he had not shown himself a friend to Czech Catholics. This ambiguous view of Masaryk paralleled an ambiguous understanding of the Church's place in the republic. Prague clergy expressed criticism of modern society and culture, while at the same time they claimed to have a relevant role in the modern Czech nation. In the 1930s, more and more parishioners agreed with them. While observers of Czech society still wrote of an indifference or even hostility to religion, other evidence showed increased identification with the Catholic Church. After the hostility of the early 1920s and the expectation of Masaryk and others that this backward, un-Czech religion would continue to decline, Catholicism in the 1930s showed signs of life in Prague. In Vinohrady, it grew vibrantly.

Once construction on Plečnik's church was completed, people did come to sing and pray. Parish records show that the opening of the new church in 1932, called the Church of the Sacred Heart, enlivened Catholic practice in Vinohrady. During the 1920s, when services were held at the St. Alois Chapel, Škarda and Titl had served communion to roughly 20,000 people each year. After construction of the new church commenced in 1928, the number of people taking communion steadily increased. In 1932, the priests served 43,500 people. By 1936, the number of communicants had climbed to 62,500—in more than two thousand services during the year.[125] People not only came to church, they also gave to the work of the church. In addition to their donations for completion of the new sanctuary, parishioners gave more than 20,000 crowns for charity each year in the mid-1930s. At the height of the Depression, the Church of the Sacred Heart was able to provide one thousand pounds of food and five thousand pounds of coal each month to more than sixty families in need.[126]

The picture we gain from Vinohrady parish records is of a community of Catholics that provided support for a new church building during the hard years of the Depression, and was then invigorated by the opening of that new church. This active religious participation among Prague

---

125 Annual statistics on the numbers of sacraments served were published in the February issues of *Farní věstník*, AHMP, Church of the Sacred Heart Collection.

126 *Farní věstník*, 1 February 1933; and *Farní věstník*, 1 February 1935, AHMP, Church of the Sacred Heart Collection.

Catholics goes against the common view, expressed anecdotally by observers of the time and seconded by scholars today, that most Czechs who claimed to be Catholics—particularly in the republic's modern capital—had only a nominal affiliation with the Church. The Vinohrady parish was not an isolated example in Prague. According to the 1930 census, the number of Catholic adherents in Prague grew by more than 100,000 over the 1921 census. In that same period, there was also a decrease in the number of people in Prague who claimed no religious affiliation. In contrast, across Bohemia and Moravia as a whole the number of people without a declared religion increased.[127] Surely, many of these Prague Catholics were the kind of indifferent adherents that observers had noted for years, people who had been baptized into the Church but paid little attention to it as adults. Yet there was evidence of active participation. Ordinations in the Prague archbishopric increased in the 1930s, as did the number of men entering monasteries. Seven new churches were built in Prague, in addition to the Church of the Sacred Heart, in districts that had been incorporated within the city's municipal boundaries in the 1920s.[128] And Catholics asserted their place in the public arena with major gatherings: commemoration of St. Václav's martyrdom in 1929 brought tens of thousands of pilgrims to Prague; that same year, over 100,000 young Catholics came to the capital for the July festival of the Orel (Eagle) athletics club; and hundreds of thousands visited Prague in 1935 for both the first republic-wide Catholic congress and an international conference of Catholic university students. A special Mass during the Catholic congress—with scripture readings in six languages—drew 300,000 people to Prague's Strahov Stadium.[129]

127 The overall Catholic population across Bohemia and Moravia grew by roughly 173,000 in that same period. The number in Prague who indicated no religious affiliation declined by 1,000, while the number across the rest of the Czech Lands increased by more than 100,000. Brotánková, "Religiozita v okresech ČR v období 1921–2001," appendices.

128 These were the churches of St. Václav in Vršovice (consecrated in 1930), Christ the King in Vysočany (1930), St. Elizabeth in Kbely (1932), St. Agnes of Bohemia in Spořilov (1935), Mary, Queen of Peace, in Lhota (1937), St. Francis of Assisi in Chodov (1938), and St. Theresa in Kobylisi (1938). See Boháč, "Vystavba katolických kostelů v zazemí pražských měst v letech," map 12 in *Atlas církevních dějin českých zemí, 1918–1999*. On ordinations and monastic vocations, see sections 7–8 and 13 of Boháč's book.

129 Klimek, *Velké dějiny zemí koruny české*, 14:330–31; and Šebek, "Der tschechische Katholizismus," 148–52. On the 1929 St. Václav jubilee, the 1935 Catholic congress, and their importance for Czech national politics, see Paces, *Prague Panoramas*, 129–38 and 149–56.

The history of the Vinohrady parish shows that Catholic clergy sought to be both relevant to and critical of contemporary society and culture. Tomáš Masaryk, however, saw no role for the Catholic Church in the moral republic. The president remained an opponent of the Roman Church to the end of his life (Jože Plečnik was unique as a Catholic who had gained the president's favor). Masaryk found great significance in the fact that the first president of Czechoslovakia was a Protestant. "The Reformation is *de facto* fulfilled in me," he told Alice in 1934. "And the Catholics are well aware of what that means."[130] But Masaryk did not hold a favorable opinion of non-Catholic churches either, despite the claims of both the unified Protestant Church and the breakaway Czechoslovak Church to follow in his legacy. As commentators like Ferdinand Peroutka and Josef Hromádka recognized, Masaryk's ideas did not fit with any conception of church. Masaryk himself understood this: in private conversation, he spoke of how he had tried to attend services after entering the Reformed Church, but his understanding of God was too subjective.[131] The irony is that he attempted to turn his subjective, individual experience of God into a universal theory of religion and a political philosophy at the foundation of a new state. The core of his religion was the individual's conviction of God and sense of moral behavior. In a sense, this vision of a new, wholly individualized religion was fulfilled in his circle of supporters. Masaryk was surrounded by people with their own, personal understandings of the divine: the atheist Peroutka believed that Masaryk's views on religion approached his own; the Catholic Plečnik described Masaryk to his students as a man of unique wisdom, someone on a different plane; and the Protestant Hromádka called him the nation's greatest philosopher of religion. They all found something in Masaryk's thinking that resonated with their own beliefs. But they were not bound by shared acceptance of his ideas. All they had in common was reverence for Masaryk himself.

---

130 Gašparíková-Horáková, diary entry of 15 March 1934, in *U Masarykovcov*, 223.

131 Gašparíková-Horáková, diary entry of May Sunday 1931, in *U Masarykovcov*, 107.

Chapter Seven

The War of the Absolute

In May 1934 the Czechoslovak parliament elected Tomáš Masaryk president for the fourth time. At age eighty-four, Masaryk was in declining health. He had suffered a stroke three weeks before the election and wanted to step aside. But with Czechoslovakia's industrial economy hit hard by the Depression, particularly in German-populated regions, and with the rise of the Nazis in neighboring Germany, the republic faced profound challenges. A transition from the revered President-Liberator to a new president would only add to the uncertainty. Moreover, there was no clear successor. Antonín Švehla, leader of the Agrarian Party and three-time prime minister, had been the republic's leading political figure after the president. But he had passed away from illness in 1933. Masaryk's preferred candidate was the foreign minister, Edvard Beneš. Yet while Beneš had the president's trust, he was a divisive and unpopular figure—something Masaryk was aware of. In part, Masaryk decided to stand for a fourth election in the hope that Beneš would be able to build a base of support among the Czech and Slovak parties. Masaryk's election in 1934 thus was a sign of Czechoslovakia's political weakness. Even though he was little more than a figurehead by that point, he was a necessary figurehead, the symbol of the republic's authority. In the words of historian Peter Bugge, Masaryk stood alone "as the incarnation and guardian of Czechoslovak democracy."[1]

---

[1] Bugge, "Czech Democracy," 22. On Masaryk's illness and the presidential election of 1934, see Klimek, *Velké dějiny zemí koruny české*, 14:283–93.

As the problems facing Czechoslovakia grew more ominous, Masaryk's supporters reasserted what they saw as the principles he had established: democracy over authoritarian rule, tolerance over prejudice, compromise over violence. Statements of the republic's ideals by writers and journalists affiliated with the Castle, especially Karel Čapek and Ferdinand Peroutka, were intended to reinforce the unique purpose of Czechoslovakia as a democratic state. But just as Masaryk's election indicated the weakness of the Czechoslovak political structure, reassertions of the republic's principles revealed the limits of Czechoslovakia's political program, at least the program that Masaryk had envisioned. If the stability of Czechoslovak democracy required Masaryk as its embodiment, this was all the more the case with his ideas of politics and morality. As president, Masaryk had advocated a civil religion for the Czechoslovak state, drawing upon the far-reaching ideas he had formulated as a philosopher, critic, and politician—ideas about nationhood, history, theology, ethics, and politics. Yes, this program had its disciples. But as members of Masaryk's own circle recognized, people such as the atheist journalist Peroutka and the Protestant theologian Hromádka, the president's ideas did not correspond to the thinking of most Czechs. The republic had not ushered in a new partnership of citizen and state, built on the ideals of *humanita* and *sub specie aeternitatis*. At the start of the 1930s, even Masaryk conceded that the Czechs had not embraced the nation's religious purpose, the meaning of its history. "Sometimes I wonder how it's possible that our deep religious tradition has been completely lost," he admitted privately.[2]

What then would be Masaryk's legacy? In the 1930s, his supporters offered varied interpretations of his life and thought. The different views reflected disagreement over Masaryk's lessons for the nation, and they led to disputes with the president's closest circle. The president's daughter Alice assumed guardianship over his legacy, keeping close watch over how he was presented in his final years. She also envisioned an expansion of the castle project—with Plečnik acting as architect—that would transform the district surrounding Hradčany into a lasting monument to her father. But the days of building monu-

---

2   Gašparíková-Horáková, diary entry of 17 April 1931, in *U Masarykovcov*, 110.

ments were over. Czechoslovakia had to strengthen itself against an aggressive Nazi Germany. Internally, the leaders of the republic faced economic crisis, German and Slovak parties demanding autonomy, and right-wing Czech nationalism (a coup attempt by fascist officers was put down in 1933). Plans for more construction in honor of Masaryk did not have a place amidst the tumult and uncertainty of the mid-1930s. Was that the case for Masaryk's ideas as well?

Convictions of the President-Liberator

In the spring of 1930, fresh from his triumph as author of the novel *Wandering*, Jaroslav Durych got himself into trouble again. Writing in *Akord*, the literary journal he had founded, he ventured back into the prickly issue of Catholics and the Czechoslovak state. This time, he directed his statements not to Karel Čapek, the representative of official Czech culture, but to the president himself. In light of continued criticism of Czech Catholics, including statements from the president's close supporters, Durych asked Masaryk to explain his own opinions. Masaryk's harsh writings against Catholicism were decades past. But where did the president stand now? Did he support the words of his friends and followers, or reject them?[3]

Again the pro-Masaryk press launched attacks on Durych. This time, Čapek did not come to the defense. Instead, he wrote in *Lidové noviny* (in an unsigned piece) that it was improper for a serving army officer to demand such a declaration from his commander in chief, "especially on a matter so delicate and deeply personal as his relation to religion and the church."[4] Army authorities took the cue, and filed charges against the troublesome Durych. The case, however, was eventually dropped on the president's intervention. Still, Masaryk did not answer Durych's request for an update on his views of the Catholic Church.[5]

---

3   Jaroslav Durych, "Spravedlnost" [Justice], *Akord*, 1 May 1930, reprinted in *Jaroslav Durych—publicista*, 275–78.

4   "To snad být nemusí" [Perhaps it must not be], *Lidové noviny*, 22 May 1930, in *Od člověka k člověku II*, 408–9.

5   By this time, Masaryk and Durych had met personally. Čapek had arranged for the novelist to visit Masaryk's summer retreat in Slovakia in 1927. There is no record of their conversation.

Masaryk did reply, though, to another appeal concerning religion, at roughly the same time. In December 1929, Christian von Ehrenfals, a professor of philosophy at the German university in Prague, wrote an open letter to the president in the journal *Philosophische Schriften*. According to Ehrenfals, the modern age demanded a new religion based upon scientific principles, one that would guide people to a cultivated altruism and sense of cooperation with God. Ehrenfals insisted that his old university colleague was the only person capable of launching this "realist Catholicism." Masaryk refused the request. The president wrote in reply that he had diagnosed the religious crisis of the age but had not formulated a "timeless creed." Masaryk explained his interest in religious questions: "I believe that I am by nature a man of politics, and because I want to have a political position on morality—love for one's neighbor—I must understand all matters of morality. But that does not require me to understand all matters of religion. Insofar as I understand myself correctly, I am a 'political builder'—that is to say, I would diminish to a certain point your notion of a builder of religion."[6]

The fact that both the traditional Catholic Durych and the pantheist philosopher Ehrenfals called for an explicit statement from Masaryk suggests that after a lifetime of writing about religion, the president still left people confused. "Often I cannot accept for myself Masaryk's theoretical views on religion," recorded the president's personal archivist, Anna Gašparíková, after one of many long conversations with the president.[7] In the eight years that Gašparíková lived in the Masaryk household at the Lány palace, she spoke often with the president about religion and listened to his conversations with others. A Slovak Protestant, she recognized the depth of his conviction and learned from his practical approach to religion, but she still remained unsettled by his opinions. For those outside the house of Masaryk, who did not hear his nightly discourses on church history, the Old and New Testaments, Dostoevsky, American religion, and the contemporary Czech churches, Masaryk's public statements on religion could be even more confusing. The president's interpreters sought to bring clar-

---

6   Quoted in Pauza, "Von Ehrenfelsova výzva T. G. Masarykovi k založení tzv. reálného katolicismu," 5.

7   Gašparíková-Horáková, diary entry of May Sunday 1931, in *U Masarykovcov*, 108.

ity to these views, with mixed success. Masaryk's religion, the new religion, remained elusive.

At the turn of the 1920s–30s, two loyal followers of Masaryk published volumes that canvassed the president's views on a broad range of issues, including religion. Their books, coming from very different perspectives, both stumbled on the matter of Masaryk's beliefs. One of these authors was theologian Josef Hromádka, who published in 1930 a comprehensive analysis of the president's philosophical, religious, and political thought. Hromádka regarded himself—to the end of his life—as Masaryk's student, and his appraisal was overwhelmingly positive. His book praised the president's unbending moral character, the heroic stances he had taken in his early career as a politician, journalist, and academic, and his ceaseless defense of the individual's dignity and freedom of conscience. "Masaryk is our greatest philosopher, our greatest philosopher of religion, and the greatest European in our country," he declared.[8] Masaryk was far-reaching in his knowledge and well reasoned in his criticism of romanticism, positivism, and liberalism. In contrast to those philosophies, Masaryk's ideal of *humanita* was a sound philosophy for moral action in the modern age, one that rejected the tendencies toward determinism and titanism in nineteenth-century thought. "*Humanita* is activity, never quietness," Hromádka wrote. "It is not sentimentalism, but work, and still more work. Masaryk is right."[9] Like many Czech followers of Masaryk, Hromádka placed the president among Europe's greatest modern thinkers, even above them. Hume, Hegel, Comte, Nietzsche, Dostoevsky—Masaryk had taken on all of them, criticizing and synthesizing, and he had set before the Czechs a better understanding of Europe and its purpose.[10] According to Hromádka, Masaryk understood that Europe was a set of ideas—personal freedom, the imperatives of rights and justice, the obligations to responsibility and criticism—and his great contribution to the nation had been in steering the Czechs toward a place in this Europe.[11]

---

8 Hromádka, "Masaryk as European," in *The Field Is the World*, 122.
9 Hromádka, *Masaryk*, 144.
10 Ibid., 147.
11 Hromádka, "Masaryk as European," in *The Field Is the World*, 121–22.

Hromádka's book was based on years of serious study. He had written his doctoral dissertation and numerous articles on Masaryk's religious thought. Yet even though he was an admirer, Hromádka was also a sharp, scholarly critic, especially in the chapter on the president's religious ideas. Yes, Hromádka acknowledged, Masaryk was correct in his fight against religious indifference, against empty formalism, and against the Catholic Church's association with state power. He understood that Masaryk wanted religion to be "neither a mood nor an emotional sensation, a dreamy delusion or an ornament of life."[12] But Hromádka judged Masaryk's attempts at a theory of religion as mistaken. The theologian admitted that Masaryk was a critic and analyst rather than "a builder of cathedrals."[13] At the same time, however, Hromádka understood that Masaryk had sought to build something of a cathedral, and he saw his own task as exposing that structure's faulty foundations.

Although he did not repeat the term in his study, Hromádka replied to Masaryk's idea of a new religion. The theologian admitted that Masaryk's vision was admirable, in the sense that he wanted a religion of critical rationalism as opposed to unthinking naturalism, a religion of moral autonomy as opposed to "pantheistic slush." But in his harangues against institutional religion, Masaryk revealed the instinctive judgments of a nineteenth-century rationalist, rather than someone who truly understood belief and practice. Hromádka charged that Masaryk showed his lack of knowledge of ecclesiology in his criticism of churches. He did not see the significance of the church as a community of believers, rather than a refuge for mystics or conservator of tradition.[14] Hromádka also countered Masaryk's repeated declaration that faith in revelation was an escape into myth. Belief in the God revealed in scripture required constant self-criticism, Hromádka rebutted. This faith brought recognition of the limits of humanity.[15]

According to the theologian, the principal errors of Masaryk's religious philosophy were its central tenets—his notions of the human

---

12   Hromádka, *Masaryk*, 114.
13   Ibid., 121.
14   Ibid., 144–46.
15   Ibid., 138–39.

and the divine. Masaryk concentrated his theories on humanity, on the individual's moral responsibility and freedom of conscience. The individual did not need grace—according to Masaryk, this led to fatalism. Nor did the individual need redemption. In Masaryk's vision, the person of religious conviction was in the process of becoming a fully conscious collaborator with God. This individual subject was the true center of Masaryk's philosophy of religion, argued Hromádka.[16] God offered wisdom, providential administration of the universe, and guarantee of eternity and the immortality of the soul. God was, in Hromádka's reading of Masaryk, the capstone of a philosophical system. Masaryk's God was more like that of Plato and Aristotle, rather than the God of Hus and Komenský. As the God of philosophers, Masaryk's deity was ultimately displaced from the center of the new religion. Hromádka concluded: "Masaryk's *sub specie aeternitatis* means that not God but man alone, by the light of his rational and moral norms, is judge of himself, humanity, and the world... Man is the measure of God."[17]

Hromádka's criticism of Masaryk represented a larger theological struggle in European Protestantism during the interwar period. In his understanding of revelation and the nature of Christ, Hromádka aligned with the Swiss theologian Karl Barth, the leading figure in the emerging body of thought known as neo-orthodoxy or dialectical theology. Masaryk, in contrast, was a product of nineteenth-century liberal Protestantism. When Hromádka faulted Masaryk for his privileging of rationalism and skepticism over revelation and community, the theologian showed his opposition to the older stream of Protestant thought, which had been founded on a historical-critical approach to scripture. In the shared view of Hromádka and Barth, liberal Protestantism had exhausted itself by the First World War; in seeking a rational understanding of God, it offered little more than optimism. Nevertheless, the established liberal school of theology still held sway in seminaries across Europe after the war, including in Prague. Hromádka's senior colleagues at the Protestant theological faculty

16   Ibid., 122–23.
17   Ibid., 151.

voiced firm opposition to the brash young theologian, his attacks on Masaryk, and the ideas of neo-orthodoxy. According to František Linhart, a historian of religion at the Protestant theological faculty, Masaryk's religious and moral thought offered a synthesis that is "the aim of our [Czech] spiritual life," while Hromádka's religious ideas were mired in tradition, scholasticism, and dogma. "It is necessary to get past this metaphysical dualism," Linhart wrote of Hromádka's theology.[18] The Czechs were the nation of Masaryk, the established Protestant scholars insisted, not of Karl Barth.

For his own part, Masaryk also did not appreciate Hromádka's critiques. The president had a number of Hromádka's books in his library, and the surviving copies show that he read the theologian attentively. For example, he marked most pages of Hromádka's 1922 book *Christianity and Scientific Knowledge*, based on the theologian's dissertation. Masaryk used red and blue pencils to underline phrases and sentences, and then he would frequently pick up a regular pencil to write in the margins. Masaryk did find statements with which he agreed, statements that sounded much like his own, on the necessity of faith in the modern age and the relevance of Christianity to contemporary social thought. But for most of the book, Masaryk disputed Hromádka's claims. In particular, the president took exception to the passages that discussed his own ideas. He underlined Hromádka's statement, "Masaryk's ideal of *humanita* is not a Christian ideal." Masaryk wrote "<u>is</u>" next to the sentence. Where Hromádka wrote that the foundations of *humanita* are reason and moral philosophy, the president added "also revelation of God." To Hromádka's interpretation that his religious philosophy was a "worldly, cultural ideal," Masaryk noted "but *sub specie aeternitatis*."[19] Although the president maintained ties with Hromádka (the theologian visited Masaryk at his country retreat on a few occasions), he did not appreciate the consistent critiques of his own religious ideas. Masaryk stated after one conversation with Hromádka that he had no patience for the theologian's

---

18 Linhart, "Masaryk a Křest'anství," 278. On the disagreements between Hromádka and the Czech liberal Protestants, see Funda, "František Žilka, František Linhart, Alois Spisar, František Kovář."

19 Masaryk's comments are on pages 36–7 of Hromádka's *Křest'anství a vědecké myšlení*, from the remnants of the president's personal library, MÚA AV ČR. Underlining in original.

FIGURE 7.1. Jan Masaryk, Alice Masaryková, Tomáš Masaryk, and Karel Čapek at the president's summer palace, 1931. Masaryk Institute and Archive, Academy of Sciences, Czech Republic.

"scholarly formulations."[20] Hromádka himself recognized that he was not well received in the house of Masaryk, despite his longstanding relationships with Alice Masaryková and Vasil Škrach. After publication of his book on Masaryk, the theologian acknowledged a "cold wind" from the castle.[21]

In contrast to Hromádka's systematic and critical analysis, Karel Čapek's popular biography offered a portrait of the president seemingly on Masaryk's own terms. One of the most celebrated books of interwar Czechoslovakia, and indeed of all twentieth-century Czech literature, *Hovory s T. G. Masarykem* (*Conversations with T. G. Masaryk*) was the product of a unique collaboration of the sitting head of state and the country's most acclaimed writer. Starting in 1926, Čapek conducted a series of interviews with Masaryk and then crafted his notes into a cohesive first-person narrative, with the president himself de-

---

20 Gašparíková-Horáková, diary entry of 9 April 1929, in *U Masarykovcov*, 15.
21 Šimsa, "J. L. Hromádka jako Masarykův žák," 29.

scribing the events of his life.[22] In the books (the *Conversations* were originally published in three volumes, in 1928, 1931, and 1935), Masaryk appears at once noble and folksy. He describes rural life in the mid-nineteenth century with matter-of-fact honesty, admitting his own childhood belief in witches and spirits and his fear of Jews using Christian blood in rituals. The text often detours from the biographical narrative to observations on contemporary life or straightforward lectures, with Masaryk coming across at once as a widely read intellectual and a man of common-sense wisdom.

Masaryk is also shown as a man of genuine faith. The first volume of the *Conversations* offers the president's fond memories of church services in the villages of his youth, his account of the questioning that led him to leave the Church, and his great love for the American Charlie Garrigue, a devout woman of firm principles. In volume two, Masaryk recounted his struggles at the turn of the century against conservative clerics who, in his telling, had less understanding of the Catholic faith than he did. The narrative then turns to a discourse on Christianity and the churches. In his talks with Čapek, Masaryk expressed a sense of loss at the passing of traditional religiosity. Remembering Sunday-morning services in the village, he acknowledged the function they had in binding the community, and he lamented that they had been made obsolete by sports teams, films, and radio. "Instead of the divine service they have a fat Sunday paper," he said regretfully. "I wonder as I thumb through it, 'Can this really take the place of the services I knew as a child?'"[23] Masaryk also seemed to regret the limitation of the Church's role in contemporary social welfare, education, and scholarship. The Church's expansive tasks and its far-reaching organization had established a Pan-European identity, but secularization of those functions had brought that "universal program of organization" to an end. "For better or for worse, economic interests now hold the world together."[24] Despite these changes, Masaryk ar-

---

22 On the genesis of the *Conversations*, see Orzoff, *Battle for the Castle*, 180–83; the editorial note by Jiří Opelík to *Hovory s T. G. Masarykem* (2013), 277–91; and Pohorský, "Karel Čapek a jeho T. G. M., Masaryk a jeho K. Č."

23 Čapek, *Talks with T. G. Masaryk*, 186.

24 Ibid., 187.

gued in his conversations with Čapek for the continued relevance of Christianity. The relevance of churches, on the other hand, was still uncertain. "The task of Christianity—the task of all churches—is as great (if not greater than) it has been these two thousand years," the president declared: "its task is to become the true herald of practical love and reviver of souls. How to go about this is for the churches themselves to decide."[25]

In later essays describing the process behind *Conversations with T. G. Masaryk*, Čapek depicted Masaryk as a humble and taciturn collaborator. "Do whatever you like," the president said, laughing, when Čapek first suggested the idea for the book. "You'll help me fill in the gaps, won't you?" asked Čapek. "I'll do what I can," Masaryk replied.[26] But the president was not as nonchalant about the project as Čapek suggested. In the late summer and early autumn of 1928, as he and Čapek were exchanging drafts of the first volume, Masaryk described the project in letters to his friend Oldra Sedlmayrová. A writer living in Moravia, Sedlmayrová served as something of a literary collaborator to the president. Masaryk regularly published opinion pieces in newspapers under pseudonyms, and Sedlmayrová would edit the texts to disguise his writing style. In the course of exchanging manuscripts and letters, Masaryk had come to see Sedlmayrová, who was the age of his children, as a confidante in matters literary, political, and personal.[27] In his letters to Sedlmayrová, the president confided that the interviews with Čapek were a chore. He recognized that Čapek's view of the world was different than his and feared that the writer did not understand him. Above all, Masaryk wrestled with how to express his life and ideas. How would he describe his love for Charlotte? She was "uncommonly noble, perhaps a modern saint," he wrote to Sedlmayrová. "And now I cannot and do not want to retouch her portrait."[28] The letters to Sedlmayrová show that Masaryk was not a man of settled views,

---

25 Ibid.

26 Ibid., 18.

27 Masaryk's letters often read like love letters, revealing him as an isolated, even lonely old widower, eager for emotional connection with someone outside his family. For instance, when Alice travels to London, Masaryk implores Sedlmayrová to visit him at the castle.

28 Masaryk to Sedlmayrová, 27 September 1928, in *Dopisy Oldře*, 24.

contrary to the picture in the *Conversations*. He wrestled with concern about the future of the republic, with the foundations of his moral thinking, and with his family.[29]

Masaryk also sought help in defining the portrait that Čapek created in the *Conversations*. While Čapek acknowledged Masaryk's participation in the rewrites, he did not mention publicly that the editors included more than just the president. Masaryk passed manuscript pages to his children Alice, Olga, and Jan, to staff members Gašparíková and Škrach, to Oldra Sedlmayrová, and even to Edvard Beneš. The writer griped to his friends about these interventions, especially those of Alice Masaryková.[30] But according to Gašparíková, everyone in the house of Masaryk recognized the deficiencies of Čapek's work. Masaryk himself pronounced, after reading the draft of the second volume, "Often it is him in there and not me."[31] A particular weakness in the drafts, according to Masaryk's family and staff, was Čapek's misrepresentation of his religious ideas. The household found laughable the writer's intimation in one section that Masaryk remained at heart a Catholic. "He did not understand Protestantism," the president judged.[32] Gašparíková expressed surprise at "how excellently Čapek captured Masaryk in the objective chapters ... [but] what a confused and false picture he offers when he speaks of Masaryk's internal, spiritual character."[33]

Indeed, the section in volume two of the *Conversations* in which Masaryk comments on Christianity and churches changed dramatically from Čapek's original draft. But it is difficult to identify passages in the original manuscript that could be read as embellishments or distortions by the writer. There are lines in Čapek's five handwritten pages that echo statements Masaryk had made throughout his life. And then there are lines that run counter to the religious biography Masaryk had crafted over the decades, such as his decision to enter the

---

29 See Miloš Pohorský's interpretation of Masaryk's inner struggles, as revealed in his letters to Sedlmayrová, in his essay "Karel Čapek a jeho T. G. M.—Masaryk a jeho K. Č.," 577–81.

30 Firt, *Knihy a Osudy*, 263.

31 Gašparíková-Horáková, diary entry of 14 February 1930, in *U Masarykovcov*, 57.

32 Ibid.

33 Gašparíková-Horáková, diary entry of 30 October 1930, in *U Masarykovcov*, 89.

Reformed Church: "I decided on the Reformed confession because it's closer to church tradition than Lutheranism," the original manuscript states. "But Protestantism always remained foreign to me. I just did not want to be without a confession. To me that's somewhat loathsome. I wanted to be something, whether this or that." The text then meanders from topic to topic. On the differences in the Christian traditions: Protestantism is more rational, less supernatural than Catholicism. But the Catholic Mass compels all of the senses: "It is such a human celebration, Protestantism is poorer." Catholicism also appeals to the fullness of a person, while Protestantism is "simpler, if you want, more empty," albeit more modern. As for the Bible, there is "almost nothing" that one can take from the Old Testament, while the New Testament has to be stripped of everything supernatural. And the churches? According to Čapek's first draft, Masaryk declared that they had to do more missions work if they were to remain alive. "But not to somewhere in Africa. They must preach the faith at home, from pub to pub, from person to person. It would be of greater value to have Christianity here, rather than among a few of those blacks in the forest."[34]

All of these comments were cut from the final version. Was it the case that Čapek did not understand Masaryk? Or was it that Masaryk was not understandable? In either case, Masaryk's remarks on religion in the published version of this section were more in line with his earlier writings, from his postwar memoir and academic project *Russia and Europe* back to his turn-of-the-century lectures. Masaryk envisioned a progressive development of religion, along the lines he had been plotting for decades. "The future of Christianity?" he said in reply to Čapek's question. According to the original draft, Masaryk replied simply: "I believe in the love of Jesus. I believe in the progress of humanity." The published version developed this answer more fully. The reply echoed Masaryk's long-held views on religion. But rather than speaking of the new religion, he spoke in the language of Somethingism: "Religion, now and in the future, will be more individual; it will

---

34 Čapek, handwritten draft of *Hovory II*, chapter seven, "1900–1910," MÚA AV ČR, TGM Collection, box 654, folder L-95.

tend to personal, spiritual needs. I am not a prophet, but I see myself as one of those future believers. What we need is freedom of scholarship and research, intellectual integrity in matters of religion, tolerance; not spiritual indifference, no, but faith, living faith in something higher [*v něco vyššího*] than ourselves, in something great, sublime, and eternal."[35]

Reigniting the Culture War

Amidst the uncertainty of the 1930s, the language of "struggle" and "conflict" appeared often in cultural journals of various stripes. Writers urged that Czechs had to fight for convictions, for democracy, for the faith and the traditions of the nation. Underlying these belligerent appeals was the sense that the founding ideals of Czechoslovakia were fading. Whether Masaryk's ideals had not been fulfilled, or were ill suited for the times, or were flawed from the start, there were concerns in the 1930s—even among the president's supporters—that the project of the moral republic had failed. As the threats of Nazism and Fascism loomed, old foes blamed each other for Czechoslovakia's weakness, while at the same time exhorting their own followers to brace themselves for a fight.

Even Masaryk doled out blame. When he remarked that the Czechs' religious tradition had been completely lost, he did not reflect on his own role in that failure. Instead, he pointed the finger at the Protestant churches. "The Protestants have not restored it," he said of the nation's religious heritage.[36] Although he praised Protestantism for advancing the progress of Christianity, Masaryk did not view the unified Czech Church favorably. "I am constantly disappointed by a certain deadness in Czech Protestantism today," he told Alice one evening, "an insufficiency of initiative, resoluteness."[37]

The leading Protestant intellectuals of the day might have agreed—in part—with Masaryk's assessment. Josef Hromádka and Emanuel Rádl also recognized that the Czech Church of the Brethren, founded

---

35 Translation is from Čapek, *Talks with T. G. Masaryk,* 187. Original Czech text is found in *Hovory s T. G. Masarykem* (1990), 147.

36 Gašparíková-Horáková, diary entry of 17 April 1931, in *U Masarykovcov,* 110.

37 Gašparíková-Horáková, diary entry of 15 March 1934, in *U Masarykovcov,* 223.

in the moment of national euphoria, had not emerged as a robust institution able to advance Protestant Christianity. Divisions between liberal Protestants and supporters of Karl Barth's neo-orthodoxy, between those open to foreign influences and those who wanted a church built solely on Czech traditions, had undermined the attempt at unification.[38] In the 1930s the Protestant Church in the Czech Lands did not experience the same revival that the Catholic Church did. The number of people who claimed affiliation with the Church of the Brethren remained stagnant, disappointing those who had expected an increase in Protestant adherents to match the rhetoric of Masaryk. The only community that saw a significant increase in Protestants was Prague, where the number of adherents to the Protestant churches climbed by more than 13,000 between 1921 and 1930.[39] But overall, in Prague as in much of Bohemia and Moravia, most Czech refugees from Catholicism chose adherence to the Czechoslovak Church over Protestantism.

At the same time, though, Hromádka and Rádl would have certainly disputed the president's claim that Protestants lacked initiative. Rádl had led the YMCA through its initial period of rapid growth, and then he and Hromádka had joined together to launch a branch of the organization in 1926, called the Academic YMCA, aimed specifically at university students and intellectuals. By the 1930s, the Academic YMCA was a significant cultural institution in Prague. Its seminars and lectures attracted students who would become the leading dissident intellectuals of the communist period, both professing Christians, such as theologian Božena Komárková, and nonbelievers like philosopher Jan Patočka. Students and intellectuals valued the openness of the Academic YMCA meetings, where voicing one's own convictions while respecting those of another was fundamental (although some criticized the individualistic direction of the organization and the strong American influence).[40] The aim of

---

38 Hromádka, *Cesty českých evangelíků*, 41–5.

39 Brotánková, "Religiozita v okresech ČR v období 1921–2001," appendices one and two.

40 Šiklová discusses the individualist and Barthian slants in her study of the organization, "Akademická YMCA v Československu," 74–5. One YMCA member reported that the organization finally had a Czech atmosphere, rather than American, only in 1931. Report by Joe Firt, Národní Archiv, YMCA Collection, box 7, folder 22.

this open exchange of ideas was that young people would understand themselves as autonomous, moral, and self-aware individuals. As the philosopher Rádl explained: "Conscious individuals are the architects of the social world, the builders of civilization, and they are responsible for what they build."[41]

Of course, Masaryk's religious, ethical, and political ideas were central to the program of the Academic YMCA, but they were cast in intellectual trends current in the late 1920s: personalist philosophy, Karl Barth's dialectical theology, and Christian socialism, inspired by another Swiss theologian, Leonhard Ragaz. Thanks to Hromádka, both Barth and Ragaz visited Prague in the 1930s and spoke to members of the Academic YMCA. Hromádka himself attempted something of a middle path between the two. Although Hromádka embraced Barth's theological ideas on the radical otherness of God, he held that Christians received revelation and grace from God within specific cultural, political, and economic contexts. Christian faith did not bring escape from history; instead, it demanded greater engagement with issues of the day. Therefore, Hromádka was drawn to Ragaz's ideas of socialism as a step toward justice, toward the kingdom of God. The Czech theologian even went so far as to argue that Christians had much to learn from the communists. In his judgment, the Bolsheviks in Russia and socialists in Europe had succeeded because the churches had failed. Christians had not spoken against the economic and social sins of liberal capitalism. They failed to act, resolutely and radically, to bring the kingdom of God to earth. "The beliefs of the Czech Brethren should have had bolder consequences than the riskiest demands of socialists," he declared. "Only then would we have the right to criticize and reject Bolshevism."[42]

Hromádka's advocacy of socialism and his favorable remarks about Soviet communism would later gain him notoriety during the Cold War. But his statements were not the product of some pragmatic, political alliance—or, in his view, a compromise of Christian principle. According to the theologian, serving God meant serving hu-

---

41 Quoted in Šiklová, "Akademická YMCA v Československu," 76.
42 Quoted in Neumärker, *Josef L. Hromádka*, 67. On Hromádka and socialism, see ibid., 63–8; and Nishitani, *Niebuhr, Hromadka, Troeltsch, and Barth*, 58–64 and 153–63.

manity; it meant struggling for social justice, acting against inequality and helplessness, and entering the public arena. This call to political action was in accord with the struggle of the Christian life: self-examination, discipline, and sacrifice, followed by creative, courageous work to challenge injustice and penetrate modern culture. As a theologian and former minister, Hromádka spoke consistently against the Protestant fixation on the mercy of God and salvation of the individual. The question "do you love Jesus?" diluted the gospel to a weak, emotional balm, he argued. "The agony of the religious life is that nothing is ever fully conquered. Faith must ceaselessly fight for its internal victory, it must be borne by ever-new growth, liveliness, and relevance."[43] Czech Protestants could not content themselves with praise songs and prayer groups. They had to speak to the world. They had to engage with the world.

This engagement, in Hromádka's view, was all the more important for Czech Protestants because the state had been founded on principles close to their own. By the 1930s, however, it was clear that these ideas did not correspond to the reality of Czech society and politics. "Masaryk's fight is not yet completed among us," Hromádka wrote in 1934. "His ideal of the state and the political order has not yet come to fruition."[44] Both he and Rádl saw their task as building awareness of these unfulfilled ideals and urging Czech Protestants to fight for them. Protestants could not be indifferent to the fate of the state's foundations. "This is not a contest of pure theory or one that is solely about partisan politics," wrote Hromádka. "It is a *battle* for the Czech soul, for the spirit of our cultural development, for the spiritual content of Czech identity."[45] Rádl extended the prognosis more broadly: if the Czechs were to have a dynamic culture that contributed ideas to the world, it had to be founded on the determined fight for principles. "People must fight; without struggle there is no culture. These people act in public, setting a new program for life, fighting publicly for truth, justice, honesty; they build a cultural ideal with their work."[46] This

43   Hromádka, "Náboženská zatuchlost," 226.
44   Hromádka, *Cesty českých evangelíků*, 58.
45   Ibid., 59. Emphasis in original.
46   Rádl, "Smysl kultury," 168.

was the lesson of Masaryk—ideas put into practice with energetic, serious work, with determined opposition to the spiritual weakness of the modern age. As Hromádka wrote in summarizing Masaryk's political legacy, "Democracy cannot live without passion and faith, courage and heroism."[47]

In the view of Hromádka and Rádl, this is where Masaryk's liberal supporters failed. They saw democracy simply as negotiation and compromise, as political transactions aimed toward practical ends, without any foundation in lasting principles. The representative of this thinking was Ferdinand Peroutka. In his reaction against the violence of war and revolution, in his love for G. K. Chesterton's humor and humanity, in his preference for English practicality over German dogmatism, Peroutka longed for Czechoslovakia to be an oasis of decent cooperation, free from fanaticism. According to Rádl and Hromádka, these instincts were admirable, but they also led Peroutka to reject any deeper convictions. Peroutka judged this or that action only by whether it brought happiness and peace. But Rádl the philosopher and Hromádka the theologian asked: What are happiness and peace? What are the lines between good and evil, between lies and truth? In Rádl's judgment, Peroutka took the position of a spectator who admires the skills of the contestants, whether writing on Masaryk, Beneš, the communists, Catholics, or Protestants, but he did not pay attention to "the spiritual struggle of the contest."[48] With no belief in fundamental principles, with no belief in truth, there was nothing for Peroutka to fight for.

Peroutka in turn fired the same charge at Czech Protestants, that they did not stand on their own principles. Leaders of the Protestant Church had been too motivated by politics, rather than religion, in forging their union. In opposing Catholicism, they had joined forces with their own enemies, the freethinkers, and devoted too much effort to speaking against Rome rather than for Christ. When Protestants did speak of religion, Peroutka charged, it was a broad humanism without distinct religious meaning. Even though he appreciated the

---

47 Hromádka, "Masarykova pochodeň," 165.
48 Rádl, "Krise inteligence VII," 202.

president's individual religious commitment, Peroutka faulted those Czech Protestants who believed too deeply in Masaryk's predictions of a religious revival and adhered too strongly to his religious ideas. Those people were mistaken, he wrote, who "confused religion with philosophy, with a meditative spirit, with *humanita* or something similar, or with something soft and vague, and disregarded that the fundamental, essential religious fact is belief in God."[49] One of the things that Peroutka the atheist so admired about Masaryk the believer was his unwavering dedication to putting faith into action. For Peroutka, Masaryk was a heroic figure. He argued, though, that Protestants had failed to follow that model. Peroutka had a favorable view of Hromádka, at least for his honesty in criticizing the faults of his fellow Protestants. But he was unrelenting in his criticism of Rádl, with whom he had been feuding since the early 1920s. In his view, Rádl was an out-of-touch philosopher as well as an old-fashioned believer, "like a granny." Whereas Masaryk made moral statements like a man, Rádl was a priggish goody-goody. According to Peroutka, Masaryk's religion had compelled him to action and engagement. Rádl's religion, on the other hand, led him to something like a monastery.[50]

In criticizing the lack of conviction of Peroutka and his liberal allies, Rádl and Hromádka wrote favorably of the committed struggle of Czech Catholics. Hromádka cited in particularly the appeal of Jaroslav Durych to his fellow Catholics: they were essentially foreigners in their own land, fighting to revive the faith; therefore, they had to act as Jesuits. Hromádka urged that Protestants think of themselves in the same way as they entered the fight in the public arena. Durych, of course, did not return the kindness—he had no regard for contemporary Protestants. Nevertheless, the author did hold similar views as Hromádka and Rádl on the republic's failings. Czechoslovakia's weakness was caused by the lack of solid principles among those who defined its culture. And while the Protestants targeted Peroutka for his unwillingness to stand for anything, Durych pointed to the journalist's partner, Karel Čapek.

---

49   Peroutka, *Budování státu,* 1: 275.
50   Peroutka, "Masarykova osobnost IV," 242. Peroutka writes about Hromádka in *Budování státu,* 276.

At the start of the 1930s, Jaroslav Durych was finally enjoying success. His novel *Wandering* had brought him prestige and prosperity. He was the central, even guiding figure in the blossoming of Czech Catholic literature, writing for new Catholic journals that emerged at the time, along with his own literary journal, *Akord*. He moved to a new, larger publishing house, which began to republish his collected writings. In 1936 he earned the state's highest cultural honor, membership in the Academy of Sciences. And he received a transfer to the military hospital in Prague, allowing him to return to the capital more than a decade after the scandal of his essay on the Jan Hus statue in Old Town Square. But at the same time, in the early to mid-1930s, Durych felt that he was creatively drained. The author who had been so direct in leveling criticism against others now confronted his own limitations. "This time of my artistic life came to a definitive end with *Wandering*," he declared. He was too young to retire, Durych conceded. He would not put down his pen. But the author's output, once a raging torrent, now slowed to a gentle stream: memoirs, travel writing, and essays. He no longer felt able to create novels. "I left the life of selling beautiful, entertaining, and useful literature," he declared, "and retreated to a little shop to sell goods to pilgrims."[51]

But the world did not allow Durych to settle down. In July 1936 civil war erupted in Spain between the Republican government and the Nationalist rebels claiming to defend the interests of the Catholic Church. Durych had a deep love for Spain; he had visited in the 1920s to conduct research for *Wandering* and later described the country in a travel book, *Pout' do Španělska* (Pilgrimage to Spain, 1929). He believed that Spain had filled a special role in the recatholicization of the Bohemian lands, an idea he portrayed with the character of Angela in *Wandering*, the devout Spanish woman who leads the faithless Jiří to the Church. As a devotee of Catholic Spain, Durych had deplored the Republican government's secularization policies.[52] And when fight-

---

51   Durych, "Masopust 1932" [Shrovetide 1932], *Akord*, February 1932, reprinted in *Jaroslav Durych—publicista*, 106–7.

52   Durych already wrote about the persecution of Catholics in Spain five years before the outbreak of the war: "Miliony" [The millions], *Akord*, June 1931, 314. On Durych's travel writings on Spain, compared to Čapek's *Vylet do Španěl*, see Voisine-Jechova, "Dvě cesty do Španělska. Jaroslav Durych a Karel Čapek."

ing opened, he fumed at the Czech press's defense of the Republicans and their attacks on Spanish Catholics. He felt compelled to act: "I did what I recognized as my duty."[53]

In January 1937 Durych launched another new journal, *Obnova*. The title can be translated as "revival," "renaissance," or "restoration," indicating that Durych had religious, cultural, and political aims for the journal. Unlike with his earlier journal of political and cultural commentary, *Rozmach*, Durych now had a full complement of talented collaborators: Jan Čep, Jan Zahradníček, Václav Renč, and other young Catholic writers who had followed his lead and were established figures in Czech letters by the mid-1930s. *Obnova* also differed from *Rozmach* in that it did not claim to be nonpartisan, casting judgment on both the Right and the Left. Instead, *Obnova* positioned itself firmly on the political Right; its writers condemned socialism and communism, mainstream liberals, and Catholics willing to collaborate with the government. Quickly, opponents branded *Obnova* not simply as reactionary Catholic but as fascist. For his own part, Durych still avoided any political labels or movements. Instead, he and his fellow Catholic writers targeted a state they saw as morally bankrupt.

In staking out his position, Durych reopened his feud with Karel Čapek. Responding to the writer's support of the Republicans over Spain's Nationalists and his pacifist criticism of the war in general, Durych went on the offensive. Describing the Civil War as a contest between evil powers and persecuted believers, the forces of Hell and Heaven, Durych declared that Spanish Catholics were fighting for their very existence. In such a fight, even God and the saints could not stand by idly. "The sword is an instrument," he declared, "which is not only possible but even necessary to use in the service of God, with all of one's heart, soul, and mind, until the moment your head is split."[54] Those who suggested that the issues in Spain were too complex to choose sides, or that both sides were at fault, were deluded. The fight in Spain was a matter of life and death for Spanish Catholics and the Church as a whole.

---

53 Durych, "Hlídač bez čísla" [An unofficial watchman], *Národní obnova*, 17 December 1938, reprinted in *Jaroslav Durych—publicista*, 240.

54 Durych, "Pláč Karla Čapka" [The tears of Karel Čapek], *Akord*, 1937, reprinted in *Jaroslav Durych—publicista*, 222.

Here Durych turned his attack: Who was Karel Čapek to criticize people fighting for their own survival—and for the survival of God's church? Who was Karel Čapek, a man who had never served in the military, to criticize those who fight for what is right and true? "I am a military physician," Durych stated. "For me, men are categorized into three groups: A, B, and C. Over the years, I've recognized that each of these groups has its own morality."[55] People of class A were of sound body and character, ready for service; while people of class C were not only physically but also morally unable to serve. He granted that there were people of class A, of full physical health, who showed the morality of class C and shirked their duty. And there were those who could not serve in the military due to physical limitations but exhibited the moral strength of someone of class A, showing discipline, commitment, and loyalty. This was not Karel Čapek. "I read Karel Čapek not as a writer but as a military physician," wrote Durych. "I recognize him as a C, and I'm afraid. I'm afraid of everything that C represents."[56]

Again, the response to Durych's biting polemic was thunderous. Čapek's chronic health problems were well known, and it appeared that Durych was cruelly attacking the writer for his physical condition. As Durych's son later wrote, his father "earned the hatred of the entire nation," which lasted for decades.[57] However, Durych's attack was not directed at Čapek's physical condition but rather at his moral outlook. The morality of Čapek, of someone of class C, "the morality of the unfit, with whom our nation is bursting," was a sin against the Czech name. The morality of class C was well mannered, Durych admitted, even humane, charitable, and kind at first look. But it was also dangerous. Karel Čapek represented—and shaped—the main current of Czech culture. If, as Durych speculated at the close of his essay, the nation followed Čapek's lead, then the nation's future was dim.[58]

Like others at the time, Durych saw the war in Spain as a harbinger, a conflict that carried warnings for his own nation and for all of Europe. But he read the war not as a struggle between democracy and fas-

---

55 Ibid.
56 Ibid., 223.
57 Václav Durych, *Vzpomínky na mého otce*, 324.
58 Durych, "Pláč Karla Čapka," 222.

cism, or between the Left and Right. Instead, the Spanish Civil War was a precursor to the looming fight between those who held faith in God and the Church and those who stood opposed. Published in the Catholic literary journal *Akord*, Durych's criticism of Čapek was not a challenge to the writer himself or to the other guardians of official Czech culture. In Durych's view, they had shown their mettle by this time. Just as with his provocative essay "Old Town Square," Durych set the challenge before Czech Catholics. When he later recalled those first months of the Civil War and his decision to speak up, Durych saw it as his obligation as a Catholic *and* a Czech, believing that support of "Red Spain" would bring horrible punishment on Czechoslovakia.[59] All of Europe faced a war—a conflict of absolutes. But in their "intellectual prostitution" and "rental of moralities," the leaders of the Czechoslovak Republic had already failed.[60] The Czech nation was unprepared, Durych wrote presciently in January 1938. It would be one of the nations to be wiped off the earth—and no amount of humanitarian or peace-loving ideas could prevent it. If the nation were to survive, it would need to adopt the traits of class A. Such a change in the morality of the nation, Durych argued, could come only from the Catholic faith.[61]

Jaroslav Durych's essays of 1937 and 1938 showed none of the over-the-top humor and irony of his political writings of the 1920s. Instead, his essays for the journal *Obnova* were dark and acerbic. The republic was collapsing, and Durych responded with judgment. When the end came in the autumn of 1938 with the Munich Agreement, the writer declared: "I told you so." Czechoslovakia had been built on flawed foundations. The philosophy of the state—and its author—had been dilettantish. Referring to Masaryk as "the philosopher," Durych denounced his realist political program as a fraud and his supposed wisdom as bogus. For twenty years, students, journalists, soldiers, teachers, and government clerks had done their work under a counterfeit morality, a counterfeit culture. Durych pointed to Somethingism as

---

59 Durych, "Hlídač bez čísla" *Národní obnova*, 17 December 1938, in *Jaroslav Durych—publicista*, 240.

60 Durych, "Dům a domácí" [House and landlord], *Obnova*, April 1937, in *Jaroslav Durych—publicista*, 224.

61 Durych, "Funkce národu" [Function of the nation], *Obnova*, January 1938, in *Jaroslav Durych—publicista*, 232–33.

the root of this false philosophy. "Certainly, they say that they believe in something," he said of the men of the "old regime." There was talk of democracy and progress. "But none of these people believe in democracy, *humanita*, or universal ideals," Durych charged. "Everything for them is just a sham slogan."[62]

Josef Hromádka made a similar assessment, after all had been lost. Writing after the war about Emanuel Rádl, who died of illness in occupied Prague in 1942, Hromádka insisted that his friend had been correct in urging Czechs to fight for principle. Unlike Durych, Hromádka held that the foundations of Czechoslovakia had been correct, that its leader had been true. Throughout his life, Masaryk had contended that people are not simply material, that there is more than the concrete world. He had turned Czechs' attention away from narrow concern with the nation to universal questions, to questions of humanity. He believed the state should be fixed to a moral standard, and that this should shape the actions of both the ordinary citizen and the statesman. But Hromádka agreed with Durych that Masaryk's supporters had lacked any real convictions. "How is it that his supporters and friends did not follow after him?" asked the theologian.[63] They had not understood the spiritual, moral core of Masaryk's ideas; instead, they skewed those ideas to solely national or political ends. The president's men had not believed in his ideas, and they did not defend those ideas when they were challenged. Throughout his life, Masaryk had fought against indifference, the theologian insisted. In the end, indifference brought down his republic.

T. G. Masaryk—Mortal and Immortal

Dear father,

I hope you will have a quiet Sunday. I <u>feel sure,</u> that just a little patience & everything will be all right. Things & people need understanding. God loves you, & you do love him. The unseen, unthought <u>Essence</u> of the world—Love, Justice, Truth in Him, Life

---

62 Durych, "Očista duší" [Cleansing the soul], *Lumír*, 30 November 1938, in *Jaroslav Durych—publicista*, 237.

63 Hromádka, *Don Quijote české filosofie*, 149.

itself. And when You <u>love Him </u>in the depths of your soul, there is no danger & no fear. I can say just those simple words of Cordelia: I love you as the salt—for You are my dear father. God is with You and *pravda vítězí*.[64]

Alice Masaryková's reference to Cordelia in *King Lear* was an absolute pledge to her father: Just as salt is indispensable, so is my love for you—I am always by your side, and will always work for your kingdom. As Tomáš Masaryk advanced into old age, her letters to him often included such declarations. Like in the note above, she sometimes wrote in English, the language of Masaryk's wife, and sometimes in Slovak, the language of Masaryk's youth. The letters included her doodles, clipped newspapers photographs, and the whimsical remarks of a daughter who dearly loved her father. She reminisced of her mother. She reread her father's books and commented on lines that struck her. She wrote of her travel for international conferences, of her work with Edvard Beneš and Jan Masaryk, now serving as ambassador to London. In one visit to London, she reported that a man stopped her on the street to shake her hand, "on account of your father." Throughout the correspondence with her father, Masaryková declared her own love and affirmed the rightness of his mission.

Alice Masaryková held steadfastly to her father's ideals, his all-encompassing vision of politics, religion, history, and culture. She saw this as the foundation for her own work with the Red Cross. During a long trip in 1929 to various European capitals for conferences, she reported to her father that she was "progressing in worldly wisdom without losing the truth."[65] Although an idealist, Masaryková understood that work on public health and welfare required attention to practicality, to the concrete. She was aware of the tension—between ideals and practical demands, between timeless truth and "worldly wisdom," between the goal of a healthy, active, responsible citizenry and the realities of poverty, disease, and unemployment. The work of creating a democracy, as her father had intended it, was a matter of addressing those

---

64 AGM to TGM, 9 June 1928, MÚA AV ČR, TGM Collection, Korespondence III, box 54, folder 3. Underlining in original.

65 AGM to TGM, 6 October 1929, MÚA AV ČR, TGM Collection, Korespondence III, box 54, folder 4.

everyday problems with an eye toward the greater goal. Masaryková recognized that the path to truth had to navigate these shoals. Still, she found the work emotionally draining. "I cannot change," she wrote to her father during a 1932 visit to London; "the unemployment on the streets hurts me sometimes too deeply for words."[66]

In the 1930s, as she entered her fifties, Alice Masaryková remained committed to the goals she had pursued as a young woman: helping those mired in poverty, disease, and unemployment. She still understood this work within the larger goal of building a democratic society. One of Masaryková's most cherished projects with the Red Cross was an annual campaign aimed at bringing broad-reaching change in the republic. In 1921 she had founded an event called the Red Cross Truce. Each year the organization mobilized various civic groups to bring attention to a particular goal, such as "health and peace," "respect for the elderly," or "cleanliness everywhere and in everything." During each truce, Masaryková hosted events at the castle for representatives of student and civic organizations as well as government officials and members of the National Assembly. Key to the success of the truce was the participation of the press. Masaryková invited journalists to the castle and wrote letters to the editors of more than twenty periodicals, asking them to refrain from publishing invective and polemics during the three-day truce. The political divisions in the republic and the rhetoric in the Czech press were particular concerns to Masaryková. As someone of self-described aristocratic outlook, she found the vitriol of the partisan press to be unfitting of the moral republic. "I see from day to day what devastation it creates," Masaryková wrote to her father. She asked him to speak—"with power"—against the rancor in the country's newspapers.[67] Likewise, during one of Karel Čapek's visits to the Masaryk household, she appealed to him to lift the overall level of discourse in the press.[68]

Editors and journalists did comply in observing the truce in their writing, and they advanced the message of the annual event in their

---

66　AGM to TGM, 6 November 1932, MÚA AV ČR, TGM Collection, Korespondence III, box 54, folder 5.

67　AGM to TGM, 22 October 1931, in MÚA AV ČR, TGM Collection, Korespondence III, box 54, folder 4.

68　Gašparíková-Horáková, diary entry of 27 September 1929, in *U Masarykovcov*, 38.

newspapers. Typically held over Easter weekend, the Red Cross Truce adapted the holiday's traditional message of renewal and turned it toward a deliberate program of social and cultural improvement. The event was such a success that Red Cross representatives from other countries visited Czechoslovakia to observe the truce, and at the 1934 conference in Tokyo, the International Red Cross encouraged member organizations to adopt the event in their own countries (the resolution was the genesis of the current World Red Cross and Red Crescent Day). In the mid-1930s, Masaryková lobbied Red Cross organizations and foreign ministers to follow through on the resolution, arguing that the truce was a valuable antidote to rising international tensions. At home, meanwhile, Masaryková saw the Red Cross Truce as a means of reminding the people of Czechoslovakia that their state was founded upon truth and morality. As she declared in a speech for the castle luncheon: "The freedom of our nation and its political independence were restored by a courageous love for truth, justice, humanity, and an innate, elemental resistance to lies, evil, and any form of violence. This is how we would characterize the nature of our people."[69] Keeping with this nature and with the principles of the republic, it was therefore necessary to act with love, kindness, and service to others.

At the same time that Alice Masaryková worked toward fulfilling her father's vision—for Czechoslovakia and the world—she also took steps to ensure that this vision and Masaryk's legacy would be forever remembered. First, there was the matter of the published testament of his life and ideas: Karel Čapek's *Conversations with T. G. Masaryk*. Čapek had planned for the *Conversations* to conclude with a direct statement of Masaryk's philosophical and religious ideas. The president had written a thirty-one-page draft of this statement early in 1927, as their interviews were just starting. This "metaphysical sketch," as it was called, was set aside until 1930, when Čapek was preparing the second volume of the project. Masaryková and Vasil Škrach took responsibility for editing this statement, clarifying Masaryk's views and in some places adding their revisions. As editor of the president's published

---

69 Masaryková, "Československý červený kříž—mír—válka" [The Czechoslovak Red Cross—Peace—War], n.d., LA PNP AGM Collection, box 2. This file includes other records pertaining to the Red Cross Truce.

texts, Škrach was most familiar with the contours of Masaryk's thought. He added whole sentences to the philosophical statement, in Masaryk's voice. For example, Škrach added a declaration at the end of one paragraph on politics: "I will say that I am a political person, but I will not say that politics, that the state is higher, more worthwhile than religion and the church." With a tick of his red pencil, the president approved the amendment. To another paragraph, where Masaryk discussed his views on the different churches, Škrach added the Reformation-era motto of the Brethren Church: "In essentials, unity; in nonessentials, liberty; and in all things, love." Giving it a Masaryk-style turn, he clarified: "in the modern expression: tolerance, patience."[70]

Masaryk's philosophical statement was never published in his lifetime. Instead of including it in the second volume of the *Conversations*, Čapek decided to produce an entirely new book devoted to Masaryk's thought. Rather than an autobiographical narrative written in Masaryk's voice, like the first two volumes, this third book would be structured in a question-and-answer format, with Čapek posing direct questions about the president's ideas on philosophy, religion, morality, and politics. The president agreed, and there were further conversations between him and Čapek. Again, Masaryk confided his weariness with the whole process in letters to Oldra Sedlmayrová.[71] Čapek likewise found the project taxing. By this time, the writer had begun to drift from Masaryk's orbit due to political disagreements; Čapek was impressed with Antonín Švehla, leader of the powerful Agrarian Party, whereas the president and his circle were wary of any partisan challenge to the Castle.[72] Meanwhile, from a writing standpoint, Čapek found it difficult to create a coherent statement out of Masaryk's far-reaching comments, wistful silences, and observations on the particular day's news.[73]

---

70   Drafts of Masaryk's "Náčrt metafyziky" [Metaphysical sketch], with comments by Škrach and Masaryková, are collected in MÚA AV ČR, TGM Collection, box 654, folder L-95. The document was not published until the 2013 edition of *Hovory s T. G. Masarykem*, 233–56.

71   See Masaryk's letters to Sedlmayrová dated 22 June 1933, 9 July 1933, and 12 October 1933, in *Dopisy Oldře*.

72   Orzoff, *Battle for the Castle*, 186–89.

73   Čapek hinted at these difficulties in an essay about *Hovory s T. G. Masarykem*, which remained unpublished. See Jiří Opelík, "Ediční poznámka" [Editorial note], in *Hovory s T. G. Masarykem* (2013), 286–87.

Čapek's revisions of the first typewritten draft show how hard it was to coalesce the scattered comments into cogent prose. He rewrote paragraphs in order to clarify remarks, and he cut entire pages in order to eliminate Masaryk's professorial tangents. Nevertheless, for all this work, members of Masaryk's family and staff still found the text to be full of errors when they received it in February 1935. Anna Gašparíková, the president's archivist, judged that the manuscript was so mangled only Masaryk himself could repair it.[74] By this time, however, Masaryk was in poor health, having suffered another stroke the previous August. Although he was able to read the manuscript (and apparently dictated the cutting of an entire chapter, following his son's urging), he was not able to take up the work of editing. Again, Vasil Škrach did much of the revision work. He also passed the text to another person, outside the household, who was deeply familiar with Masaryk's philosophy: Emanuel Rádl.

When it was published later in 1935, much of the third volume of *Conversations with T. G. Masaryk*, subtitled *Thought and Life*, was devoted to religious questions. Many of his remarks—on the necessity of religion in modern times, the history of the Christian churches, the nature of the divine—echoed those of past decades. At the same time, though, the president's statements in the *Conversations* were no longer the sharp barbs of the confrontational professor and parliamentarian. Absent from the book are the censorious rebukes of Catholicism. There is not arrangement of religious ideas and practice into categories of the "primitive" and the "modern," nor is there talk of the "blindness" of the faithful. Gone are the appeals to "we" as opposed to an ignorant and backward "them." Gone as well is the phrase "new religion." Instead, the book speaks of the "free church" and a religion of Jesus (*Ježíšství*).[75]

In his discussion of religion, Masaryk also used the word "faith," a term he had once avoided. Faith *is* conviction, he explained, as it is also examination and discernment. Throughout the chapters are references to the object of that faith. Masaryk still held to a philosopher's no-

74 Gašparíková-Horáková, diary entry, undated [1935], in *U Masarykovcov*, 239.

75 Masaryk's discussions of religion and Christianity comprise the heart of the third volume, titled *Myšlení a život* (Thought and Life). Čapek, *Hovory s T. G. Masarykem* (1990), 254–305.

tion of God, describing the deity in terms of Platonic mind and Aristotelian mover. But Masaryk's God, according to the *Conversations*, is also the Creator, the Director of the World, the Omnipotent and Omniscient, and Father. Masaryk referred repeatedly to a relationship to this God. True religious faith, he insisted, was characterized by "a personal and intimate relation to God."[76] He described his own stance toward God as one of *reverentia*. He insisted upon the Latin term, with its connotations of "honor, complete trust, thankfulness, and hopefulness."[77] Along with that reverence to God came love—for God and for others. Masaryk maintained that religion must encourage people according to a "moral law of love," toward the creation of a "culture of love." These were the articles of his faith. "You would like to hear my creed," Masaryk told Čapek; "its final word is *reverentia*: a conscious honoring of God and of man."[78]

"Every actual conversation turned in the end to political praxis, or to God," Karel Čapek remarked on his interviews with the president, "to the active concerns of today and tomorrow, or to the eternal."[79] At the end of his published essay on the making of *Conversations with T. G. Masaryk*, Čapek spoke of Masaryk's words as the "wise and beautiful" stones of a building, just as Alice Masaryková had done in her letters to Jože Plečnik. But he also allowed that there were some (perhaps thinking of himself) who could not accept the substance of those stones. What was there in Masaryk's philosophy for those "who found no resonance in Platonic antiquity and Jesus's preaching of love?" For those people, Čapek stated, the value of Masaryk's ideals was found in their order, their breadth of vision, their grasp for the fullness of truth. What resonated was the "harmony" of Masaryk's thought.[80] Ultimately, Karel Čapek's own longing was for harmony. As a pragmatist, a philosophical relativist, he longed for the harmony of multiple perspectives within a truly tolerant, democratic environment. As a moral-

---

76 Ibid., 296.

77 Ibid., 301.

78 Ibid., 303.

79 Čapek, "Mlčení s T. G. Masarykem" [Silences with T. G. Masaryk] (1936), in *Hovory s T. G. Masarykem* (1990), 357.

80 Ibid., 362.

ist, he longed for forbearance among his fellow citizens, sympathy, and mutual kindness. In the democratic society that Čapek envisioned, people would be guided in their everyday actions by deeply held convictions, while at the same time respecting others' convictions. He recorded Masaryk as expressing a similar vision: "If I believe in the teachings of Jesus, I believe, then I must also believe in the future of religion... I must also plead for tolerance—not tolerance out of religious indifference, but a positive tolerance: everyone holds to his own convictions, but they also respect the genuine convictions of others. None of us are infallible."[81] In Čapek's view, Masaryk's tolerant religiosity overlapped with his own pragmatic relativism. Perhaps to emphasize that reading by tying it to Czech tradition, Čapek crossed out the last sentence above and replaced it with a line from Jan Hus: "Wish the truth to everyone—this was taught to us and it remains valid forever."[82]

In the final, published statement of Masaryk's ideas, a good part of the credit for their harmony has to go to Čapek, for drawing together the president's scattered remarks. Even though Alice Masaryková and other members of the household were upset with Čapek's presentation of the president's religious views, the early drafts and revisions show that the writer did masterful work in bringing Masaryk's remarks into coherence. Many of the edits and rewrites in Čapek's hand in the manuscripts are in the published version of the interviews. Whether these changes were his own inspiration or suggestions from one of his uncredited coeditors—Vasil Škrach, Anna Gašparíková, Emanuel Rádl, Alice Masaryková, Jan Masaryk, or Edvard Beneš— we cannot tell. All of the contributors to the *Conversations* came to Masaryk's ideas from different perspectives. Indeed, they sometimes disputed those ideas with each other or with Masaryk himself. But they all wanted the erratic and increasingly crotchety remarks of an old man to be received as a coherent body of thought. They wanted Masaryk of the *Conversations* to speak of both principles and tolerance, to encourage healthy faith and healthy skepticism, to warn of

---

81 First draft of *Hovory III*, typewritten, with Čapek's handwritten revisions, MÚA AV ČR, TGM Collection, box 654, file L-95.

82 Ibid.

coercive authority while at the same time exhorting people to civility, discipline, and self-improvement. They wanted a book of wisdom for the modern age, the words of a revered sage—the father figure, the leader, the liberator—passed on to citizens of a democratic state. Čapek wrote of Masaryk's words as a cathedral: "Each sentence can be weighed like a block of stone, but we shall fail to understand it fully if we fail to see the pillars and buttresses, the steeples and spires of the structure as a whole. Only then can we appreciate the beautiful, wise order present in even the most simple building block."[83] In the end, this cathedral was the work of Čapek and the members of the house of Masaryk. Like the students of ancient prophets and philosophers who recorded and redacted their masters' words, Masaryk's disciples sought to bring lasting order and contemporary relevance to his wisdom. They put the final stones into place.

Conclusion

Alice Masaryková also believed that her father's legacy was like a grand structure. To ensure that legacy, she looked to have real stones moved and real structures built, not only within the castle but also outside its confines in the surrounding districts of Prague. With the work inside the castle nearing completion, Jože Plečnik submitted his plans for another project, one that Tomáš Masaryk had wanted from the start: the complete renovation of the areas surrounding the castle, from the banks of the Vltava to the developing neighborhoods of Bubeneč, Dejvice, and Střešovice on the north side of Hradčany. Years earlier, Plečnik had dabbled with a development plan for the southeast face of the castle hill, site of the present-day Malostranská metro stop. Despite the president's backing for his plans, Plečnik's aversion to deadlines and committees drained the patience of city planners, resulting in the shelving of the project. The planning committee went forward with other development plans, such as the building of military staff headquarters at Victory Circle in Dejvice. Its members recognized the need for an overall plan for the area between Dejvice—to

---

83   Čapek, *Talks with T. G. Masaryk*, 32.

FIGURE 7.2. Plečnik's plan for the district surrounding Prague Castle, 1934.
Jože Plečnik Collection, Museums and Galleries of Ljubljana, Slovenia.

the northwest—and the castle, but they had to keep an ear tuned to
any signal from Plečnik. Municipal projects stalled if there was word
of some idea from the castle's architect.[84] At the start of 1935, the
long-expected plan was finally ready, arriving with the endorsement of
Masaryk. Of far greater scope and ambition than his earlier plans,
Plečnik's design cast Prague as a great European capital, with the areas
surrounding the castle its monumental center.

In his project, Plečnik returned to the area that he had worked on
earlier: the southeast side of the castle, from the Vltava River up to
Chotkovy Sady. This steep slope (where tram cars today make the slow
trip up a sharp, hairpin curve) was to be completely reshaped to open
a route for a new ascending street. At the bottom of the street, alongside the river, was to be a large, first-class hotel, while at the top there
would be a concert hall dedicated to composer Bedřich Smetana. From
that point westward, the architect planned a grand boulevard, forty
meters wide, suitable for automobile traffic and military parades. A
paved square in the former royal gardens would be the entrance to the
castle, with two parallel bridges (somewhat like Plečnik's three bridg-

---

84 Record of meeting of members of the State Planning Commission and the President Office, 7 February 1934, APH KPR, SV, box 45.

es in the center of Ljubljana) crossing the Deer Moat directly into the castle—one at Prašný Most into the second courtyard (site of the current bridge) and a second entering into the third courtyard, just in front of the portal of St. Vitus Cathedral. At the opposite end of this entrance square, a street would connect to the northwest, all the way to Victory Circle in Dejvice. To the west of the square, the open area between the Deer Moat and the Nový Svět neighborhood was to be an area for a new presidential estate, called the White House. And at the far end of the boulevard, at the center of a traffic circle, would be a monument to the President-Liberator.[85]

After receiving the drawings from Ljubljana, Alice Masaryková pressed Plečnik's plan on top officials in the presidential chancellery. With the same exultant imagery she used in her earlier letters to the architect, she described how Prague would look after the project's completion: the old royal gardens and the castle would burst with flowers, artwork, and polished stone, creating her long-imagined ideal of a beautiful acropolis. The project would require the outlay of twenty million crowns to start and four million crowns annually over the next five years. Masaryková insisted that the whole structure of the presidential office would have to be reorganized in order to expedite the redevelopment, which would be launched to coincide with her father's eighty-fifth birthday. She telephoned the chancellery staff and appeared in their offices with eager suggestions, disappeared, and then returned later in the day with new suggestions. Members of the chancellery reported the interventions with patience, although the frustration was implicit in their memos. Masaryková pushed the project at a time of economic crisis, rising international tension, and internal political division. The government was committed to increases in defense and infrastructure spending. Chancellery officials understood that Plečnik's plan would never gain approval in the assembly—in fact, it would open them to attack. "Even if we had the money," advised the finance minister, Karel Trapl, "it would not be recommended to commence with this work, especially at this time,

---

85 Office of the President of the Republic, "Statement on Prague Castle and Its Environs," 5 March 1935, APH KPR, SV, box 45.

since it would certainly lead to attacks on the Castle from the Right and Left."[86]

But Alice Masaryková did not relent. That March, in time for her father's birthday, the presidential chancellery sent Plečnik's full redevelopment plan to the planning commission. The plans were also published in various periodicals. *Lidové noviny*, the newspaper of Karel Čapek, endorsed the project, arguing that it would bring a needed, general solution to the space east and north of Hradčany.[87] But *Lidové noviny* was alone. In the spring and summer of 1935, newspaper editorials excoriated the development project. *Národní listy* derided the project as absurd and naïve. *Národní politika* offered the judgment of architect Antonín Engel, designer of the military buildings in Dejvice: the plans were "conglomeration of various ideas and motifs."[88] The president's office received letters of complaint from neighborhood associations and preservation groups. A persistent theme in these objections, from both civic groups and newspapers, was that further development in and around the castle had to respect "Czech feelings and attitudes."[89] In other words, the foreigner Plečnik was no longer welcome. Years earlier, when newspapers had published objections to the monolith or other aspects of the castle renovation, Plečnik's name was never mentioned. But in 1935, nationalist opposition to the Slovene architect was explicit. The Czech press raised a storm over the "fantastic" plans of this foreigner. Perhaps tired of the mystical pretensions of the castle project, one editorialist jibed: "Certainly it is due to God's Providence that the public has received the plans of Jože Plečnik for the further modification of the area around Prague Castle."[90]

The grand development project died amidst the turbulent politics of the mid-1930s. Reaction against Plečnik's plans came mainly from the nationalist Right, which had become more aggressive with Czechoslovakia's economic problems. The acclaim that Czech artists such as Pav-

---

86 Přemysl Šamal, 18 February 1935, AKPR, T 23/21, part III, box 19. The box contains the other communications within the chancellery from February 1935.

87 *Lidové noviny*, 5 August 1935.

88 *Národní Listy*, 12 May 1935; and *Národní Politika*, 15 August 1935. Clippings of hostile editorials fill a thick folder in the records of the Castle Building Administration. APH KPR, SV, box 45, folder 532.

89 Klub přátel Malé strany to Presidential Chancellery, 15 April 1935, APH KPR, SV, box 45, folder 532.

90 *Národní listy*, 12 May 1935.

el Janák and Max Švabinský had once bestowed on Plečnik could no longer offset nationalist opposition. *Lidové noviny* tried that approach again in their endorsement of the project, but their reference to the architect as a "magnificent spirit" was drowned out. However, the failure of Plečnik's project was not only due to Czech criticism of the foreign architect, or Alice Masaryková's naiveté in pushing the plan. The construction surrounding the physical castle reached its limits due to the weakness of the political Castle. When the president's chief of staff discussed the development plans with Prime Minister Jan Malypetr, the conservative premier objected that the government had already directed plenty of funds to projects honoring Masaryk.[91] And when Finance Minister Trapl advised against forwarding the plan, he warned against the opposition that the Castle would encounter. "These attacks would be especially unwelcome at the time of the president's birthday," he cautioned.[92] It was a sign of the Castle's decreased power that instead of using Masaryk's milestone birthday to advance a project, the president's men had to shield themselves from critics. With Masaryk weakened by old age and illness, the personal authority he had once commanded was lost. It did not pass to those who worked in his name.

In the mid-1920s, Jože Plečnik had wide respect among Czech artists and architects. Designers and dignitaries repeatedly asked for personal tours through the castle grounds—requests that Plečnik always refused. He had a blank check—if he had wanted it—to carry out his work at Hradčany. But the architect did not return to Prague after 1931, choosing instead to pass instructions for both the castle and the Vinohrady church through his assistant (and former student), Otto Rothmayer. The arrangement worked as long as Masaryk's unyielding support shielded Plečnik from opposition. But as Masaryk's condition steadily worsened, it became clear that he would have to relinquish the office. On December 14, 1935, he resigned the presidency and was succeeded by his trusted accomplice, Edvard Beneš. Plečnik's resignation as castle architect came soon afterward. "I arrived at Prague Castle as if in a dream—and left without a sound," he wrote in May 1936. "Be-

91 Přemysl Šamal, memorandum, 22 February 1935, AKPR, T 23/21, part III, box 19.

92 Přemysl Šamal, memorandum, 18 February 1935, AKPR, T 23/21, part III, box 19.

lieve me, I never walked its grounds without respect." He had been attentive to the divine during the project, he claimed, just as he was in leaving. "It is one's duty to have an ear ready for the least vibration of the voice of Providence. I heard the voice of Providence—do not expect me anymore."[93]

Less than two years after the end of his presidency, on September 14, 1937, Tomáš Garrigue Masaryk passed away. Among the many tributes published in the days that followed—in newspapers across the political spectrum—were a series of reminiscences and encomia by Karel Čapek, published in *Lidové noviny*.[94] In his characteristic gentle style, Czechoslovakia's most famous writer described the mourners who came by the thousands to pay their respects, and the slow journey of Masaryk's casket from the castle to the cemetery in Lány. He published snippets from his conversations with the "Old Man": moments that revealed Masaryk's humanity, humor, and everyday wisdom. And he wrote longer essays that reminded readers of Masaryk's character and convictions. In these essays, Čapek wrote of Masaryk's devotion to truth, his humanism, his moral strength, his rationalism, even his beauty. But above all else, Čapek remembered Masaryk as a man of faith. Masaryk's search for truth, his moral sense, his dedication to democracy, his love for people were all products of his faith. "He did not proclaim his faith," Čapek wrote, "but his life conformed to it. His courage and confidence, his prudence and rationality, his austerity, his trustfulness, optimism, and mettle, everything he accomplished and thought about and aspired after, it was all substantiated, in the deepest way, by his humble faith in the divine order of the world."[95] This faith was not just a vital part of Masaryk's singular character—it was his legacy for the Czech people. In his portrait of Masaryk as a man of devotion, Čapek pointed to the president as model, one that was particularly apt in a time of a rising, dynamic "paganism" in Europe. "Our small nation," the writer stated,

---

93 Plečnik to Presidential Chancellery, 14 May 1936, APH KPR, SV, folder 446, box 20.

94 Jonathan Bolton discusses the themes expressed in press coverage of Masaryk's death in "Mourning Becomes the Nation."

95 Capek, "Masaryk věřil" [Masaryk believed], *Lidové noviny*, 21 September 1937, in *Hovory s T. G. Masarykem* (1990), 479.

FIGURE 7.3. Masaryk's casket lying in state in the entrance hall to the Castle, 1937. Jože Plečnik Collection, Museums and Galleries of Ljubljana, Slovenia.

"often small in faith as well, can be proud of the fact that it has given to the contemporary world this singular example of a Christian politician, hero, and ruler." Following Masaryk's example of belief meant keeping with the purposes of his republic. Czechs could never forget, Čapek wrote on the day of the president's death, that there was "something more" in the foundation of the state, as Masaryk had built it: "In the foundations of our state is God."[96]

In the days that followed Masaryk's death, an estimated 750,000 people queued at Hradčany —for up to nine hours—to pay their re-

---

96 Capek, "Věčný Masaryk" [The eternal Masaryk], *Lidové noviny*, 14 September 1937, in *Hovory s T. G. Masarykem* (1990), 461.

spects to the President-Liberator.[97] Masaryk lay in state in the castle, in the room now known as the Plečnik Hall. Although visible to today's visitors of the castle, the hall is often overlooked. One can find it, locked behind glass doors, when passing through the Matthias Gate from the castle's first courtyard to the second. The hall is open to its full, four-story height; on the top three floors, columns with Doric and Ionic capitals are arranged along interior ledges. Unlike today, the ground floor of the hall was not enclosed; instead, the spaces between the supporting columns were open, wide enough for automobiles to enter. Plečnik's intention was that the adjacent Matthias Gate—the baroque portal to the old citadel of kings and emperors—would be closed, and the new hall would be a *propylaea*, a ceremonial entrance to the inner courts.

For three days after Masaryk's death, even through the night, mourners filed past the coffin set in the middle of the columned hall. Draped in black, it was a fitting choice for the president's place of repose. The hall evoked the classical and the modern, the noble and the simple. It was a ceremonial hall, intended to inspire respect, but it was also unobstructed, opening to the democratic castle. Here were Masaryk's ideas expressed in stone: the beautiful, the rational, the eternal. Throughout his life, Masaryk had sought to achieve a harmony with his body of thought, just as Jan Amos Komenský had done. Such a harmony of political, moral, and religious ideals was elusive in the realms of philosophy and statecraft. In contrast, as both commentators of the time and architectural historians have observed, Jože Plečnik achieved a timeless harmony with his designs for Prague Castle. "When we walk through the courtyards of the castle, it is as if we sense another world," wrote Vasil Škrach.[98] Tomáš Masaryk and Alice Masaryková hoped that their republic would likewise be another world, and a model for the world—a political state that brought the kingdom of God to earth. But Czechoslovakia was all too human, weakened by internal division, external tumult, and uncertainty over the state of its soul.

---

97 Bolton, "Mourning Becomes the Nation," 116–18.
98 *České slovo*, 23 January 1932.

Conclusion

"**O**ur age, friends, will be celebrated as a golden age," Karel Čapek wrote in late September 1937, "because it was the age of Masaryk."[1] One year later, the golden age came to an end. With Germany threatening to invade and Britain and France refusing to fight for his country, President Edvard Beneš accepted the terms of the Munich Agreement on September 30, 1938, allowing cession of the border regions known as the Sudetenland to the Reich. Within the week, Beneš resigned the presidency. He went abroad, first to America and then to England, where he formed a government-in-exile after the wider European war began. Beneš argued that Hitler's aggression in defiance of the Munich Agreement had annulled that document. Czechoslovakia was therefore still a legitimate part of Europe, in the same form it had been before September 1938, and he was still its rightful president. As chosen successor to the President-Liberator, Beneš was hailed in the government-in-exile's propaganda as the President-Continuator (*President-Pokračovatel*). The government-in-exile declared that the borders would be restored and the republic of Masaryk would again be a beacon of progress and democracy in Europe.

But restoring the golden age would prove impossible. Masaryk's supporters were scattered or lost during the war. Some said the first casualty was Karel Čapek, who succumbed to illness on Christmas Day 1938, just after the republic's end. Ferdinand Peroutka was detained immediately after the Germans occupied the rest of the Czech Lands,

---

[1]   Čapek, "Masaryk věřil", *Lidové noviny*, 21 September 1937, in *Hovory s T. G. Masarykem* (1990), 478.

in March 1939. He was arrested again in September, after the start of the war, and spent the next five and a half years in the Dachau and Buchenwald concentration camps. Vasil Škrach did not survive the camps; he was imprisoned for three years and executed in 1943.

Alice Masaryková reached the safety of America. She received an honorary doctorate from the University of Pittsburgh in 1939 and traveled the country, giving speeches. But after devoting two decades to the health of the republic, her own health failed. She collapsed during her speaking tour and spent the rest of the war convalescing in a familiar place: the University Settlement House in Chicago. Josef Hromádka also reached America, where he taught theology at Princeton. His colleague and friend Emanuel Rádl remained behind. Following a severe illness in 1935, Rádl was confined to his home in Prague, under the care of his wife. During the occupation, he found refuge in his books. He wrote a testament just before his death in 1942, reflecting on the great works of philosophy, the paths his generation had taken, and the loss of the world's moral order in an age of technical progress. Imprisoned by illness, his city occupied by a foreign army, Rádl contemplated a God who did not intervene with force in the world's events, a God who was, in Rádl's words, "a perfectly unarmed being." His realization paralleled that of another Protestant thinker living in isolation during the war, the German theologian Dietrich Bonhoeffer. For Bonhoeffer, the awareness of God as weak and powerless had to be the foundation of an honest religion in a violent, secular age.[2] For Rádl, it brought personal consolation at the end of his life: "An unarmed God; an unarmed cosmic moral order; an unarmed philosophy; an unarmed culture—once more I experience the sacred rapture I once knew when as a boy I stood in a church crowded with people in festive dress as all of them sang until the windows rattled and the walls shook with pious respect: *Te, Deum, laudamus!*"[3]

---

2   Bonhoeffer discusses his realization of the powerless God in his letter to Eberhard Bethge, 16 July 1944, in *Letters and Papers from Prison*, 360–61.

3   Rádl, "Consolations from Philosophy" (1942; published in 1947), trans. by Erazim Kohák, unpublished manuscript provided by Professor Kohák. Theologian Jan Milič Lochmann points out this connection between Bonhoeffer's and Rádl's ideas in "Aktualita Rádlova odkazu pro ekologii, politiku a teologii," 513–14.

Jaroslav Durych did not believe in a powerless God. In the fateful year 1938, he pointed to the "Spanish sword," wielded by the Nationalists, as an example of the defense of the faith against its enemies. After the end of the First Republic, he demanded a cleansing away of its failed, godless liberalism and those who had opposed Christianity in the name of progress and patriotism. Durych became the leading cultural figure in the rump state that remained after Munich, known as the Second Republic. The nationalist and Catholic politicians who gained authority turned the state in an authoritarian direction, away from the partisan bickering of the interwar period. Durych gained the position he had wanted all along, the position that Karel Čapek had held in the First Republic: the literary voice of the Czech nation. He became cochair of the National Cultural Council, created to guide the nation's return to the Catholic moral order and the "clearing away of all the erroneous ideas of the past."[4] And he launched attacks on his old adversaries. In a November 1938 essay titled "Očista duší" (Cleansing the Soul), Durych attacked the "convinced unbeliever" and the "philosopher" who had peddled a fake morality in the old republic.[5] Although he did not mention them by name, the attack on Čapek and Masaryk was clearly understood. Other Catholic writers took Durych's lead, firing barbs at the First Republic and especially at Čapek. When the war ended and Beneš returned to Prague as president, Durych's vigorous calls for a purging of the nation's soul were remembered. In 1947 a tribunal cited his article from years earlier as cause for disciplining him for actions against the nation. Durych continued to write (his historical novel on the Jesuit mission in Japan, for example, totaled four volumes and more than a thousand pages), but his work no longer appeared in print, both in the immediate postwar years and after the Communist coup in 1948. Thanks to an unknown protector, he was never arrested, unlike other Catholic intellectuals, and he was able to work as a physician. In the 1950s, he tried to reach out to Karel Čapek's widow. She refused his apology.

---

4 Quoted in Gebhart and Kuklík, *Druhá republika 1938–1939*, 185. On the Catholic reaction against the First Republic as a foundation of the short-lived Second Republic, see Rataj, *O autoritativní národní stát*, especially 129–37.

5 Durych, "Očista duší" *Lumír*, 30 November 1938, in *Jaroslav Durych—publicista*, 237–38.

War and occupation did not come to Yugoslavia until two years after the fall of Czechoslovakia. During that time, Jože Plečnik saw some of his most notable projects brought to completion, works that have come to be landmarks of Plečnik's Ljubljana: the National and University Library, the locks on the Ljubljanica River, the colonnaded market in the city's center, and the expansive Žale cemetery. After the invasion and partition of the kingdom in April 1941, Plečnik was able to go on with his work teaching and designing. Ljubljana came under the authority of the Italians, who allowed the university to open. But with the fall of Italy in September 1943, the Germans took direct control over all of Slovenia. The architecture school became a barracks, and Plečnik isolated himself in his home, fearing for his safety.

After the war Tito and the Partisans claimed power, and Yugoslavia became a communist state. In the years that followed, Plečnik took commissions from the new rulers: he designed a pavilion for Tito's retreat on the Brioni Islands and monuments to fallen soldiers. One such monument in Ljubljana has the geometric form characteristic of Plečnik's designs, along with the addition of communist stars. But the architect also continued to design projects for Catholic parishes, at a time when the church was under state suppression and other architects were reluctant to jeopardize their careers by taking on sacral projects. The old professor had admirers in state office who allowed him to hold his university chair and even arranged publication of his work. But as architecture moved in bold, socialist directions, Plečnik became irrelevant and forgotten.

Alice Masaryková did not forget Plečnik. In 1947 she wrote from Prague, where she was living in retirement not far from the castle gates. People were talking, she wrote to the architect, Czechs as well as visiting foreigners. They were wondering what the purpose of the monolith was. She recalled that Plečnik and her father had been considering an inscription, suitable for a memorial to the first ten years of the republic. "I know that there was still mention of the triple definition of God expressed by the simple sentences—God is truth, God is love, God is light. To stress these three things, the legacy of father's and your era, would be beautiful." The inscription would be "a credo

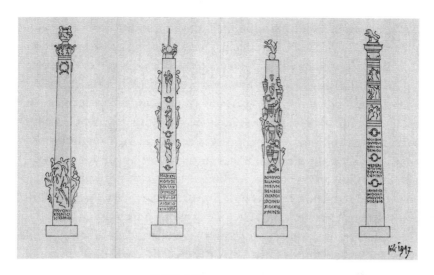

FIGURES C.1 AND C.2. Plečnik's plans for completion of the monolith, 1947.
Jože Plečnik Collection, Museums and Galleries of Ljubljana, Slovenia.

and a warning."[6] Plečnik responded to Masaryková's concerns about the monolith with a set of drawings, each featuring a different inscription and arrangement of sculptures on the sides and top of the pillar.

In one drawing, Plečnik provided scale by adding the figure of a well-dressed older woman—perhaps Alice Masaryková herself. But there were no additions to the monolith. Within a year Masaryková was again in exile, her brother Jan was dead, and the Communist Party leader, Klement Gottwald, was in the castle as president. She returned to the United States, speaking occasionally on Radio Free Europe broadcasts to her homeland.[7] In 1956 she wrote again to Plečnik, after hearing that he was still teaching at the university in Ljubljana. He replied in turn, reflecting on how Providence had brought him to work for Masaryková's father. Once more, Alice wrote of the monolith, its original purpose, and the fact that, in her view, it had never been completed. She returned to an idea that had so fascinated her three decades earlier, the eternal flame that would burn within the monolith. "It is possible that an error can turn into something good," she wrote, that even though the monolith was inside the castle courtyard, it could shine a light of truth, peace, and love. "Perhaps some time in a free moment you will take your pencil and at a time of inspiration draw a sketch of the eternal light above the monolith. You are not afraid of new achievements."[8]

There were to be no more achievements. Five months after receiving Masaryková's letter, on January 7, 1957, Jože Plečnik passed away. Alice Masaryková lived another nine years in the United States. She wrote a memoir of her childhood, and directed publication of new editions of her father's writings. There were also difficult times; her financial resources were limited, she was at times estranged from her sister Olga, and she moved from place to place, finding care with other exiles or with the American social workers she had welcomed to Prague in the first months of independence. She died in Chicago on November 29, 1966.

---

6   Masaryková to Plecnik, 6 May 1947, PC MGL. Translation by Wilma Iggers.

7   The manuscripts of Masaryková's talks over Radio Free Europe from the 1950s are in the Alice Masaryk Collection, Lilly Library, box 4.

8   Masaryková to Plecnik, 19 August 1956, PC MGL. Translation by Wilma Iggers. The earlier letter in that same year was dated 13 February.

Years ago, when I arrived in Prague to conduct research for this book, a Czech academic at a reception asked about my project. "Why do you want to study Czech religious history?" he asked after I had explained my research. "Don't you know that all Czechs are atheists?" The remark—more serious than joking—was rooted in the conventional understanding of religion in the Czech Republic. Today, the nation is overwhelmingly secularized, with a large majority of Czechs claiming no religious affiliation or even belief. This current absence of religion is typically seen as the result of the inexorable process of modernization: industrial and urban development in the nineteenth century, along with the anti-Habsburg and anti-Catholic platforms of the nationalist movement, combined to turn Czechs away from the Church. And really, most Czechs had little allegiance to the Church all along. After the defeat of the Czech Protestant nobility at the Battle of White Mountain in 1620, the Habsburgs had instituted a program of forced re-Catholicization in the lands of the Bohemian Kingdom. Jesuits opened schools, baroque churches were built, and statues of saints were raised, such as the monument to the Virgin Mary on Prague's Old Town Square. But the Czechs never accepted this religion imposed by foreign rulers. I once asked a respected Czech scholar of philosophy and religion for his interpretation of the nation's secularization, and he recited the creedal statement of this conventional narrative: "It all goes back to 1620 and White Mountain." Whatever the starting point, whether the seventeenth-century wars of religion or the nineteenth-century advances of industry, science, and nationalism, the end result was the same: by the time of the Communist takeover in 1948 most Czechs had only a nominal affiliation to the Catholic Church. Communist oppression and cooption simply administered the death blow. In the words of an American sociologist of religion: "With very little popular support for the Roman Catholic Church, it was easy for communists to begin depleting church resources and promoting atheistic alternatives."[9]

There are Czech scholars who do conduct research on religion in their own country, despite the high rates of nonbelief, and they give a

---

9 Froese, "Secular Czechs and Devout Slovaks," 278.

more nuanced view of the arc of religious decline. To be sure, active identification with the Catholic Church had declined among Czechs by the early twentieth century. As the preceding chapters show, Masaryk, Peroutka, Hromádka, and Durych all recognized a lack of religiosity among their fellow Czechs. The observations of an outsider like Jože Plečnik were matched by the comments of Bohemian Germans on the lax practice of their Czech neighbors. Growth of industrial cities in Bohemia was an important factor in this drop in religious participation (according to census data from the First Republic, the industrial areas of Kladno and Karlín were among the districts with the lowest numbers of adherents). Anti-Habsburg nationalism also contributed to the weakening of the Church. But this nationalist anticlericalism was stirred by more than animosity toward the Austrians. For many Czechs, especially the educated, Catholicism was seen as backward, as un-modern.[10] Going back to the nineteenth century, the main current of Czech nationalist thinking cast the nation as an integral part of modern Europe. Jan Hus thus was a symbol of freedom of conscience, of resistance to authority, rather than a martyr for a more pious church. This equation of the Czech nation with modernity was central to the ideology of the interwar republic. Government propaganda presented the republic as democratic, industrial, educated, and prosperous. "From the very outset of her independent existence, Czechoslovakia has based her whole life on democratic principles," wrote Karel Čapek in an essay aimed at foreign readers. "Alone among the states which surrounded her, she has never for a moment swerved from the great European tradition of spiritual and intellectual liberty, of civic equality and of social rights."[11] The priests at the Vinohrady parish recognized this strain in Czech self-definition: we are a modern people; our church is one of the most modern buildings in the city—so modern that conservative Catholics do not like it; therefore, you can come to our church and still be modern. But Fathers Titl and Škarda were fighting a strong and long-running current in Czech culture. As sociologist Zdeněk Nešpor points out, the Czechs offer the "perfect

---

10   On religion in nineteenth-century Bohemia, see Nešpor, *Příliš slábi ve víře*, 50–9; and Nešpor, "Religious Processes in Contemporary Czech Society," 282–84.

11   Čapek, "At the Crossroads of Europe" (1938), in *Toward the Radical Center*, 406.

example" of José Casanova's idea of secularization as a self-fulfilling prophesy. Beginning in the nineteenth century, nationalist writers planted the seed that to be Czech was to be modern, and to be modern was to be secular. As this idea gained acceptance, more and more Czechs viewed the Church negatively.[12]

Yet, even though nationalist ideology of the early to mid-twentieth century posed Catholicism and modernity as antagonistic, most Czechs maintained their formal adherence to the Catholic Church through the First Republic. According to one source of social data, many even attended church in the prewar and war years, suggesting that the attendance figures at the Church of the Sacred Heart in the 1930s were not unique. The 1999 version of the European Values Survey administered in the Czech Republic included questions on the religious atmosphere of a respondent's family and upbringing. One question asked: "Apart from weddings, funerals, and christenings, about how often did you attend religious services when you were twelve years old?" Of Czech respondents born between 1924 and 1935, over sixty percent answered that they had gone to services regularly at age twelve, meaning at least once a week, while over eighty percent answered that they had attended services occasionally, which included attendance once a month or on special days.[13] The survey data corresponds to Callum Brown's analysis of religion in Britain and elsewhere in Western Europe at mid-century. As Brown shows from records of church membership, baptisms, communicants, and confirmations, there was a significant resilience to the Christian churches as late as the 1950s. At the same time, people in Britain continued to frame their life narratives with reference to religious faith and church involvement well into the middle of the last century. It has only been since the 1960s, Brown argues, that people have forsaken the Christian religion, left the churches, and come to understand themselves and their world in largely nonreligious terms.[14]

Of course, one key distinction from Britain is that the rule of the Communist Party played a significant role in religious decline in

---

12 Nešpor, "Religious Processes in Contemporary Czech Society," 284.

13 See Spousta, "Changes in Religious Values in the Czech Republic." A summary of the survey data is available at www.worldvaluessurvey.org.

14 Brown, *The Death of Christian Britain*, chapter eight.

Czechoslovakia. In the 1950s, the government imprisoned Czech and Slovak bishops, interned thousands of monks and nuns, and arrested Catholic intellectuals. In 1948, the year the Communists took power, there were roughly 3,000 priests in Bohemia and Moravia; by 1968, that number was reduced by a thousand. In 1987, the number of serving Czech priests was down to 1,462, less than half what it had been four decades earlier.[15] Churches that lost a serving pastor were left unfilled. This was particularly catastrophic in the borderlands of northern and western Bohemia, which had been populated largely by Germans before the war. Among the nearly three million Germans deported from Czechoslovakia after the war were more than seven hundred Catholic priests. With these German priests gone, vicariates and parishes were depleted of clergy.[16] As the Czech and Slovak settlers in these regions were loyal to the Communist authorities who provided jobs and homes, they were not inclined to revive church life. And even if some of the new settlers had wanted to go to church, they would have had a hard time finding a serving priest. Even today, these formerly German-populated districts have the lowest rates of religious adherence and participation in the Czech Republic.

The government's aggressive steps against religion, particularly the Catholic Church, were reflected in church attendance, as demonstrated in responses to the European Values Survey on the question of childhood participation in services. The graph below shows a correlation between church attendance and the periods of government repression: the Stalinist rule of the 1950s corresponded with a sharp downturn in participation; the liberalization of the 1960s brought a brief breathing space for the churches; but repression returned during the period of normalization in the 1970s, following the Soviet invasion that ended the Prague Spring reforms of 1968.

We should not, however, see communist repression alone as the cause of religious decline in the Czech Lands. Various indices of religious participation in West European countries show similar declines over the postwar decades. Granted, the drops in church attendance, in-

---

15   Nešpor, *Příliš slábi ve víře*, 92. Nešpor devotes a large section of the book (68–101) to the communist state's persecution of the Christian churches, particularly the Catholic Church.

16   Boháč, sections 28–29, in *Atlas církevních dějin českých zemí 1918–1999*.

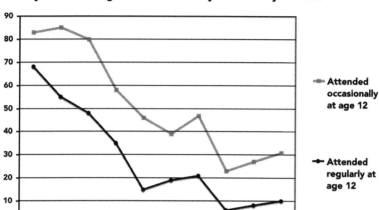

"Apart from weddings, funerals and christenings, about how often did you attend religious services when you were 12 years old?"

Sources: Jan Spousta, "Changes in Religious Values in the Czech Republic," *Sociologický časopis*, 38, no. 3 (2002): 345-363; and 1999 World Values Survey, <www.worldvaluessurvey.org>

FIGURE C.3. World Values Survey graph, www.worldvaluessurvey.org; Spousta, "Changes in Religious Values in the Czech Republic."

fant baptism, and other demonstrations of religiosity came later, in the 1960s rather than the 1950s. But the fact that Europeans in the democratic West and the communist East turned away from the traditional churches in such large numbers and at roughly the same time suggests that there were some common factors. Increased material well-being, development of the welfare state, expanded higher education, and the spread of popular culture, from films and music to sports, all contributed to the decline of religious participation and adherence in Europe. Even in the Vinohrady parish in the 1930s, when participation climbed dramatically, there were signs of the deeper social trends that would undermine religious life in the Czech Lands and throughout Europe in the postwar period. First, the Church of the Sacred Heart faced a crisis of future membership. In the decade of 1927–1936, the parish newsletter reported a yearly average of 178 member deaths, as opposed to only 29 births in the parish. The number of children born to members of the parish declined steadily, from 46 in 1927 to 18 in 1936. Priests in other parishes in Prague recognized the same trend and called on their flocks to stem the decline in births, framing their appeals in the language of building national strength. Surely, though, the priests recognized that the greater threat was to the Church. Since churches gained most members by the raising of new generations in the faith rather than conversions, the low birth rates foretold shrinking congregations. The second portent of the church's future struggles was that the parish's most deeply invested members, as indicated by their contributions to the building project, were overwhelmingly women. The fact that more women than men attend church is commonly recognized. But as Callum Brown argues in the case of Britain, the problem for the Christian churches was that once women began to leave the church, whether to go to work or university, the pews were left empty.[17]

Czech sociologists point out that the contemporary religious situation in their country is also similar to Western Europe. They apply Grace Davie's observation of West Europeans "believing without belonging," maintaining religious faith but not active links to religious institutions.[18] As in West European countries, there has been a movement away from religion—with ties to a tradition, an institution, or a group of fellow believers—in the direction of an individualized spirituality. And the Czech Republic has an expanded religious marketplace, with various groups promoting sources of religious comfort to willing customers.[19] A distinct feature of the Czech Republic is the resistance not only to traditional religion but also to any traditional conception of God. Surveys show large percentages of respondents stating they do not believe in a personal God, but at the same time large percentages of respondents say that they do believe in some supernatural power. Even many people who identify themselves as members of a traditional church indicate no belief in—or knowledge of—the tenets of historical Christianity, but instead claim belief in amulets, horoscopes, and fortune-tellers. The general picture gained from sociological research is that Czechs are strong opponents of church-based

---

17 Brown, *The Death of Christian Britain*, 183–92.
18 Nešpor, "Religious Processes in Contemporary Czech Society," 282.
19 Ibid., 285–87.

religion, but they do maintain belief in a transcendent power, although they are uncertain about what that power is. The national religion of the Czech Republic is indeed Somethingism.

By its very name, Somethingism would appear to be a disconnected set of beliefs and practices. But there are recognizable principles, a theology even, that have developed within Czech culture. Take for example the statement of a contemporary faith healer and seller of dietary supplements in the north Bohemian city of Česká Lípa:

> In my view, the grounds of church-based religion ... are simply flawed, despite the fact that originally such religion might have meant well, since it relies upon its extensive power and authority and this is not good. It does not reconcile itself with either divine or spiritual principles. It is said that to judge is something that God gave up in the name of love. Nobody has the right to judge his fellow man in terms of what he does or how he does it... And from this perspective the church does not act spiritually. The church judges, evaluates and asserts its interests and concepts and does not allow man the opportunity to disagree.[20]

This view of churches echoes what Tomáš Masaryk said more than a century earlier. Masaryk did not invent Somethingism. His ideas of a new religion borrowed from various theological sources, mixed with observation of the spiritual longings and skepticism of the age. But with his authority as president, his statements on religion gained a firm place in Czech culture, giving sanction to sentiments like those expressed above. Masaryk declared that modern people could attain spiritual fulfillment, experienced in a wholly individual manner. He argued that people could live moral lives, in reverence to the divine, without restriction by any church's theology, doctrine, or ritual—indeed, as the statement above says, living apart from a church would allow someone to be *even more* spiritual and moral. Forcefully and repeatedly, he voiced this distrust of churches, which is one of the

---

20 Quoted in Nešpor and Nešporová, "Religion: An Unsolved Problem for the Modern Czech Nation," 1229.

fundamental beliefs of Somethingism. And according to Ferdinand Peroutka, he expressed privately another tenet of Somethingism: that a person can live a moral, fulfilled, and spiritual life even without belief in a personal God. In his memoirs, Peroutka wrote of conversations with Masaryk on God and religion (he published accounts of these conversations in a *Přítomnost* article commemorating Masaryk's eightieth birthday). In the journalist's telling, Masaryk expressed the creedal statement of Somethingism: yes, there is a higher power, but I cannot claim to define it.

> Every so often he returned to the question: does God exist? He picked a flower from the vase and said, "Look, there must be something." He said "something." I also knew that there must be "something," but the problem was, what is it, this "something." Masaryk never answered that. He said, "Never for a second was I an atheist." But whenever people pressed themselves on him and asked, what is God, he said, "I don't know." In private, he sometimes even said that religion without God was possible.
> On the other hand, he had for himself different words, different expressions for God. He said that God is internal life. Or that God is real power. Or that God—and this was his favorite word—is synergy, the unity of all strength that is in people. But he did not believe in a personal God. People with religious questions came up to him and asked for specific instruction. I know they left disappointed, since he did not have a specific instruction for them.[21]

Somethingism does not require a deity, but it does have saints. Foremost among them is Masaryk. The President-Liberator entered the pantheon of national immortals immediately after his death—the embodiment of the wise, moral, and faithful leader. In Czech religious and moral thought, he is an essential authority: Protestant theologians, the Czechoslovak Church (now called the Czechoslovak Hussite Church), and intellectuals with no religious affiliation all acknowl-

---

21 Peroutka, "Ze vzpomínek zaznamenaných pro vysílání svobodné Evropy" in *Deníky, dopisy, vzpomínky*, 153.

edge Masaryk's influence. Even the Czech Catholic Church now recognizes Masaryk as a religious thinker and an example of faith. Masaryk was "the lone believing professor at the university," stated the
archbishop of Prague, Dominik Duka, in a 2011 essay on Czech atheism; "he realized his relationship to God outside of the Catholic
Church."[22] As the archbishop acknowledged in that statement, a life
of faith is possible apart from the Church, and Masaryk offers a model. Another saint of Somethingism, Václav Havel, offers a similar example. Havel wrote and spoke regularly of matters spiritual and moral. Like Masaryk, he looked to a transcendent measure as the guide for
individual and social ethics, and he posed the idea of the spiritual or
moral state. He shared Masaryk's aversion to institutional religion and
even avoided use of the term "God."[23] As anthropologist Ladislav
Holy observes, figures like Havel and Masaryk provide models of morality and cultivation that Czechs can access vicariously. Ordinary
Czechs did not necessarily adjust their behavior to follow the example
of Havel or Masaryk (both presidents came to recognize this, as did
their critics). Instead, these saints of Somethingism allow Czechs the
assurance that because their leaders are cultured, moral, and even
spiritual, so is their nation—so are they. The great Czech hero, Holy
writes, "relieves others from the necessity to live up to their ideals and
makes it possible to maintain the credibility of an ideal which would
otherwise be challenged by the historical experience of the masses."[24]

Somethingism has its saints, and it has its sacred place. When Václav Havel entered Prague Castle as president in 1989, the majesty of
Masaryk's presidency had been lost. "It was so strange," recalled one of
Havel's fellow dissidents, "sparsely furnished in the communist style
of a taste for the distasteful, with huge fake-leather chairs that made
you freeze in the winter and stuck to the back of your trousers in
summer."[25] As in 1918, restoration work was needed. Havel the play-

---

22 Duka, "S naším ateismem to není tak žhavé." Duka has referred to Masaryk several times in speeches
     and articles.
23 Martin Putna examines Havel's moral and spiritual thinking, and the influences on his ideas, in *Vá-
     clav Havel: Duchovní portrét v rámu české kultury 20. století.*
24 Holy, *The Little Czech and the Great Czech Nation*, 167.
25 Remnick, "Exit Havel."

wright brought distinct touches: a costume designer created new uniforms for the castle guards; Mick Jagger and Keith Richards purchased new chandeliers for one of the historic halls; and the president appointed as castle architect Bořek Šípek, a designer whose colorful carpets, furniture, and fixtures brightened the interior rooms. Even with Havel's irreverence, the castle regained its symbolic power as the seat of a wise ruler, as the center of the nation, and a place that welcomed the world's luminaries. In 1997, Havel opened the Forum 2000 conference with an introduction of Prague—"a true crossroads of European spiritual trends, if not its center"—and the castle—"the center of our life, both spiritual and cultural."[26] There was, Havel said, no other place more appropriate for such an event, which brought together Nobel Prize–winning writers Elie Wiesel and Wole Soyinka, intellectuals and scholars, former presidents and prime ministers, and the archbishop of Paris and the Dalai Lama. Until the end of his presidency in 2003, Havel hosted these annual meetings at the castle to discuss the challenges facing humanity. Many of the participants in these meetings returned to the castle in 2011 to pay their respects after Havel's death. They were joined by thousands of Czechs who filed past as the former president lay in state in the castle's medieval Vladislav Hall. Archbishop Dominik Duka, a friend from the time both he and Havel were imprisoned by the Communists, performed the funeral mass in St.Vitus Cathedral, and Havel's casket was borne away by the same gun carriage that had carried Masaryk's through Prague.

Although Havel's successors as president have not had the same moral and intellectual authority he did, Prague Castle remains a place of symbolic power, a place at the center of Europe where cultural and political ideals are concentrated. Barack Obama used this language in his 2009 address on Hradčany Square, just outside the castle gates. Prague was "the center of a Europe that is peaceful, united, and free," a fitting place for his speech introducing a new proposal on nuclear disarmament.[27] At the start of his address, Obama acknowledged Tomáš Masaryk. The statue of Czechoslovakia's first president stood

---

26 Havel, "Address at the Opening Session of Forum 2000."

27 Remarks by President Barack Obama, 5 April 2009, http://www.whitehouse.gov/the_press_office/Remarks-By-President-Barack-Obama-In-Prague-As-Delivered.

nearby, overlooking the dais where the American president spoke. At least in this one respect, Masaryk's grand vision had been fulfilled—the vision shared by his daughter and their architect: Prague and its castle have become recognized around the world as a sacred, mystical precinct, a site that embodies ideals of democracy, of rights over power, of the intermingling of the poetic and the political. As Obama declared in his address, "Prague has set itself apart from any other city in any other place."

On the hill overlooking the Czech capital, some six million people each year enter the courtyards, churches, staterooms, gardens, and galleries of Prague Castle. On many days while researching this book, I watched these tourists making their way through the citadel. Many paused to take photos of specific elements of Jože Plečnik's work: the monolith, the massive granite bowl, the columned belvedere in the garden. There are features of Plečnik's work whose meaning is clear, such as the sculpture of the Good Shepherd on the garden wall. But other details, I could see, left people perplexed. Nearly a century after Plečnik began his work at Prague Castle, we can say that Alice Masaryková's charge to the architect has been met: the stones of the castle do express the ideals of her father. Those ideals are inspiring, but they are also ambiguous, just like the stones Plečnik placed in the castle. There is meaning to them, to be sure. They have symbolic significance. Yet there is no inscription to explain that significance. They suggest a transcendence, a harmony. What are these stones pointing us toward? We can only say they point to Something.

Bibliography

Archives

PRAGUE, CZECH REPUBLIC

Archiv Hlavního města Prahy (Archive of the City of Prague)
    Church of the Sacred Heart Collection
Archiv Kancelář Prezidenta Republiky (Archive of the Chancellery of the President of the Republic)
    Protokol T (tajné), 1921–1944
Archiv Pražského Hradu, Kancelář Prezidenta Republiky (Archive of Prague Castle, Chancellery of the President of the Republic)
    Stavební věci 1919–1947 (S-HLF)
Archiv Národního Galerie (Archive of the National Gallery)
    Stanislav Sucharda Collection
Literarní Archiv, Pamatník národního pisemnictví (Literary Archive, Museum of National Literature)
    Jakub Deml Collection
    Jaroslav Durych Collection
    Alice Garrigue Masaryková Collection
    Tomáš Garrigue Masaryk Collection
Masarykův Ústav a Archiv Akademie věd ČR (Masaryk Institute and Archive, Academy of Sciences, Czech Republic)
    Alice Garrigue Masaryková Collection
    Charlotte Garrigue Masaryková Collection
    Tomáš Garrigue Masaryk Collection
Národní archiv (National Archive)
    YMCA Collection
    YWCA Collection

LJUBLJANA, SLOVENIA

Jože Plečnik Collection, Museums and Galleries of Ljubljana

BLOOMINGTON, INDIANA

Lilly Research Library, Indiana University
    Alice Masaryk Collection
    Tomáš Masaryk Collection
    Ruth Mitchell Collection

Published Primary Sources
(Essays, Speeches, Memoirs, Literature)

Addams, Jane. *Twenty Years at Hull House with Autobiographical Notes.* Urbana: University of Illinois Press, 1990.

Bane, Suda Lorena, and Ralph Haswell Lutz, eds. *Organization of American Relief in Europe, 1918–1919.* Stanford: Stanford University Press, 1943.

Beneš, Edvard. *My War Memoirs.* Translated by Paul Selver. Boston: Houghton Mifflin, 1928.

Benson, Timothy O., and Éva Forgács, eds. *Between Worlds: A Sourcebook of Central European Avant-Gardes, 1910–1930.* Cambridge: MIT Press and the Los Angeles County Museum of Art, 2002.

Bonhoeffer, Dietrich. *Letters and Papers from Prison.* New York: Touchstone, 1997.

Čapek, Karel. *The Absolute at Large.* Lincoln: University of Nebraska Press, 2005.

———. *Apocryphal Tales.* Translated by Norma Comrada. North Haven, CT: Catbird Press, 1997.

———. *Hovory s T. G. Masarykem* [Conversations with T. G. Masaryk]. Vol. 20 of *Spisy Karla Čapka* [Collected works of Karel Čapek]. Prague: Československý spisovatel, 1990.

———. *Hovory s T. G. Masarykem.* Vol. 37 of *Spisy T. G. Masaryka* [Collected works of T. G. Masaryk]. Prague: Ústav T. G. Masaryka, 2013.

———. *O umění a kultuře I* [On art and culture]. Vol. 17 of *Spisy Karla Čapka.* Prague: Československý spisovatel, 1984.

———. *O umění a kultuře III.* Edited by Emanuel Macek and Miloš Pohorský. Vol. 19 of *Spisy Karla Čapka.* Prague: Československý spisovatel, 1986.

———. *Od člověka k člověku I* [From person to person]. Edited by Emanuel Macek and Miloš Pohorský. Vol. 14 of *Spisy Karla Čapka.* Prague: Československý spisovatel, 1988.

———. *Od člověka k člověku II.* Edited by Emanuel Macek and Miloš Pohorský. Vol. 15 of *Spisy Karla Čapka.* Prague: Československý spisovatel, 1991.

———. *Talks with T. G. Masaryk.* Translated by Michael Henry Heim. North Haven, CT: Catbird Press, 1995.

———. *Toward the Radical Center: A Karel Čapek Reader.* Edited by Peter Kussi. Highland Park, NJ: Catbird Press, 1990.

Čapková, Jarmila. *Vzpomínky* [Memoirs]. Prague: Torst, 1998.

Crawford, Ruth. "Pathfinding in Prague." *The Survey* 46, no. 11 (11 June 1921): 328–32.

Dandová, Marta, ed. "Korespondence Karla Čapka s Arne Novákem, Otokarem Fischerem, Jaroslavem Durychem, a Františkem Xaverem Šaldou" [Karel Čapek's correspondence with Arne Novák, Otokar Fischer, Jaroslav Durych, and František Xaver Šalda]. *Literární archiv* 24 (1990): 23–121.

Duka, Dominik. "S naším ateismem to není tak žhavé" [Our atheism is not so fervid]. *Dnes,* 31 January 2011, http://www.dominikduka.cz/clankyc/s-nasim-ateismem-to-neni-tak-zhave.

Durych, Jaroslav. *Bloudění* [Wandering]. Brno: Atlantis, 1993.

———. *The Descent of the Idol.* Translated by Lynton Hudson. New York: E. P. Dutton, 1936.

———. *Ejhle člověk!* [Behold the man!]. Prague: Ladislav Kuncíř, 1928.

———. "Genese 'Bloudění'" [The genesis of *Wandering*]. *Akord* 2, no. 10 (1928–29): 290–97.

———. *Jaroslav Durych—Publicista.* Edited by Zuzana Fialová. Prague: Academia, 2001.

———. "Uvod" [Introduction]. *Rozmach* 1, no. 1 (15 October 1923).

Durych, Václav. *Vzpomínky na mého otce: Životopis Jaroslava Durycha* [Reminiscences of my father: The biography of Jaroslav Durych]. Olomouc: Votobia, 2001.

Durych, Václav, Karel Komárek, Jiří Kudrnáč, Jan Šulc, Jitka Uhdeová, and Věra Vladyková. *Jaroslav Durych: život, ohlasy, soupis díla a literatury o něm* [Jaroslav Durych: His life, reviews, and and an index of his works and literature about him]. Brno: Atlantis, 2000.

Filla, Emil. *Práce oka* [The work of the eye]. Edited by Cestmír Berka. Prague: Odeon, 1982.

Fischl, Viktor. *Hovory s Janem Masarykem* [Conversations with Jan Masaryk]. Chicago: Kruh přátel československých knih, 1952.

Grabrijan, Dušan. *Plečnik in njegova šola* [Plečnik and his school]. Maribor: Obzorja, 1968.

Gašparíková-Horáková, Anna. *U Masarykovcov: Spomienky osobnej archivárky T. G. Masaryka* [Among the Masaryks: Memoirs of T. G. Masaryk's personal archivist]. Bratislava: Academic Electronic Press, 1995.

Gutfreund, Otto. "Surface and Space." In *Between Worlds: A Sourcebook of Central European Avant-Gardes, 1910–1930,* edited by Timothy O. Benson and Éva Forgács, 92–95. Cambridge: MIT Press and the Los Angeles County Museum of Art, 2002.

Halík, Tomáš. "O ateismu, pochybnostech a víře" [On Atheism, doubt, and faith]. Transcript of lecture held at the Protestant Theological Faculty, Charles University, Prague, January 26, 2005, http://halik.cz/cs/tvorba/clanky-eseje/clanek/45/.

Havel, Václav. "Address at the Opening Session of Forum 2000," 3 September 1997. *Forum2000,* http://www.forum2000.cz/en/projects/forum-2000-conferences/1997/transcripts1/opening-session.

Havel, Václav M. *Mé vzpomínky* [My memoirs]. Prague: Lidové noviny, 1993.

Hromádka, Josef Lukl. *Cesty českých evangelíků* [Paths of Czech Protestants]. Prague: Kalich, 1934.

———. *Don Quijote české filosofie: Emanuel Rádl, 1873–1942* [The Don Quixote of Czech philosophy: Emanuel Rádl, 1873–1942]. Prague: Jan Laichter, 1947.

———. *The Field Is the World: Selected Writings from the Years 1918–1968*. Edited by Milan Opočenský. Prague: Christian Peace Conference, 1990.

———. *Křesťanství a vědecké myšlení* [Christianity and scientific thought]. Valašské Meziříčí: Českobratrského naklad, 1922.

———. *Masaryk*. Brno: L. Marek, 2005.

———. "Masarykova pochodeň" [Masaryk's torch]. *Křesťanská revue* 9 (1936): 165.

———. "Náboženská zatuchlost" [Religious mustiness]. *Křesťanská revue* 4 (April 1931): 226.

Janák, Pavel. "Josef Plečnik v Praze" [Josef Plečnik in Prague]. *Volné směry* 26 (1928–29): 97–108.

———. "Od moderní architektury do architektuře" [From Modern architecture to architecture]. *Styl* 2 (1910): 108–9.

———. "The Prism and the Pyramid." In *Between Worlds: A Sourcebook of Central European Avant-Gardes, 1910–1930*, edited by Timothy O. Benson and Éva Forgács, 86–91. Cambridge: MIT Press and the Los Angeles County Museum of Art, 2002. Firt, Julius. *Knihy a osudy* [Books and fates]. Brno: Atlantis, 1991.

Keller, Helen. *The Story of My Life*. Garden City, NY: Doubleday, 1923.

Koželuhová, Helena. *Čapci očima rodiny* [The Čapeks in the eyes of their family]. Prague: B. Just, 1995.

Kubišta, Bohumil. "The Intellectual Basis of Modern Time." In *Between Worlds: A Sourcebook of Central European Avant-Gardes, 1910–1930*, edited by Timothy O. Benson and Éva Forgács, 99–103. Cambridge: MIT Press and the Los Angeles County Museum of Art, 2002.

League of Nations Health Organization. *The Official Vital Statistics of the Republic of Czechoslovakia*. League of Nations Statistical Handbooks Series, no. 8. Geneva: League of Nations, 1927.

Lenarčič, Vinko. *Plečnik: Spomini na Plečnika* [Memoirs of Plečnik]. Ljubljana: AccordiA, 1998.

Linhart, František. "Masaryk a Křesťanství" [Masaryk and Christianity]. *Naše doba* 34, no 5 (February 1927): 278.

Ludwig, Emil. *Defender of Democracy: Masaryk of Czechoslovakia*. New York: R. M. McBride, 1936.

———. *Duch a čin: Rozmluvy s Masarykem* [Spirit and deed: Talks with Masaryk]. Edited by Jana Malínská. Vol. 38 of *Spisy T. G. Masaryka*. Prague: Masarykův ústav a Archiv AV ČR, 2012.

Masaryk, Tomáš Garrigue. *Česká otázka, Naše nynější krize, Jan Hus* [The Czech question, our current crisis, Jan Hus]. Edited by Jiří Brabec. Vol. 6 of *Spisy T. G. Masaryka*. Prague: Masarykův ústav AV ČR, 2000.

———. *Cesta demokracie I: Projevy, články, rozhovory, 1918–1920* [The Path of democracy I: Speeches, articles, interviews]. Edited by Vojtěch Feljek and Richard Vašek. Vol. 33 of *Spisy T. G. Masaryka*. Prague: Masarykův ústav AV ČR, 2003.

———. *Dopisy Oldře* [Letters to Oldra]. Edited by Dagmara Hájková. Prague: In Život, 2006.

———. *The Ideals of Humanity and How to Work*. Translated by Marie J. Kohn-Holoček. New York: Arno Press, 1971.

———. *Ideály humanitní a texty z let 1901–1903* [Ideals of humanity and texts from 1901–1903]. Edited by Michal Kosák. Vol. 25 of *Spisy T. G. Masaryka*. Prague: Masarykův ústav a Archiv AV ČR, 2011.

———. *Inteligence a náboženství: Náboženská diskuse v Královéhradeckém Adalbertinu 23. října 1906* [Intellectuals and religion: A religious discussion in the Adalbert Hall, Hradec Králové, 23 October 1906]. Prague: Čas, 1907.

———. *The Lectures of Professor T. G. Masaryk at the University of Chicago, Summer 1902*. Edited by Draga B. Shillinglaw. Lewisburg, PA: Bucknell University Press, 1978.

———. *Masaryk on Marx: An Abridged Edition of T. G. Masaryk; The Social Question: Philosophical and Sociological Foundations of Marxism*. Edited by Erazim V. Kohák. Lewisburg, PA: Bucknell University Press, 1972.

———. *The Meaning of Czech History*. Edited by René Wellek. Translated by Peter Kussi. Chapel Hill: University of North Carolina Press, 1974.

———. *Modern Man and Religion*. Translated by Ann Bibza and Václav Benes. London: G. Allen & Unwin, 1938.

———. *Parlamentní projevy, 1907–1914* [Parliamentary speeches, 1907–1914]. Edited by Vratislav Doubek, Zdeněk Kárník, and Martin Kučera. Vol. 29 of *Spisy T. G. Masaryka*. Prague: Masarykův ústav AV ČR, 2002.

———. *Přehled nejnovější filosofie náboženství* [Survey of the most recent philosophy of religion]. Prague: Spolek Augustin Smetana, 1906.

———. *The Spirit of Russia: Studies in History, Literature and Philosophy*. Translated by Eden and Cedar Paul. London: George Allen & Unwin, 1919.

———. *Suicide and the Meaning of Civilization*. Translated by William B. Weist and Robert G. Batson. Chicago: University of Chicago Press, 1970.

———. *Světová revoluce: Za války a ve válce 1914–1918* [The world revolution: During the war and in the war, 1914–1918]. Edited by Jindřich Srovnal. Vol. 15 of *Spisy T. G. Masaryka*. Prague: Masarykův ústav Akademie věd, 2005.

———. *V boji o náboženství* [In the battle over religion]. Prague: Jan Laichter, 1904.

Masaryková, Alice Garrigue. *Československý Červený kříž* [The Czechoslovak Red Cross]. Prague: Československý Červený kříž, 1935.

———. *Dětství a mládí: Vzpomínky a myšlenky* [Childhood and youth: Memoirs and thoughts]. Prague: Ústav T. G. Masaryka, 1994.

———. "From an Austrian Prison." *The Atlantic Monthly*, November 1920, 577–86.

——— [Jan Skála, pseud.]. *Helena Kellerová: Případ slepé a hluchoněmé spisovatelky a socialistiky* [Helen Keller: The case of a blind, deaf, and dumb writer and socialist]. Prague: Ústředního dělnického knihkupectví a nakladatelství, 1915.

———. "The Prison House." *The Atlantic Monthly*, December 1920, 770–79.

Masaryková, Alice Garrigue, and Charlotte Garrigue Masaryková. *Drahá mama/ Dear Alice: Korespondence Alice a Charlotty Masarykových, 1915–1916* [Dear Mama/Dear Alice: The Correspondence of Alice and Charlotte Masaryková, 1915–1916]. Edited by Dagmara Hájková and Jaroslav Soukup. Prague: Ústav T. G. Masaryka, 2001.

Masaryková, Charlotte Garrigue. *Listy do vězení* [Letters to prison]. Prague: Vladimír Žikeš, 1948.

McDowell, Mary. *Mary McDowell and Municipal Housekeeping: A Symposium.* Edited by Caroline Miles Hill. Chicago: Millar, 1937.

———. "How the Living Faith of One Social Worker Grew." *Survey* 60 (April 1928): 40–53, 57–60.

Pécaut, Félix. "Horace Mann." In *Life and Works of Horace Mann.* Vol. 5, edited by George Comb Mann, 527–49. Boston: Lee and Shepard, 1891.

Pelc, Hynek J. *Organization of the Public Health Services in Czechoslovakia.* Geneva: League of Nations Health Organization, 1924.

Peroutka, Ferdinand. *Budování státu* [Building the State]. Prague: Lidové noviny, 1991.

———. *Deníky, dopisy, vzpomínky* [Diaries, letters, memoirs]. Prague: Lidové noviny, 1995.

———. *Jací jsme* [What we are like]. Prague: Středočeské nakládatelství, 1991.

———. "Je pokrok ohrožen?" [Is progress in danger?]. *Přítomnost,* 25 February 1926.

———. "Masarykova osobnost II" [Masaryk's personality]. *Přítomnost,* 2 April 1930.

———. "Masarykova osobnost III." *Přítomnost,* 16 April 1930.

———. "Masarykova osobnost IV." *Přítomnost,* 23 April 1930.

Plečnik, Jože. *Kotěra/Plečnik: korespondence* [Kotěra/Plečnik: Correspondence]. Edited by Jindřich Vybiral and Damjan Prelovšek. Prague: Vysoká škola uměleckoprůmyslová, 2001.

———. "Kronika" [Chronicle]. *Styl* I (1908): 115–6.

———. *Nejměnujte me nikdy... Dopisy Josipa Plečnika Alexandru Titlovi 1919–1947* [Never mention me: Letters of Josip Plečnik to Alexander Titl 1919–1947]. Edited by Jiří Horský. Prague: Přátelé Prahy, 2011.

———. *Výběr prací školy pro dekorativní architekturu v Praze z roku 1911–1921* [Selection of works of the School for Decorative Architecture in Prague, 1911–1921]. Prague: Vysoká škola uměleckoprůmyslová, 1927.

Rádl, Emanuel. "Consolations from Philosophy." Translated by Erazim Kohák. Unpublished manuscript.

———. "Krise inteligence VII" [Crisis of the intelligentsia]. *Křesťanská revue* 1 (1928): 202.

———. "O nehistoričnosti naší doby" [On the ahistoricity of our times]. *Křesťanská revue* 7 (1934): 41–5.

———. "O smysl našich dějin" [On the meaning of our history]. In *Spor o smysl českých dějin* [The debate over the meaning of czech history], edited by Miloš Havelka. Prague: Torst, 1995.

———. "Smysl kultury" [The meaning of culture]. *Křesťanská revue* 4 (1931): 168.

———. *Válka čechů s němci* [The Czechs' war with the Germans]. Prague: Melantrich, 1995.

Remnick, David. "Exit Havel." *The New Yorker,* 17 February 2003.

Sinclair, Upton. *The Jungle.* New York: Heritage Press, 1965.

Soutěž na druhý katolický kostel na Král. Vinohradech [Competition for the second Catholic church in Kralovské Vinohrady]. Vol. 2. Publication of Knihovna *Stylu.* Prague: Společnost Architektů, 1920.

Stepanek, Bedrich. "Social and Economic Problems: How Czecho-Slovakia Is Trying to Meet Them." *The Survey* 46, no. 11 (11 June 1921): 349.

Štěpánek, Josef. "Plečnik, učitel a mistr" [Plečnik, teacher, and master]. *Architektura* 18 (13 May 1942): 60.

Teige, Karel. *Modern Architecture and Other Writings.* Translated by Irena Žantovská Murray. Los Angeles: Getty Research Institute, 2000.

Secondary Sources

Atkinson, David, and Denis Cosgrove. "Urban Rhetoric and Embodied Identities: City, Nation, and Empire at the Vittorio Emanuele II Monument in Rome, 1870–1945." *Annals of the Association of American Geographers* 88, no. 1 (1988): 28–49.

Axt-Piscalar, Christine. "Liberal Theology in Germany." In *The Blackwell Companion to Nineteenth-Century Theology*, edited by David A. Fergusson, 468–85. Chichester, UK: Wiley-Blackwell, 2010.

Bachstein, Martin K. "Die soziologische Struktur der 'Burg'—Versuch einer Strukturanalyse." In *Die "Burg": Einflußreiche politische Kräfte um Masaryk und Beneš*. Vol. 1, edited by Karl Bosl, 47–68. Munich: R. Oldenbourg, 1973.

Barnard, Frederick M. "Humanism and Titanism: Masaryk and Herder." In *T. G. Masaryk (1850–1937)*. Vol. 1, *Thinker and Politician*, edited by Stanley B. Winters, 23–43. London: Macmillan, 1990.

Bellah, Robert. "Civil Religion in America." *Dædalus: Journal of the American Academy of Arts and Sciences* 96, no. 1 (1967): 1–21.

Beller, Steven. "The Hilsner Affair: Nationalism, Anti-Semitism and the Individual in the Habsburg Monarchy at the Turn of the Century." In *T. G. Masaryk (1850–1937)*. Vol. 2, *Thinker and Critic*, edited by Robert B. Pynsent, 52–76. New York: St. Martin's Press, 1989.

Boháč, Zdeněk. *Atlas církevních dějin českých zemí, 1918–1999* [Atlas of the Church history of the Czech Lands, 1918–1999]. Prague: Karmelitánské, 1999.

Bolton, Jonathan. "Mourning Becomes the Nation: The Funeral of Tomáš G. Masaryk in 1937." *Bohemia: Jahrbuch des Collegium Carolinum* 45 (2004): 115–31.

Bosl, Karl. "Der Burgkreis: Leitende Figuren, Minoritäten, gesellschaftlich-wirtschaftliche Kräfte." In *Die "Burg": Einflußreiche politische Kräfte um Masaryk und Beneš*. Vol. 2, edited by Karl Bosl and Martin K. Bachstein, 197–208. Munich: R. Oldenbourg, 1974.

Boyer, John. *Culture and Political Crisis in Vienna: Christian Socialism in Power, 1897–1918*. Chicago: University of Chicago Press, 1995.

Broklová, Eva. *Mám jen knihy a skripta, cenná práce životní: 70 let Masarykovo ústavu: Studie a dokumenty* [I have only books and notes, the valuable work of a lifetime: 70 years of the Masaryk Institute: Studies and documents]. Prague: Masarykův ústav AV ČR, 2002.

Brotánková, Helena. "Religiozita v okresech ČR v období 1921–2001" [Religiosity in the districts of the Czech Republic, 1921–2001]. MA thesis, Charles University, 2004.

Brown, Callum. *The Death of Christian Britain: Understanding Secularisation, 1800–2000.* London: Routledge, 2001.

Bugge, Peter. "Czech Democracy, 1918–1938—Paragon or Parody?" *Bohemia: Jahrbuch des Collegium Carolinum* 47 (2006–7): 17–22.

Burkhardt, François, Claude Eveno, and Boris Podrecca, eds. *Jože Plečnik, Architect: 1872–1957.* Translated by Carol Volk. Cambridge: MIT Press, 1989.

Čapková, Kateřina. *Czechs, Germans, Jews? National Identity and the Jews of Bohemia.* Translated by Derek and Marzia Paton. Oxford: Berghahn, 2014.

Casanova, José. "Religion, European Secular Identities, and European Integration." In *Religion in an Expanding Europe,* edited by Timothy A. Byrnes and Peter J. Katzenstein, 65–92. Cambridge: Cambridge University Press, 2006.

Čižinská, Helena. "Zbožnost a liturgie v díle Josipa Plečnika" [Piety and liturgy in the work of Josip Plečnik]. In *Josip Plečnik a česká sakrální architektura první poloviny 20. století,* edited by Jiří Horský, 28–33. Prague: Výsoká škola uměleckopřůmyslová, 2012.

Curtis, Susan. *A Consuming Faith: The Social Gospel and Modern American Culture.* Baltimore: Johns Hopkins University Press, 1991.

Davis, Donald E., and Eugene P. Trani. "The American YMCA and the Russian Revolution." *Slavic Review* 33, no. 3 (1974): 469–91.

Demetz, Peter. *Prague in Black and Gold: Scenes from the Life of a European City.* New York: Hill and Wang, 1997.

Dorrien, Gary. *Social Ethics in the Making: Interpreting an American Tradition.* Chichester, UK: Wiley–Blackwell, 2009.

Feinberg, Melissa. *Elusive Equality: Gender, Citizenship, and the Limits of Democracy in Czechoslovakia, 1918–1950.* Pittsburgh: University of Pittsburgh Press, 2006.

Felak, James. *After Hitler, Before Stalin: Catholics, Communists, and Democrats in Slovakia, 1945–1948.* Pittsburgh: University of Pittsburgh Press, 2009.

———. *"At the Price of the Republic": Hlinka's Slovak People's Party, 1929–1938.* Pittsburgh: University of Pittsburgh Press, 1995.

Firt, Julius. "Die 'Burg' aus der Sicht eines Zeitgenossen." In *Die "Burg": Einflußreiche politische Kräfte um Masaryk und Beneš.* Vol. 1, edited by Karl Bosl, 85–107. Munich: R. Oldenbourg, 1973.

Frankl, Michal. "The Background of the Hilsner Case: Political Antisemitism and Allegations of Ritual Murder, 1896–1900." *Judaica Bohemiae* 36 (2000): 34–118.

Froese, Paul. "Secular Czechs and Devout Slovaks." *Review of Religious Research* 46, no. 3 (March 2005): 269–83.

Fry, Edward F. "Czech Cubism in the European Context." In *Czech Cubism, 1909–1925: Art, Architecture, Design,* edited by Jiří Švestka and Tomáš Vlček, with Pavel Liška, 12–5. Prague: i3 CZ: Modernista, 2006.

Frýdl, David. *Reformní náboženské hnutí v počátcích československé republiky: snaha o reformu katolicismu v Čechách a na Moravě* [The reformist religious movement at the beginnings of the Czechoslovak Republic: The attempt at a reform of Catholicism in Bohemia and Moravia]. Brno: L. Marek, 2001.

Funda, Otakar A. "František Žilka, František Linhart, Alois Spisar, František Kovář: Náboženství pro moderního člověka" [František Žilka, František Linhart, Alois Spisar, František Kovář: Religion for the modern person]. In *Náboženství v českém myšlení—první polovina 20. století* [Religion in Czech thought in first half of the 20th century], edited by Jiří Gabriel and Jiří Svoboda, 60–6. Brno: Ústav etiky a religionistiky FF MU, 1993.

———. *Thomas Garrigue Masaryk: Sein philosophisches, religiöses und politisches Denken.* Bern: Peter Lang, 1978.

Gebhart, Jan, and Jan Kuklík. *Druhá republika 1938–1939: Svár demokracie a totality v politickém, spolenčském, a kultrním životě* [The Second Republic 1938–1939: The conflict of democracy and totalitarianism in political, social, and cultural life]. Prague: Paseka, 2004.

Güllendi-Cimprichová, Zuzana. "Architekt Josip Plečnik und seine Unternehmungen in Prag in Spannungsfeld zwischen denkmalpflegerischen Prinzipien und politischer Indienstnahme." PhD diss., University of Bamberg, 2010.

———. "Památková hodnota, religiozita: K památkářskému postoji Josipa Plečnika" [Commemorative value, religiosity: On the preservationist position of Josip Plečnik]. In *Josip Plečnik a česká sakrální architektura první poloviny 20. století*, edited by Jiří Horský, 42–45. Prague: Vysoká škola uměleckopřůmyslová, 2012.

Gubser, Michael. *The Far Reaches: Phenomenology, Ethics, and Social Renewal in Central Europe.* Stanford: Stanford University Press, 2014.

Hajek, Hanus J. *T. G. Masaryk Revisited: A Critical Assessment.* Boulder, CO: East European Monographs, 1983.

Hamplová, Dana. "Čemu Češi věří: dimenze soudobé české religiozity" [What Czechs believe: Dimensions of contemporary Czech religiosity]. *Sociologický Časopis/Czech Sociological Review* 44, no. 4 (2008): 703–23.

Hanak, Harry, ed. *T. G. Masaryk (1850–1937).* Vol. 3, *Statesman and Cultural Force.* London: Macmillan, 1989.

Havránek, Jan. "Akademická mládež mezi křesťanstvím a atheismem a Rádlova profesura na universitě" [Young academics between Christianity and atheism and Rádl's professorship at the university]. In *Emanuel Rádl: vědec a filosof: Sborník z mezinárodní konference konané u příležitosti 130. výročí narození a 60. výročí úmrtí Emanuela Rádla*, edited by Tomáš Hermann and Anton Markoš, 523–32. Prague: Oikoymenh, 2003.

Heimann, Mary. *Czechoslovakia: The State that Failed.* New Haven, CT: Yale University Press, 2009.

Herben, Jan. *T. G. Masaryk: Život a dílo Presidenta Osvoboditele* [T. G. Masaryk: The life and work of the president liberator]. Prague: Sfinx, Bohumil Janda, 1946.

Hermann, Tomáš, and Anton Markoš, eds. *Emanuel Rádl: vědec a filosof: Sborník z mezinárodní konference konané u příležitosti 130. výročí narození a 60. výročí úmrtí Emanuela Rádla* [Emanuel Rádl: scientist and philosopher: Proceedings of the international conference on the 130th anniversary of the birth and 60th anniversary of the death of Emanuel Rádl]. Prague: Oikoymenh, 2003.

Hojda, Zdeněk, and Jiří Pokorný. *Pomníky a zapomníky* [Monuments and memorials]. Prague: Paseka, 1997.

Holy, Ladislav. *The Little Czech and the Great Czech Nation: National Identity and the Post-Communist Social Transformation*. Cambridge: Cambridge University Press, 1996.

Horský, Jiří, ed. *Josip Plečnik a česká sakrální architektura první poloviny 20. století* [Josip Plečnik and Czech sacral architecture in the first half of the 20th century]. Prague: Výsoká škola uměleckopřůmyslová, 2012.

Hrejsa, Ferdinand. *Dějiny české evanjelické církve v Praze a ve středních Čechách v posledních 250 letech* [History of the Czech Protestant Church in Prague and Central Bohemia in the last 250 years]. Prague: Českobratrské evanjelické církve, 1927.

Huber, Augustin Kurt. "Die 'Burg' und der Kirchen." In *Die "Burg": Einflußreiche politische Kräfte um Masaryk und Beneš*. Vol. 2, edited by Karl Bosl and Martin K. Bachstein, 181–96. Munich: R. Oldenbourg, 1974.

Kadushin, Charles. "Networks and Circles in the Production of Culture." In *The Production of Culture*, edited by Richard A. Peterson, 107–22. London: Sage, 1976.

Kieval, Hillel J. "Death and the Nation: Ritual Murder as Political Discourse in the Czech Lands." *Jewish History* 10, no. 1 (1996): 75–91.

———. *The Making of Czech Jewry: National Conflict and Jewish Society in Bohemia, 1870–1918*. New York: Oxford University Press, 1988.

Klíma, Ivan. *Karel Čapek: Life and Work*. Translated by Norma Comrada. North Haven, CT: Catbird Press, 2002.

Klimek, Antonín. *Boj o Hrad* [The battle for the Castle]. Vol. 1, *Hrad a pětka 1918–1926* [The Castle and the five]. Prague: Panevropa, 1996.

———. *Boj o Hrad*. Vol. 2, *Kdo po Masarykovi? 1927–1938* [Who after Masaryk?]. Prague: Panevropa, 1998.

———. *Velké dějiny zemí Koruny české* [The complete history of the Bohemian Crown Lands]. Vol. 13, *1918–1929*. Prague: Paseka, 2000.

———. *Velké dějiny zemí Koruny české*. Vol. 14, *1929–1938*. Prague: Paseka, 2002.

Kohák, Erazim V. *The Embers and the Stars: A Philosophical Inquiry into the Moral Sense of Nature*. Chicago: University of Chicago Press, 1984.

———. "Masaryk and Plato in the 20th Century." In *The Czechoslovak Contribution to World Culture*, edited by Miloslav Rechcígl, 283–94. The Hague: Mouton, 1964.

Kosatík, Pavel. *Ferdinand Peroutka: život v novinách 1895–1935* [Ferdinand Peroutka: A life in newspapers 1895–1935]. Prague: Paseka, 2003.

Kostílková, Marie. "Katedrála v 19. a 20. století. Jednota pro dostavení chrámu svatého Víta" [The cathedral in the 19th and 20th centuries: The association for the completion of the Cathedral of St. Vitus]. In *Katedrála sv. Víta v Praze: K 650. výročí založení*, edited by Anežka Merhautová, 198–204. Prague: Academic, 1994.

Kovtun, Jiří. *Slovo má poslanec Masaryk* [Deputy Masaryk has the floor]. Prague: Československý spisovatel, 1991.

Krajčí, Petr. "Lány." In *Josip Plečnik—Architect of Prague Castle*, edited by Zdeněk Lukeš, Damjan Prelovšek, and Tomáš Valena, 471–75. Prague: Prague Castle Administration, 1997.

Krečič, Peter. *Jože Plečnik*. Ljubljana: Državna žal. Slovenije, 1992.

———. *Plečnik: The Complete Works*. New York: Whitney Library of Design, 1993.

Lazier, Benjamin. *God Interrupted: Heresy and the European Imagination between the Two World Wars*. Princeton: Princeton University Press, 2008.

Lehmann, Hartmut. "Die Säkularisierung der Religion und die Sakralisierung der Nation im 20. Jahrhundert: Varianten einer komplementären Relation." In *Religion im Nationalstaat zwischen den Weltkriegen 1918–1939*, edited by Hans-Christian Maner and Martin Schulze Wessel, 13–27. Stuttgart: Franz Steiner, 2002.

Liška, Pavel. "Important Prague Exhibitions, 1911–1922." In *Czech Cubism, 1909–1925: Art, Architecture, Design*, edited by Jiří Švestka and Tomáš Vlček, with Pavel Liška, 78–85. Prague: i3 CZ: Modernista, 2006.

Lochman, Jan Milič. "Aktualita Rádlova odkazu pro ekologii, politiku a teologii" [The topicality of Rádl's legacy for ecology, politics, and theology]. In *Emanuel Rádl: vědec a filosof: Sborník z mezinárodní konference konané u příležitosti 130. výročí narození a 60. výročí úmrtí Emanuela Rádla*, edited by Tomáš Hermann and Anton Markoš, 501–16. Prague: Oikoymenh, 2003.

———. "Emanuel Rádl: In Masaryk's Footsteps." In *T. G. Masaryk in Perspective: Comments and Criticism*, edited by Milič Čapek and Karel Hrubý, 83–95. New York: SVU Press, 1981.

———. "Masaryk's Quarrel with Marxism." In *T. G. Masaryk (1850–1937)*. Vol. 2, *Thinker and Politician*, edited by Stanley B. Winters, 120–33. London: Macmillan, 1990.

Lovčí, Radovan. *Alice Garrigue Masaryková: život ve stínu slavného otce* [Alice Garrigue Masaryková: Life in the shadow of a famous father]. Prague: Univerzita Karlova, Filozofická fakulta, 2007.

Löwenstein, Shimona. *Emanuel Rádl: Philosoph und Moralist, 1873–1942*. Frankfurt am Main: P. Lang, 1995.

Lukeš, Zdeněk. "Architektura." In *Praha 3: Urbanismus, Architektura*, edited by Zdeněk Lukeš and Jan Sedlák, 144–62. Prague: Argo, 2008.

Lukeš, Zdeněk, Damjan Prelovšek, and Tomáš Valena, eds. *Josip Plečnik: An Architect of Prague Castle*. Prague: Prague Castle Administration, 1997.

Machovec, Milan. *Tomáš G. Masaryk*. Prague: Melantrich, 1968.

Malá, Věra. "The Castle Architect and the Prague Castle Building Project." In *Josip Plečnik: An Architect of Prague Castle*, edited by Zdeněk Lukeš, Damjan Prelovšek, and Tomáš Valena, 123–40. Prague: Prague Castle Administration, 1997.

———. "History of the Monolith." In *Josip Plečnik: An Architect of Prague Castle*, edited by Zdeněk Lukeš, Damjan Prelovšek, and Tomáš Valena, 291–95. Prague: Prague Castle Administration, 1997.

Marek, Pavel. *Český katolicismus, 1890–1914: Kapitoly z dějin českého katolického tábora na přelomu 19. a 20. století* [Czech Catholicism, 1890–1914: Chapters from the history of the Czech Catholic Camp at the turn of the 19th and 20th centuries]. Olomouc: Rosice, 2003.

———. *České schisma: Příspěvek k dějinám reformního hnutí katolického duchovenstva v letech, 1917–1924* [Czech schism: A contribution to the history of the reform movement of Catholic clergy, 1917–1924]. Olomouc: Rosice, 2000.

―――. *Politické programy českého politického katolicismu 1894–1938* [The political programs of Czech political Catholicism]. Prague: Historický ústav, 2011.

―――. "Das Verhältnis zwischen Staat und Kirchen." In *Handbuch der Religions- und Kirchengeschichte der böhmischen Länder under Tschechiens im 20. Jahrhundert*, edited by Martin Schulze Wessel and Martin Zückert, 3–46. Munich: R. Oldenbourg, 2009.

Margolius, Ivan. *Church of the Sacred Heart: Jože Plečnik*. London: Phaidon, 1995.

Matějka, Ondřej. "Die tschechischen protestantischen Kirchen." In *Handbuch der Religions- und Kirchengeschichte der böhmischen Länder und Tschechiens im 20. Jahrhundert*, edited by Martin Schulze Wessel and Martin Zückert, 147–52. Munich: R. Oldenbourg, 2009.

McLeod, Hugh, ed. *European Religion in the Age of the Great Cities, 1830–1930*. London: Routledge, 1995.

―――. *The Religious Crisis of the 1960s*. Oxford: Oxford University Press, 2007.

―――. *Secularisation in Western Europe, 1848–1914*. New York: St. Martin's, 2000.

Merhautová, Anežka. *Katedrála sv. Víta v Praze: K 650. výročí založení* [The Cathedral of St. Vitus in Prague: On the 650th anniversary of its founding]. Prague: Academic, 1994.

Miller, Michael L. "The Rise and Fall of Archbishop Kohn: Czechs, Germans, and Jews in Turn-of-the-Century Moravia." *Slavic Review* 65, no. 3 (2006): 446–74.

Mišovič, Ján. *Víra v dějinách zemí koruny české* [Faith in the history of Czech Lands]. Prague: Slon, 2001.

Mitchell, Ruth Crawford. *Alice Garrigue Masaryk, 1879–1966: Her Life as Recorded in Her Own Words and by Her Friends*. Pittsburgh: University Center for International Studies, University of Pittsburgh, 1980.

Moravánszky, Ákos. *Competing Visions: Aesthetic Invention and Social Imagination in Central European Architecture, 1867–1918*. Cambridge: MIT Press, 1998.

Němec, Ludvík. "The Czech Jednota: The Avant-Garde of Modern Clerical Progressivism and Unionism." *Proceedings of the American Philosophical Society* 112, no. 1 (1968): 74–100.

―――. "The Czechoslovak Heresy and Schism: The Emergence of a National Czechoslovak Church." *Transactions of the American Philosophical Society* 65, no. 1 (1975): 1–78.

Nešlehová, Mahulena. "The Dostoyevsky Series and Hofman's Other Portfolios." In *Vlastislav Hofman*, edited by Mahulena Nešlehová, Rostislav Švácha, and Jiří Hilmera, translated by Derek Paton. Prague: Institute of Art History, 2005.

Nešpor, Zdeněk R. *Příliš slábi ve víře: Česká ne/religiozita v evropskám kontextu* [Too weak in faith: Czech (non)religiosity in the European context]. Prague: Kalich, 2010.

―――. "Religious Processes in Contemporary Czech Society." *Sociologický Časopis/Czech Sociological Review* 40, no. 3 (2004): 277–95.

Nešpor, Zdeněk R, and Olga Nešporová. "Religion: An Unsolved Problem for the Modern Czech Nation." *Sociologický Časopis/Czech Sociological Review* 45, no. 6 (2009): 1215–37.

Neumärker, Dorothea. *Josef L. Hromádka: Theologie und Politik im Kontext des Zeitgeschehens.* Munich: C. Kaiser, 1974.

Nishitani, Kosuke. *Niebuhr, Hromadka, Troeltsch, and Barth: The Significance of Theology of History for Christian Social Ethics.* New York: Peter Lang, 1999.

Novák, Josef. "Masaryk and the Brentano School." In *On Masaryk: Texts in English and German,* edited by Josef Novák, 27–38. Amsterdam: Rodopi, 1988.

Ort, Thomas. *Art and Life in Modernist Prague: Karel Čapek and His Generation, 1911–1938.* New York: Palgrave Macmillan, 2013.

———. "Men without Qualities: Karel Čapek and His Generation, 1911–1938." PhD diss., New York University, 2005.

Orzoff, Andrea. *Battle for the Castle: The Myth of Czechoslovakia in Europe, 1914–1948.* New York: Oxford University Press, 2009.

———. "O mimoparlamentní politice meziválečné ČSR zatím víme dost málo" [We still know quite little about the extra-parliamentary politics of the interwar Czechoslovak Republic]. Interview by Milan Ducháček. *Dějiny a současnost,* June 2010, http://dejinyasoucasnost.cz/archiv/2010/6/o-mimoparlamentni-politice-mezivalecne-csr-zatim-vime-dost-malo/.

Paces, Cynthia. *Prague Panoramas: National Memory and Sacred Space in the Twentieth Century.* Pittsburgh: University of Pittsburgh Press, 2009.

Page, Benjamin B. "The Social Philosophy of T. G. Masaryk: A Question of Suicide." In *T. G. Masaryk (1850–1937).* Vol. 2, *Thinker and Critic,* edited by Robert B. Pynsent, 19–36. New York: St. Martin's Press, 1989.

Patočka, Jan. "An Attempt at a Czech National Philosophy and Its Failure." In *T. G. Masaryk in Perspective: Comments and Criticism,* edited by Milič Čapek and Karel Hrubý, translated by Mark Suino, 1–21. New York: SVU Press, 1981.

———. "Spiritual Crises of European Humanity in Husserl and Masaryk." In *On Masaryk: Texts in German and English,* edited by Josef Novák, 97–110. Amsterdam: Rodopi, 1988.

Pauza, Miroslav. "Von Ehrenfelsova výzva T. G. Masarykovi k založení tzv. reálného katolicismu" [Von Ehrenfels's appeal to T. G. Masaryk to establish a so-called objective Catholicism]. In *Náboženství v českém myšlení–první polovina 20. století,* edited by Jiří Gabriel and Jiří Svoboda, 5–10. Brno: Ústav etiky a religionistiky: 1993.

Pencák, Marcel. "Soutěž na pomník Jana Žižky na Vítkově v roce 1913" [The competition for the Jan Žižka monument on Vítkov]. *Umění* 54, no. 1 (2006): 69–84.

Petrasová, Taťána. "Dostavba katedrály" [Final construction of the Cathedral]. In *Katedrála sv. Víta v Praze: K 650. výročí založení,* edited by Anežka Merhautová, 205–36. Prague: Academic, 1994.

Podivinský, Mirek. "Kirche, Staat und religiöses Leben der Tschechen in der Ersten Republik." In *Kultur und Gesellschaft in der Ersten Tschechoslowakischen Republik,* edited by Karl Bosl and Ferdinand Seibt, 227–40. Munich: R. Oldenbourg, 1972.

Pohorský, Miloš. "Karel Čapek a jeho T. G. M.—Masaryk a jeho K. Č." [Karel Čapek and his T. G. Masaryk, Masaryk and his Karel Čapek]. In Karel Čapek, *Hovory s T. G. Masarykem.* Vol. 20, *Spisy Karla Čapka,* 557–84. Prague: Československý spisovatel, 1990.

Polák, Stanislav. *T. G. Masaryk: Za ideálem a pravdou* [T. G. Masaryk: For ideals and truth]. 7 vols. Prague: Masarykův ústav AV ČR, 2000–2014.

Prelovšek, Damjan. "The Church of the Most Sacred Heart of Our Lord in Prague." In *Josip Plečnik: An Architect of Prague Castle*, edited by Zdeněk Lukeš, Damjan Prelovšek, and Tomáš Valena, 565–80. Prague: Prague Castle Administration, 1997.

———. "Ideological Substratum in Plečnik's Work." In *Josip Plečnik: An Architect of Prague Castle*, edited by Zdeněk Lukeš, Damjan Prelovšek, and Tomáš Valena, 89–106. Prague: Prague Castle Administration, 1997.

———. *Josef Plečnik: Wiener Arbeiten von 1896 bis 1914.* Vienna: Tusch, 1979.

———. *Jože Plečnik, 1872–1957: Architectura perennis.* Translated by Patricia Crampton and Eileen Martin. New Haven: Yale University Press, 1997.

———. "Kotěra's Viennese Period: Semper, Wagner, Plečnik." In *Jan Kotěra, 1871–1923: The Founder of Modern Czech Architecture*, 73–93. Prague: Obecní dům and Kant, 2001.

———. *Plečnikova sakralna umetnost* [Plečnik's sacral art]. Koper: Ognjišče, 1999.

Putna, Martin C. *Česká katolická literatura v evropském kontextech, 1848–1918* [Czech Catholic literature in the European context, 1848–1918]. Prague: Torst, 1998.

———. *Česká katolická literatura v kontextech, 1918–1945* [Czech Catholic literature in contexts, 1918–1945]. Prague: Torst, 2010.

———. *Jaroslav Durych.* Prague: Torst, 2003.

———. "Plečnikovo místo mezi náboženskými kulturami" [Plečnik's place between religion cultures]. In *Josip Plečnik a česká sakrální architektura první poloviny 20. století*, edited by Jiří Horský, 46–52. Prague: Výsoká škola uměleckopřůmyslová, 2012.

———. *Václav Havel: Duchovní portrét v rámu české kultury 20. století* [Václav Havel: A Spiritual Portrait in the Frame of 20th-Century Czech Culture]. Prague: Knihovna Václav Havla, 2011.

Pynsent, Robert B. "Masaryk and Decadence." In *T. G. Masaryk (1850–1937)*. Vol. 1, *Thinker and Politician*, edited by Stanley B. Winters, 60–87. London: Macmillan, 1990.

———, ed. *T. G. Masaryk (1850–1937)*. Vol. 2, *Thinker and Critic.* New York: St. Martin's Press, 1989.

Rataj, Jan. *O autoritativní národní stát: Ideologické proměny české politiky v druhé republice 1938–1939* [On the authoritarian national State: Ideological changes of Czech politics in the Second Republic, 1938–1939]. Prague: Karolinum, 1997.

Schmidt-Hartmann, Eva. *Thomas G. Masaryk's Realism: Origins of a Czech Political Concept.* Munich: R. Oldenbourg, 1984.

Schorske, Carl. *Fin-de-Siècle Vienna: Politics and Culture.* New York: Vintage, 1981.

Schuhmann, Karl. "Husserl and Masaryk." In *On Masaryk: Texts in German and English*, edited by Josef Novák, 129–56. Amsterdam: Rodopi, 1988.

Schulze Wessel, Martin. "Katholik und Staatsbürger? Zur republikanischen Loyalität der Katholiken in der Ersten Tschechoslowakischen Republik." In *Loyalitäten in der Tschechoslowakischen Republik, 1918–1938*, edited by Martin Schulze Wessel, 179–91. Munich: R. Oldenbourg, 2004.

————. "Die Konfessionalisierung der tschechischen Nation." In *Nation und Religion in Europa: Mehrkonfessionelle Gesellschaften im 19. und 20. Jahrhundert*, edited by Heinz-Gerhard Haupt and Dieter Langewiesche, 135–49. Frankfurt am Main: Campus, 2004.

————. "Konfessionelle Konflikte in der Ersten Tschechoslowakischen Republik: Zum Problem des Status von Konfessionen im Nationalstaat." In *Religion im Nationalstaat zwischen den Weltkriegen 1918–1939: Polen—Tschecho-slowakei—Ungarn—Rumänien*, edited by Hans-Christian Maner and Martin Schulze Wessel, 73–102. Stuttgart: Franz Steiner, 2002.

Schulze Wessel, Martin, and Martin Zückert, eds. *Handbuch der Religions- und Kirchengeschichte der böhmischen Länder und Tschechiens im 20. Jahrhundert.* Munich: R. Oldenbourg, 2009.

Scruton, Roger. "Masaryk, Kant, and the Czech Experience." In *T. G. Masaryk (1850–1937)*. Vol. 1, *Thinker and Politician*, edited by Stanley B. Winters, 44–59. London: Macmillan, 1990.

————. "Masaryk, Patočka, and the Care of the Soul." In *On Masaryk: Texts in German and English*, edited by Josef Novák, 111–28. Amsterdam: Rodopi, 1988.

Šebek, Jaroslav. "Die katolische Kirche in der Gesellschaft." In *Handbuch der Religions- und Kirchengeschichte der böhmischen Länder under Tschechiens im 20. Jahrhundert*, edited by Martin Schulze Wessel and Martin Zückert, 47–73. Munich: R. Oldenbourg, 2009.

————. *Mezi křížem a národem: Politické prostředí sudetoněmeckého katolicismu v meziválečném Československu* [Between the cross and the nation: Political background of Sudeten German Catholicism in interwar Czechoslovakia]. Brno: Centrum pro studium demokracie a kultury, 2006.

————. *Od konfliktu ke smíření: Česko-německé vztahy ve 20. století očima katolické církve* [From conflict to conciliation: Czech–German relations in the 20th century in the eyes of the Catholic Church]. Kostelní Vydří: Karmelitánské, 2013.

————. "Der tschechische Katholizismus im Spannungsfeld von Kirche, Staat und Gesellschaft zwischen den Weltkriegen." In *Religion im Nationalstaat zwischen den Weltkriegen 1918–1939: Polen—Tschechoslowakei—Ungarn—Rumänien*, edited by Hans-Christian Maner and Martin Schulze Wessel, 145–56. Stuttgart: Franz Steiner, 2002.

Šedivý, Ivan. *Češi, české země, a velká válka, 1914–1918* [The Czechs, the Czech Lands, and the Great War, 1914-1918]. Prague: Lidové noviny, 2001.

Šiklová, Jiřina. "Akademická YMCA v Československu a jeji příspěvek k formování studenstva a inteligence" [The Academic YMCA in Czechoslovakia and its contribution to the formation of the student class and intelligentsia]. *Acta Universitatis Carolinae—Philosophica et Historica* 1 (1967): 61–93.

Šimsa, Jan. "J. L. Hromádka jako Masarykův žák" [Hromádka as Masaryk's pupil]. In *Náboženství v českém myšlení—první polovina 20. století*, edited by Jiří Gabriel and Jiří Svoboda, 28–32. Brno: Ústav etiky a religionistiky FF MU, 1993.

Skálová, Vanda. "Sepulchral Architecture." In *Jan Kotěra, 1871–1923: The Founder of Modern Czech Architecture*, edited by Vladimír Šlapeta and Daniela Karasová. Prague: Obecní dům and Kant, 2001.

Skilling, H. Gordon. *Mother and Daughter: Charlotte and Alice Masaryk*. Prague: Gender Studies, 2001.

———. *T. G. Masaryk: Against the Current, 1882–1914*. University Park: Pennsylvania State University Press, 1994.

Šlapeta, Vladimir. "Jože Plečnik and Prague." In *Jože Plečnik, Architect: 1872–1957*, edited by François Burkhardt, Claude Eveno, and Boris Podrecca, 82–95. Cambridge: MIT Press, 1989.

Šmid, Marek. "Vztah Tomáše Garrigua Masaryka k české Katolické moderně na přelomu 19. a 20. Století" [Relation of Tomáš Garrigue Masaryk to Czech Catholic Modernism at the turn of the 19th and 20th centuries]. *Masarykův sborník* 14 (2006–2008): 267–81.

Soubignon, Alain. *Tomáš Garrigue Masaryk*. Translated from French to Czech by Helena Beguivinová. Prague: Paseka, 2004.

Spain, Daphne. *How Women Saved the City*. Minneapolis: University of Minnesota Press, 2001.

Spinka, Matthew. "Religious Movements in Czechoslovakia." *The Journal of Religion* 3, no. 6 (1923): 616–31.

———. "The Religious Situation in Czechoslovakia." In *Czechoslovakia*, edited by Robert J. Kerner, 284–301. Berkeley: University of California Press, 1945.

Spousta, Jan. "Changes in Religious Values in the Czech Republic." *Sociologický Časopis/Czech Sociological Review* 38, no. 3 (2002): 345–63.

Steiner, Peter. *The Deserts of Bohemia: Czech Fiction and Its Social Context*. Ithaca: Cornell University Press, 2000.

Surface, Frank M., and Raymond L. Bland. *American Food in the World War and Reconstruction Period*. Stanford: Stanford University Press, 1931.

Švejnoha, Josef. "Alice Masaryková a mezinárodní hnutí Červeného kříže" [Alice Masaryková and the International Red Cross Movement]. In *Červený kříž Alica G. Masaryková a Slovensko* [The Red Cross of Alice G. Masaryková and Slovakia], edited by Zora Mintalová, 50–53. Martin, SK: Ústav Milana Rastislava Štefánika, 2006.

Szporluk, Roman. "Masaryk's Idea of Democracy." *The Slavonic and East European Review* 41, no. 96 (1962): 31–49.

———. *The Political Thought of Thomas G. Masaryk*. Boulder, CO: East European Monographs, 1981.

Taylor, Charles. *A Secular Age*. Cambridge: Belknap Press of Harvard University Press, 2007.

Thomas, Alfred. *The Labyrinth of the Word: Truth and Representation in Czech Literature*. Munich: R. Oldenbourg, 1995.

Trapl, Miloš. *Political Catholicism and the Czechoslovak People's Party in Czechoslovakia, 1918–1948*. Boulder, CO: Social Science Monographs, 1995.

Trensky, Paul I. "Masaryk and Dostoevsky." In *T. G. Masaryk (1850–1937)*. Vol. 3, *Statesman and Cultural Force*, edited by Harry Hanak, 161–77. London: Macmillan, 1989.

Unterberger, Betty M. "The Arrest of Alice Masaryk." *Slavic Review* 33, no. 1 (March 1974): 91–106.

Van den Beld, Antonie. *Humanity: The Political and Social Philosophy of Thomas G. Masaryk*. The Hague: Mouton, 1976.

Vlček, Tomáš. *Praha 1900: Studie k dějinám kultury a umění Prahy v letech 1890–1914* [Prague 1900: Studies in the history of culture and art of Prague, 1890–1914]. Prague: Panorama, 1986.

Voisine-Jechova, Hana. "Dvě cesty do Španélska. Jaroslav Durych a Karel Čapek" [Two paths to Spain: Jaroslav Durych a Karel Čapek]. *Literární Archiv* 39 (2007): 215–27

Vybíral, Jindřich. "Verba et Voces: Jan Kotěra in the Realm of Ideas and Social Relationships." In *Jan Kotěra, 1871–1923: The Founder of Modern Czech Architecture*, edited by Vladimír Šlapeta and Daniela Karasová, 55–71. Prague: Obecní dům, Kant, 2001.

Warlick, M. E. "Mythic Rebirth in Gustav Klimt's Stoclet Frieze: New Considerations of Its Egyptianizing Form and Content." *The Art Bulletin* 74, no. 1 (March 1992): 115–34.

Wellek, René. "Masaryk's Philosophy." In *On Masaryk: Texts in German and English*, edited by Josef Novák, 17–26. Amsterdam: Rodopi, 1988.

Williams, Joyce E., and Vicky M. MacLean. *Settlement Sociology in the Progressive Years: Faith, Science, and Reform.* Leiden: Brill, 2015.

Wingfield, Nancy M. *Flag Wars and Stone Saints: How the Bohemian Lands Became Czech.* Cambridge: Harvard University Press, 2007.

Winters, Stanley B., ed. *T. G. Masaryk (1850–1937).* Vol. 1, *Thinker and Politician.* London: Macmillan, 1990.

Zahra, Tara. "Imagined Noncommunities: National Indifference as a Category of Analysis." *Slavic Review* 69, no. 1 (2010): 93–119.

Zahradník, Pavel, and Dobroslav Líbal. *Katedrála svatého Víta na pražském Hradě* [St. Vitus Cathedral at Prague Castle]. Prague: Unicornis, 1999.

Žantovská-Murray, Irena. "'Our Slav Acropolis': Language and Architecture in the Prague Castle under Masaryk." PhD diss., McGill University, 2002.

———. "Sources of Cubist Architecture in Bohemia: The Theories of Pavel Janák." MA thesis, McGill University, 1990.

Zumr, Josef, and Thomas Binder, eds. *T. G. Masaryk und die Brentano-Schule.* Prague: Filosofický ústav Českovslovenská akademie věd, 1991.

Subject Index